DRABBLE

SCRATCH
SCRATCH
SCRATCH
SCRATCH
SCARY, ISN'T IT?
THUMP
THUMP
THUMP
THUMP

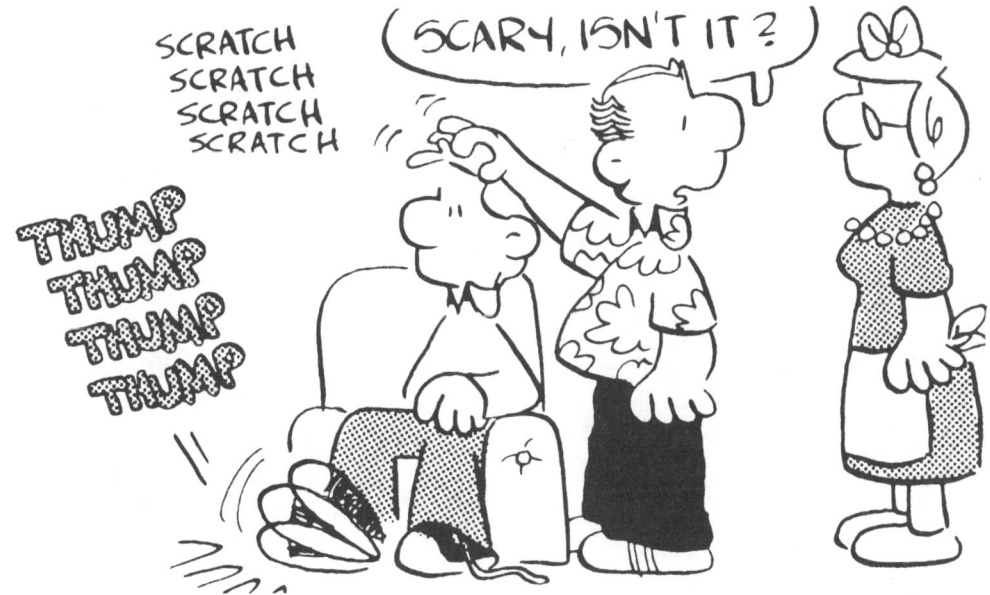

Kevin Fagan

NANTIER · BEALL · MINOUSTCHINE
Publishing inc.
new york

Also Available:
One Big Happy: "Should I Spit On Him?", $9.95 (plus $3 P&H)

NBM has over 150 graphic novels available
Please write for a free color catalog to:
NBM -Dept. S
185 Madison Ave. Ste. 1504
New York, N.Y. 10016

ISBN 1-56163-173-6
©1997 United Feature Syndicate, Inc.
Printed in Canada

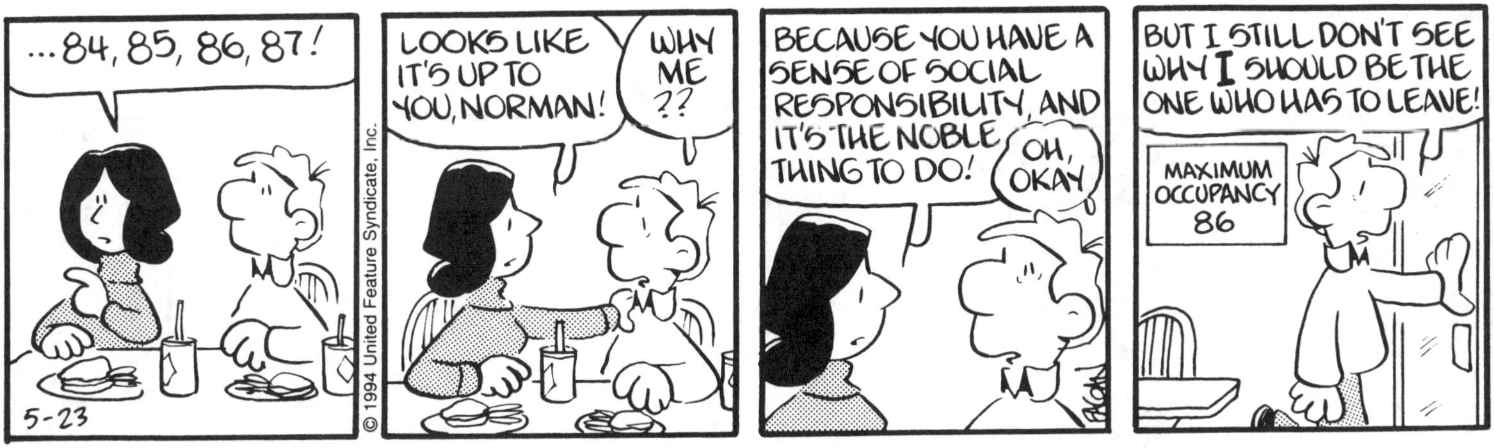
5-23
...84, 85, 86, 87!
© 1994 United Feature Syndicate, Inc.
LOOKS LIKE IT'S UP TO YOU, NORMAN!
WHY ME ??
BECAUSE YOU HAVE A SENSE OF SOCIAL RESPONSIBILITY, AND IT'S THE NOBLE THING TO DO!
OH, OKAY
BUT I STILL DON'T SEE WHY I SHOULD BE THE ONE WHO HAS TO LEAVE!
MAXIMUM OCCUPANCY 86

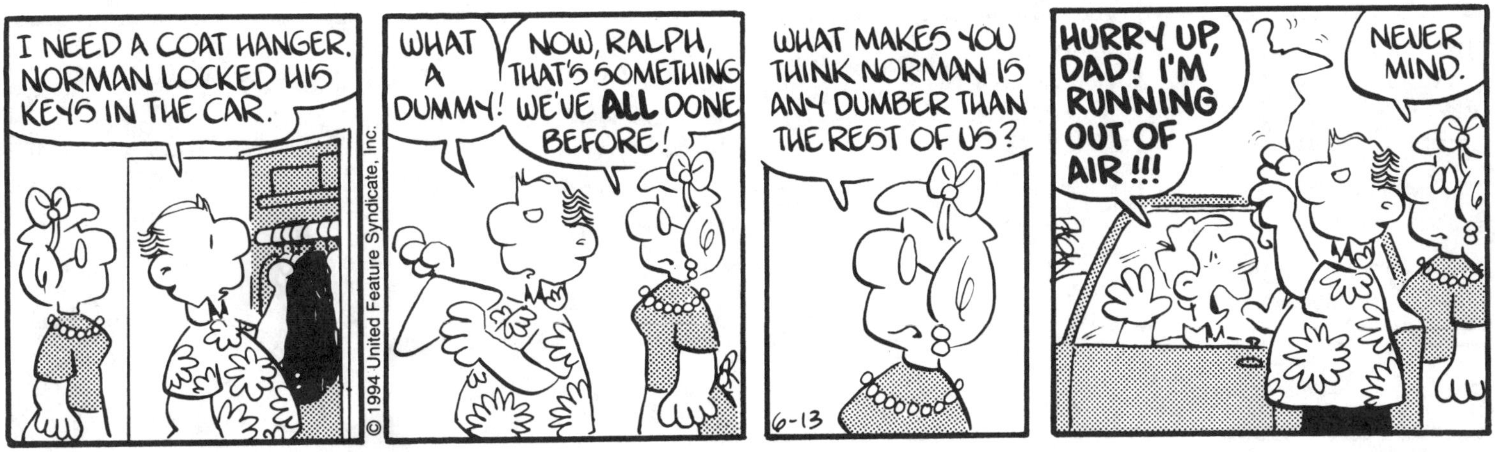
I NEED A COAT HANGER. NORMAN LOCKED HIS KEYS IN THE CAR.
© 1994 United Feature Syndicate, Inc.
WHAT A DUMMY!
NOW, RALPH, THAT'S SOMETHING WE'VE ALL DONE BEFORE!
WHAT MAKES YOU THINK NORMAN IS ANY DUMBER THAN THE REST OF US?
6-13
HURRY UP, DAD! I'M RUNNING OUT OF AIR!!!
NEVER MIND.

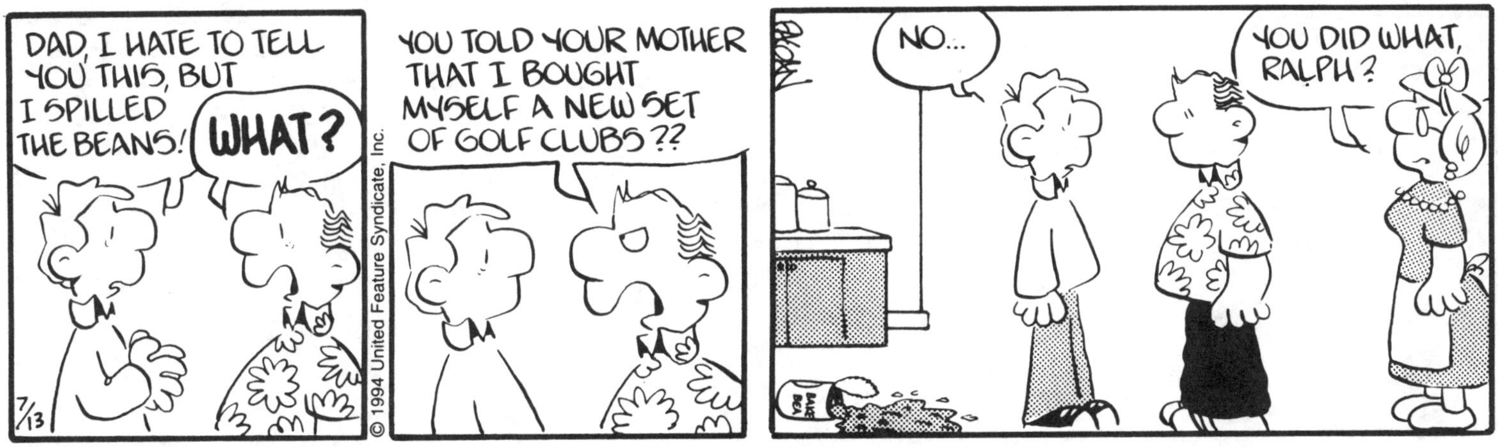
DAD, I HATE TO TELL YOU THIS, BUT I SPILLED THE BEANS!
WHAT?
7/13
© 1994 United Feature Syndicate, Inc.
YOU TOLD YOUR MOTHER THAT I BOUGHT MYSELF A NEW SET OF GOLF CLUBS??
NO...
YOU DID WHAT, RALPH?

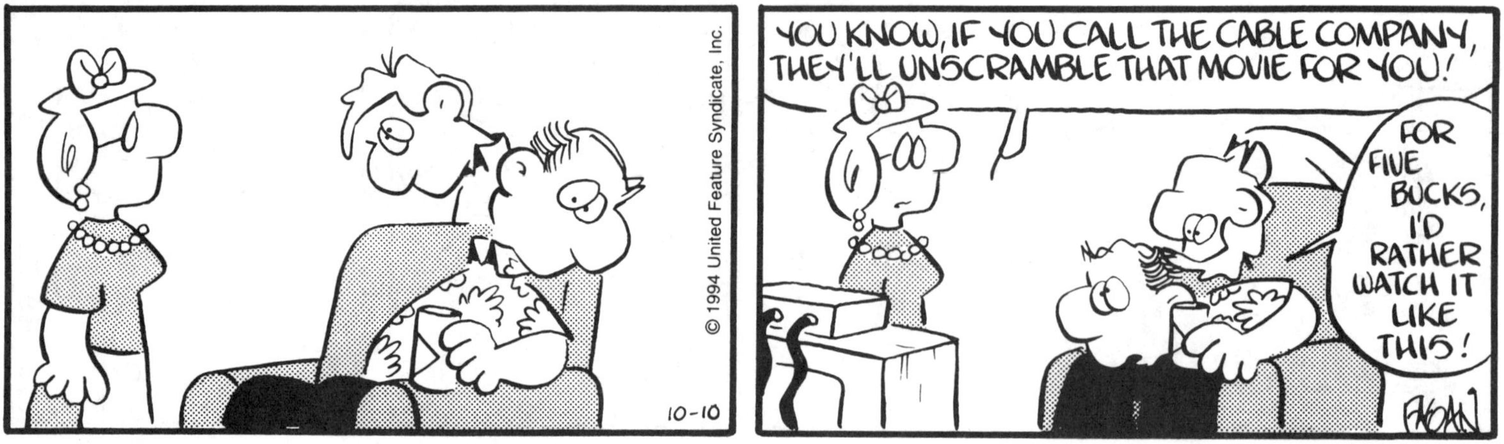
© 1994 United Feature Syndicate, Inc.
10-10
YOU KNOW, IF YOU CALL THE CABLE COMPANY, THEY'LL UNSCRAMBLE THAT MOVIE FOR YOU!
FOR FIVE BUCKS, I'D RATHER WATCH IT LIKE THIS!
FAGAN

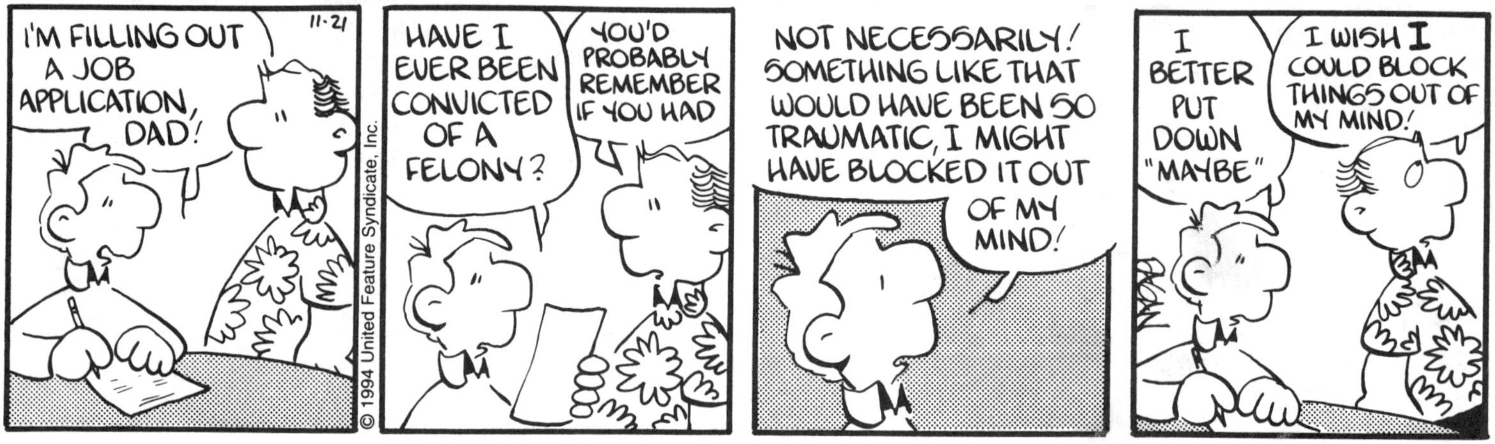
11-21
I'M FILLING OUT A JOB APPLICATION, DAD!
© 1994 United Feature Syndicate, Inc.
HAVE I EVER BEEN CONVICTED OF A FELONY?
YOU'D PROBABLY REMEMBER IF YOU HAD
NOT NECESSARILY! SOMETHING LIKE THAT WOULD HAVE BEEN SO TRAUMATIC, I MIGHT HAVE BLOCKED IT OUT OF MY MIND!
I BETTER PUT DOWN "MAYBE"
I WISH I COULD BLOCK THINGS OUT OF MY MIND!
FAGAN

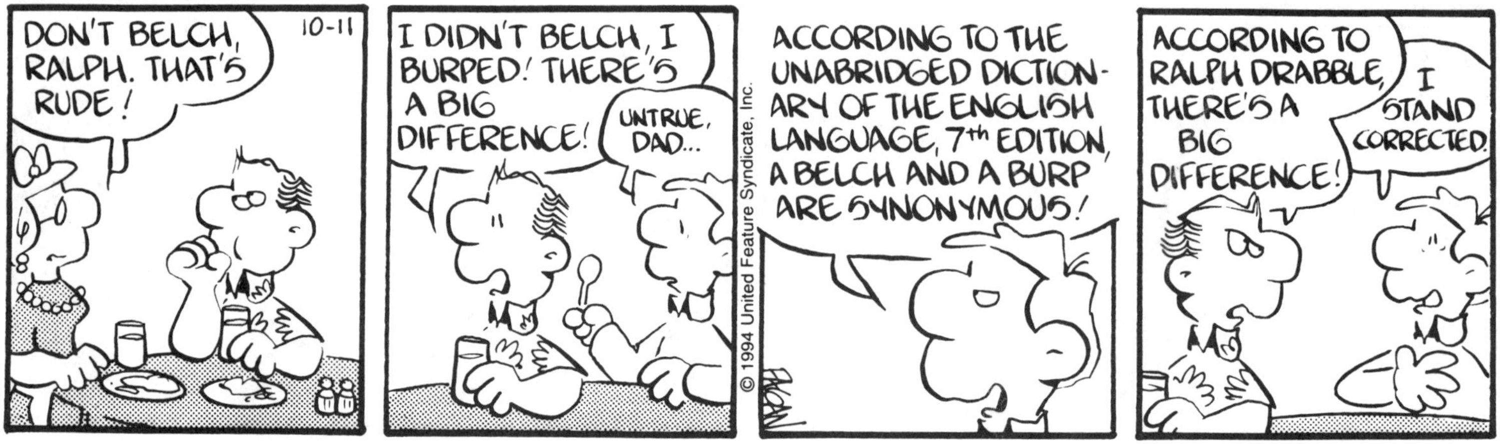
10-11
DON'T BELCH, RALPH. THAT'S RUDE!
I DIDN'T BELCH, I BURPED! THERE'S A BIG DIFFERENCE!
UNTRUE, DAD...
© 1994 United Feature Syndicate, Inc.
ACCORDING TO THE UNABRIDGED DICTIONARY OF THE ENGLISH LANGUAGE, 7th EDITION, A BELCH AND A BURP ARE SYNONYMOUS!
ACCORDING TO RALPH DRABBLE, THERE'S A BIG DIFFERENCE!
I STAND CORRECTED.
FAGAN

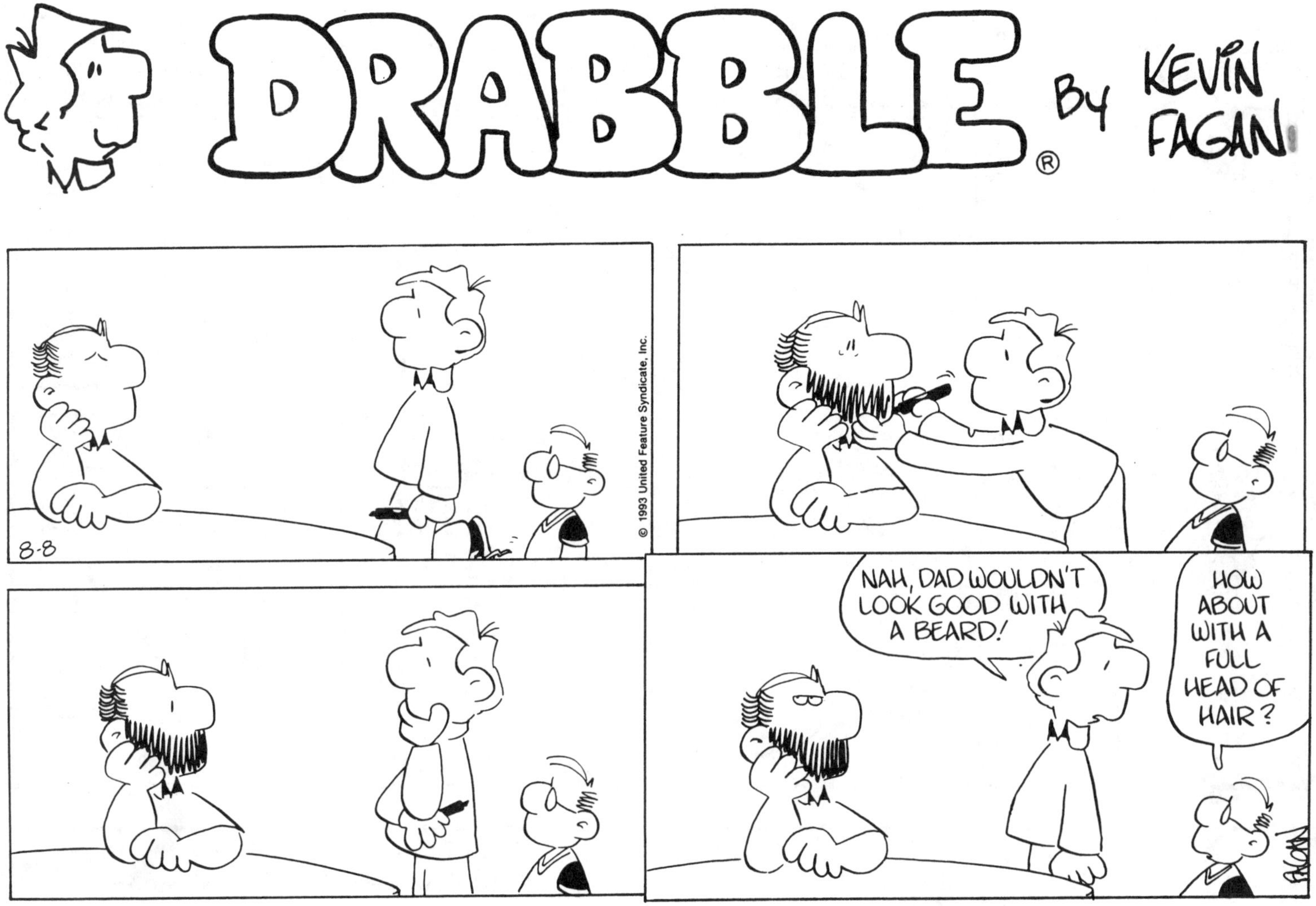
DRABBLE®
By KEVIN FAGAN
© 1993 United Feature Syndicate, Inc.
8-8
NAH, DAD WOULDN'T LOOK GOOD WITH A BEARD!
HOW ABOUT WITH A FULL HEAD OF HAIR?

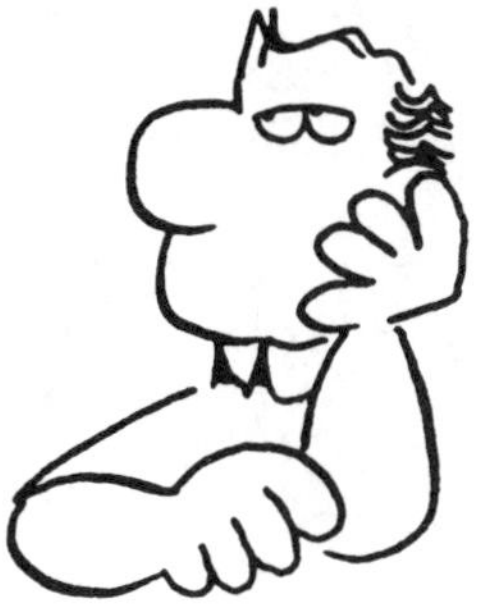

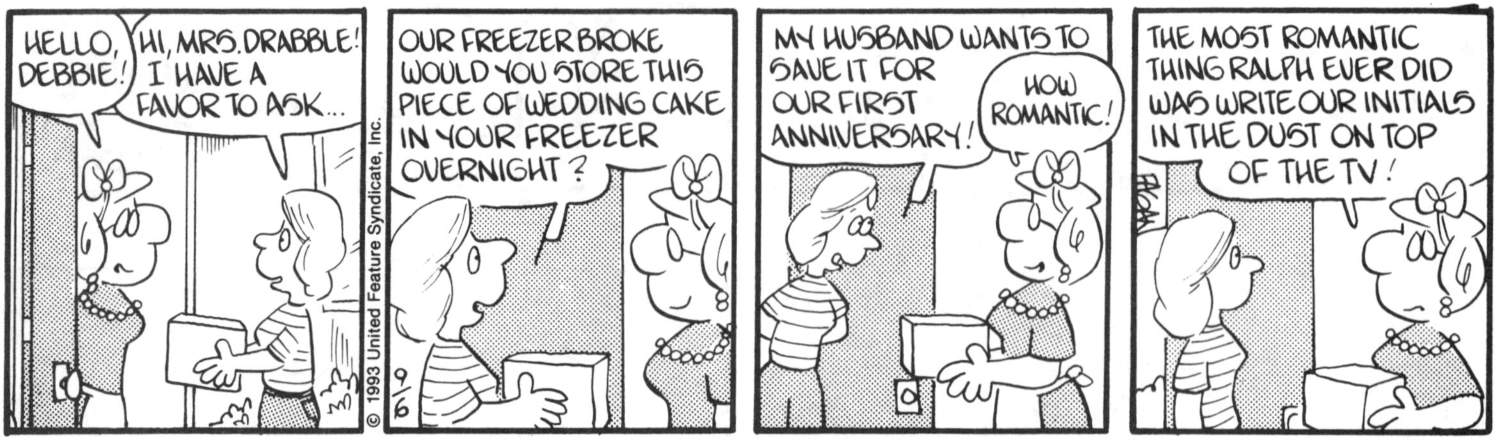
HELLO, DEBBIE!
HI, MRS. DRABBLE! I HAVE A FAVOR TO ASK...
© 1993 United Feature Syndicate, Inc.
9/6
OUR FREEZER BROKE WOULD YOU STORE THIS PIECE OF WEDDING CAKE IN YOUR FREEZER OVERNIGHT?
MY HUSBAND WANTS TO SAVE IT FOR OUR FIRST ANNIVERSARY!
HOW ROMANTIC!
THE MOST ROMANTIC THING RALPH EVER DID WAS WRITE OUR INITIALS IN THE DUST ON TOP OF THE TV!

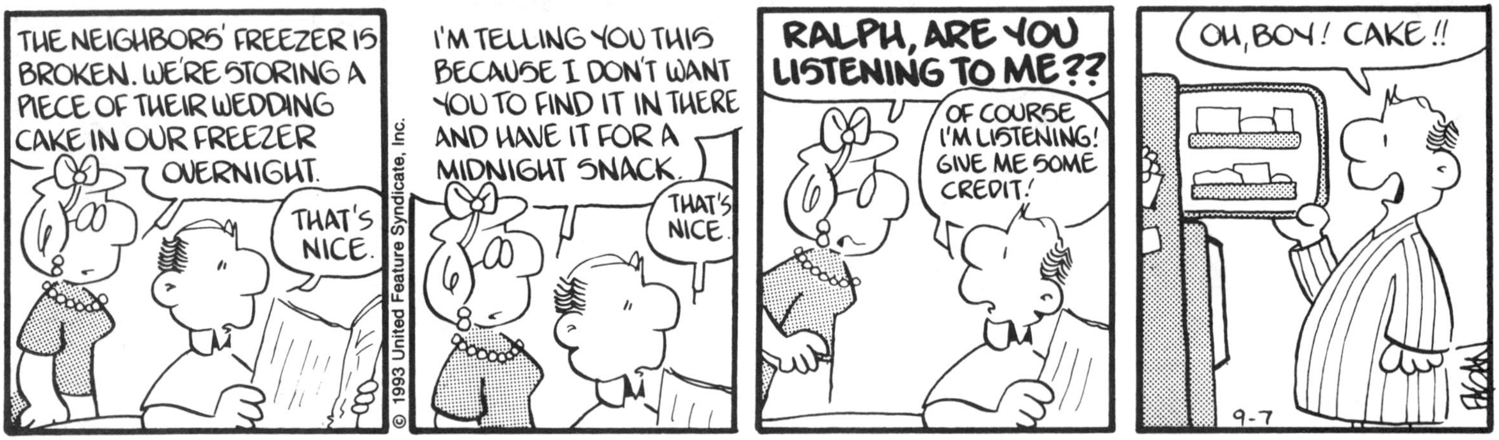
THE NEIGHBORS' FREEZER IS BROKEN. WE'RE STORING A PIECE OF THEIR WEDDING CAKE IN OUR FREEZER OVERNIGHT.
THAT'S NICE.
© 1993 United Feature Syndicate, Inc.
I'M TELLING YOU THIS BECAUSE I DON'T WANT YOU TO FIND IT IN THERE AND HAVE IT FOR A MIDNIGHT SNACK.
THAT'S NICE.
RALPH, ARE YOU LISTENING TO ME??
OF COURSE I'M LISTENING! GIVE ME SOME CREDIT!
OH, BOY! CAKE!!
9-7

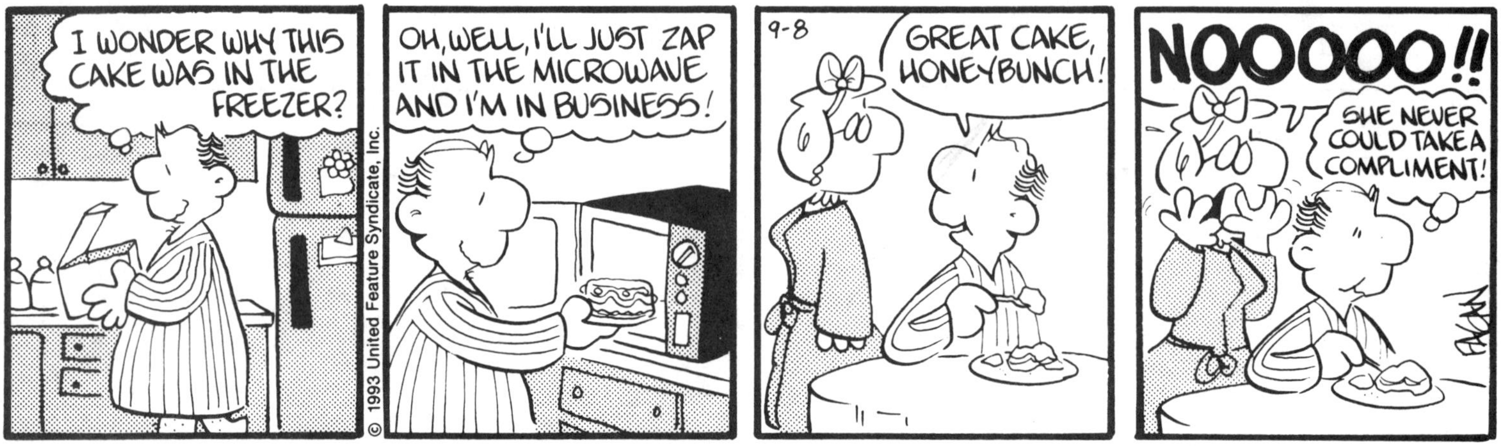
I WONDER WHY THIS CAKE WAS IN THE FREEZER?
© 1993 United Feature Syndicate, Inc.
OH, WELL, I'LL JUST ZAP IT IN THE MICROWAVE AND I'M IN BUSINESS!
9-8
GREAT CAKE, HONEYBUNCH!
NOOOOO!!
SHE NEVER COULD TAKE A COMPLIMENT!

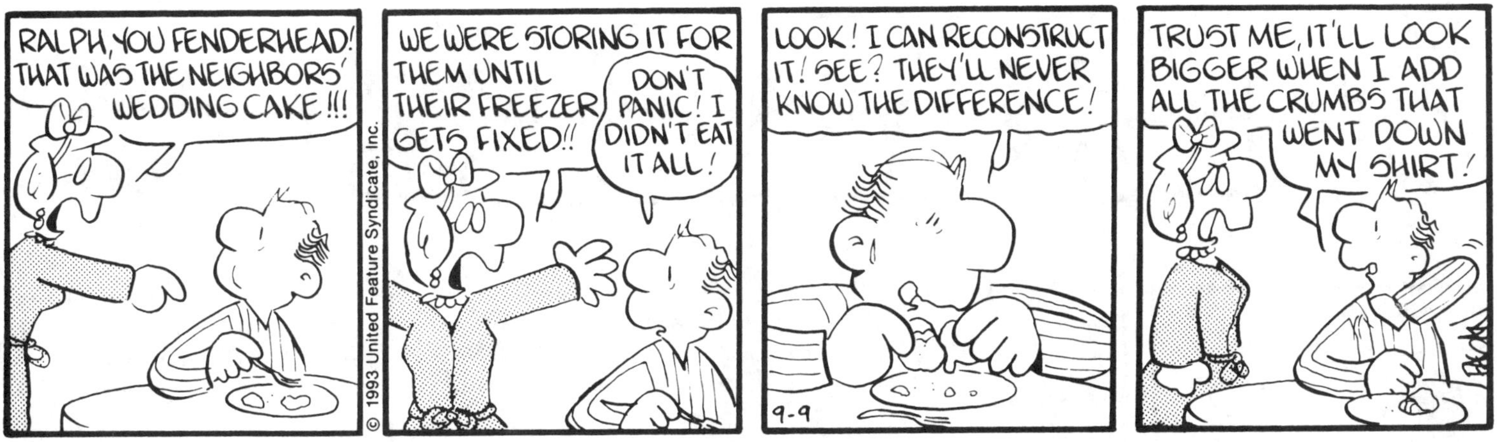
RALPH, YOU FENDERHEAD! THAT WAS THE NEIGHBORS' WEDDING CAKE!!!
© 1993 United Feature Syndicate, Inc.
WE WERE STORING IT FOR THEM UNTIL THEIR FREEZER GETS FIXED!!
DON'T PANIC! I DIDN'T EAT IT ALL!
LOOK! I CAN RECONSTRUCT IT! SEE? THEY'LL NEVER KNOW THE DIFFERENCE!
9-9
TRUST ME, IT'LL LOOK BIGGER WHEN I ADD ALL THE CRUMBS THAT WENT DOWN MY SHIRT!

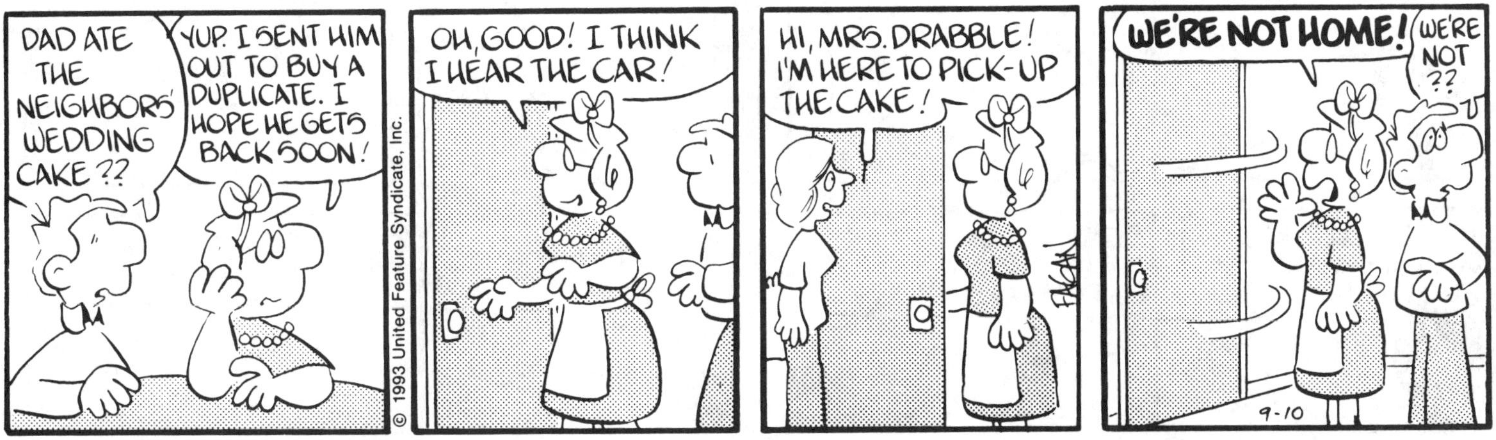
DAD ATE THE NEIGHBORS' WEDDING CAKE??
YUP. I SENT HIM OUT TO BUY A DUPLICATE. I HOPE HE GETS BACK SOON!
© 1993 United Feature Syndicate, Inc.
OH, GOOD! I THINK I HEAR THE CAR!
HI, MRS. DRABBLE! I'M HERE TO PICK-UP THE CAKE!
WE'RE NOT HOME!
WE'RE NOT??
9-10

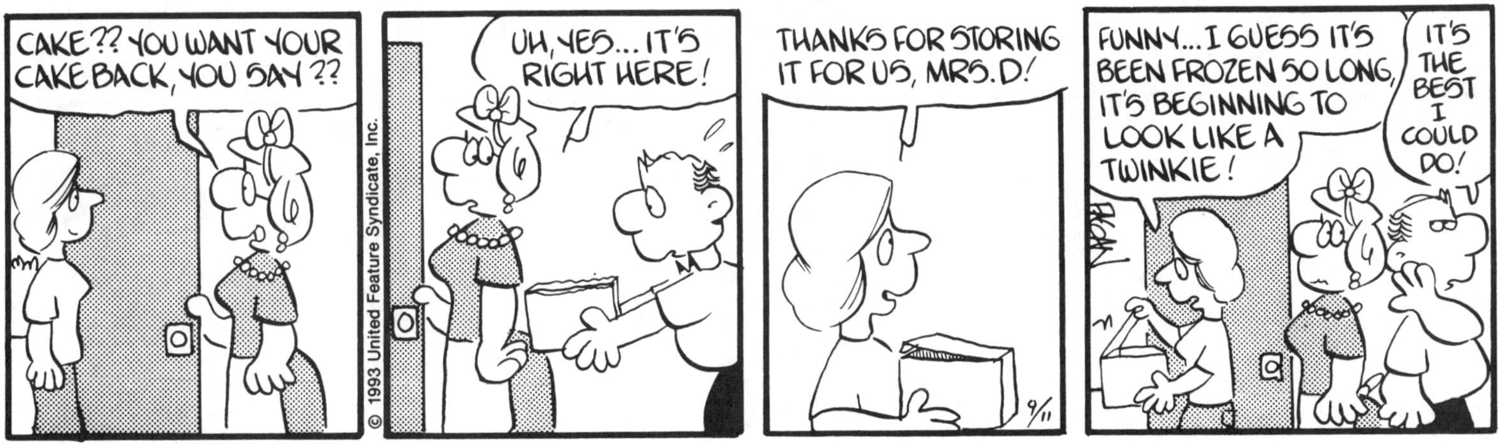
CAKE?? YOU WANT YOUR CAKE BACK, YOU SAY??
© 1993 United Feature Syndicate, Inc.
UH, YES... IT'S RIGHT HERE!
THANKS FOR STORING IT FOR US, MRS. D!
9/11
FUNNY... I GUESS IT'S BEEN FROZEN SO LONG, IT'S BEGINNING TO LOOK LIKE A TWINKIE!
IT'S THE BEST I COULD DO!

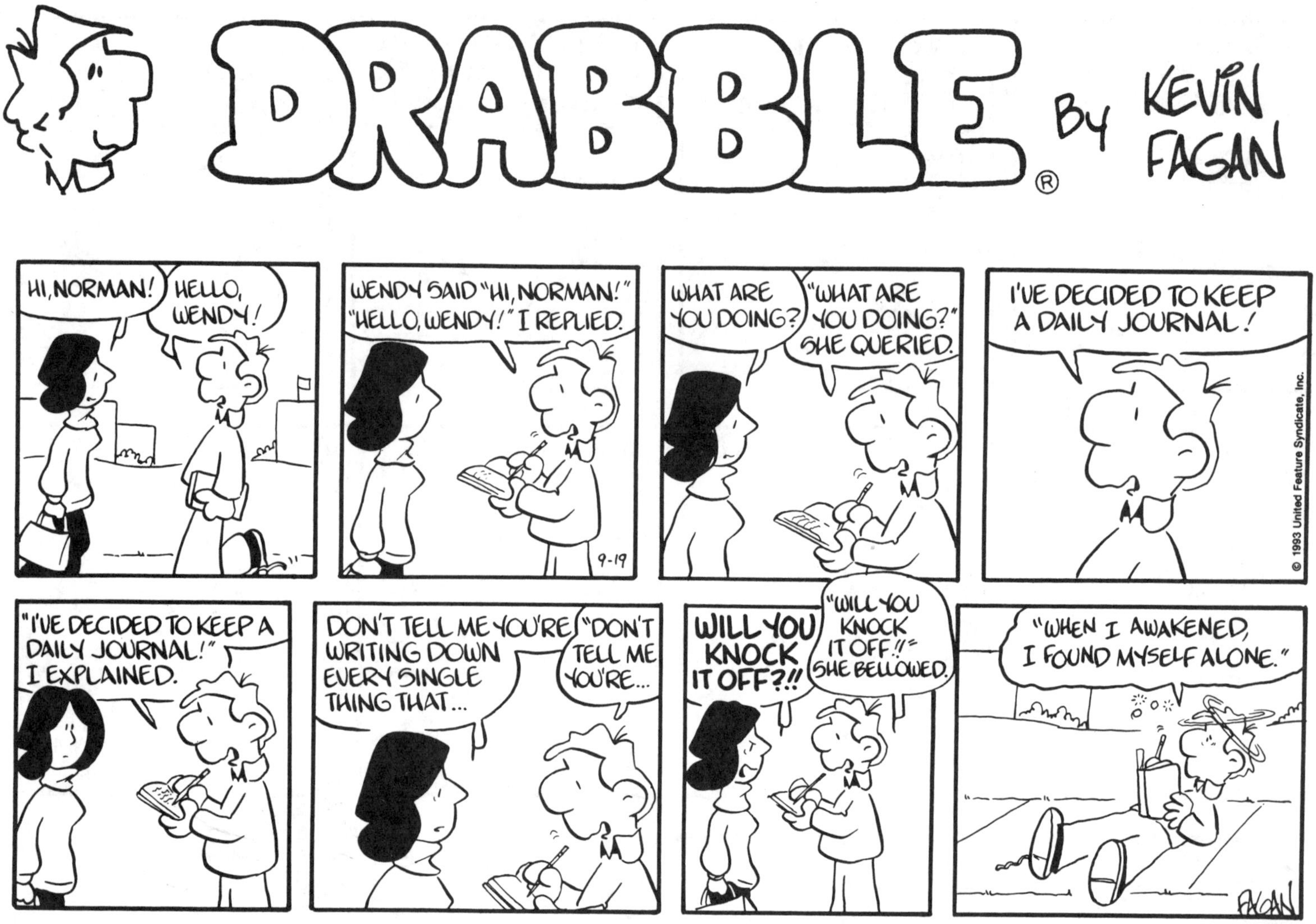
DRABBLE®
By KEVIN FAGAN
HI, NORMAN!
HELLO, WENDY!
WENDY SAID "HI, NORMAN!" "HELLO, WENDY!" I REPLIED.
9-19
WHAT ARE YOU DOING?
"WHAT ARE YOU DOING?" SHE QUERIED.
I'VE DECIDED TO KEEP A DAILY JOURNAL!
© 1993 United Feature Syndicate, Inc.
"I'VE DECIDED TO KEEP A DAILY JOURNAL!" I EXPLAINED.
DON'T TELL ME YOU'RE WRITING DOWN EVERY SINGLE THING THAT...
"DON'T TELL ME YOU'RE...
WILL YOU KNOCK IT OFF?!!
"WILL YOU KNOCK IT OFF?!!" SHE BELLOWED.
"WHEN I AWAKENED, I FOUND MYSELF ALONE."
FAGAN

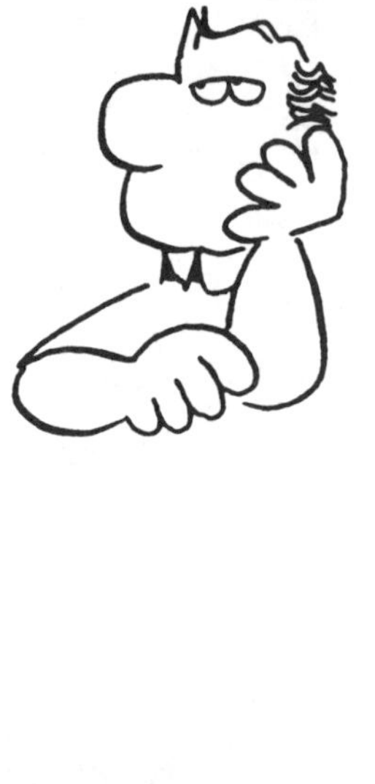

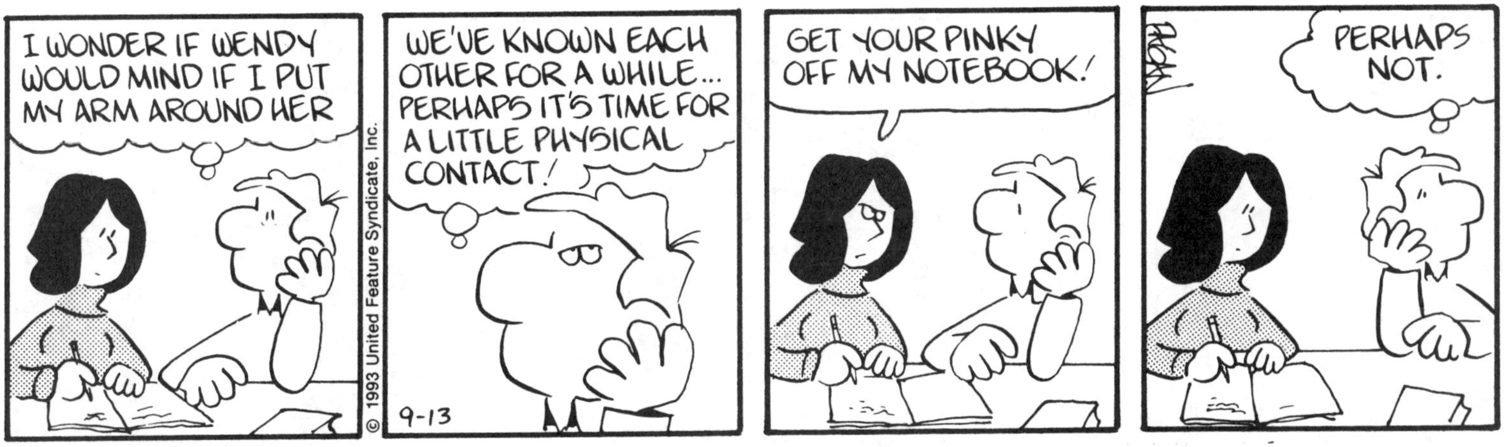
I WONDER IF WENDY WOULD MIND IF I PUT MY ARM AROUND HER
© 1993 United Feature Syndicate, Inc.
WE'VE KNOWN EACH OTHER FOR A WHILE... PERHAPS IT'S TIME FOR A LITTLE PHYSICAL CONTACT!
9-13
GET YOUR PINKY OFF MY NOTEBOOK!
PERHAPS NOT.

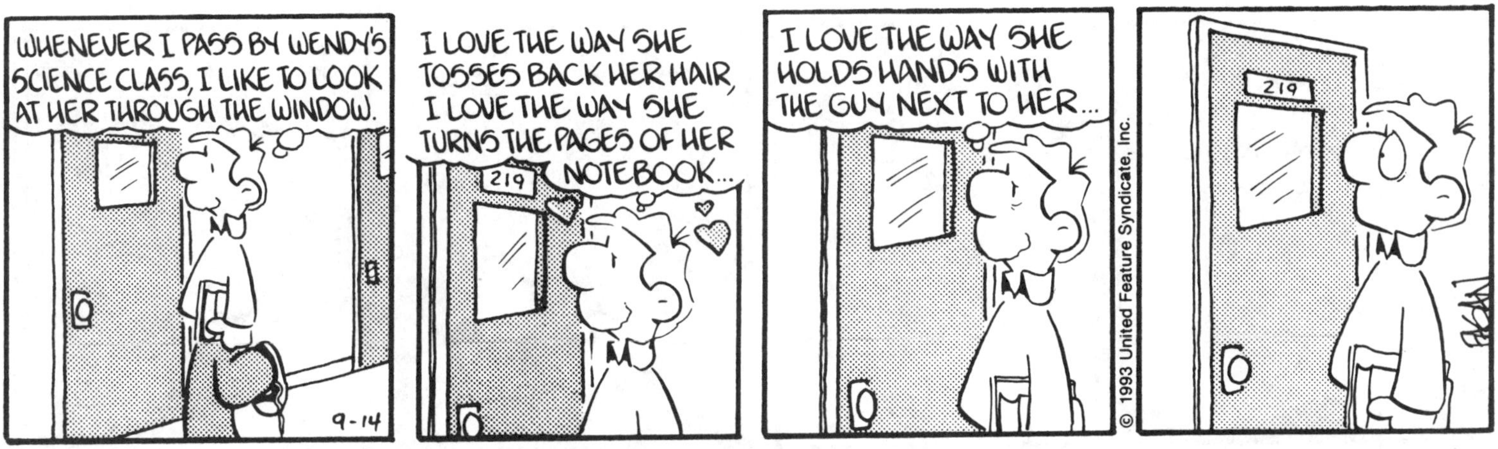
WHENEVER I PASS BY WENDY'S SCIENCE CLASS, I LIKE TO LOOK AT HER THROUGH THE WINDOW.
9-14
I LOVE THE WAY SHE TOSSES BACK HER HAIR, I LOVE THE WAY SHE TURNS THE PAGES OF HER NOTEBOOK...
219
I LOVE THE WAY SHE HOLDS HANDS WITH THE GUY NEXT TO HER...
© 1993 United Feature Syndicate, Inc.
219

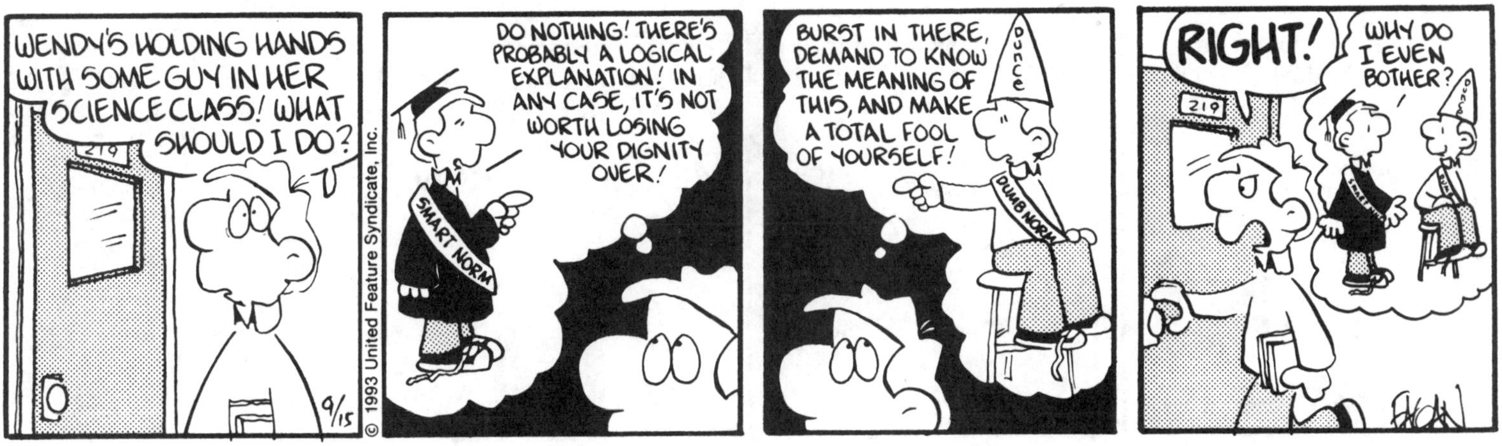
WENDY'S HOLDING HANDS WITH SOME GUY IN HER SCIENCE CLASS! WHAT SHOULD I DO?
9/15
© 1993 United Feature Syndicate, Inc.
DO NOTHING! THERE'S PROBABLY A LOGICAL EXPLANATION! IN ANY CASE, IT'S NOT WORTH LOSING YOUR DIGNITY OVER!
SMART NORM
BURST IN THERE, DEMAND TO KNOW THE MEANING OF THIS, AND MAKE A TOTAL FOOL OF YOURSELF!
DUNCE
DUMB NORM
RIGHT!
WHY DO I EVEN BOTHER?
219

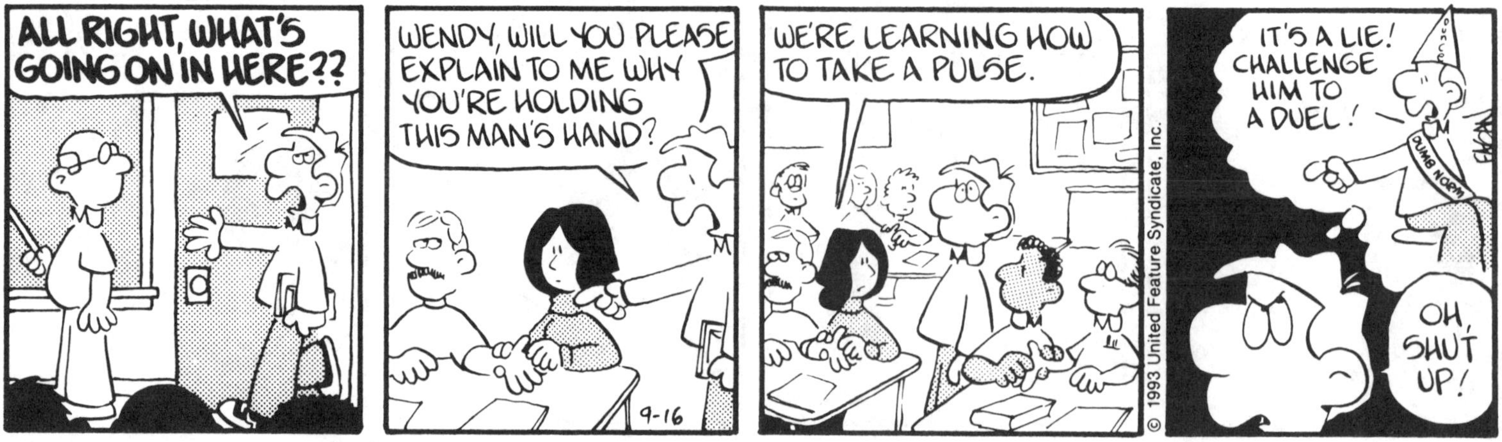
ALL RIGHT, WHAT'S GOING ON IN HERE??
WENDY, WILL YOU PLEASE EXPLAIN TO ME WHY YOU'RE HOLDING THIS MAN'S HAND?
9-16
WE'RE LEARNING HOW TO TAKE A PULSE.
© 1993 United Feature Syndicate, Inc.
IT'S A LIE! CHALLENGE HIM TO A DUEL!
DUNCE
DUMB NORM
OH, SHUT UP!

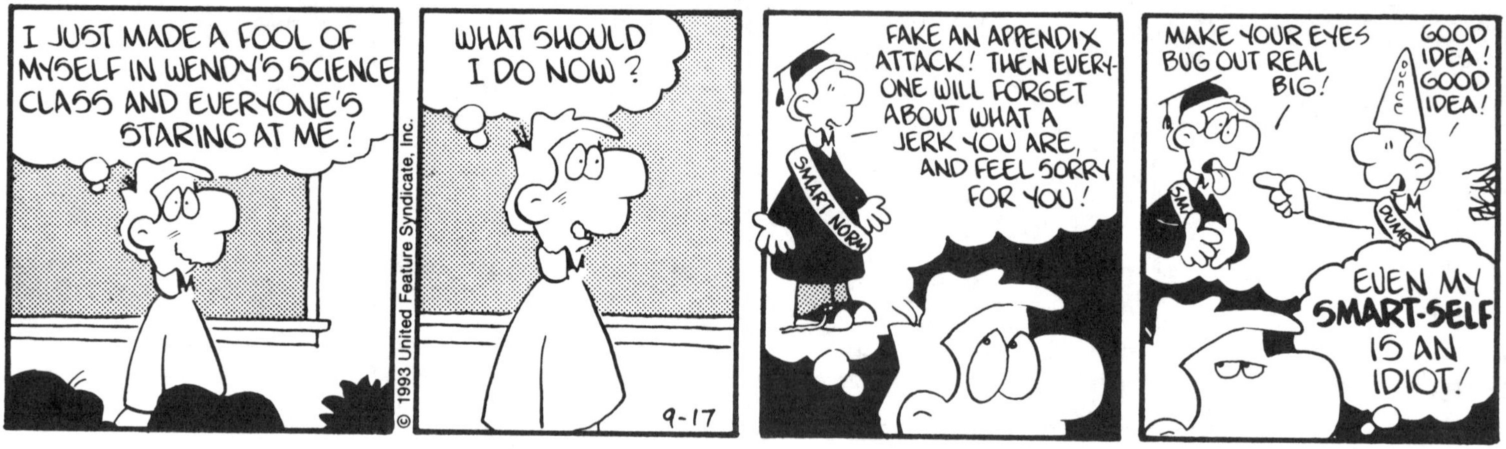
I JUST MADE A FOOL OF MYSELF IN WENDY'S SCIENCE CLASS AND EVERYONE'S STARING AT ME!
© 1993 United Feature Syndicate, Inc.
WHAT SHOULD I DO NOW?
9-17
FAKE AN APPENDIX ATTACK! THEN EVERYONE WILL FORGET ABOUT WHAT A JERK YOU ARE, AND FEEL SORRY FOR YOU!
SMART NORM
MAKE YOUR EYES BUG OUT REAL BIG!
GOOD IDEA! GOOD IDEA!
DUNCE
EVEN MY **SMART-SELF** IS AN IDIOT!

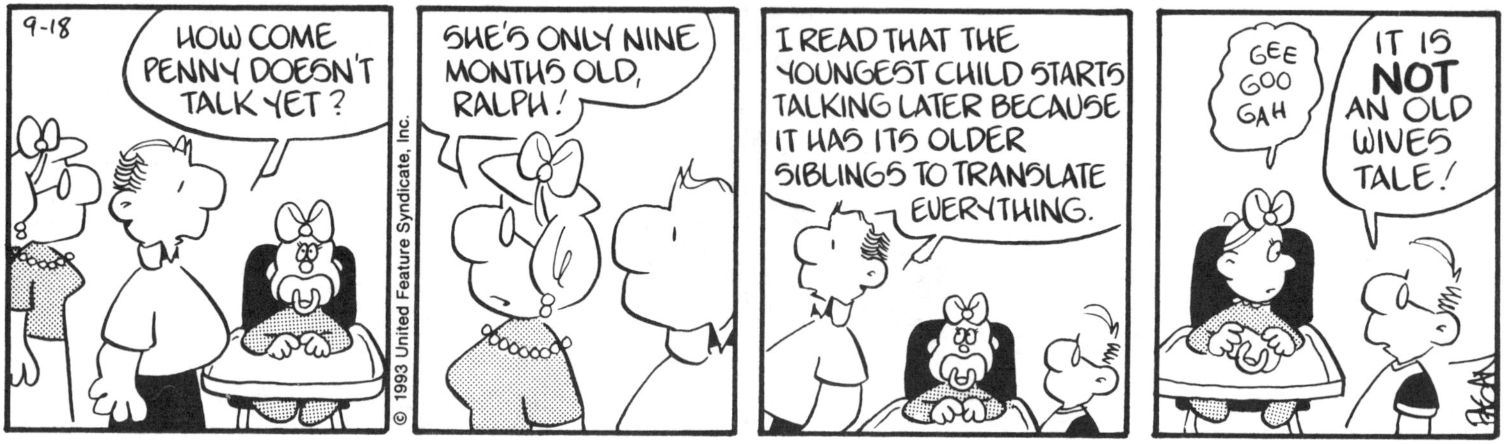
9-18
HOW COME PENNY DOESN'T TALK YET?
© 1993 United Feature Syndicate, Inc.
SHE'S ONLY NINE MONTHS OLD, RALPH!
I READ THAT THE YOUNGEST CHILD STARTS TALKING LATER BECAUSE IT HAS ITS OLDER SIBLINGS TO TRANSLATE EVERYTHING.
GEE GOO GAH
IT IS **NOT** AN OLD WIVES TALE!

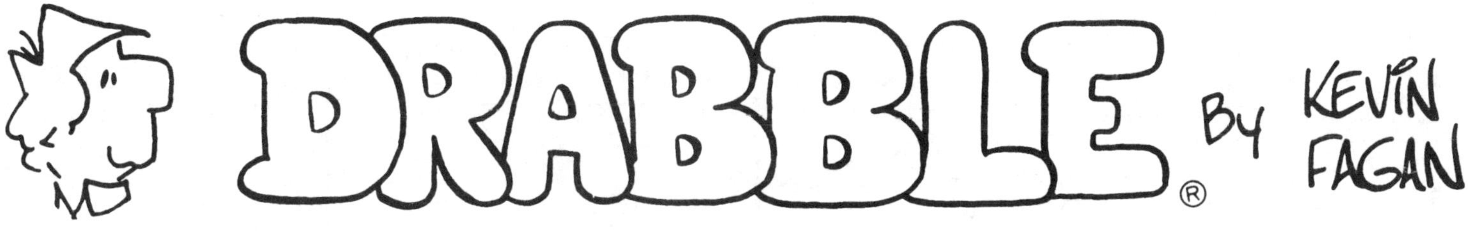
DRABBLE
By KEVIN FAGAN

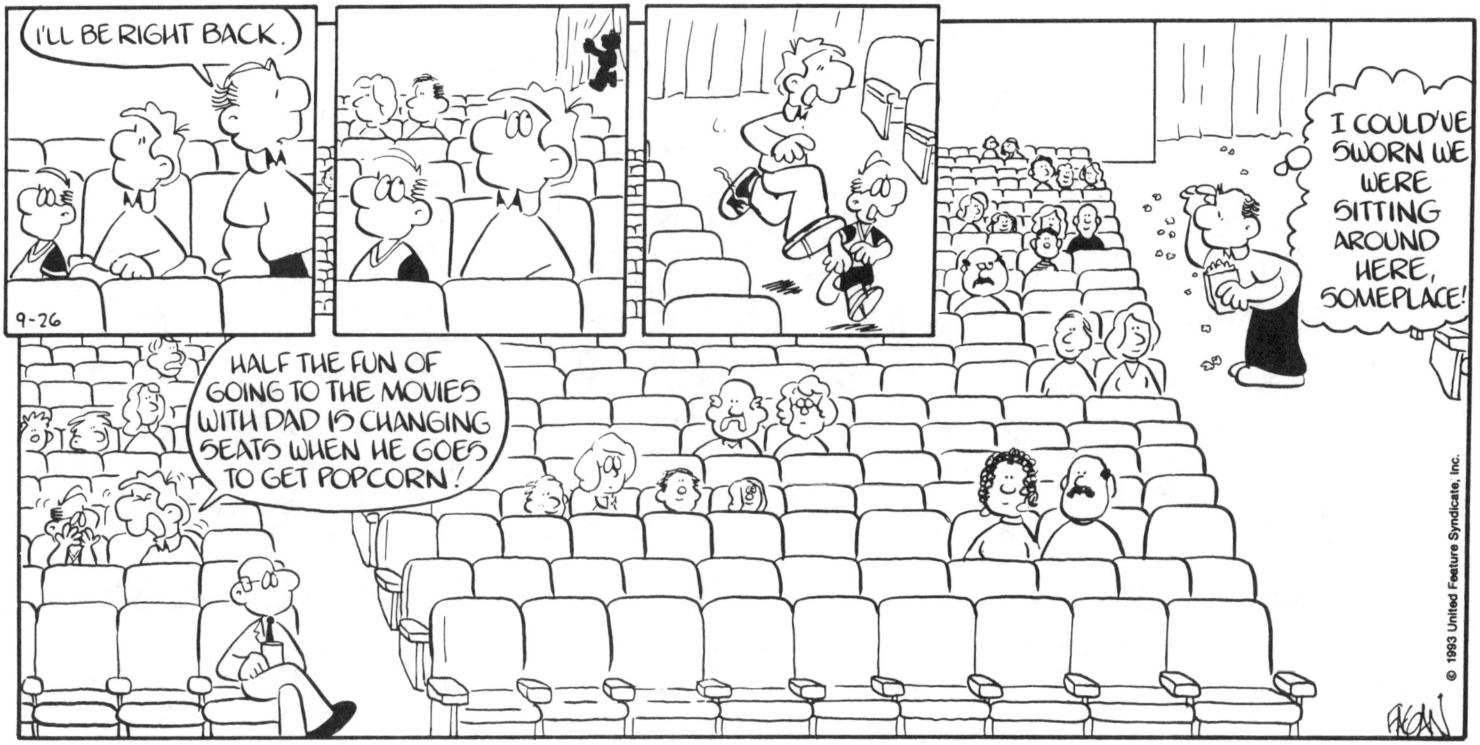
I'LL BE RIGHT BACK.
9-26
HALF THE FUN OF GOING TO THE MOVIES WITH DAD IS CHANGING SEATS WHEN HE GOES TO GET POPCORN!
I COULD'VE SWORN WE WERE SITTING AROUND HERE, SOMEPLACE!
© 1993 United Feature Syndicate, Inc.
FAGAN

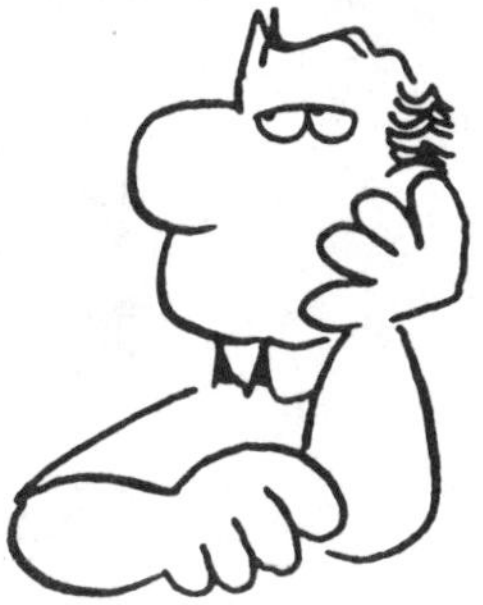

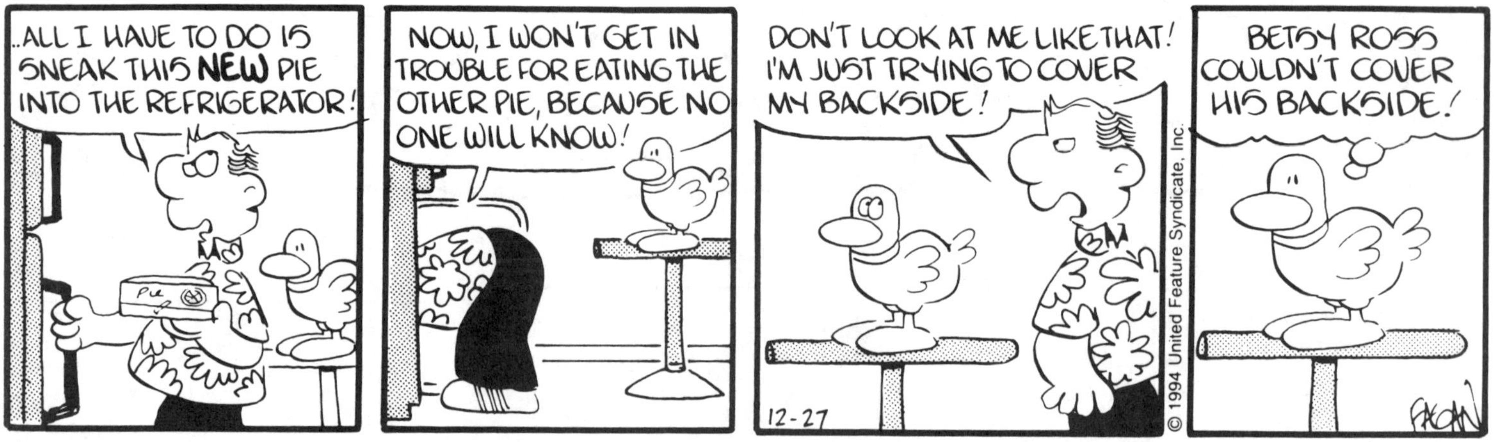
..ALL I HAVE TO DO IS SNEAK THIS NEW PIE INTO THE REFRIGERATOR!
PIE
NOW, I WON'T GET IN TROUBLE FOR EATING THE OTHER PIE, BECAUSE NO ONE WILL KNOW!
DON'T LOOK AT ME LIKE THAT! I'M JUST TRYING TO COVER MY BACKSIDE!
12-27
© 1994 United Feature Syndicate, Inc.
BETSY ROSS COULDN'T COVER HIS BACKSIDE!
FAGAN

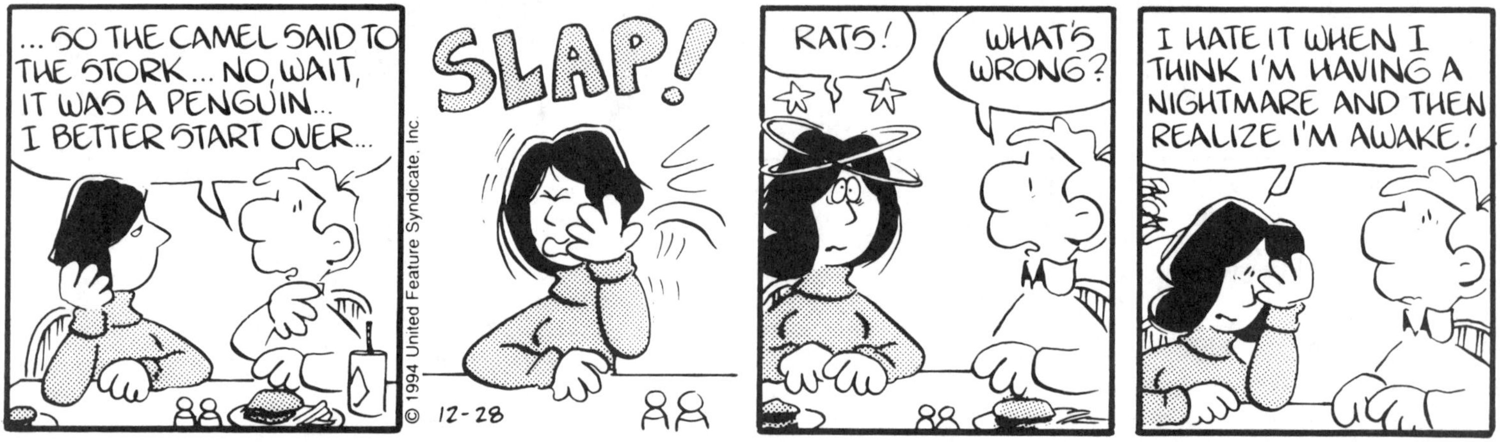
... SO THE CAMEL SAID TO THE STORK... NO, WAIT, IT WAS A PENGUIN... I BETTER START OVER...
© 1994 United Feature Syndicate, Inc.
SLAP!
12-28
RATS!
WHAT'S WRONG?
I HATE IT WHEN I THINK I'M HAVING A NIGHTMARE AND THEN REALIZE I'M AWAKE!

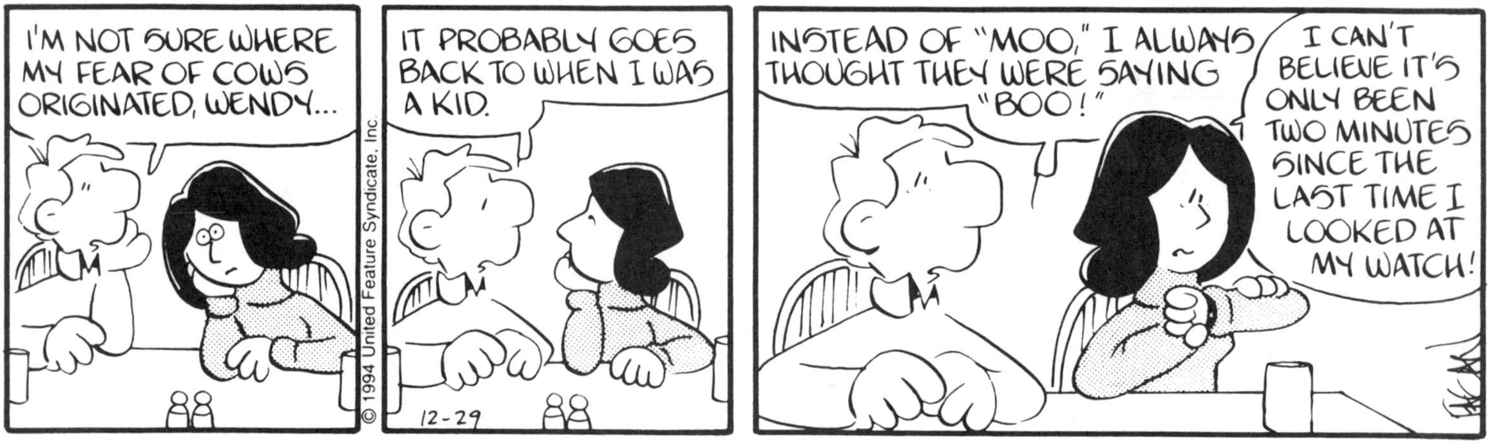
I'M NOT SURE WHERE MY FEAR OF COWS ORIGINATED, WENDY...
© 1994 United Feature Syndicate, Inc.
IT PROBABLY GOES BACK TO WHEN I WAS A KID.
12-29
INSTEAD OF "MOO," I ALWAYS THOUGHT THEY WERE SAYING "BOO!"
I CAN'T BELIEVE IT'S ONLY BEEN TWO MINUTES SINCE THE LAST TIME I LOOKED AT MY WATCH!

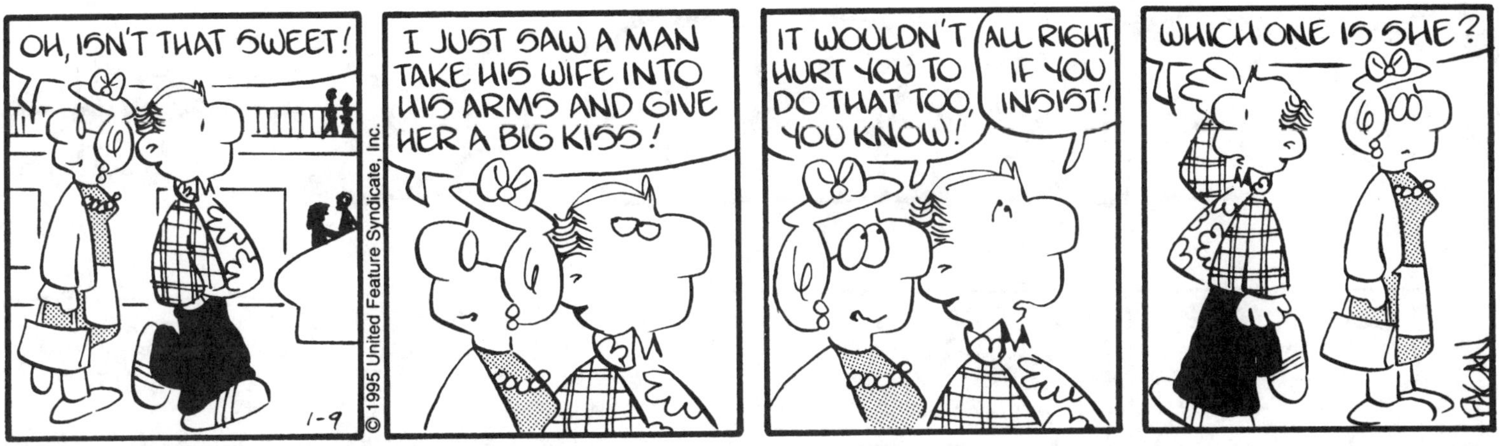
OH, ISN'T THAT SWEET!
I JUST SAW A MAN TAKE HIS WIFE INTO HIS ARMS AND GIVE HER A BIG KISS!
IT WOULDN'T HURT YOU TO DO THAT TOO, YOU KNOW!
ALL RIGHT, IF YOU INSIST!
WHICH ONE IS SHE?
1-9
© 1995 United Feature Syndicate, Inc.

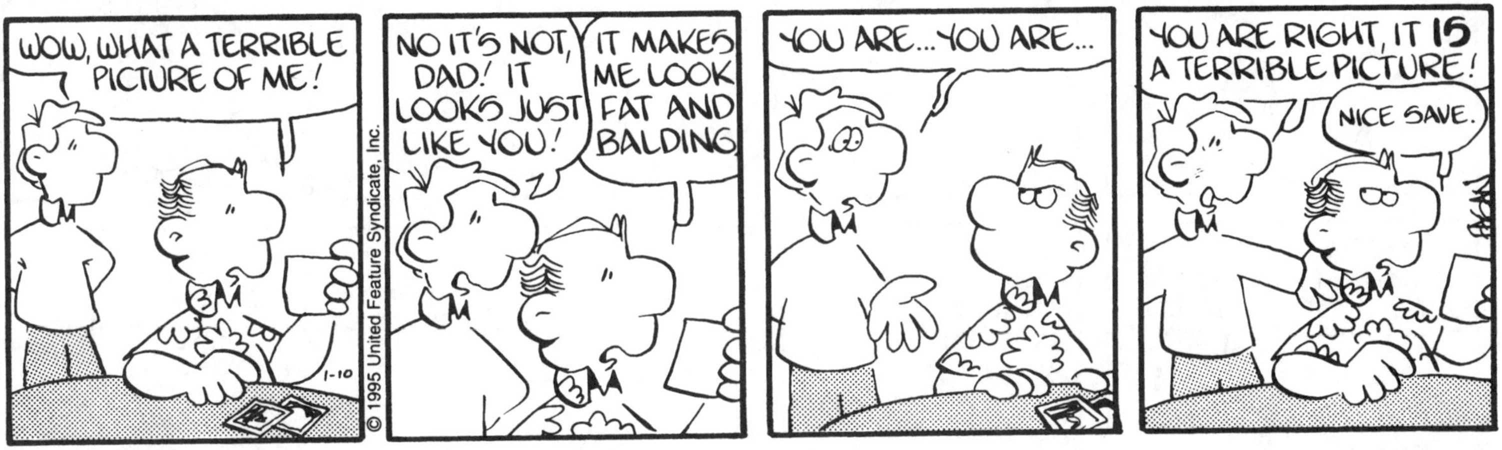
WOW, WHAT A TERRIBLE PICTURE OF ME!
NO IT'S NOT, DAD! IT LOOKS JUST LIKE YOU!
IT MAKES ME LOOK FAT AND BALDING
YOU ARE... YOU ARE...
YOU ARE RIGHT, IT **IS** A TERRIBLE PICTURE!
NICE SAVE.
1-10
© 1995 United Feature Syndicate, Inc.

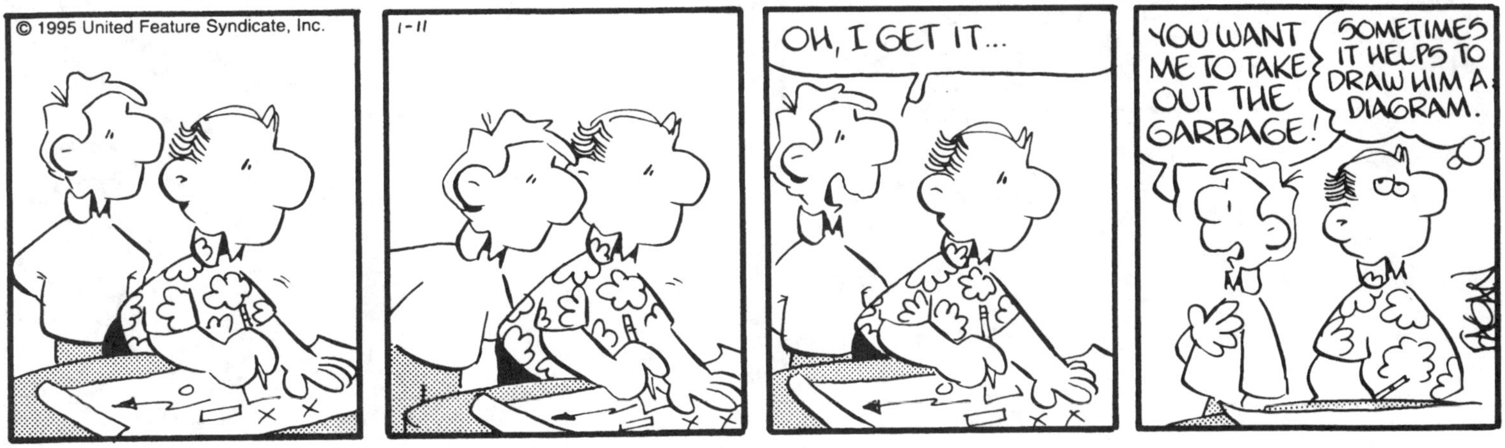
© 1995 United Feature Syndicate, Inc.
1-11
OH, I GET IT...
YOU WANT ME TO TAKE OUT THE GARBAGE!
SOMETIMES IT HELPS TO DRAW HIM A DIAGRAM.

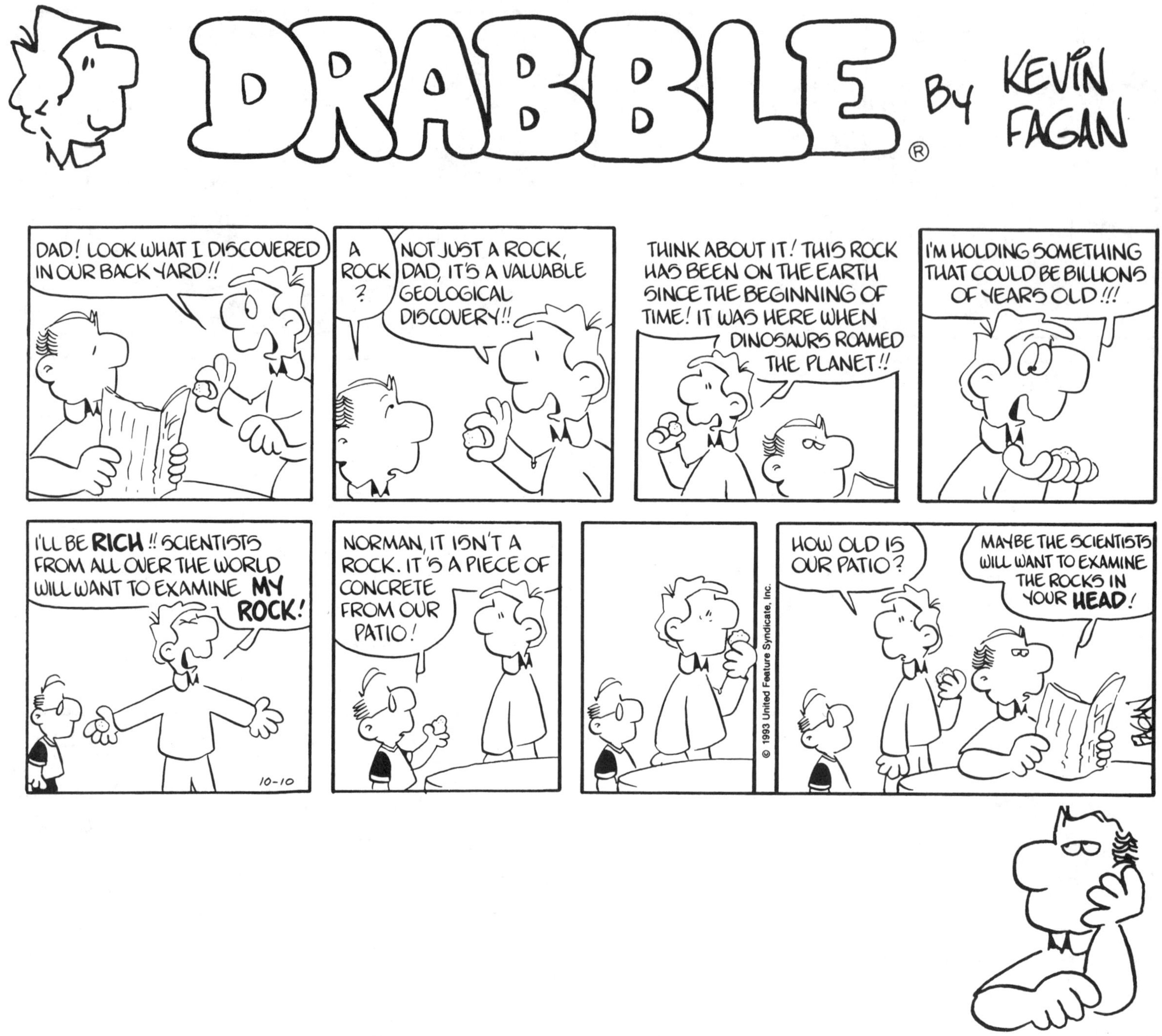

DRABBLE
By KEVIN FAGAN
®
DAD! LOOK WHAT I DISCOVERED IN OUR BACK YARD!!
A ROCK?
NOT JUST A ROCK, DAD, IT'S A VALUABLE GEOLOGICAL DISCOVERY!!
THINK ABOUT IT! THIS ROCK HAS BEEN ON THE EARTH SINCE THE BEGINNING OF TIME! IT WAS HERE WHEN DINOSAURS ROAMED THE PLANET!!
I'M HOLDING SOMETHING THAT COULD BE BILLIONS OF YEARS OLD!!!
I'LL BE **RICH**!! SCIENTISTS FROM ALL OVER THE WORLD WILL WANT TO EXAMINE **MY ROCK**!
10-10
NORMAN, IT ISN'T A ROCK. IT'S A PIECE OF CONCRETE FROM OUR PATIO!
© 1993 United Feature Syndicate, Inc.
HOW OLD IS OUR PATIO?
MAYBE THE SCIENTISTS WILL WANT TO EXAMINE THE ROCKS IN YOUR **HEAD**!
FAGAN

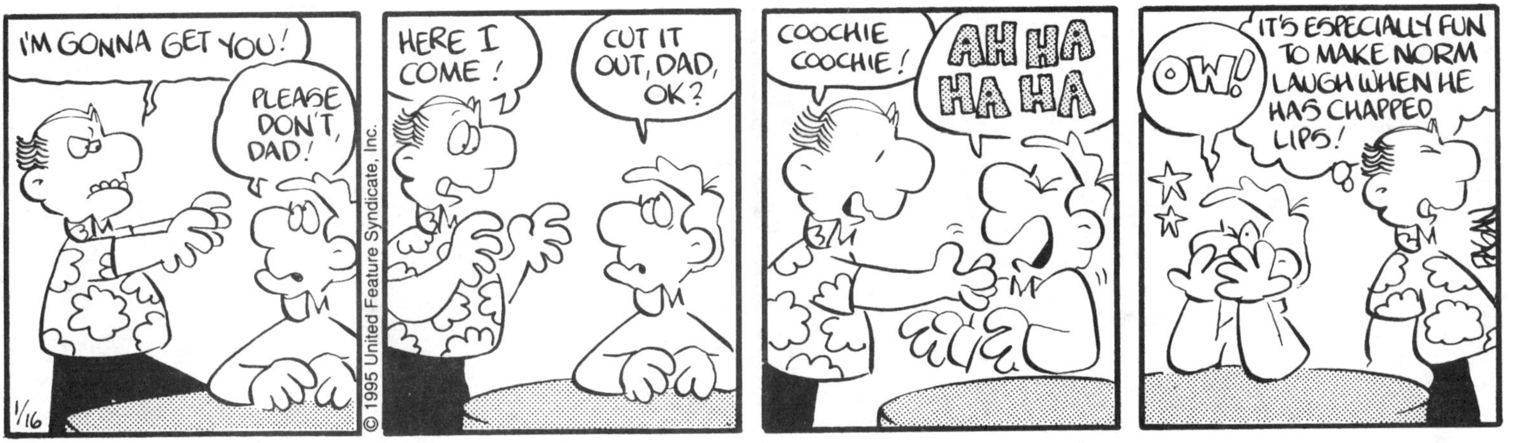
I'M GONNA GET YOU!
PLEASE DON'T, DAD!
1/16
© 1995 United Feature Syndicate, Inc.
HERE I COME!
CUT IT OUT, DAD, OK?
COOCHIE COOCHIE!
AH HA HA HA
OW!
IT'S ESPECIALLY FUN TO MAKE NORM LAUGH WHEN HE HAS CHAPPED LIPS!

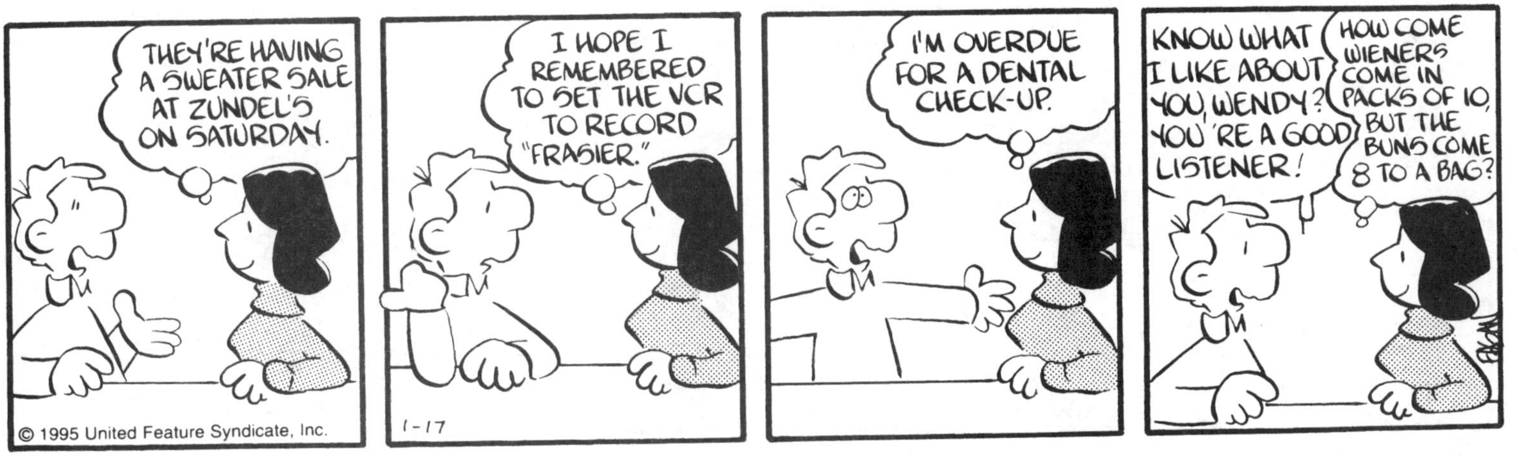
THEY'RE HAVING A SWEATER SALE AT ZUNDEL'S ON SATURDAY.
© 1995 United Feature Syndicate, Inc.
I HOPE I REMEMBERED TO SET THE VCR TO RECORD "FRASIER."
1-17
I'M OVERDUE FOR A DENTAL CHECK-UP.
KNOW WHAT I LIKE ABOUT YOU, WENDY? YOU'RE A GOOD LISTENER!
HOW COME WIENERS COME IN PACKS OF 10, BUT THE BUNS COME 8 TO A BAG?

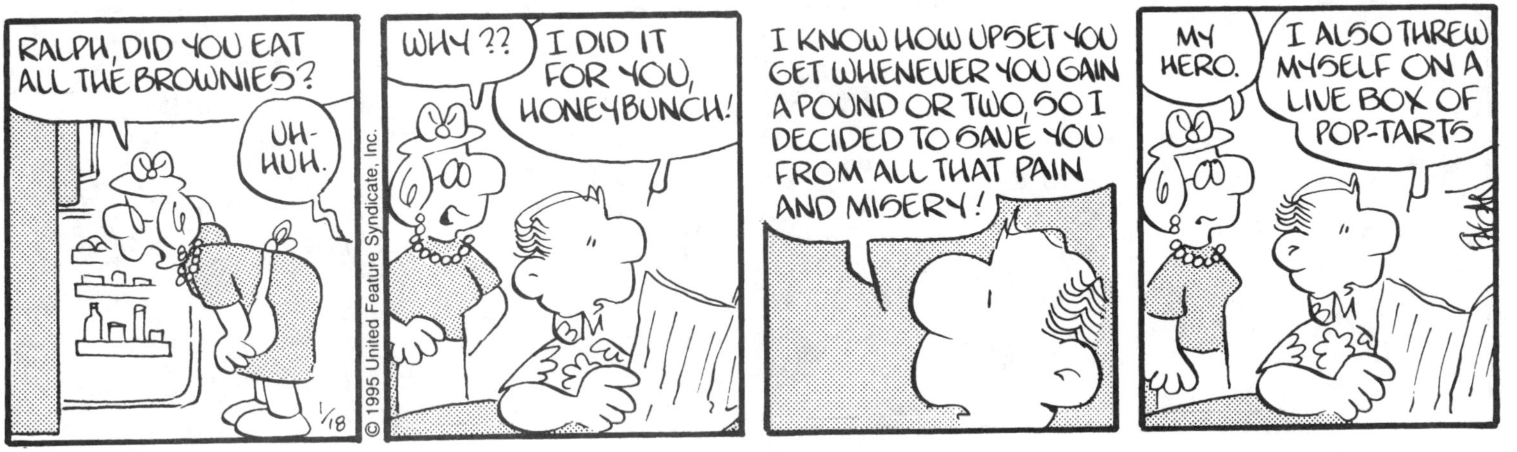
RALPH, DID YOU EAT ALL THE BROWNIES?
UH-HUH.
1/18
© 1995 United Feature Syndicate, Inc.
WHY??
I DID IT FOR YOU, HONEYBUNCH!
I KNOW HOW UPSET YOU GET WHENEVER YOU GAIN A POUND OR TWO, SO I DECIDED TO SAVE YOU FROM ALL THAT PAIN AND MISERY!
MY HERO.
I ALSO THREW MYSELF ON A LIVE BOX OF POP-TARTS

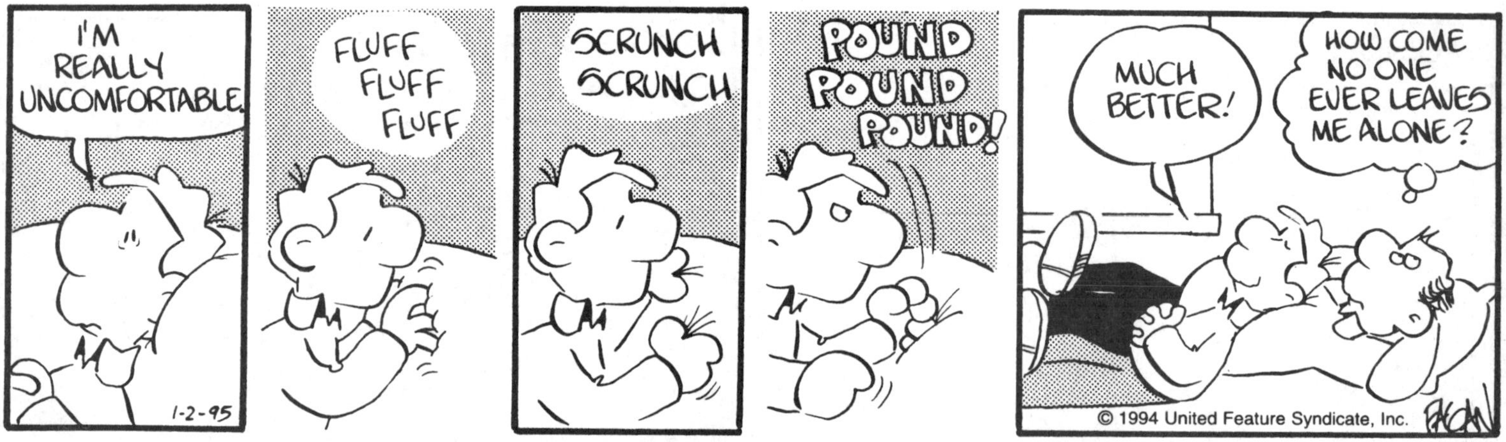
I'M REALLY UNCOMFORTABLE.
1-2-95
FLUFF FLUFF FLUFF
SCRUNCH SCRUNCH
POUND POUND POUND!
MUCH BETTER!
HOW COME NO ONE EVER LEAVES ME ALONE?
© 1994 United Feature Syndicate, Inc.

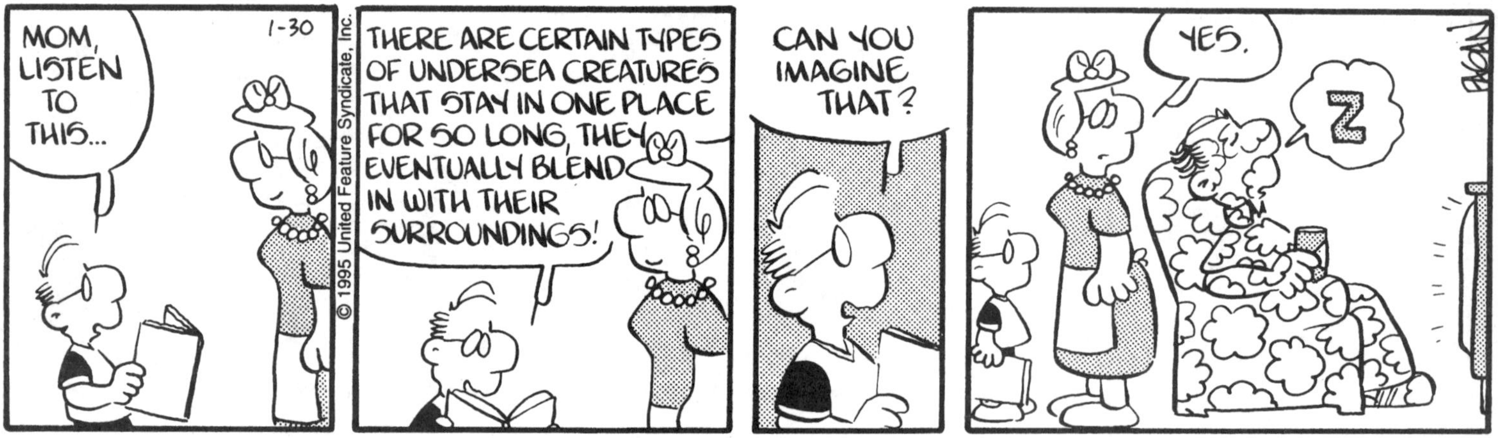
1-30
MOM, LISTEN TO THIS...
© 1995 United Feature Syndicate, Inc.
THERE ARE CERTAIN TYPES OF UNDERSEA CREATURES THAT STAY IN ONE PLACE FOR SO LONG, THEY EVENTUALLY BLEND IN WITH THEIR SURROUNDINGS!
CAN YOU IMAGINE THAT?
YES.
Z

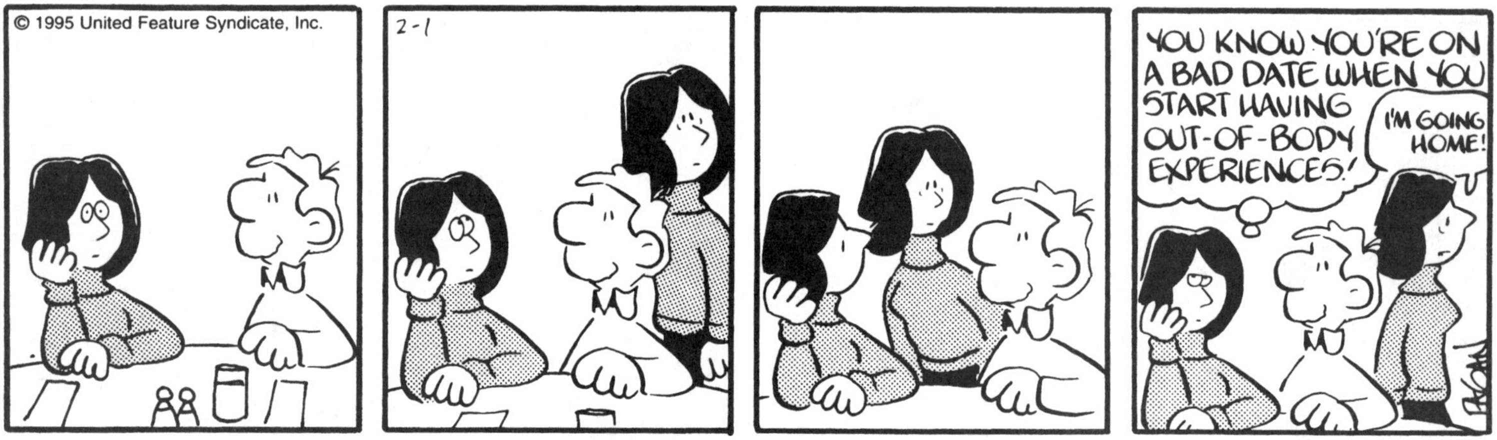
© 1995 United Feature Syndicate, Inc.
2-1
YOU KNOW YOU'RE ON A BAD DATE WHEN YOU START HAVING OUT-OF-BODY EXPERIENCES!
I'M GOING HOME!

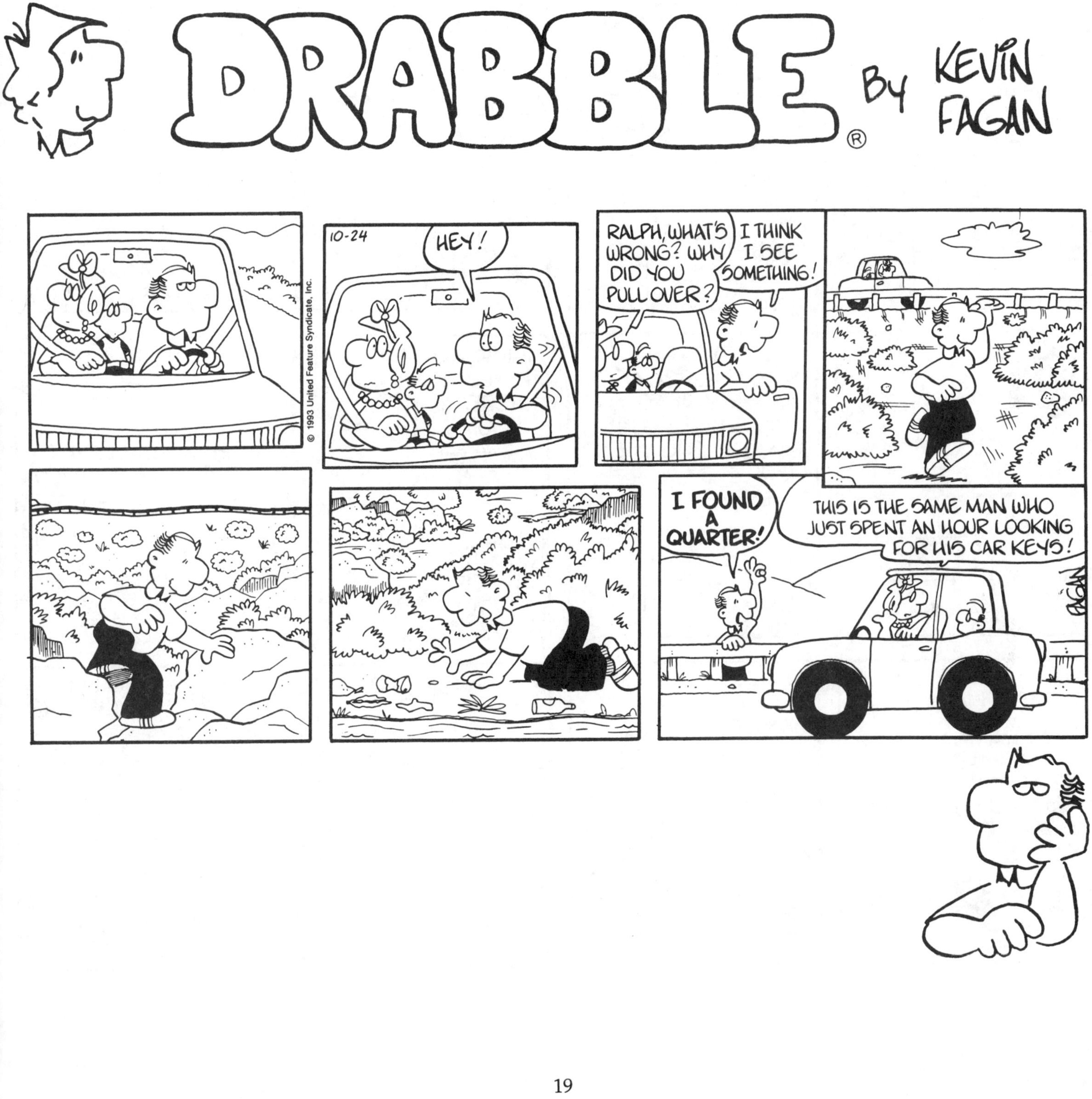
DRABBLE
By KEVIN FAGAN
© 1993 United Feature Syndicate, Inc.
10-24
HEY!
RALPH, WHAT'S WRONG? WHY DID YOU PULL OVER?
I THINK I SEE SOMETHING!
I FOUND A QUARTER!
THIS IS THE SAME MAN WHO JUST SPENT AN HOUR LOOKING FOR HIS CAR KEYS!

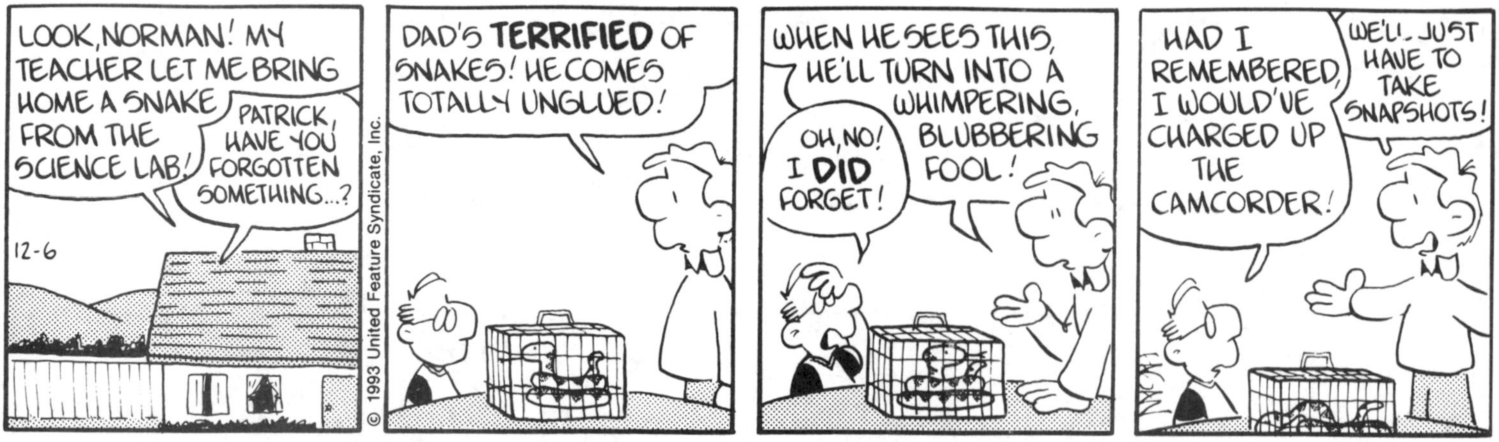
LOOK, NORMAN! MY TEACHER LET ME BRING HOME A SNAKE FROM THE SCIENCE LAB!
PATRICK, HAVE YOU FORGOTTEN SOMETHING...?
12-6
© 1993 United Feature Syndicate, Inc.
DAD'S **TERRIFIED** OF SNAKES! HE COMES TOTALLY UNGLUED!
WHEN HE SEES THIS, HE'LL TURN INTO A WHIMPERING, BLUBBERING FOOL!
OH, NO! I **DID** FORGET!
HAD I REMEMBERED, I WOULD'VE CHARGED UP THE CAMCORDER!
WE'LL JUST HAVE TO TAKE SNAPSHOTS!

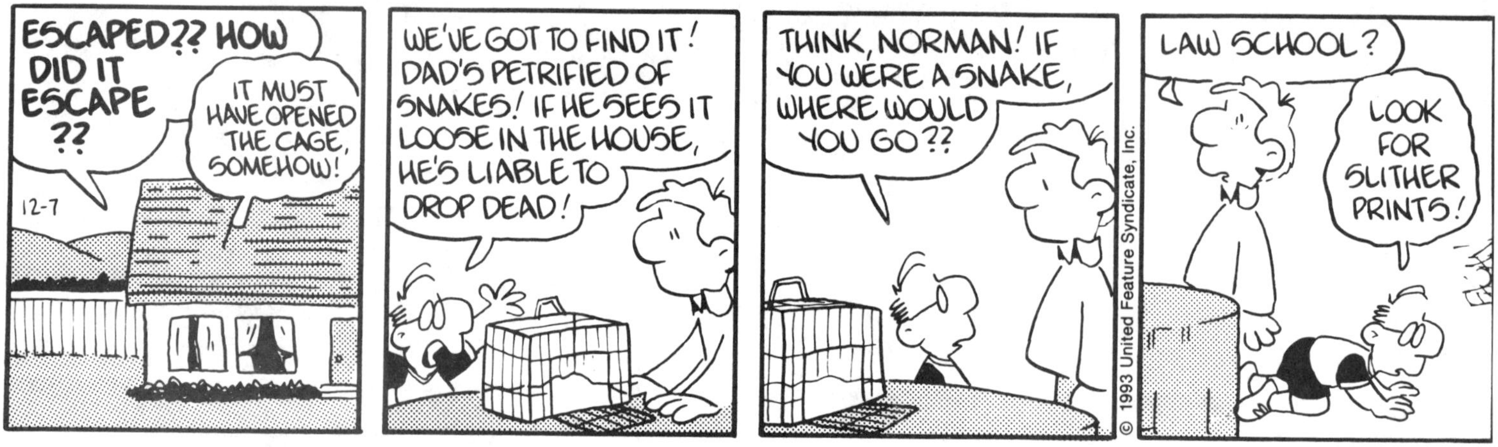
ESCAPED?? HOW DID IT ESCAPE??
IT MUST HAVE OPENED THE CAGE, SOMEHOW!
12-7
WE'VE GOT TO FIND IT! DAD'S PETRIFIED OF SNAKES! IF HE SEES IT LOOSE IN THE HOUSE, HE'S LIABLE TO DROP DEAD!
THINK, NORMAN! IF YOU WERE A SNAKE, WHERE WOULD YOU GO??
© 1993 United Feature Syndicate, Inc.
LAW SCHOOL?
LOOK FOR SLITHER PRINTS!

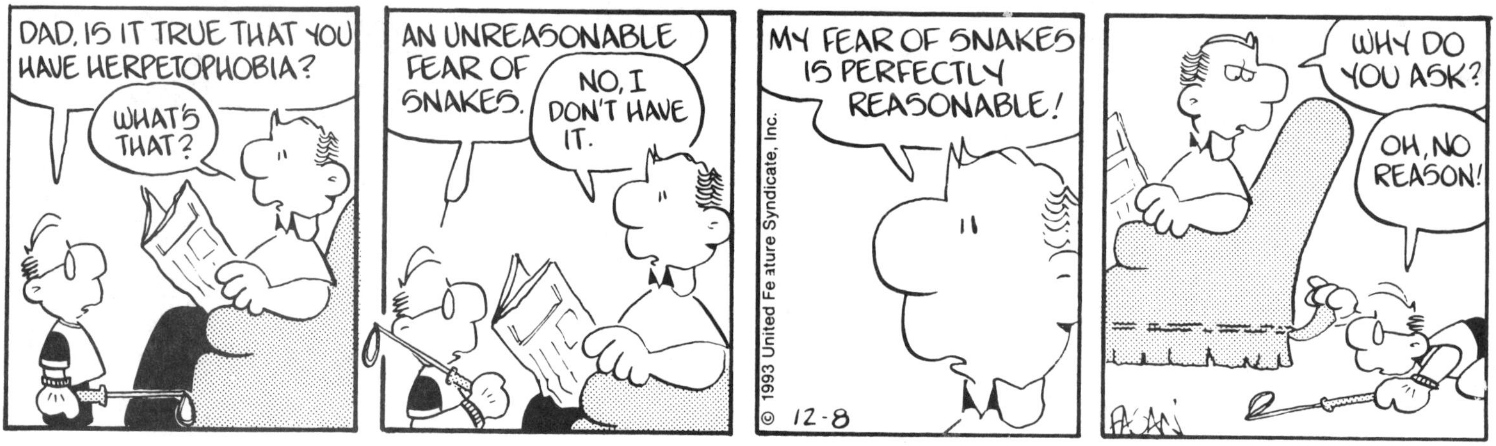
DAD, IS IT TRUE THAT YOU HAVE HERPETOPHOBIA?
WHAT'S THAT?
AN UNREASONABLE FEAR OF SNAKES.
NO, I DON'T HAVE IT.
MY FEAR OF SNAKES IS PERFECTLY REASONABLE!
© 1993 United Feature Syndicate, Inc.
12-8
WHY DO YOU ASK?
OH, NO REASON!

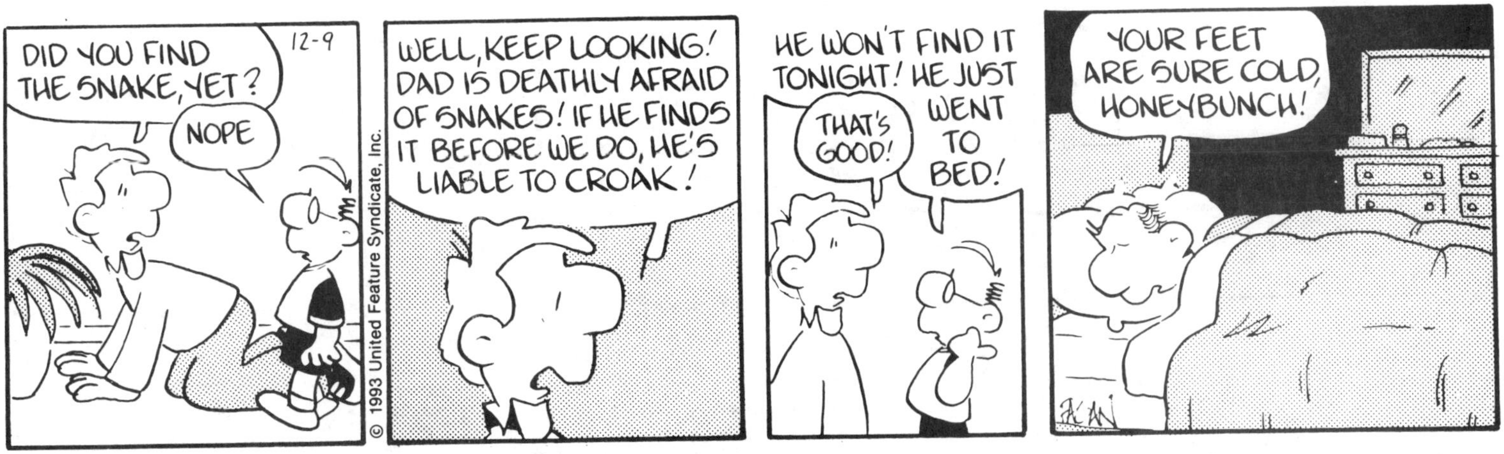
12-9
DID YOU FIND THE SNAKE, YET?
NOPE
© 1993 United Feature Syndicate, Inc.
WELL, KEEP LOOKING! DAD IS DEATHLY AFRAID OF SNAKES! IF HE FINDS IT BEFORE WE DO, HE'S LIABLE TO CROAK!
HE WON'T FIND IT TONIGHT! HE JUST WENT TO BED!
THAT'S GOOD!
YOUR FEET ARE SURE COLD, HONEYBUNCH!

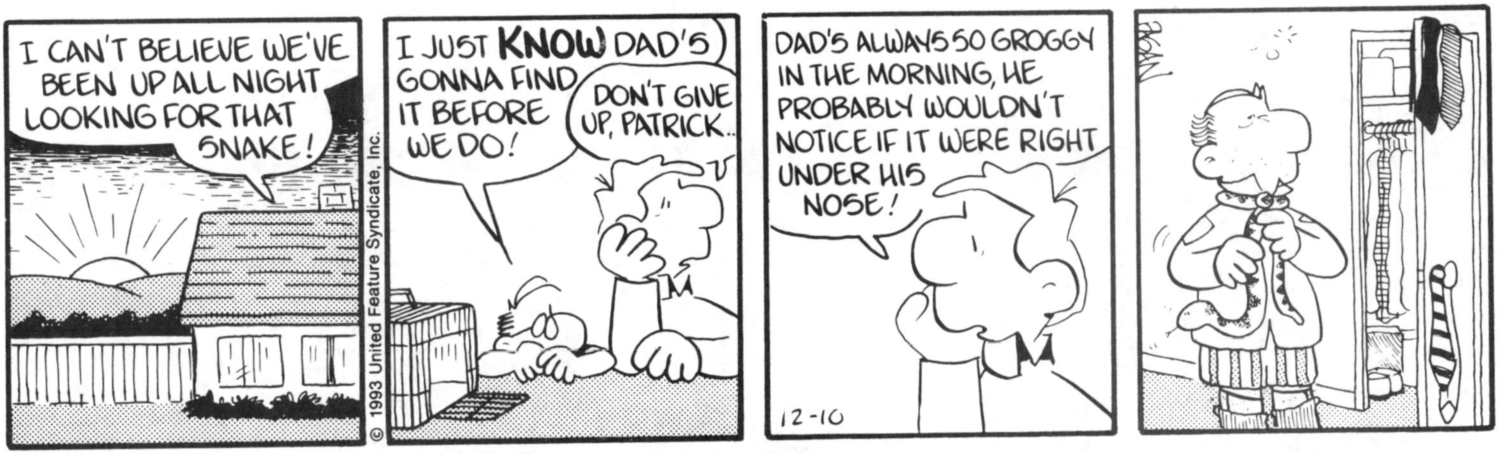
I CAN'T BELIEVE WE'VE BEEN UP ALL NIGHT LOOKING FOR THAT SNAKE!
© 1993 United Feature Syndicate, Inc.
I JUST **KNOW** DAD'S GONNA FIND IT BEFORE WE DO!
DON'T GIVE UP, PATRICK...
DAD'S ALWAYS SO GROGGY IN THE MORNING, HE PROBABLY WOULDN'T NOTICE IF IT WERE RIGHT UNDER HIS NOSE!
12-10

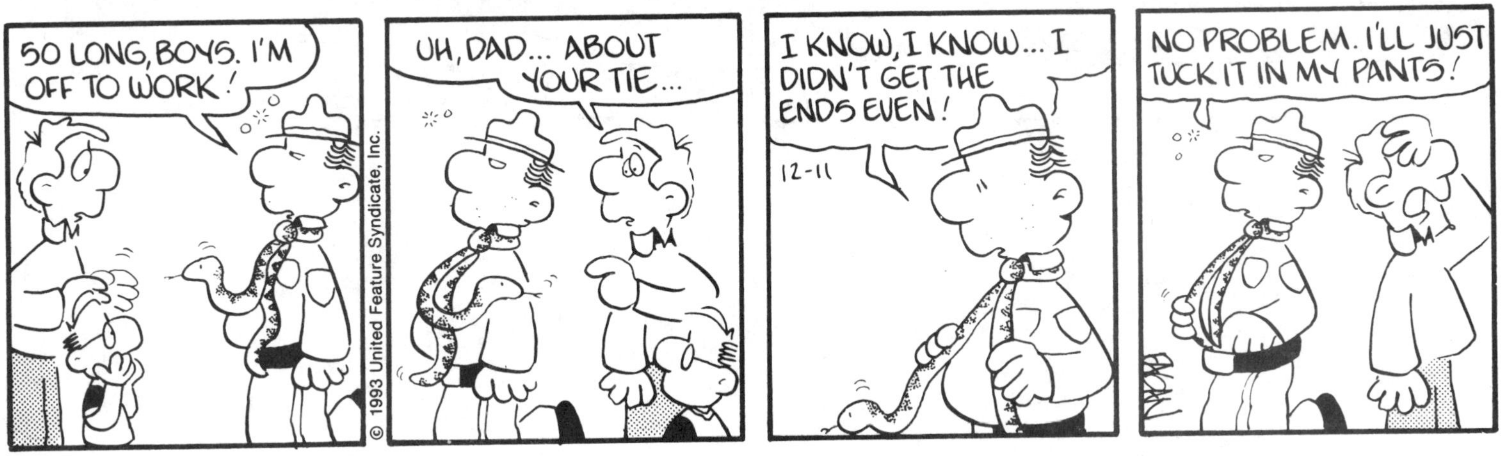
SO LONG, BOYS. I'M OFF TO WORK!
© 1993 United Feature Syndicate, Inc.
UH, DAD... ABOUT YOUR TIE...
I KNOW, I KNOW... I DIDN'T GET THE ENDS EVEN!
12-11
NO PROBLEM. I'LL JUST TUCK IT IN MY PANTS!

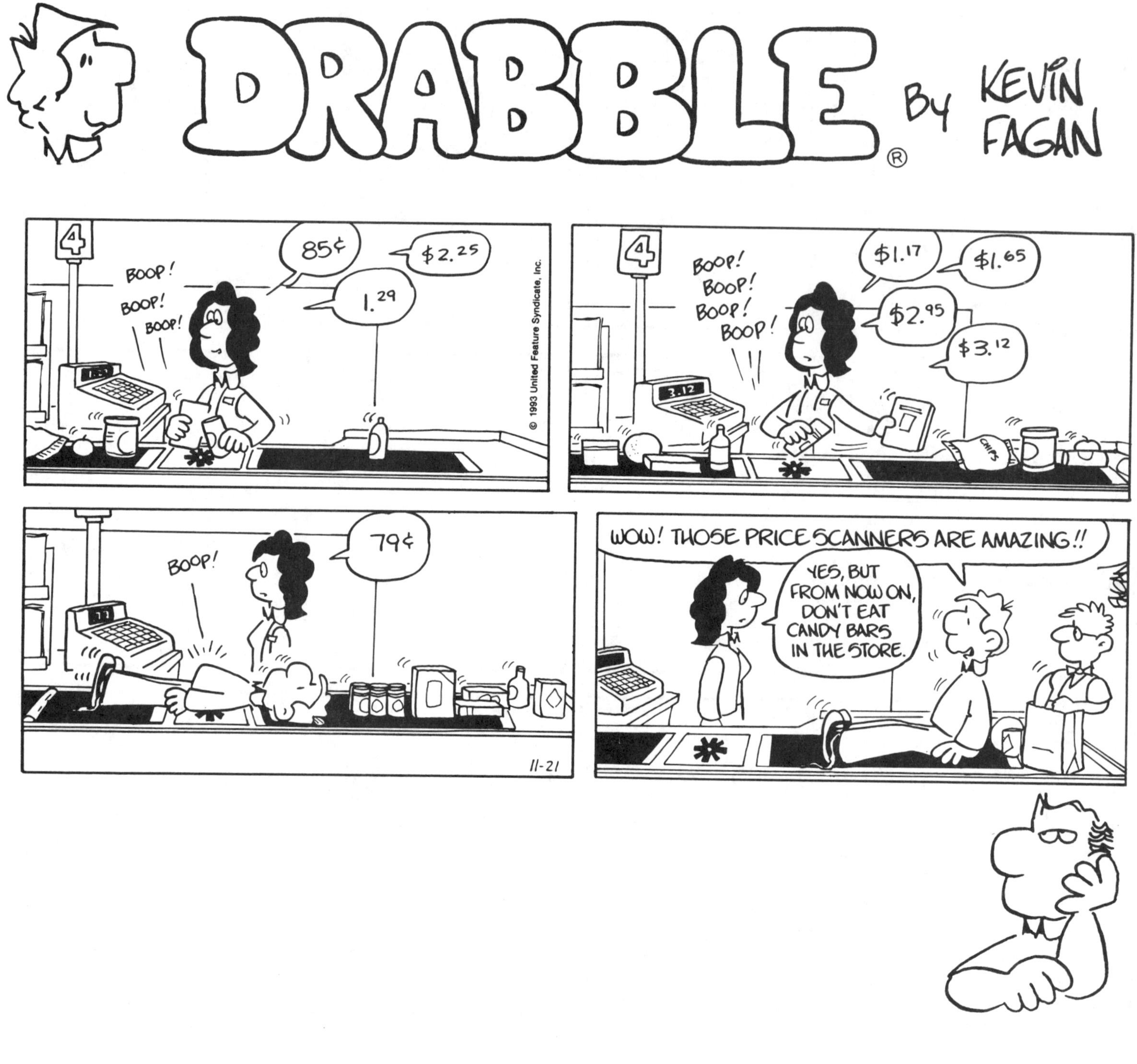
DRABBLE®
By KEVIN FAGAN
BOOP!
BOOP!
BOOP!
85¢
$2.25
1.29
© 1993 United Feature Syndicate, Inc.
BOOP!
BOOP!
BOOP!
BOOP!
$1.17
$1.65
$2.95
$3.12
CHIPS
BOOP!
79¢
11-21
WOW! THOSE PRICE SCANNERS ARE AMAZING!!
YES, BUT FROM NOW ON, DON'T EAT CANDY BARS IN THE STORE.

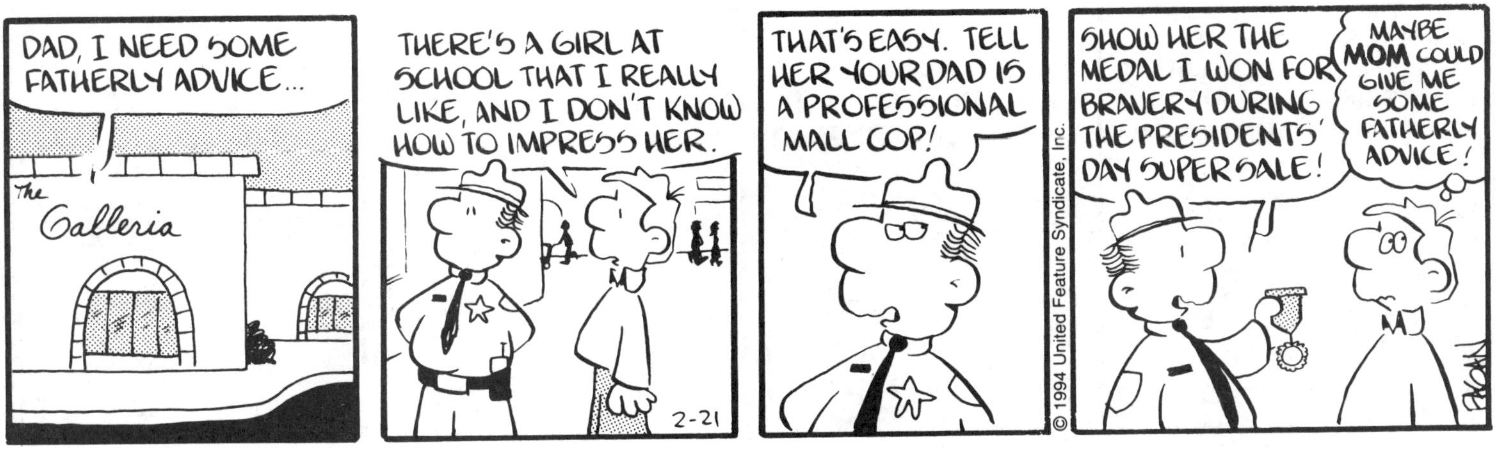
DAD, I NEED SOME FATHERLY ADVICE...
The Galleria
THERE'S A GIRL AT SCHOOL THAT I REALLY LIKE, AND I DON'T KNOW HOW TO IMPRESS HER.
2-21
THAT'S EASY. TELL HER YOUR DAD IS A PROFESSIONAL MALL COP!
© 1994 United Feature Syndicate, Inc.
SHOW HER THE MEDAL I WON FOR BRAVERY DURING THE PRESIDENTS' DAY SUPER SALE!
MAYBE MOM COULD GIVE ME SOME FATHERLY ADVICE!

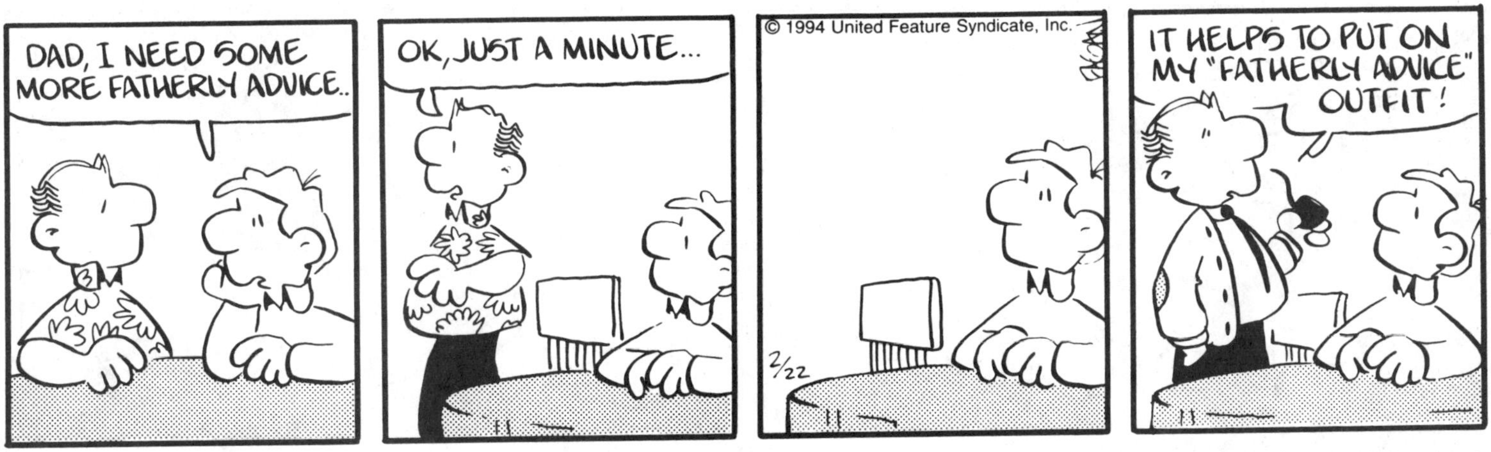
DAD, I NEED SOME MORE FATHERLY ADVICE..
OK, JUST A MINUTE...
© 1994 United Feature Syndicate, Inc.
2/22
IT HELPS TO PUT ON MY "FATHERLY ADVICE" OUTFIT!

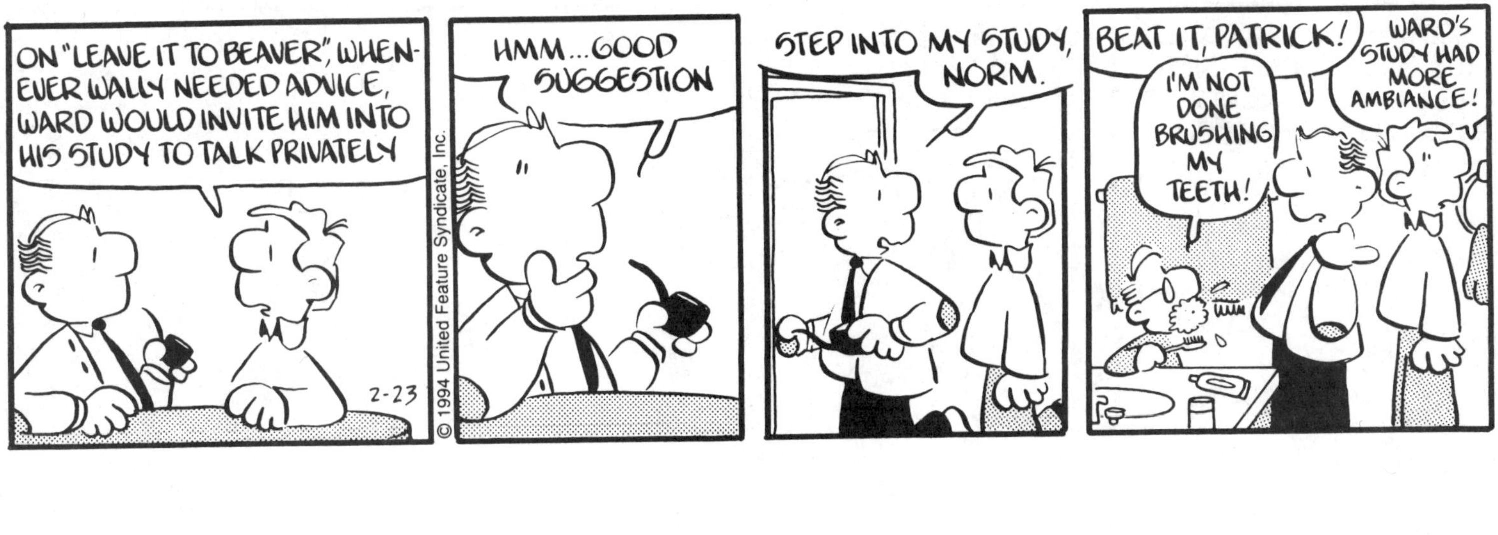
ON "LEAVE IT TO BEAVER", WHENEVER WALLY NEEDED ADVICE, WARD WOULD INVITE HIM INTO HIS STUDY TO TALK PRIVATELY
2-23
© 1994 United Feature Syndicate, Inc.
HMM...GOOD SUGGESTION
STEP INTO MY STUDY, NORM.
BEAT IT, PATRICK!
I'M NOT DONE BRUSHING MY TEETH!
WARD'S STUDY HAD MORE AMBIANCE!

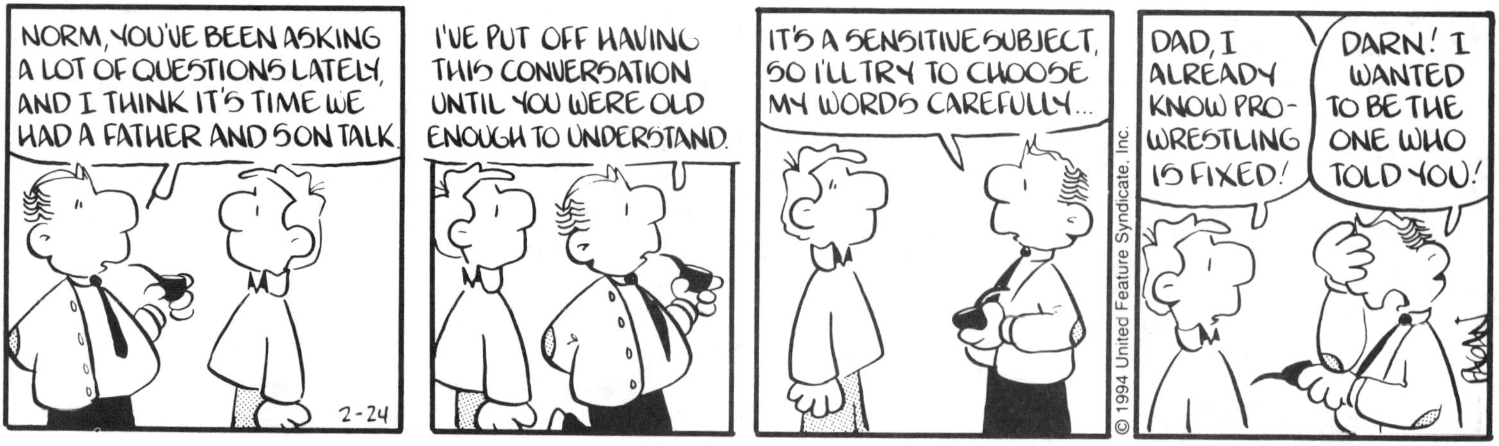
NORM, YOU'VE BEEN ASKING A LOT OF QUESTIONS LATELY, AND I THINK IT'S TIME WE HAD A FATHER AND SON TALK.
2-24
I'VE PUT OFF HAVING THIS CONVERSATION UNTIL YOU WERE OLD ENOUGH TO UNDERSTAND.
IT'S A SENSITIVE SUBJECT, SO I'LL TRY TO CHOOSE MY WORDS CAREFULLY...
© 1994 United Feature Syndicate, Inc.
DAD, I ALREADY KNOW PRO-WRESTLING IS FIXED!
DARN! I WANTED TO BE THE ONE WHO TOLD YOU!

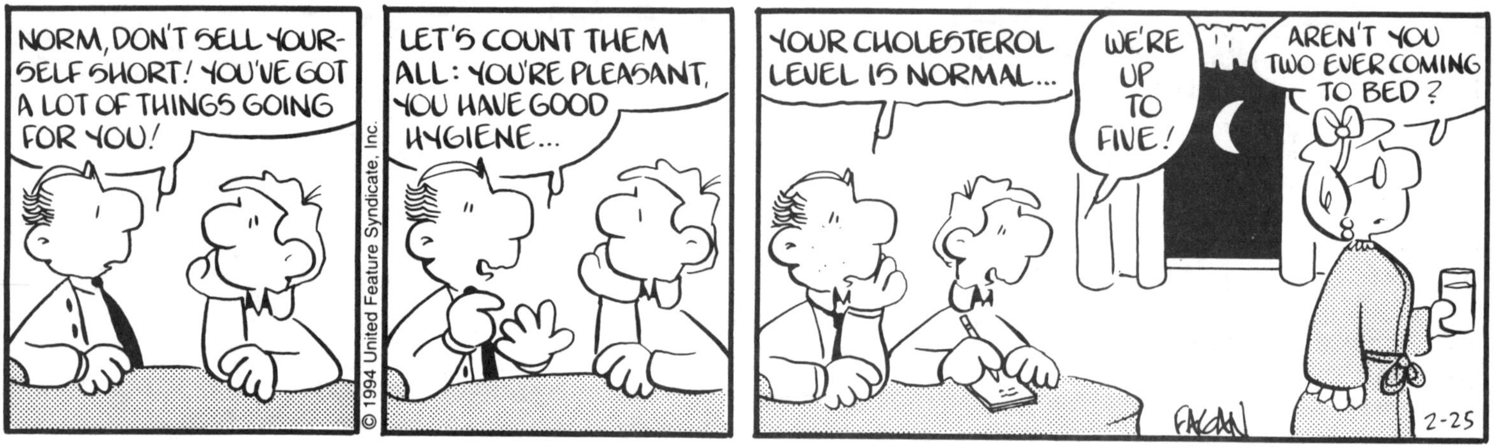
NORM, DON'T SELL YOURSELF SHORT! YOU'VE GOT A LOT OF THINGS GOING FOR YOU!
© 1994 United Feature Syndicate, Inc.
LET'S COUNT THEM ALL: YOU'RE PLEASANT, YOU HAVE GOOD HYGIENE...
YOUR CHOLESTEROL LEVEL IS NORMAL...
WE'RE UP TO FIVE!
AREN'T YOU TWO EVER COMING TO BED?
2-25

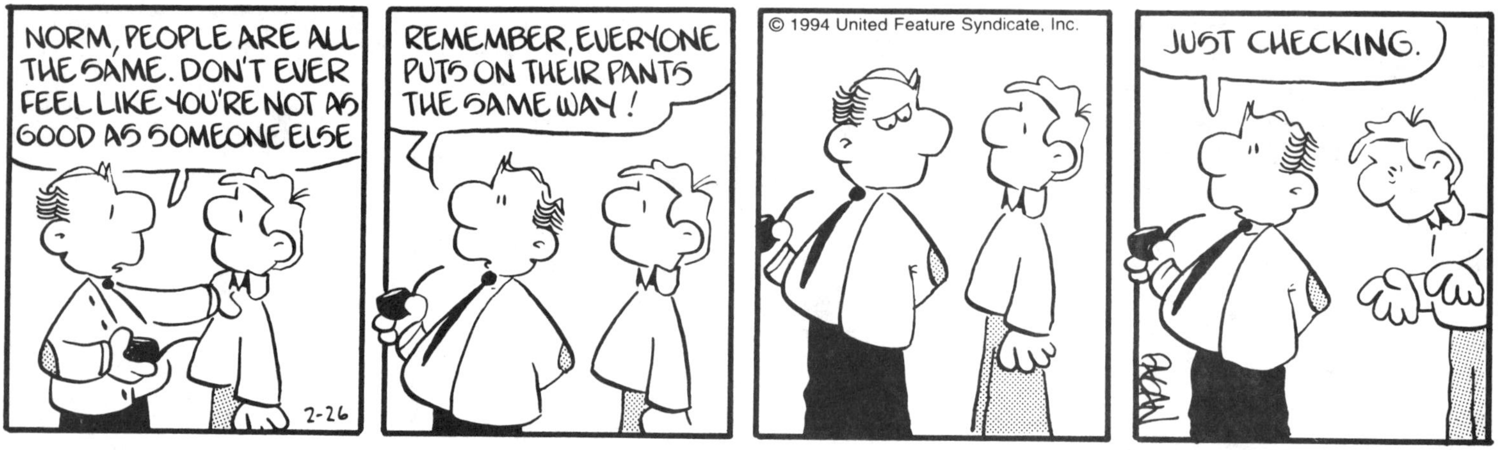
NORM, PEOPLE ARE ALL THE SAME. DON'T EVER FEEL LIKE YOU'RE NOT AS GOOD AS SOMEONE ELSE
2-26
REMEMBER, EVERYONE PUTS ON THEIR PANTS THE SAME WAY!
© 1994 United Feature Syndicate, Inc.
JUST CHECKING.

DRABBLE® By KEVIN FAGAN

RALPH, YOU FINALLY DID IT! YOU BOUGHT POPCORN WITHOUT MELTED BUTTER ON IT!
© 1993 United Feature Syndicate, Inc.
I GUESS ALL MY NAGGING ABOUT IT FINALLY PAID OFF! THANK YOU FOR LISTENING TO ME!
POPCORN
I KNOW YOU'VE ALWAYS LOVED TO DRENCH YOUR POPCORN IN MELTED BUTTER, BUT THINK OF ALL THE CALORIES YOU'RE SAVING!
POPCORN
AND IT TASTES JUST AS GOOD WITHOUT IT, DOESN'T IT?
MMM HMM!
POPCORN
THANK YOU FOR TAKING THIS IMPORTANT STEP TOWARD BETTER HEALTH!
POPCORN
11-28
ANYTHING FOR YOU, HONEYBUNCH!
POPCORN
YUK!! THAT ISN'T SODA!! IT'S MELTED BUTTER!!!
SHHH!
POPCORN
FAGAN

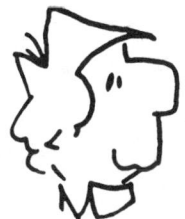

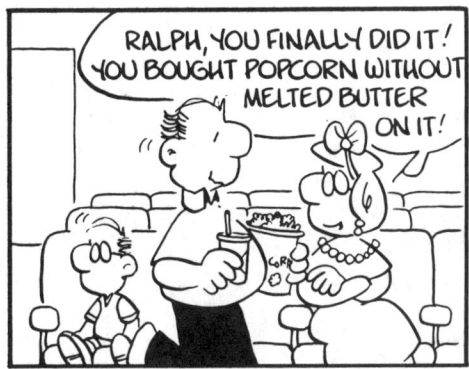

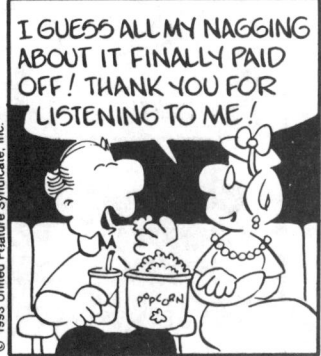

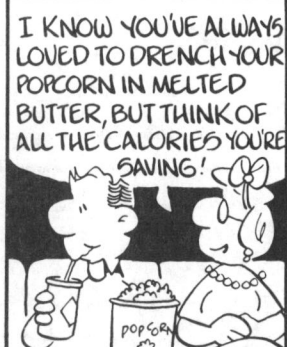

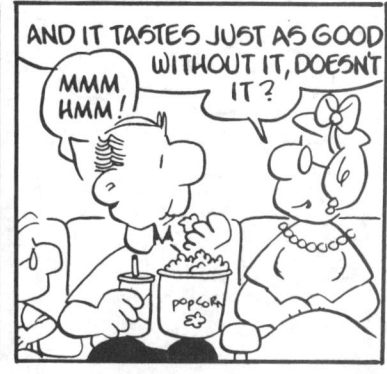

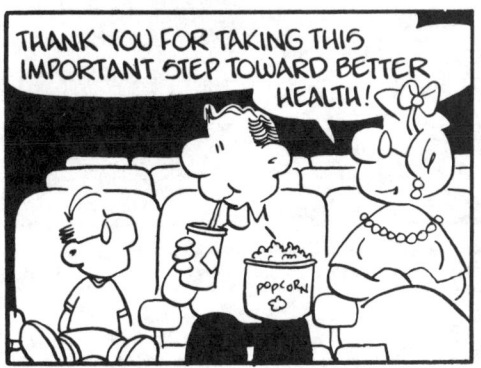

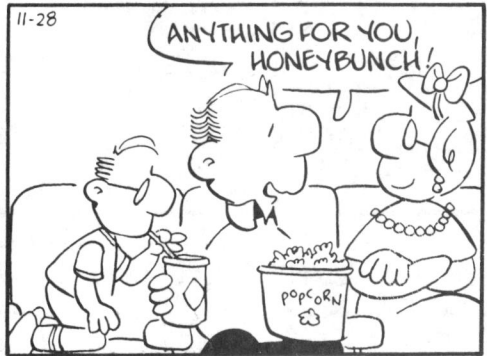

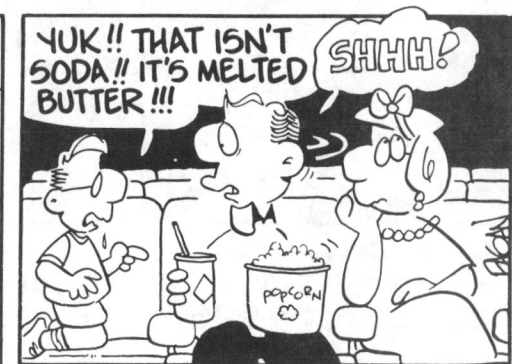

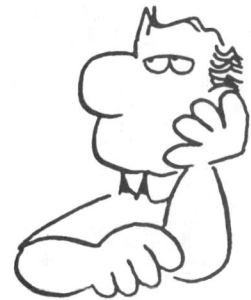

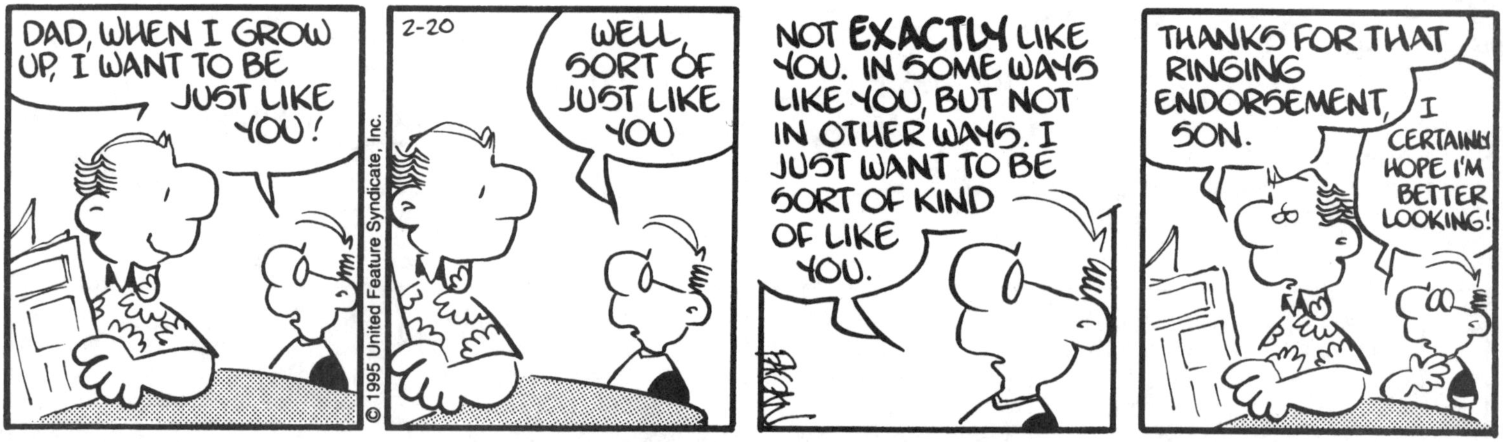
DAD, WHEN I GROW UP, I WANT TO BE JUST LIKE YOU!
© 1995 United Feature Syndicate, Inc.
2-20
WELL, SORT OF JUST LIKE YOU
NOT EXACTLY LIKE YOU. IN SOME WAYS LIKE YOU, BUT NOT IN OTHER WAYS. I JUST WANT TO BE SORT OF KIND OF LIKE YOU.
THANKS FOR THAT RINGING ENDORSEMENT, SON.
I CERTAINLY HOPE I'M BETTER LOOKING!

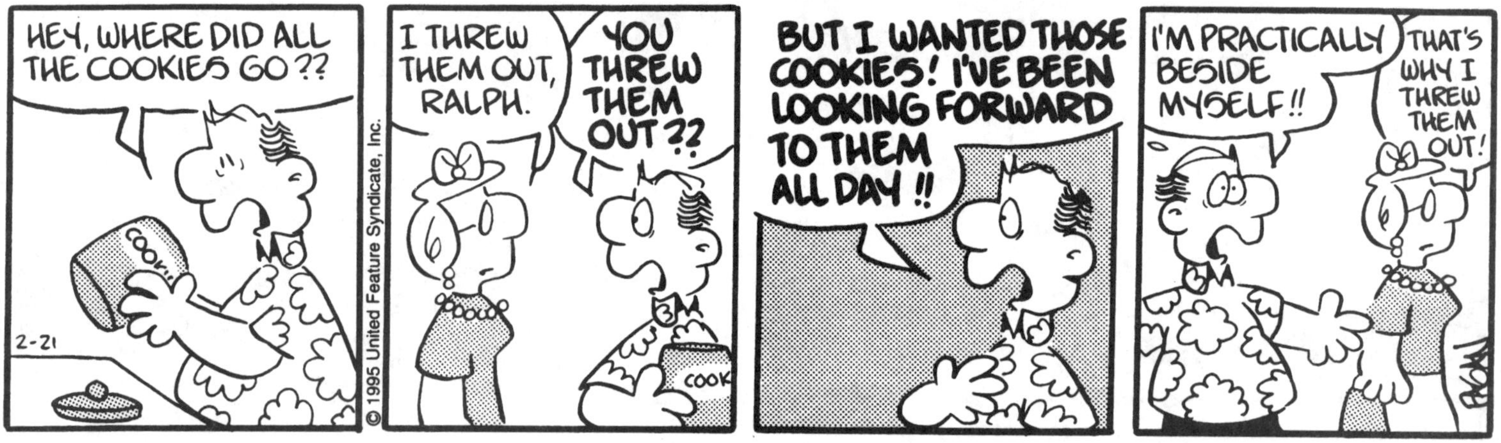
HEY, WHERE DID ALL THE COOKIES GO??
2-21
© 1995 United Feature Syndicate, Inc.
I THREW THEM OUT, RALPH.
YOU THREW THEM OUT??
COOK
BUT I WANTED THOSE COOKIES! I'VE BEEN LOOKING FORWARD TO THEM ALL DAY!!
I'M PRACTICALLY BESIDE MYSELF!!
THAT'S WHY I THREW THEM OUT!

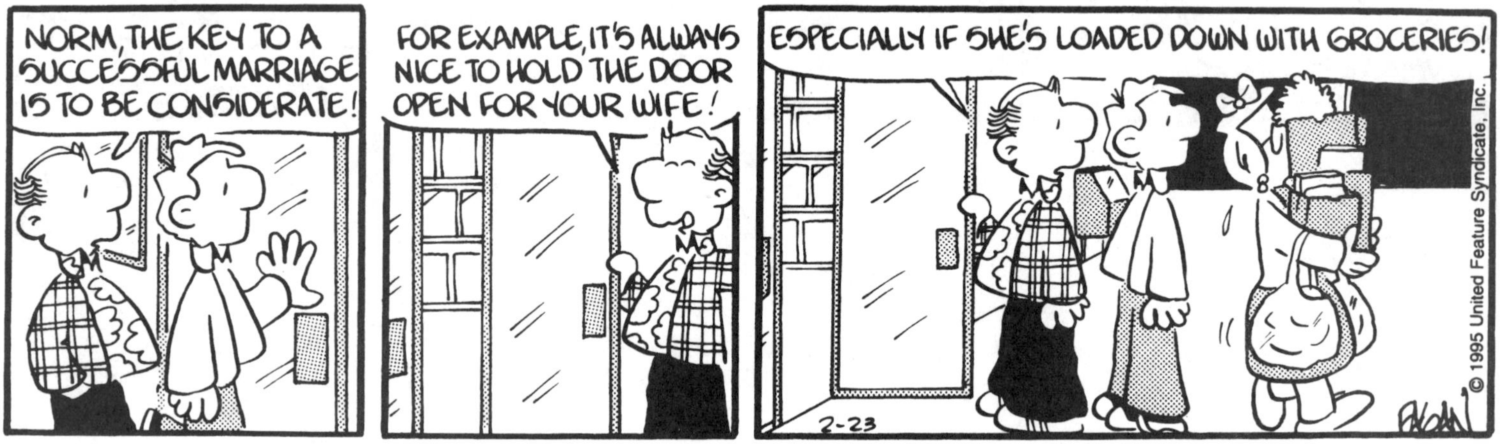
NORM, THE KEY TO A SUCCESSFUL MARRIAGE IS TO BE CONSIDERATE!
FOR EXAMPLE, IT'S ALWAYS NICE TO HOLD THE DOOR OPEN FOR YOUR WIFE!
ESPECIALLY IF SHE'S LOADED DOWN WITH GROCERIES!
2-23
© 1995 United Feature Syndicate, Inc.

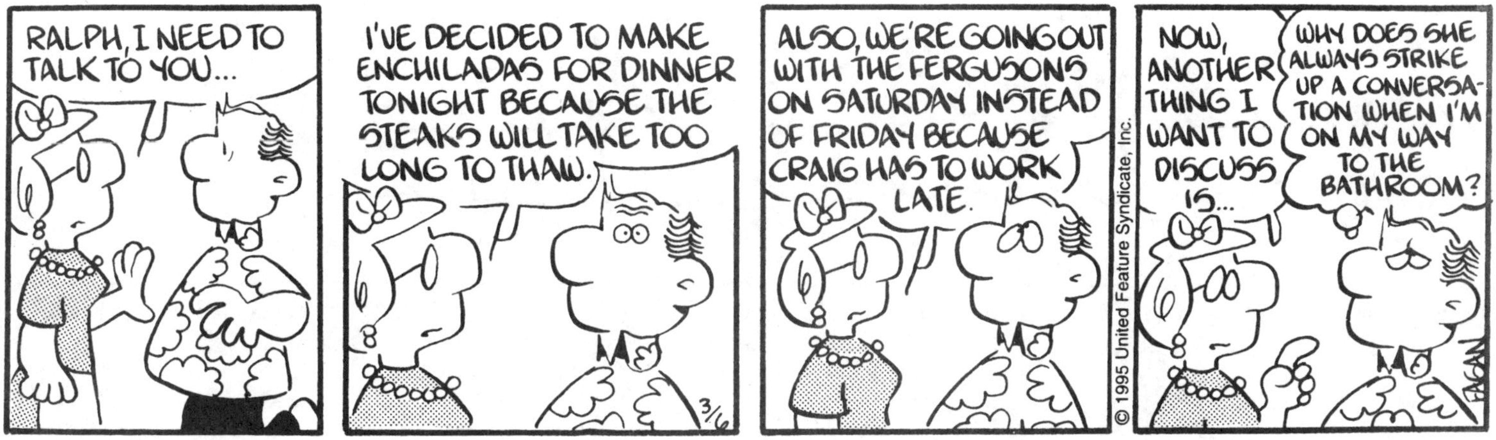
RALPH, I NEED TO TALK TO YOU...
I'VE DECIDED TO MAKE ENCHILADAS FOR DINNER TONIGHT BECAUSE THE STEAKS WILL TAKE TOO LONG TO THAW.
3/6
ALSO, WE'RE GOING OUT WITH THE FERGUSONS ON SATURDAY INSTEAD OF FRIDAY BECAUSE CRAIG HAS TO WORK LATE.
© 1995 United Feature Syndicate, Inc.
NOW, ANOTHER THING I WANT TO DISCUSS IS...
WHY DOES SHE ALWAYS STRIKE UP A CONVERSATION WHEN I'M ON MY WAY TO THE BATHROOM?
FAGAN

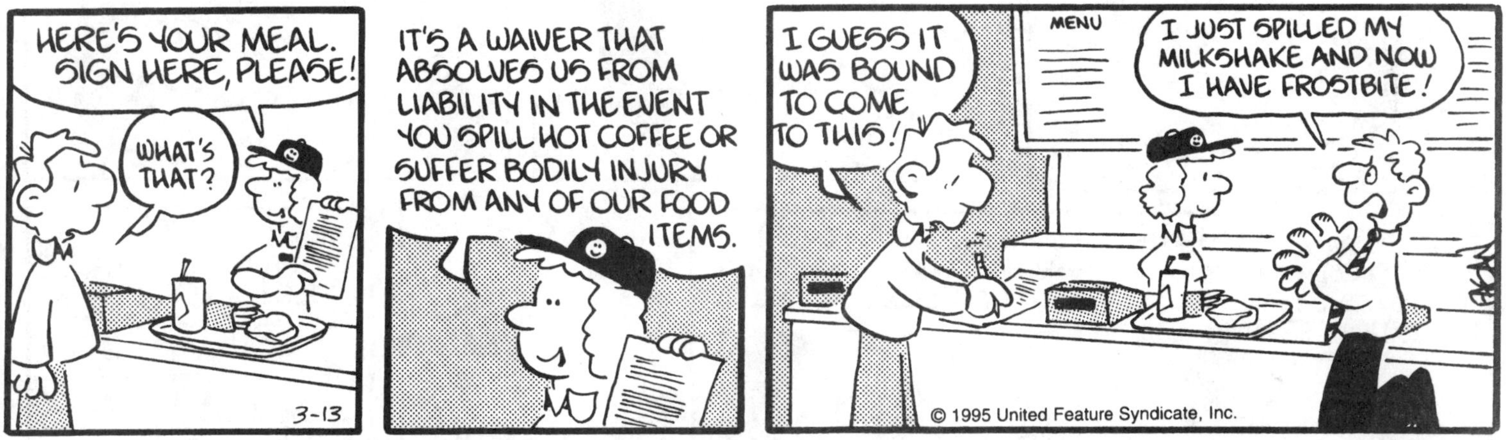
HERE'S YOUR MEAL. SIGN HERE, PLEASE!
WHAT'S THAT?
3-13
IT'S A WAIVER THAT ABSOLVES US FROM LIABILITY IN THE EVENT YOU SPILL HOT COFFEE OR SUFFER BODILY INJURY FROM ANY OF OUR FOOD ITEMS.
MENU
I GUESS IT WAS BOUND TO COME TO THIS!
I JUST SPILLED MY MILKSHAKE AND NOW I HAVE FROSTBITE!
FAGAN
© 1995 United Feature Syndicate, Inc.

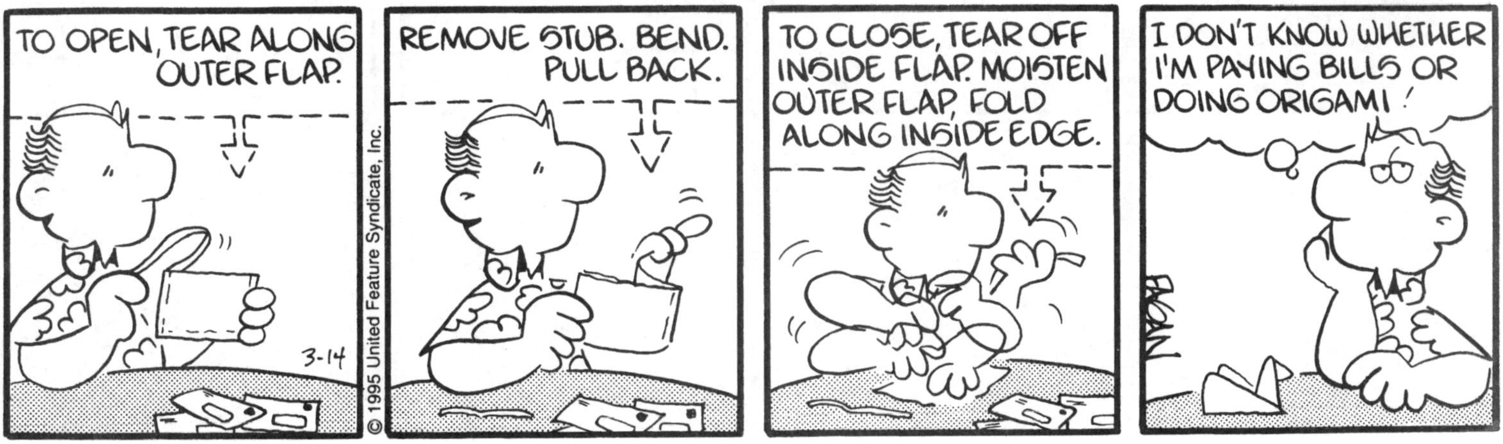
TO OPEN, TEAR ALONG OUTER FLAP.
3-14
© 1995 United Feature Syndicate, Inc.
REMOVE STUB. BEND. PULL BACK.
TO CLOSE, TEAR OFF INSIDE FLAP. MOISTEN OUTER FLAP, FOLD ALONG INSIDE EDGE.
I DON'T KNOW WHETHER I'M PAYING BILLS OR DOING ORIGAMI!
FAGAN

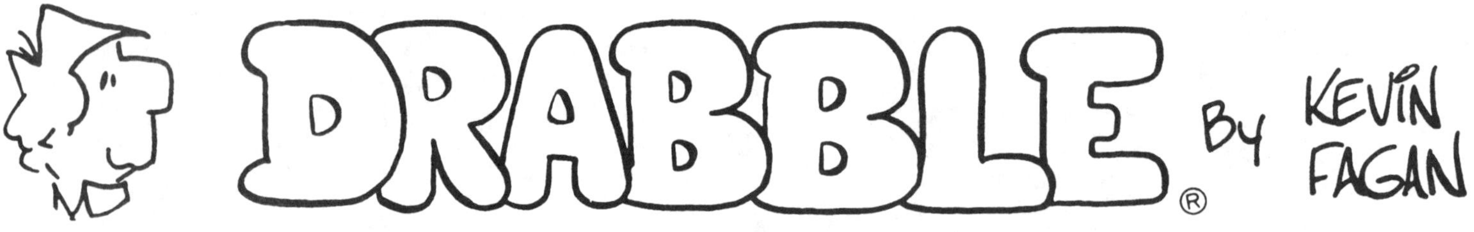
DRABBLE
By KEVIN FAGAN

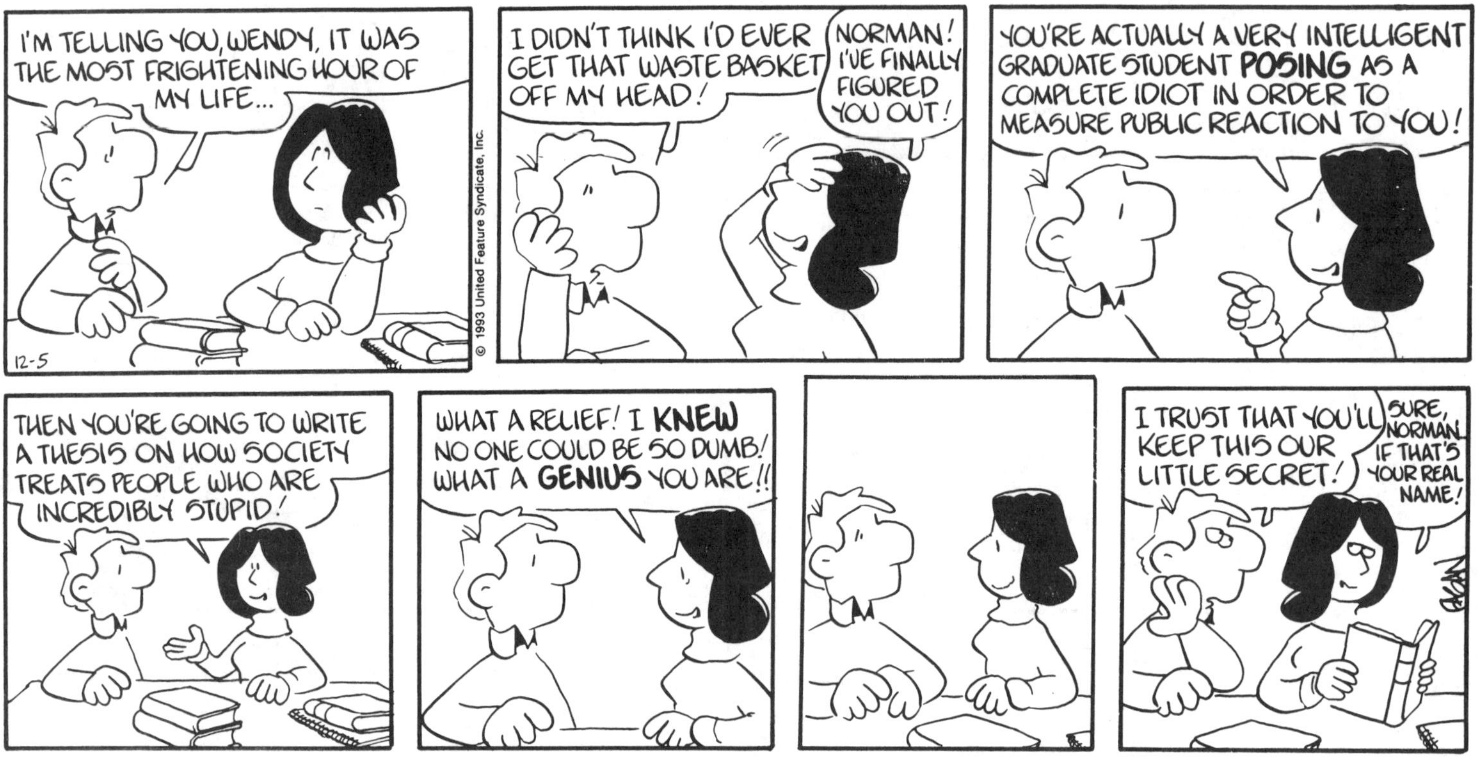
I'M TELLING YOU, WENDY, IT WAS THE MOST FRIGHTENING HOUR OF MY LIFE...
12-5
© 1993 United Feature Syndicate, Inc.
I DIDN'T THINK I'D EVER GET THAT WASTE BASKET OFF MY HEAD!
NORMAN! I'VE FINALLY FIGURED YOU OUT!
YOU'RE ACTUALLY A VERY INTELLIGENT GRADUATE STUDENT POSING AS A COMPLETE IDIOT IN ORDER TO MEASURE PUBLIC REACTION TO YOU!
THEN YOU'RE GOING TO WRITE A THESIS ON HOW SOCIETY TREATS PEOPLE WHO ARE INCREDIBLY STUPID!
WHAT A RELIEF! I KNEW NO ONE COULD BE SO DUMB! WHAT A GENIUS YOU ARE!!
I TRUST THAT YOU'LL KEEP THIS OUR LITTLE SECRET!
SURE, NORMAN... IF THAT'S YOUR REAL NAME!

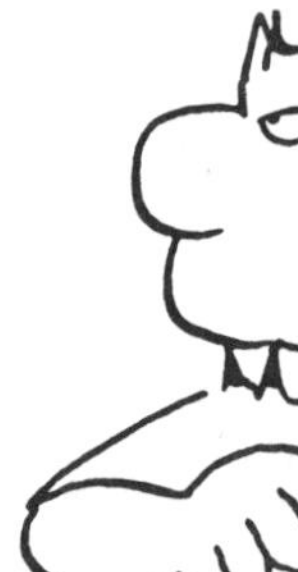

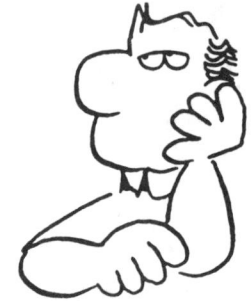

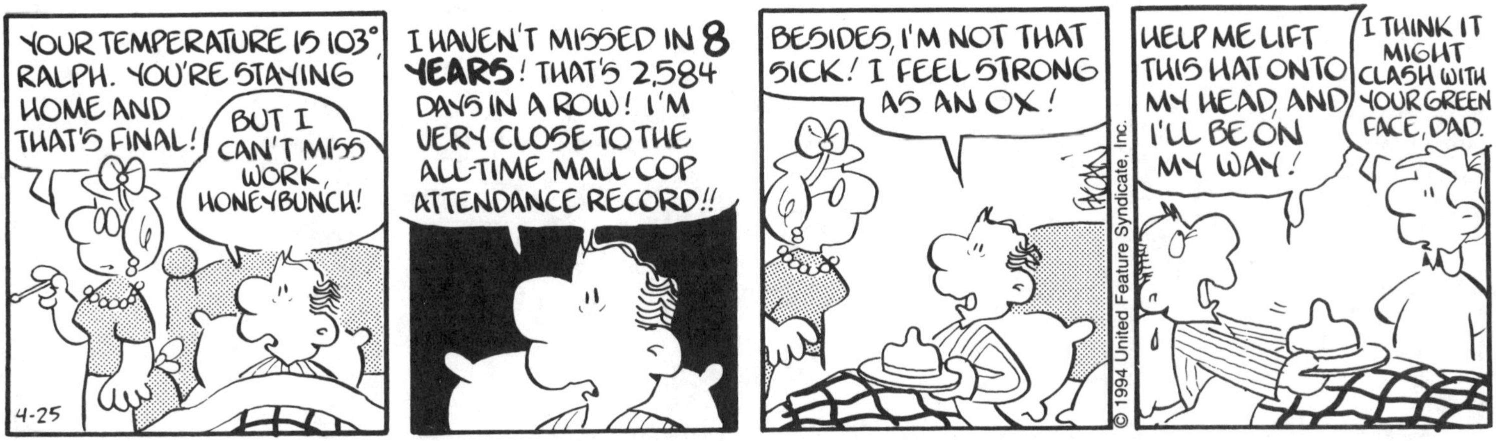
YOUR TEMPERATURE IS 103°, RALPH. YOU'RE STAYING HOME AND THAT'S FINAL!
BUT I CAN'T MISS WORK, HONEYBUNCH!
4-25
I HAVEN'T MISSED IN 8 YEARS! THAT'S 2,584 DAYS IN A ROW! I'M VERY CLOSE TO THE ALL-TIME MALL COP ATTENDANCE RECORD!!
BESIDES, I'M NOT THAT SICK! I FEEL STRONG AS AN OX!
© 1994 United Feature Syndicate, Inc.
HELP ME LIFT THIS HAT ONTO MY HEAD, AND I'LL BE ON MY WAY!
I THINK IT MIGHT CLASH WITH YOUR GREEN FACE, DAD.

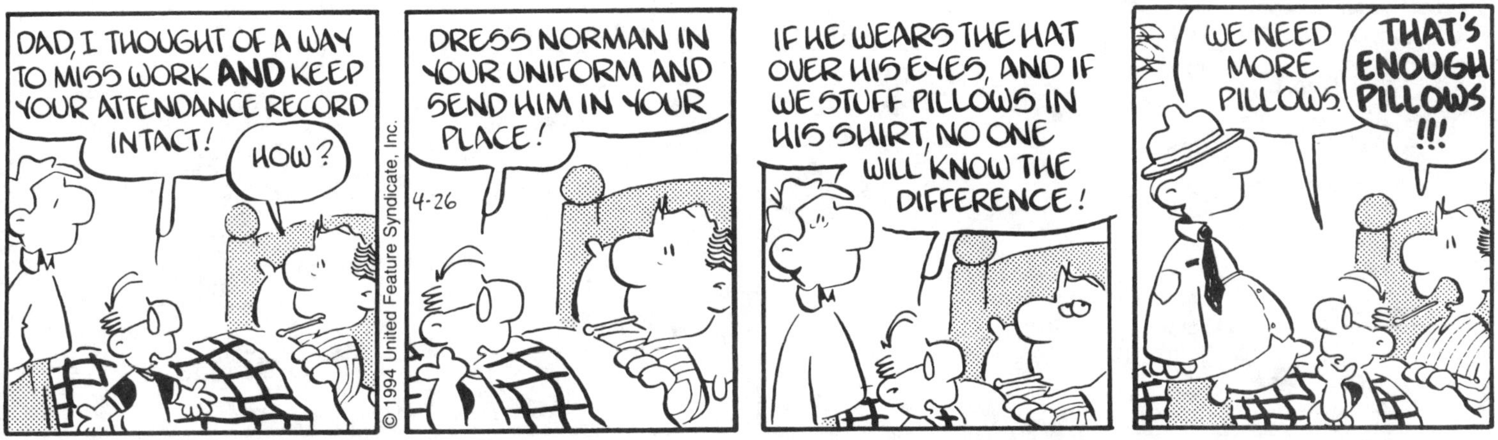
DAD, I THOUGHT OF A WAY TO MISS WORK AND KEEP YOUR ATTENDANCE RECORD INTACT!
HOW?
© 1994 United Feature Syndicate, Inc.
DRESS NORMAN IN YOUR UNIFORM AND SEND HIM IN YOUR PLACE!
4-26
IF HE WEARS THE HAT OVER HIS EYES, AND IF WE STUFF PILLOWS IN HIS SHIRT, NO ONE WILL KNOW THE DIFFERENCE!
WE NEED MORE PILLOWS.
THAT'S ENOUGH PILLOWS!!!

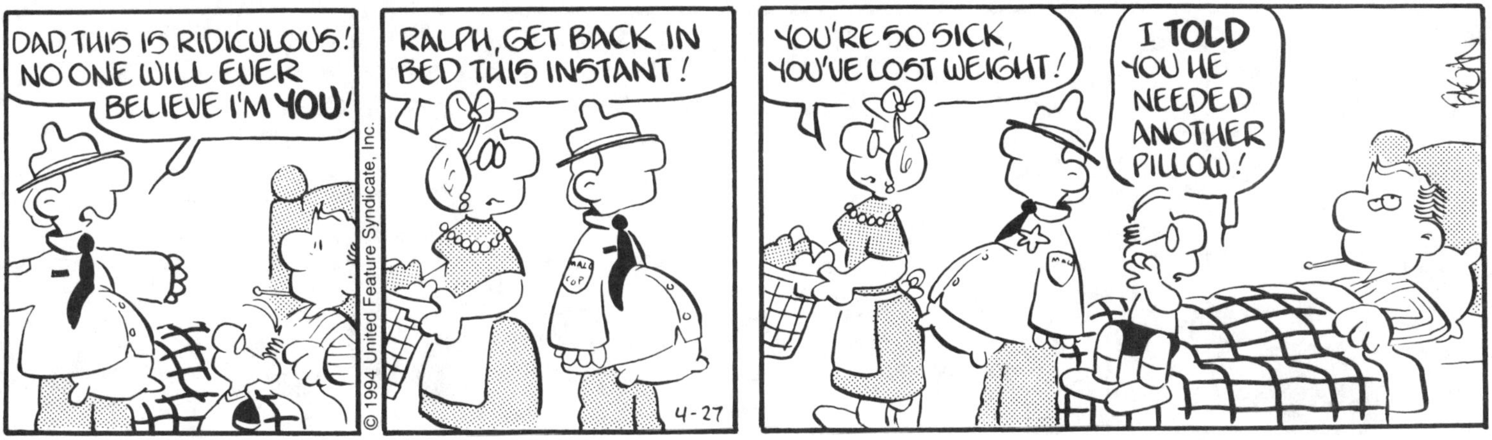
DAD, THIS IS RIDICULOUS! NO ONE WILL EVER BELIEVE I'M YOU!
© 1994 United Feature Syndicate, Inc.
RALPH, GET BACK IN BED THIS INSTANT!
4-27
YOU'RE SO SICK, YOU'VE LOST WEIGHT!
I TOLD YOU HE NEEDED ANOTHER PILLOW!

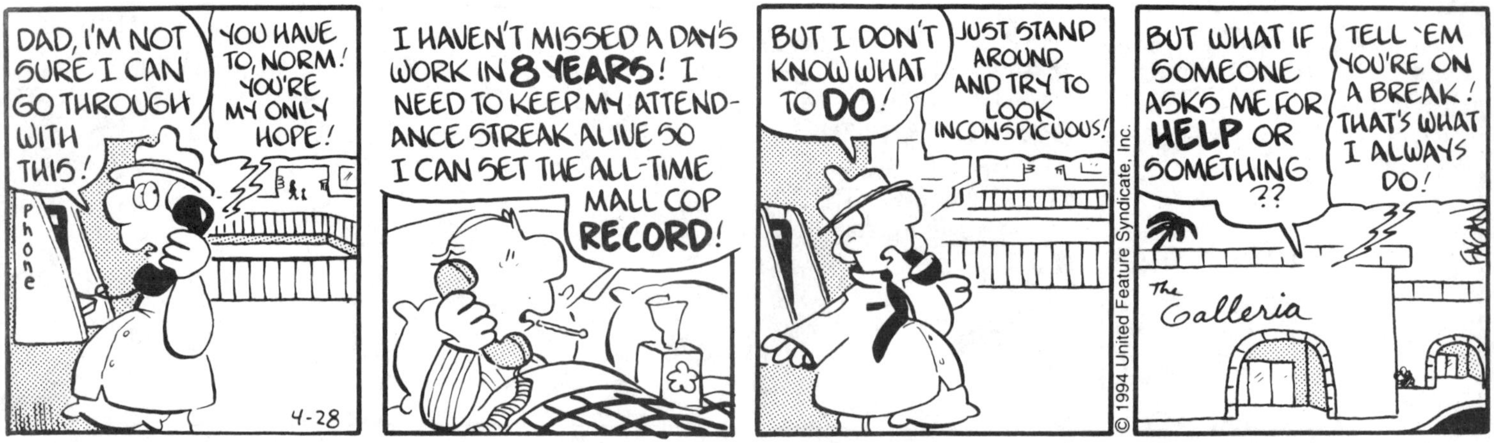
DAD, I'M NOT SURE I CAN GO THROUGH WITH THIS!
YOU HAVE TO, NORM! YOU'RE MY ONLY HOPE!
phone
4-28
I HAVEN'T MISSED A DAY'S WORK IN **8 YEARS**! I NEED TO KEEP MY ATTENDANCE STREAK ALIVE SO I CAN SET THE ALL-TIME MALL COP **RECORD**!
BUT I DON'T KNOW WHAT TO **DO**!
JUST STAND AROUND AND TRY TO LOOK INCONSPICUOUS!
© 1994 United Feature Syndicate, Inc.
BUT WHAT IF SOMEONE ASKS ME FOR **HELP** OR SOMETHING??
TELL 'EM YOU'RE ON A BREAK! THAT'S WHAT I ALWAYS DO!
The Galleria

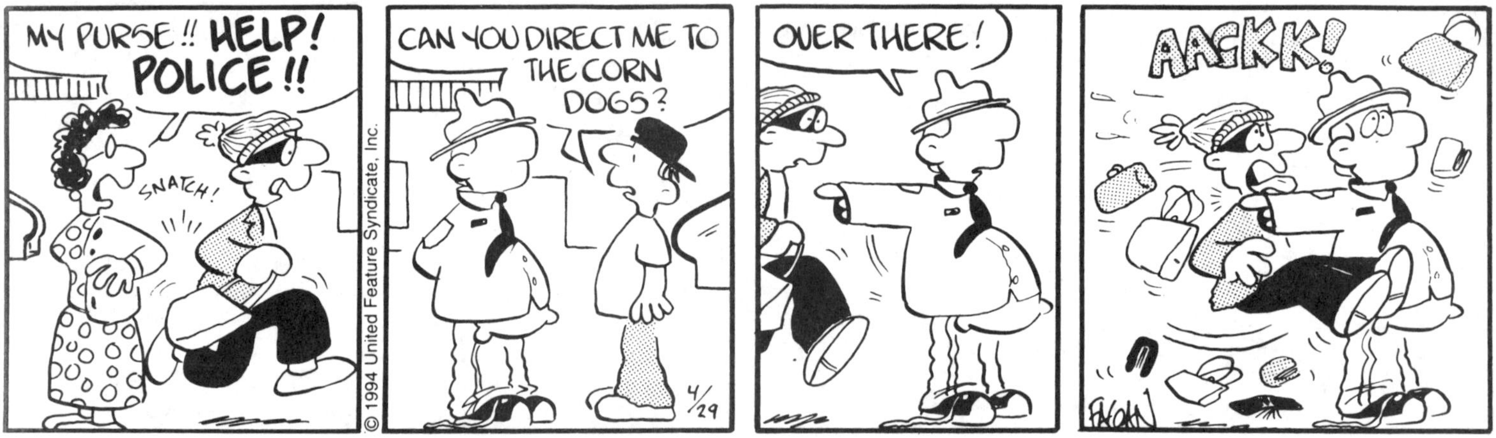
MY PURSE!! **HELP! POLICE!!**
SNATCH!
© 1994 United Feature Syndicate, Inc.
CAN YOU DIRECT ME TO THE CORN DOGS?
4/29
OVER THERE!
AACKK!

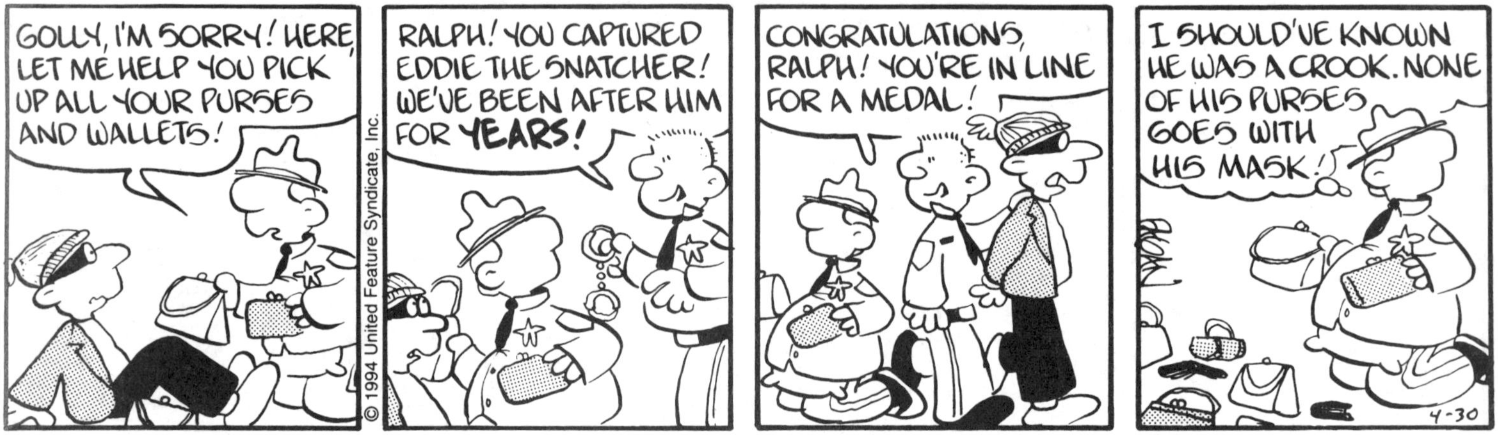
GOLLY, I'M SORRY! HERE, LET ME HELP YOU PICK UP ALL YOUR PURSES AND WALLETS!
© 1994 United Feature Syndicate, Inc.
RALPH! YOU CAPTURED EDDIE THE SNATCHER! WE'VE BEEN AFTER HIM FOR **YEARS**!
CONGRATULATIONS, RALPH! YOU'RE IN LINE FOR A MEDAL!
I SHOULD'VE KNOWN HE WAS A CROOK. NONE OF HIS PURSES GOES WITH HIS MASK!
4-30

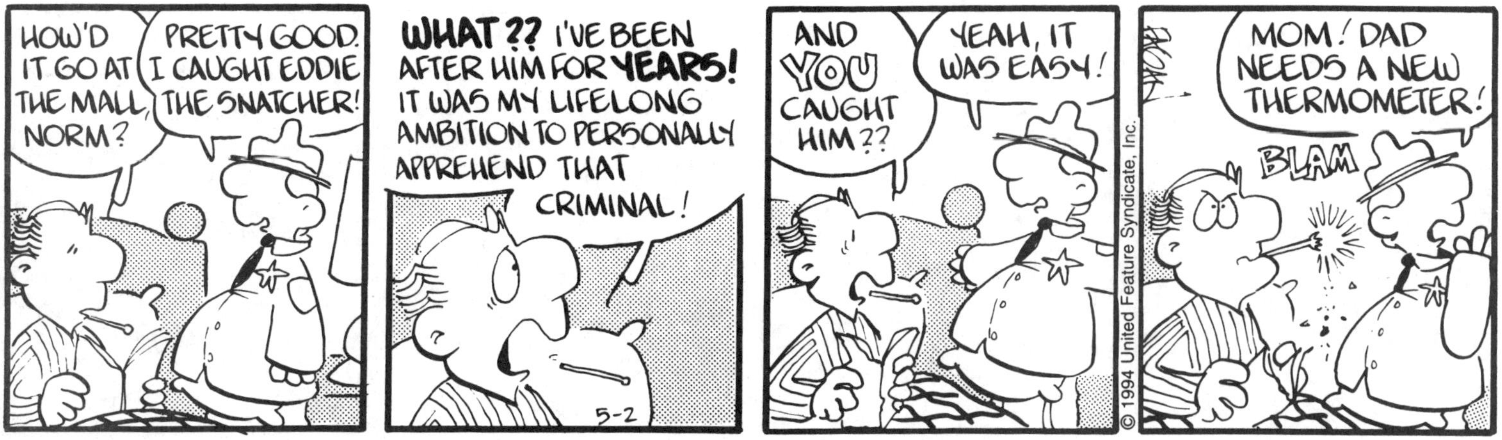
HOW'D IT GO AT THE MALL, NORM?
PRETTY GOOD. I CAUGHT EDDIE THE SNATCHER!
WHAT?? I'VE BEEN AFTER HIM FOR YEARS! IT WAS MY LIFELONG AMBITION TO PERSONALLY APPREHEND THAT CRIMINAL!
5-2
AND YOU CAUGHT HIM??
YEAH, IT WAS EASY!
© 1994 United Feature Syndicate, Inc.
MOM! DAD NEEDS A NEW THERMOMETER!
BLAM

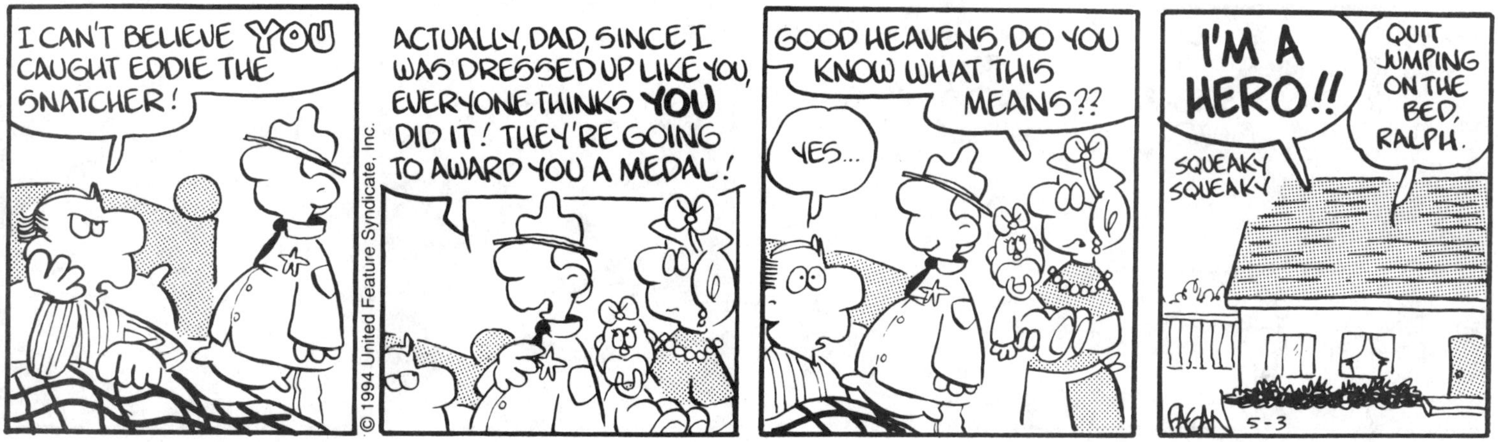
I CAN'T BELIEVE YOU CAUGHT EDDIE THE SNATCHER!
© 1994 United Feature Syndicate, Inc.
ACTUALLY, DAD, SINCE I WAS DRESSED UP LIKE YOU, EVERYONE THINKS YOU DID IT! THEY'RE GOING TO AWARD YOU A MEDAL!
GOOD HEAVENS, DO YOU KNOW WHAT THIS MEANS??
YES...
I'M A HERO!!
QUIT JUMPING ON THE BED, RALPH.
SQUEAKY SQUEAKY
FAGAN
5-3

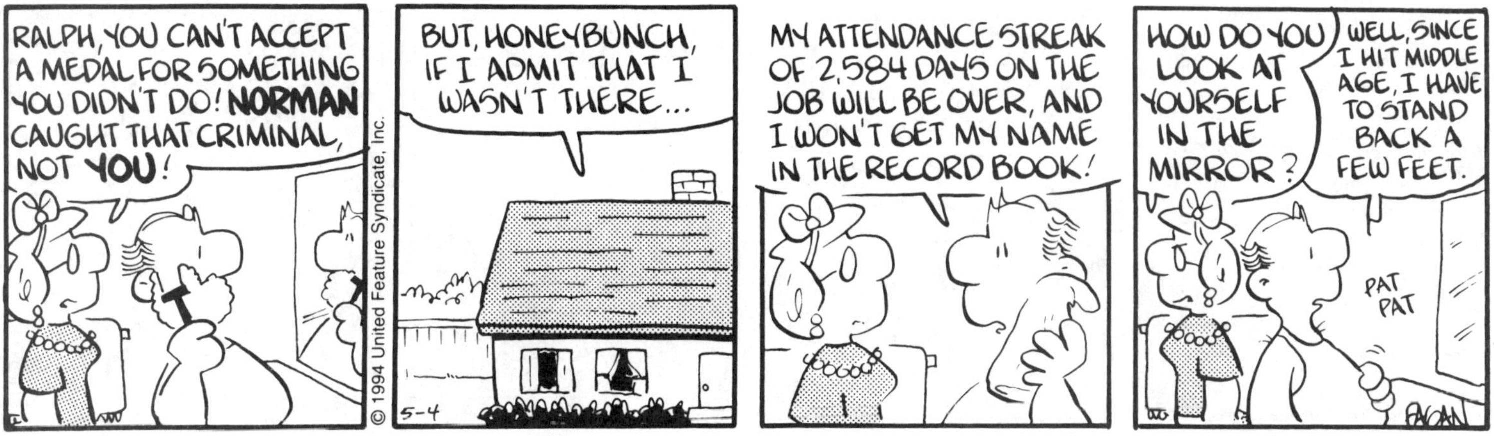
RALPH, YOU CAN'T ACCEPT A MEDAL FOR SOMETHING YOU DIDN'T DO! NORMAN CAUGHT THAT CRIMINAL, NOT YOU!
© 1994 United Feature Syndicate, Inc.
BUT, HONEYBUNCH, IF I ADMIT THAT I WASN'T THERE...
5-4
MY ATTENDANCE STREAK OF 2,584 DAYS ON THE JOB WILL BE OVER, AND I WON'T GET MY NAME IN THE RECORD BOOK!
HOW DO YOU LOOK AT YOURSELF IN THE MIRROR?
WELL, SINCE I HIT MIDDLE AGE, I HAVE TO STAND BACK A FEW FEET.
PAT PAT
FAGAN

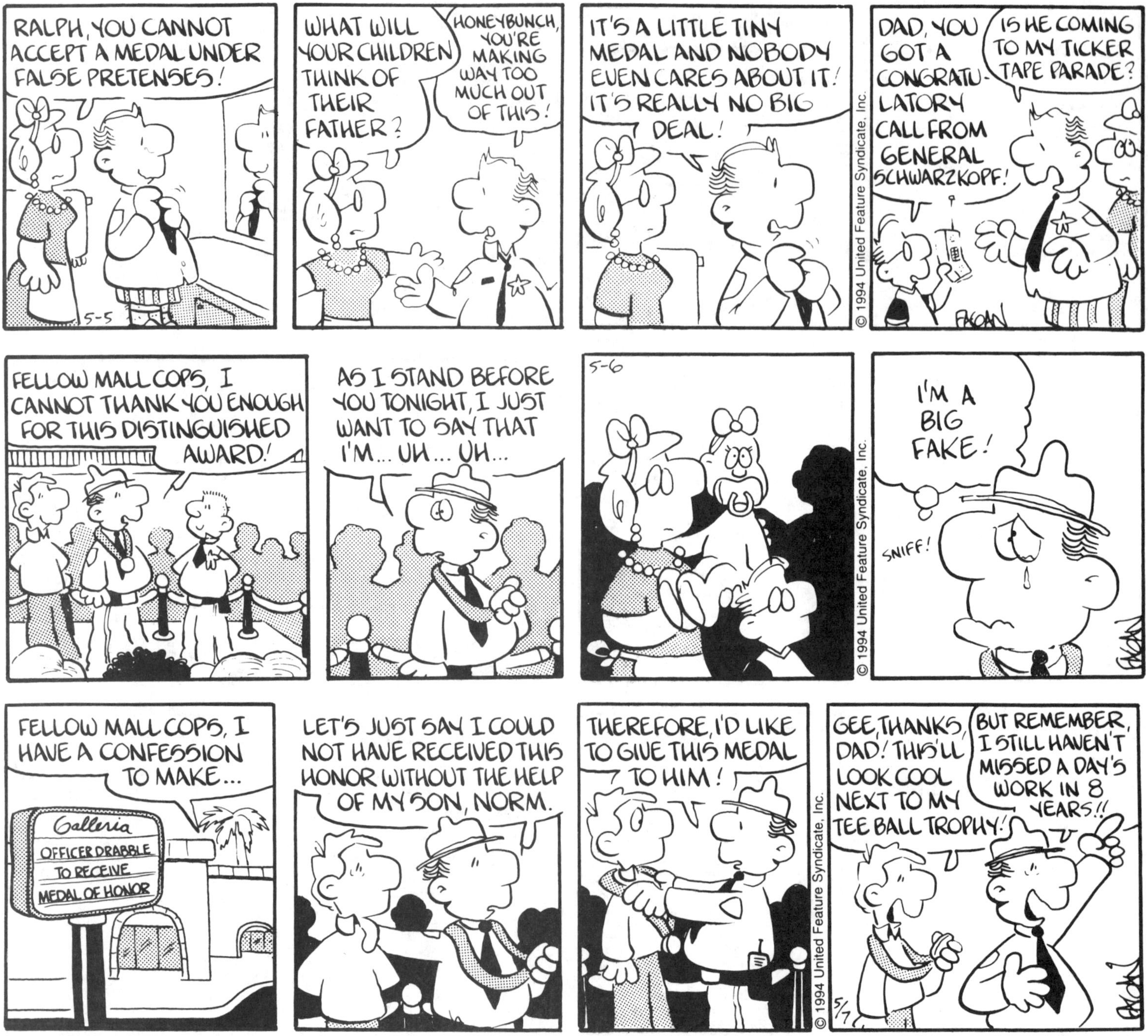
RALPH, YOU CANNOT ACCEPT A MEDAL UNDER FALSE PRETENSES!
5-5
WHAT WILL YOUR CHILDREN THINK OF THEIR FATHER?
HONEYBUNCH, YOU'RE MAKING WAY TOO MUCH OUT OF THIS!
IT'S A LITTLE TINY MEDAL AND NOBODY EVEN CARES ABOUT IT! IT'S REALLY NO BIG DEAL!
© 1994 United Feature Syndicate, Inc.
DAD, YOU GOT A CONGRATU-LATORY CALL FROM GENERAL SCHWARZKOPF!
IS HE COMING TO MY TICKER TAPE PARADE?
FAGAN
FELLOW MALL COPS, I CANNOT THANK YOU ENOUGH FOR THIS DISTINGUISHED AWARD!
AS I STAND BEFORE YOU TONIGHT, I JUST WANT TO SAY THAT I'M... UH... UH...
5-6
© 1994 United Feature Syndicate, Inc.
I'M A BIG FAKE!
SNIFF!
FAGAN
FELLOW MALL COPS, I HAVE A CONFESSION TO MAKE...
Galleria
OFFICER DRABBLE
TO RECEIVE
MEDAL OF HONOR
LET'S JUST SAY I COULD NOT HAVE RECEIVED THIS HONOR WITHOUT THE HELP OF MY SON, NORM.
THEREFORE, I'D LIKE TO GIVE THIS MEDAL TO HIM!
© 1994 United Feature Syndicate, Inc.
5/7
GEE, THANKS, DAD! THIS'LL LOOK COOL NEXT TO MY TEE BALL TROPHY!
BUT REMEMBER, I STILL HAVEN'T MISSED A DAY'S WORK IN 8 YEARS!!
FAGAN

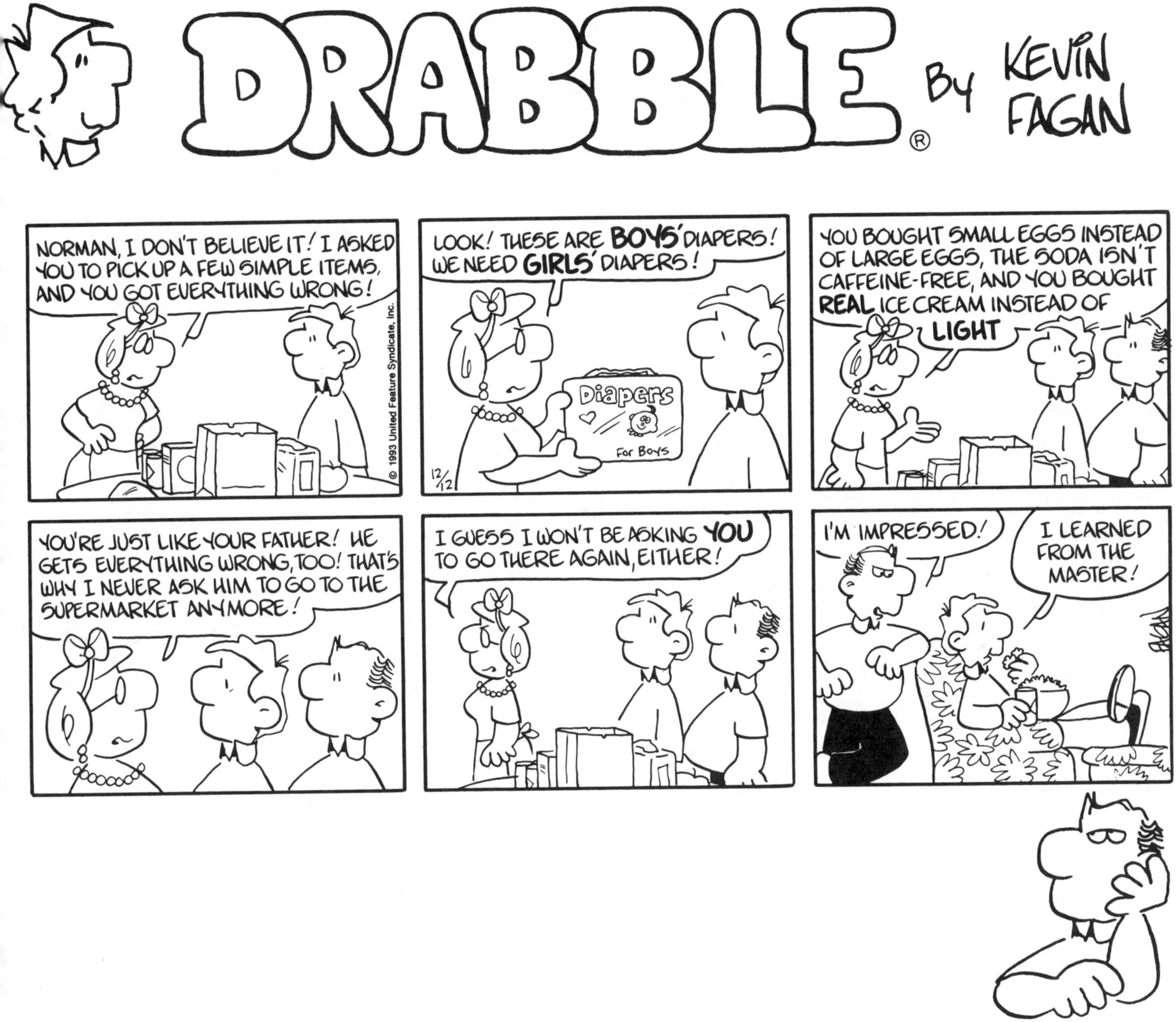
DRABBLE
By KEVIN FAGAN
NORMAN, I DON'T BELIEVE IT! I ASKED YOU TO PICK UP A FEW SIMPLE ITEMS, AND YOU GOT EVERYTHING WRONG!
© 1993 United Feature Syndicate, Inc.
LOOK! THESE ARE BOYS' DIAPERS! WE NEED GIRLS' DIAPERS!
Diapers
For Boys
12/12
YOU BOUGHT SMALL EGGS INSTEAD OF LARGE EGGS, THE SODA ISN'T CAFFEINE-FREE, AND YOU BOUGHT REAL ICE CREAM INSTEAD OF LIGHT
YOU'RE JUST LIKE YOUR FATHER! HE GETS EVERYTHING WRONG, TOO! THAT'S WHY I NEVER ASK HIM TO GO TO THE SUPERMARKET ANYMORE!
I GUESS I WON'T BE ASKING YOU TO GO THERE AGAIN, EITHER!
I'M IMPRESSED!
I LEARNED FROM THE MASTER!

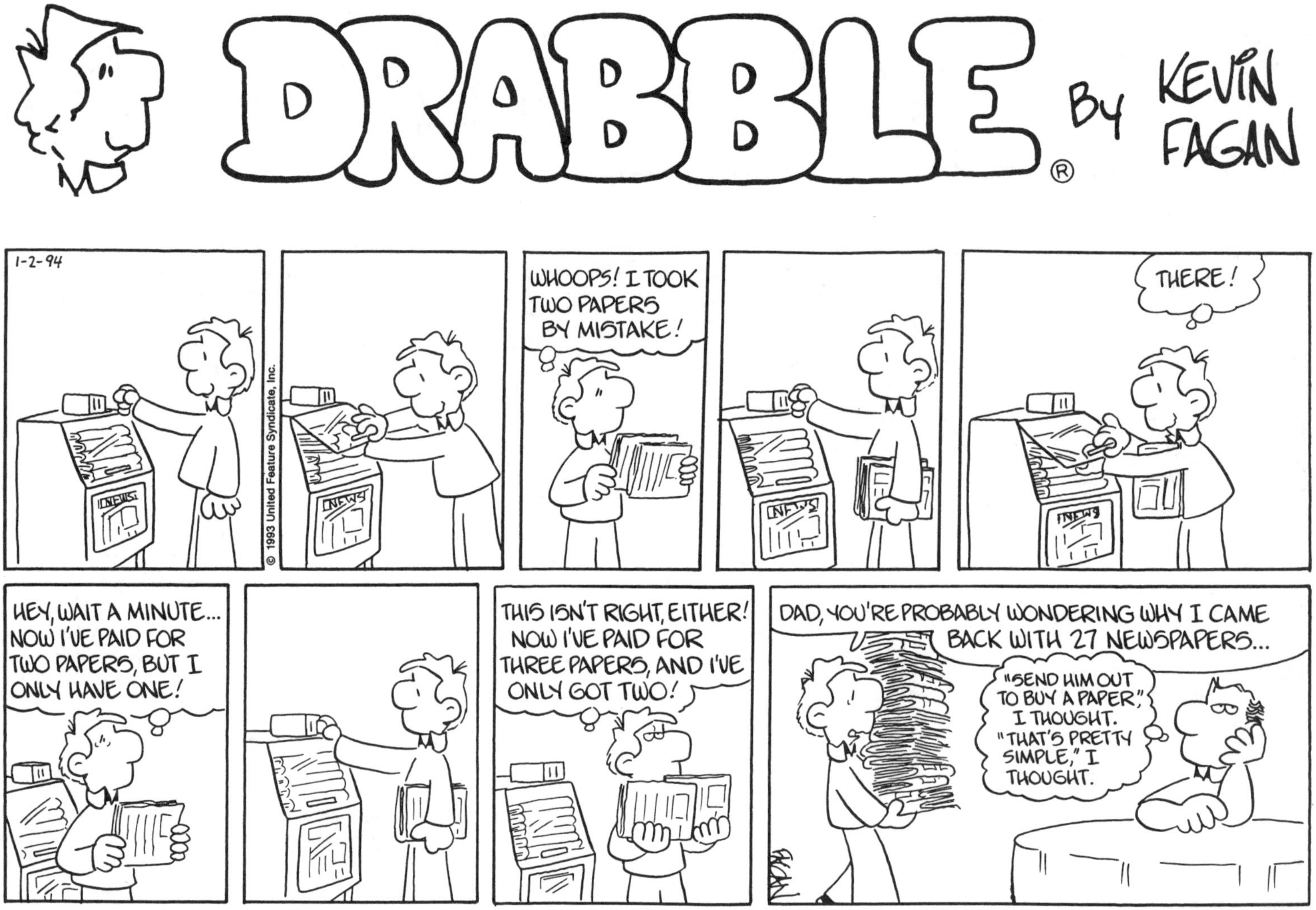
DRABBLE
By KEVIN FAGAN
1-2-94
© 1993 United Feature Syndicate, Inc.
WHOOPS! I TOOK TWO PAPERS BY MISTAKE!
THERE!
HEY, WAIT A MINUTE... NOW I'VE PAID FOR TWO PAPERS, BUT I ONLY HAVE ONE!
THIS ISN'T RIGHT, EITHER! NOW I'VE PAID FOR THREE PAPERS, AND I'VE ONLY GOT TWO!
DAD, YOU'RE PROBABLY WONDERING WHY I CAME BACK WITH 27 NEWSPAPERS...
"SEND HIM OUT TO BUY A PAPER," I THOUGHT. "THAT'S PRETTY SIMPLE," I THOUGHT.

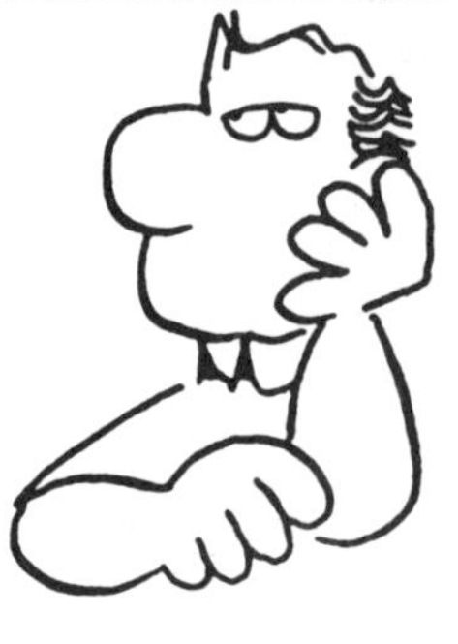

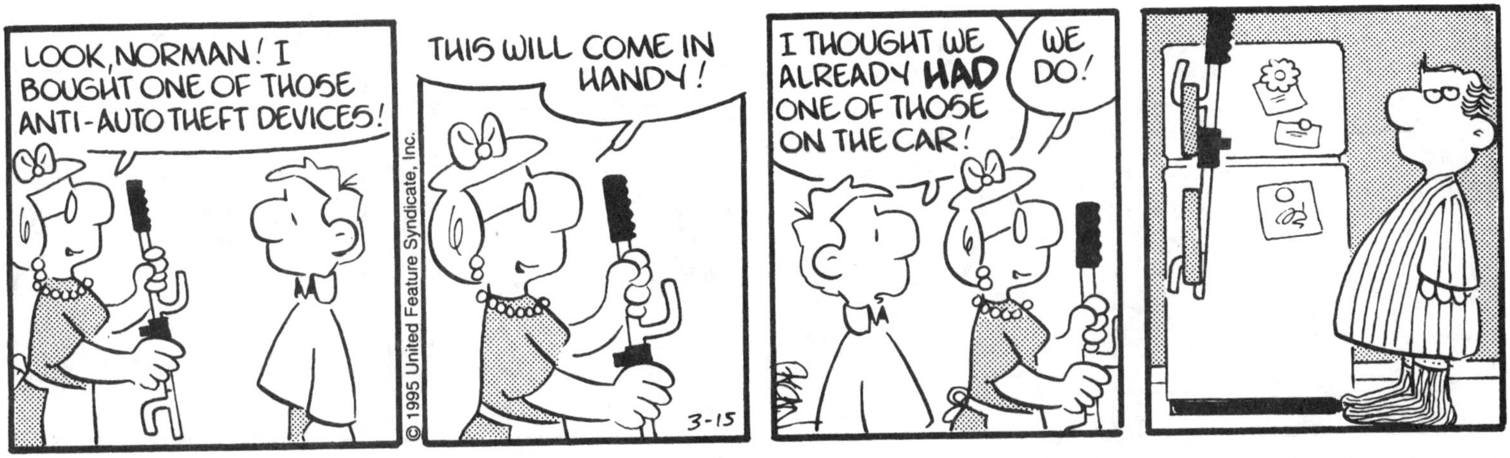
LOOK, NORMAN! I BOUGHT ONE OF THOSE ANTI-AUTO THEFT DEVICES!
© 1995 United Feature Syndicate, Inc.
THIS WILL COME IN HANDY!
3-15
I THOUGHT WE ALREADY HAD ONE OF THOSE ON THE CAR!
WE DO!

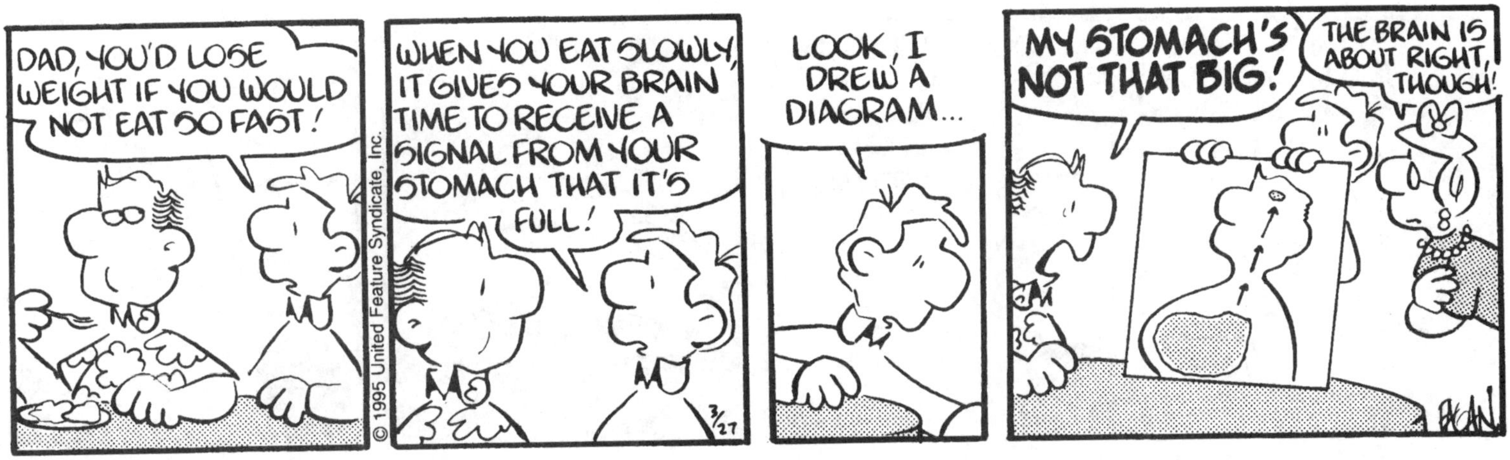
DAD, YOU'D LOSE WEIGHT IF YOU WOULD NOT EAT SO FAST!
© 1995 United Feature Syndicate, Inc.
WHEN YOU EAT SLOWLY, IT GIVES YOUR BRAIN TIME TO RECEIVE A SIGNAL FROM YOUR STOMACH THAT IT'S FULL!
3/27
LOOK, I DREW A DIAGRAM...
MY STOMACH'S NOT THAT BIG!
THE BRAIN IS ABOUT RIGHT, THOUGH!

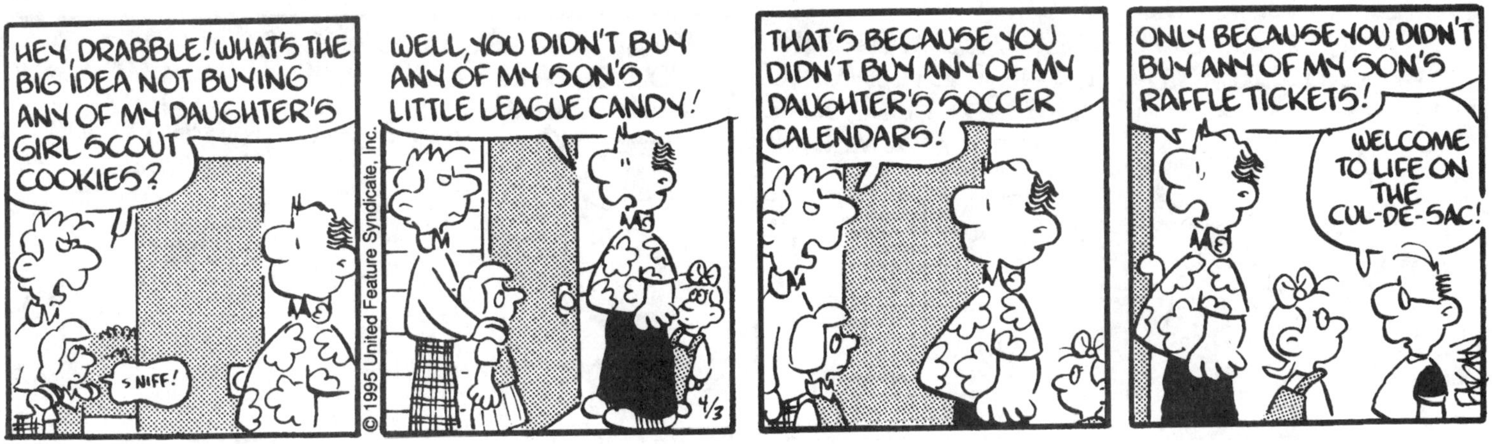
HEY, DRABBLE! WHAT'S THE BIG IDEA NOT BUYING ANY OF MY DAUGHTER'S GIRL SCOUT COOKIES?
SNIFF!
© 1995 United Feature Syndicate, Inc.
WELL, YOU DIDN'T BUY ANY OF MY SON'S LITTLE LEAGUE CANDY!
4/3
THAT'S BECAUSE YOU DIDN'T BUY ANY OF MY DAUGHTER'S SOCCER CALENDARS!
ONLY BECAUSE YOU DIDN'T BUY ANY OF MY SON'S RAFFLE TICKETS!
WELCOME TO LIFE ON THE CUL-DE-SAC!

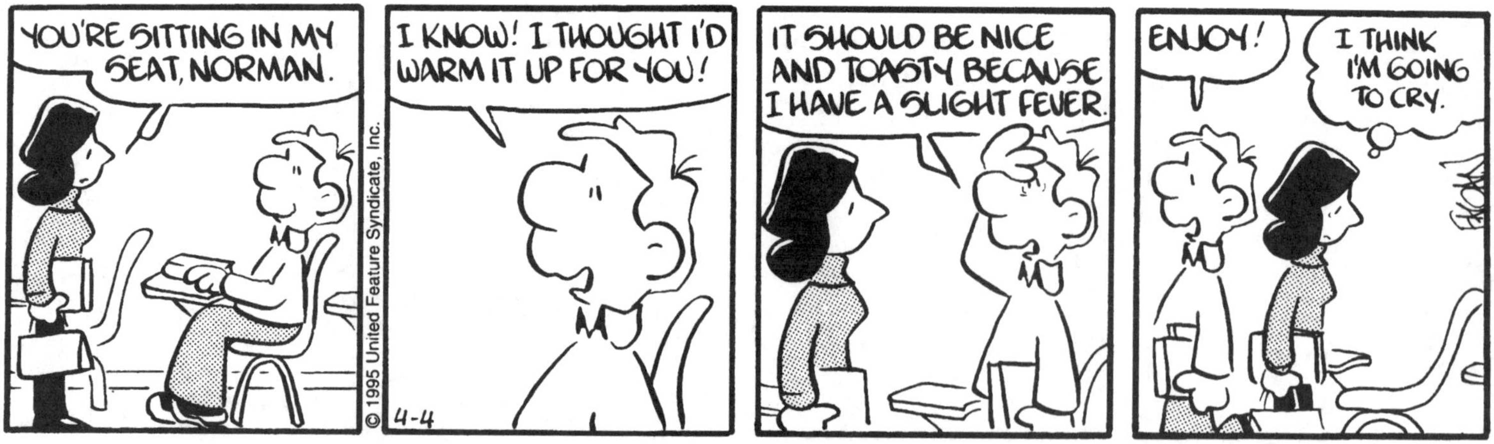
YOU'RE SITTING IN MY SEAT, NORMAN.
© 1995 United Feature Syndicate, Inc.
I KNOW! I THOUGHT I'D WARM IT UP FOR YOU!
4-4
IT SHOULD BE NICE AND TOASTY BECAUSE I HAVE A SLIGHT FEVER.
ENJOY!
I THINK I'M GOING TO CRY.

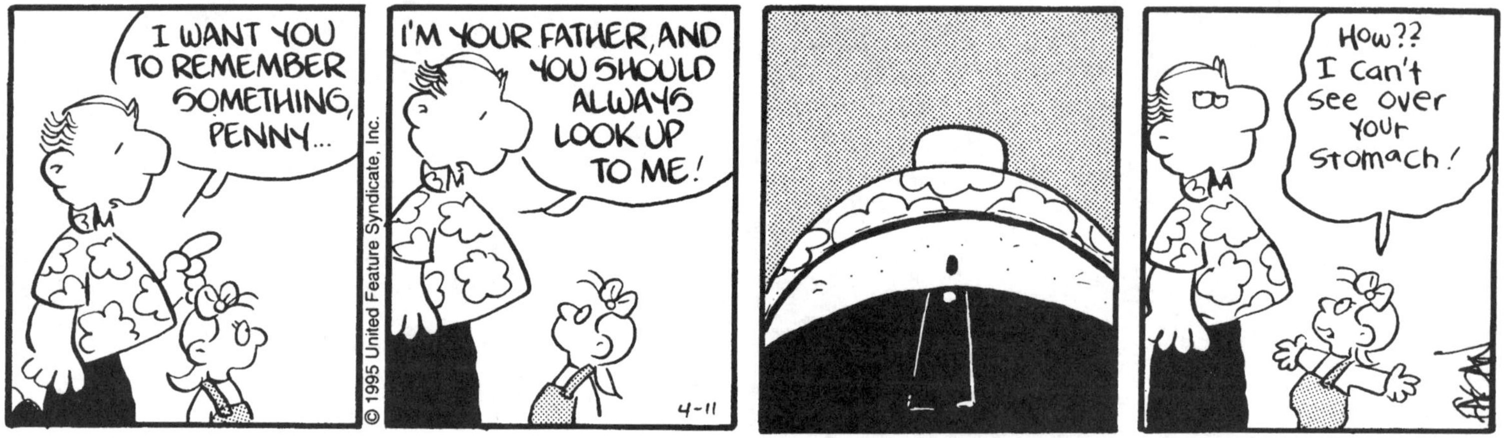
I WANT YOU TO REMEMBER SOMETHING, PENNY...
© 1995 United Feature Syndicate, Inc.
I'M YOUR FATHER, AND YOU SHOULD ALWAYS LOOK UP TO ME!
4-11
How?? I can't see over your stomach!

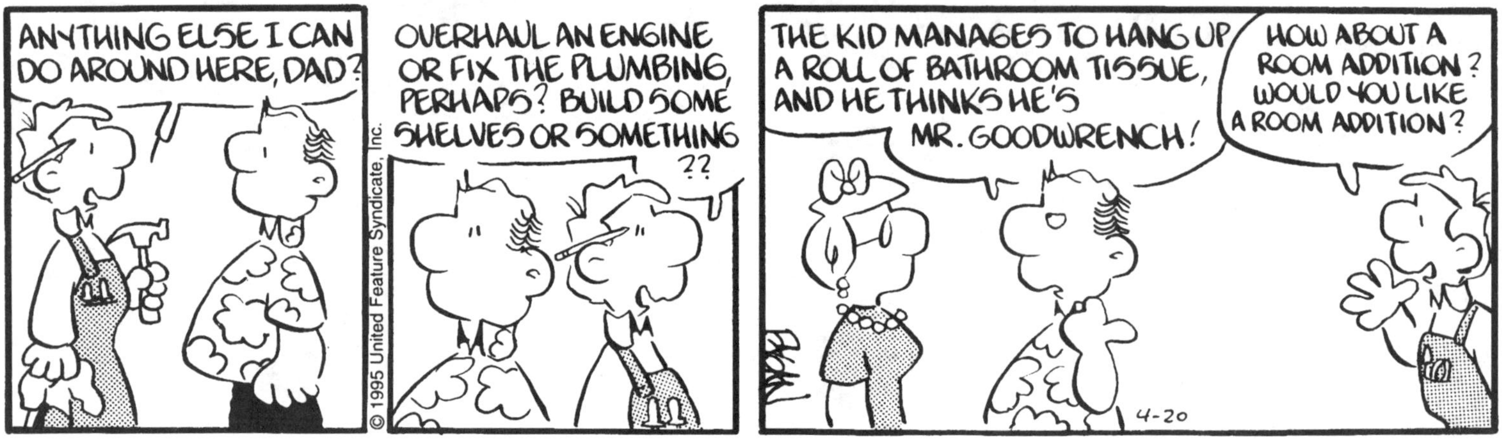
ANYTHING ELSE I CAN DO AROUND HERE, DAD?
© 1995 United Feature Syndicate, Inc.
OVERHAUL AN ENGINE OR FIX THE PLUMBING, PERHAPS? BUILD SOME SHELVES OR SOMETHING
??
THE KID MANAGES TO HANG UP A ROLL OF BATHROOM TISSUE, AND HE THINKS HE'S MR. GOODWRENCH!
HOW ABOUT A ROOM ADDITION? WOULD YOU LIKE A ROOM ADDITION?
4-20

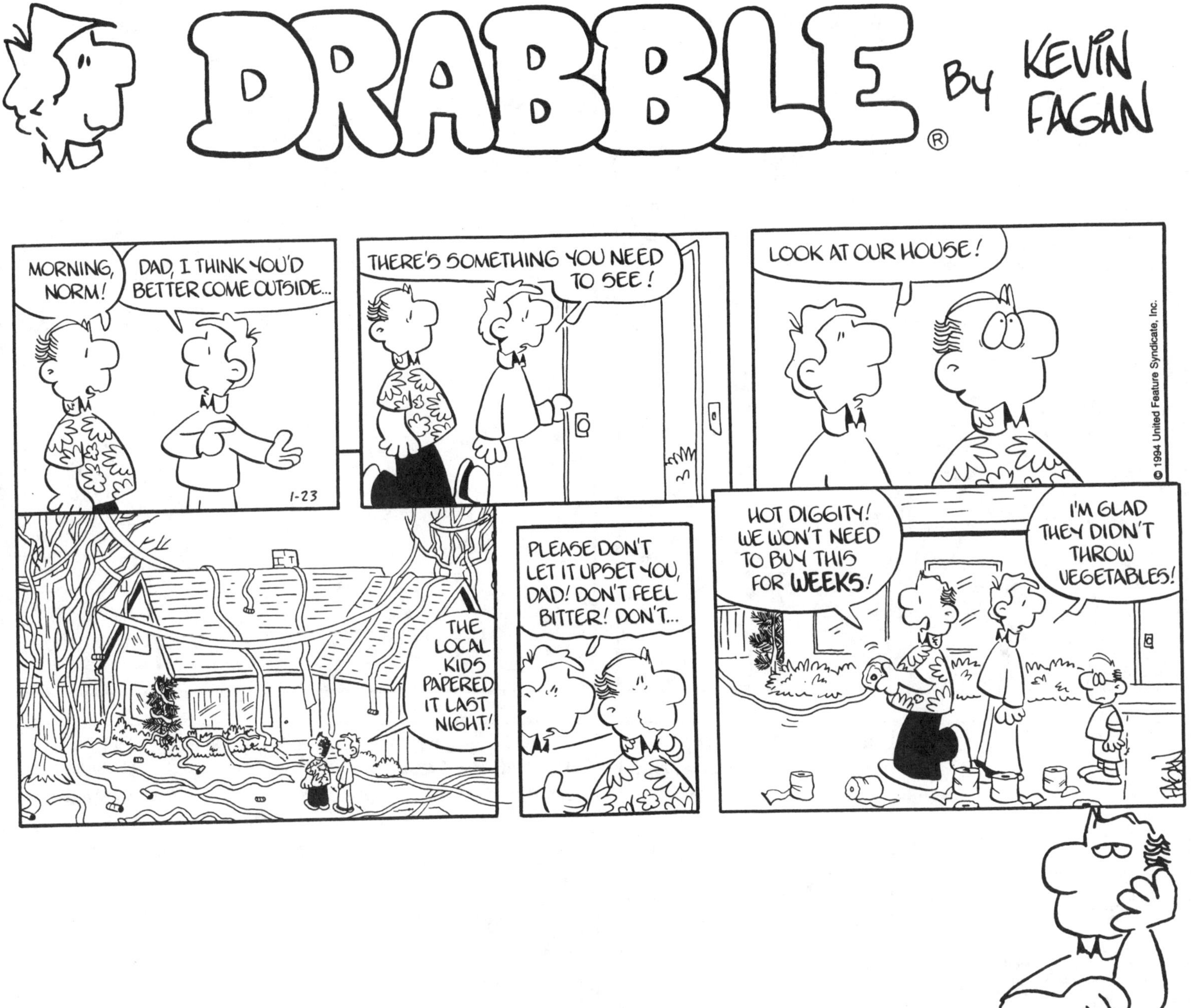
DRABBLE®
By KEVIN FAGAN
MORNING, NORM!
DAD, I THINK YOU'D BETTER COME OUTSIDE...
1-23
THERE'S SOMETHING YOU NEED TO SEE!
LOOK AT OUR HOUSE!
© 1994 United Feature Syndicate, Inc.
THE LOCAL KIDS PAPERED IT LAST NIGHT!
PLEASE DON'T LET IT UPSET YOU, DAD! DON'T FEEL BITTER! DON'T...
HOT DIGGITY! WE WON'T NEED TO BUY THIS FOR **WEEKS**!
I'M GLAD THEY DIDN'T THROW VEGETABLES!

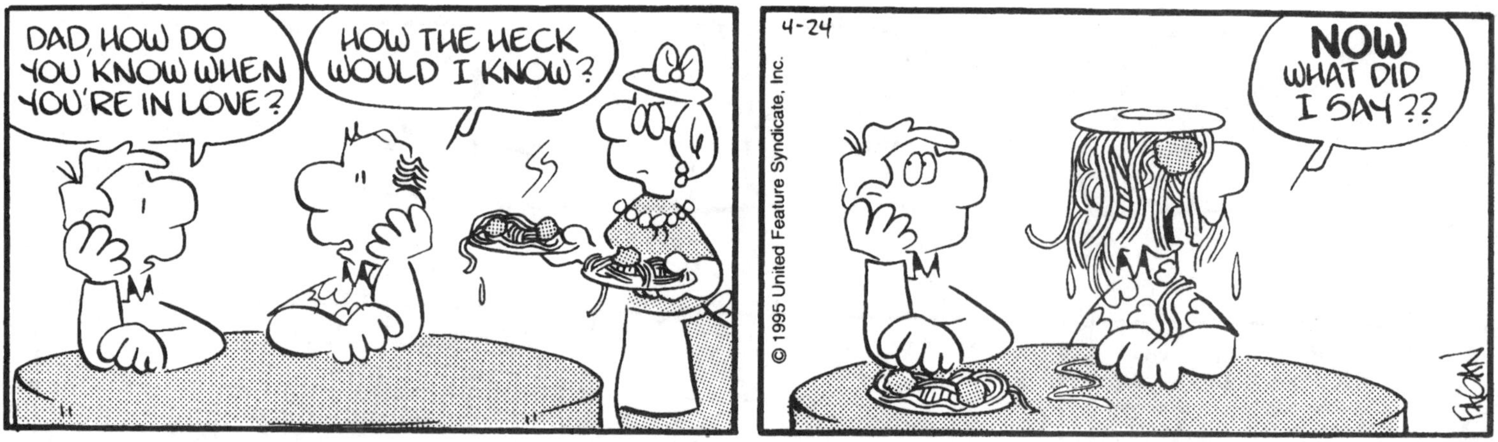
DAD, HOW DO YOU KNOW WHEN YOU'RE IN LOVE?
HOW THE HECK WOULD I KNOW?
4-24
© 1995 United Feature Syndicate, Inc.
NOW WHAT DID I SAY??

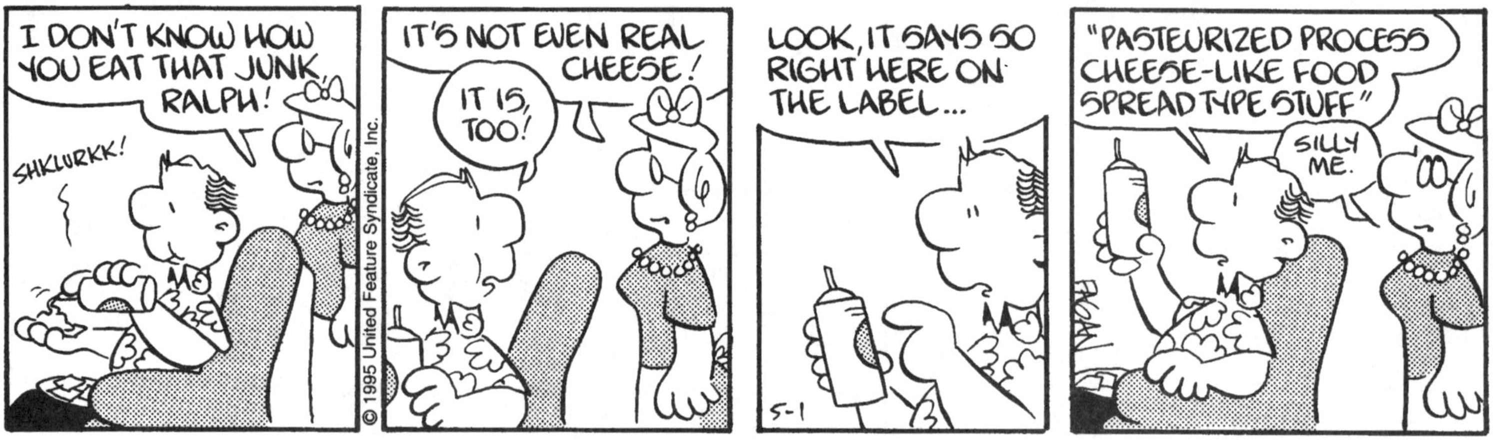
I DON'T KNOW HOW YOU EAT THAT JUNK, RALPH!
SHKLURKK!
© 1995 United Feature Syndicate, Inc.
IT'S NOT EVEN REAL CHEESE!
IT IS, TOO!
LOOK, IT SAYS SO RIGHT HERE ON THE LABEL...
5-1
"PASTEURIZED PROCESS CHEESE-LIKE FOOD SPREAD TYPE STUFF"
SILLY ME.

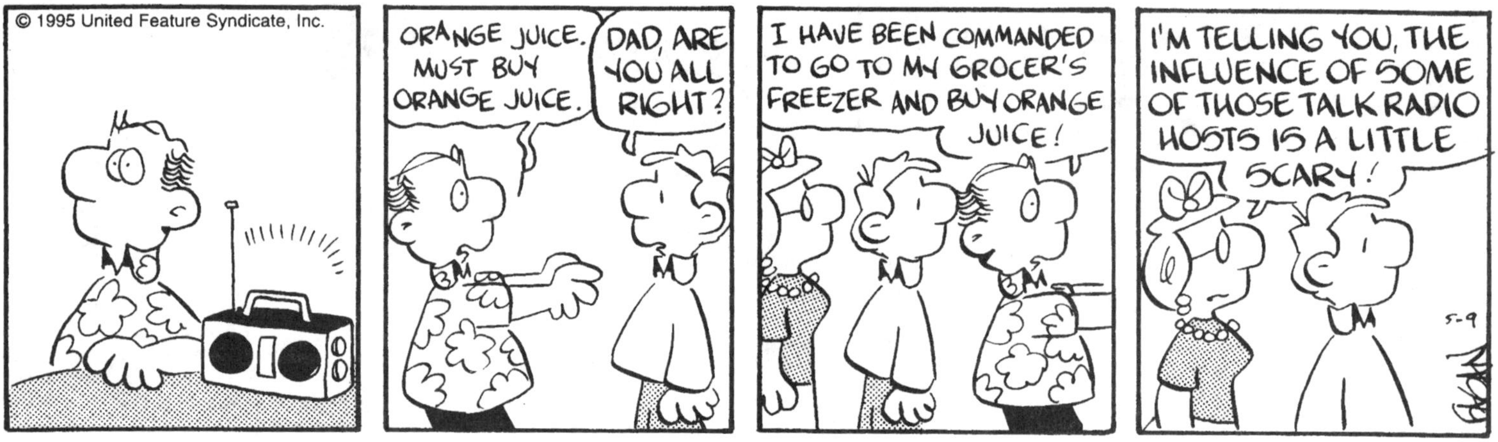
© 1995 United Feature Syndicate, Inc.
ORANGE JUICE. MUST BUY ORANGE JUICE.
DAD, ARE YOU ALL RIGHT?
I HAVE BEEN COMMANDED TO GO TO MY GROCER'S FREEZER AND BUY ORANGE JUICE!
I'M TELLING YOU, THE INFLUENCE OF SOME OF THOSE TALK RADIO HOSTS IS A LITTLE SCARY!
5-9

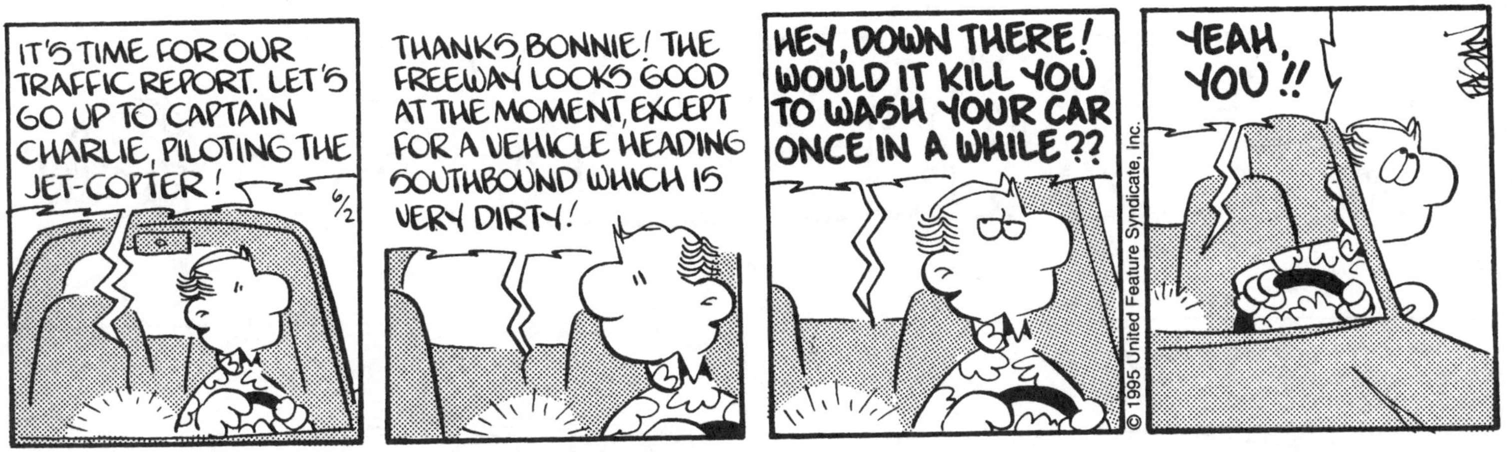
IT'S TIME FOR OUR TRAFFIC REPORT. LET'S GO UP TO CAPTAIN CHARLIE, PILOTING THE JET-COPTER!
6/2
THANKS, BONNIE! THE FREEWAY LOOKS GOOD AT THE MOMENT, EXCEPT FOR A VEHICLE HEADING SOUTHBOUND WHICH IS VERY DIRTY!
HEY, DOWN THERE! WOULD IT KILL YOU TO WASH YOUR CAR ONCE IN A WHILE??
© 1995 United Feature Syndicate, Inc.
YEAH, YOU!!

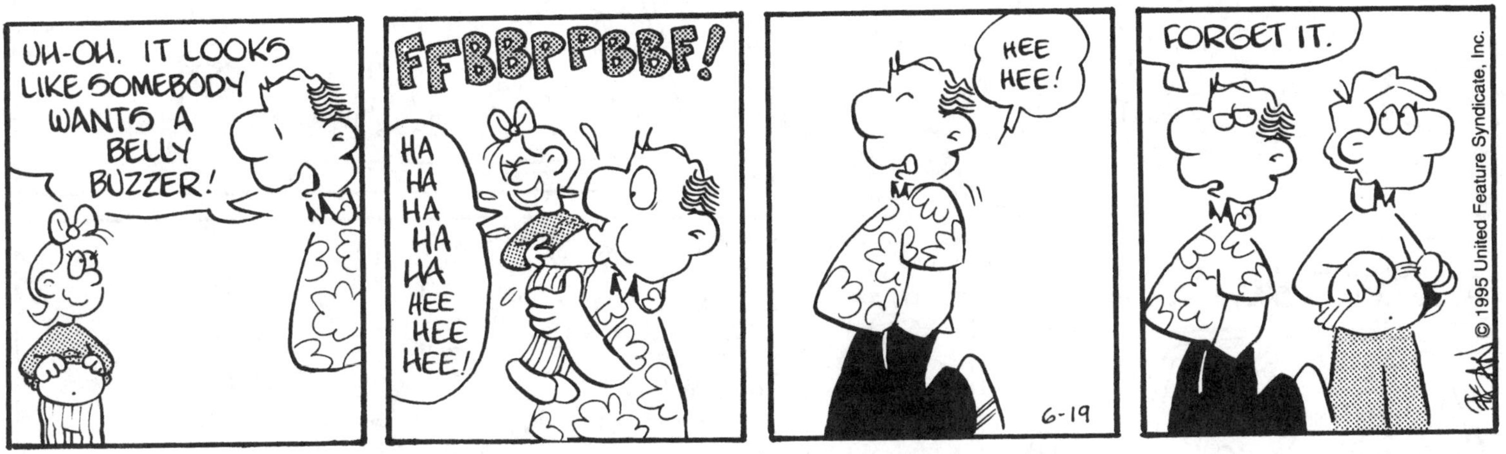
UH-OH. IT LOOKS LIKE SOMEBODY WANTS A BELLY BUZZER!
FFBBPPBBF!
HA HA HA HA HA HEE HEE HEE!
HEE HEE!
6-19
FORGET IT.
© 1995 United Feature Syndicate, Inc.

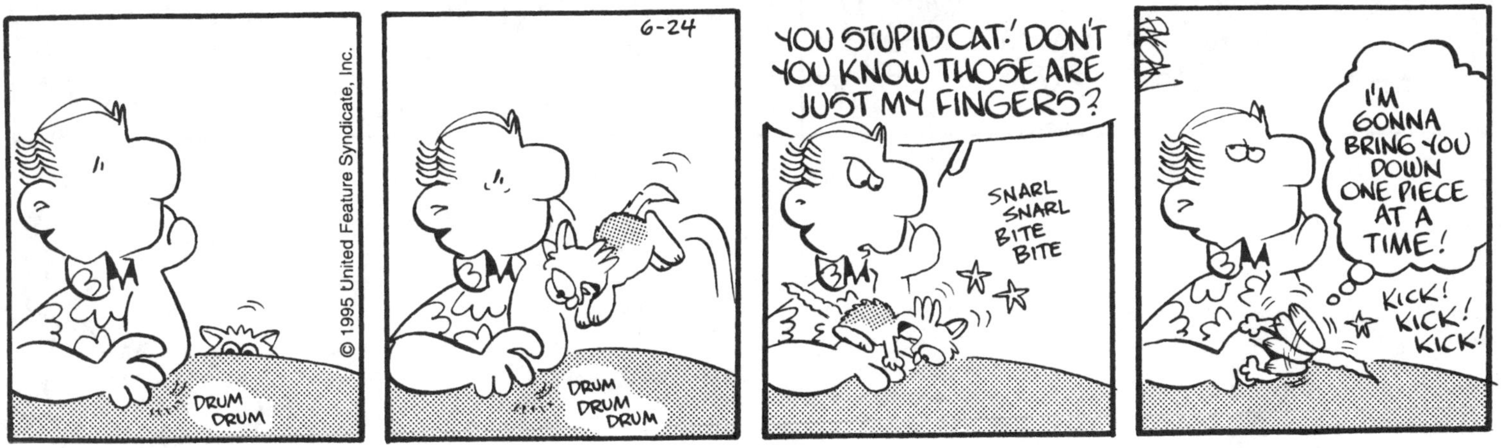
DRUM DRUM
© 1995 United Feature Syndicate, Inc.
6-24
DRUM DRUM DRUM
YOU STUPID CAT! DON'T YOU KNOW THOSE ARE JUST MY FINGERS?
SNARL SNARL BITE BITE
I'M GONNA BRING YOU DOWN ONE PIECE AT A TIME!
KICK! KICK! KICK!

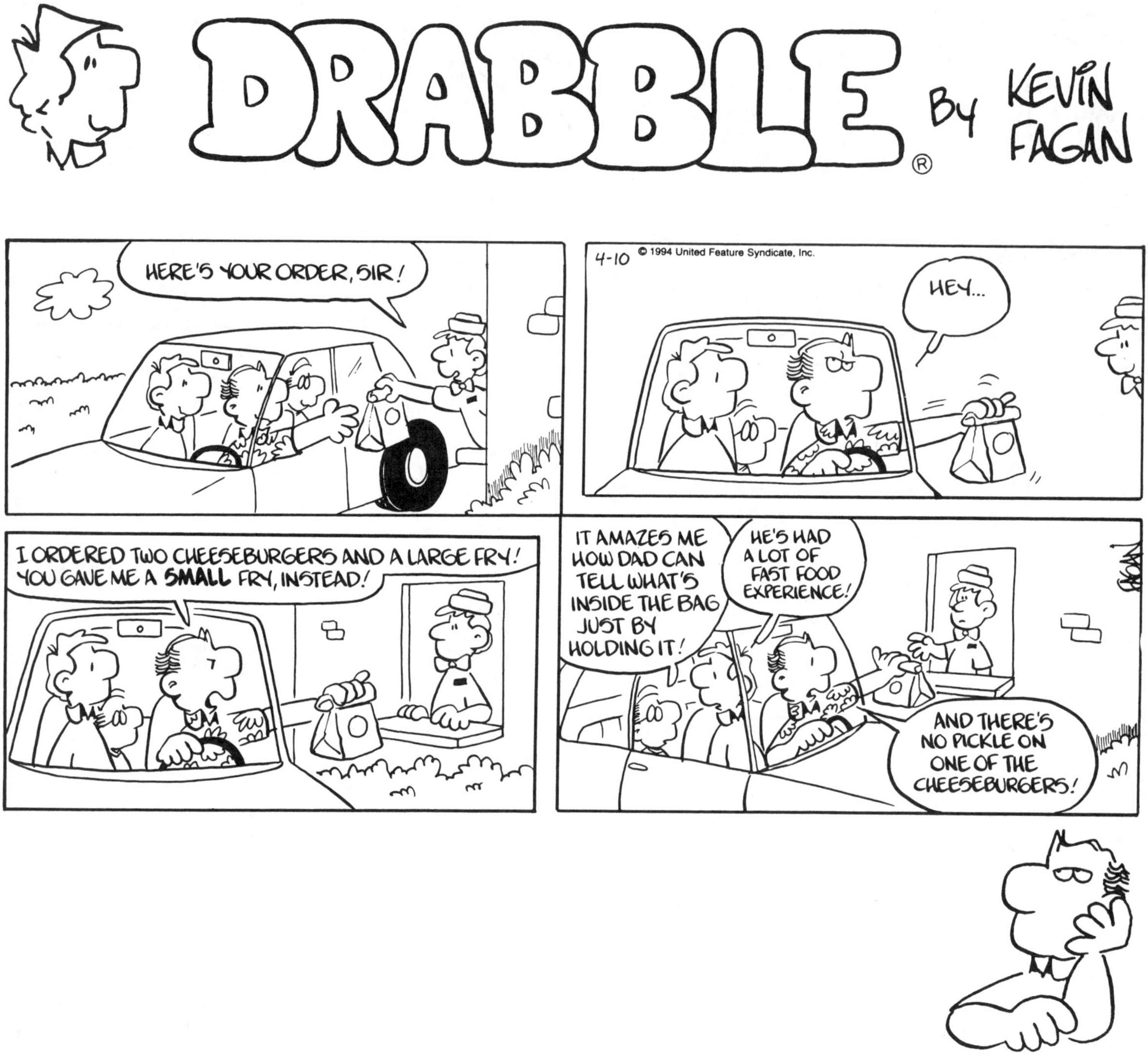
DRABBLE
By KEVIN FAGAN
HERE'S YOUR ORDER, SIR!
4-10
© 1994 United Feature Syndicate, Inc.
HEY...
I ORDERED TWO CHEESEBURGERS AND A LARGE FRY! YOU GAVE ME A **SMALL** FRY, INSTEAD!
IT AMAZES ME HOW DAD CAN TELL WHAT'S INSIDE THE BAG JUST BY HOLDING IT!
HE'S HAD A LOT OF FAST FOOD EXPERIENCE!
AND THERE'S NO PICKLE ON ONE OF THE CHEESEBURGERS!
FAGAN

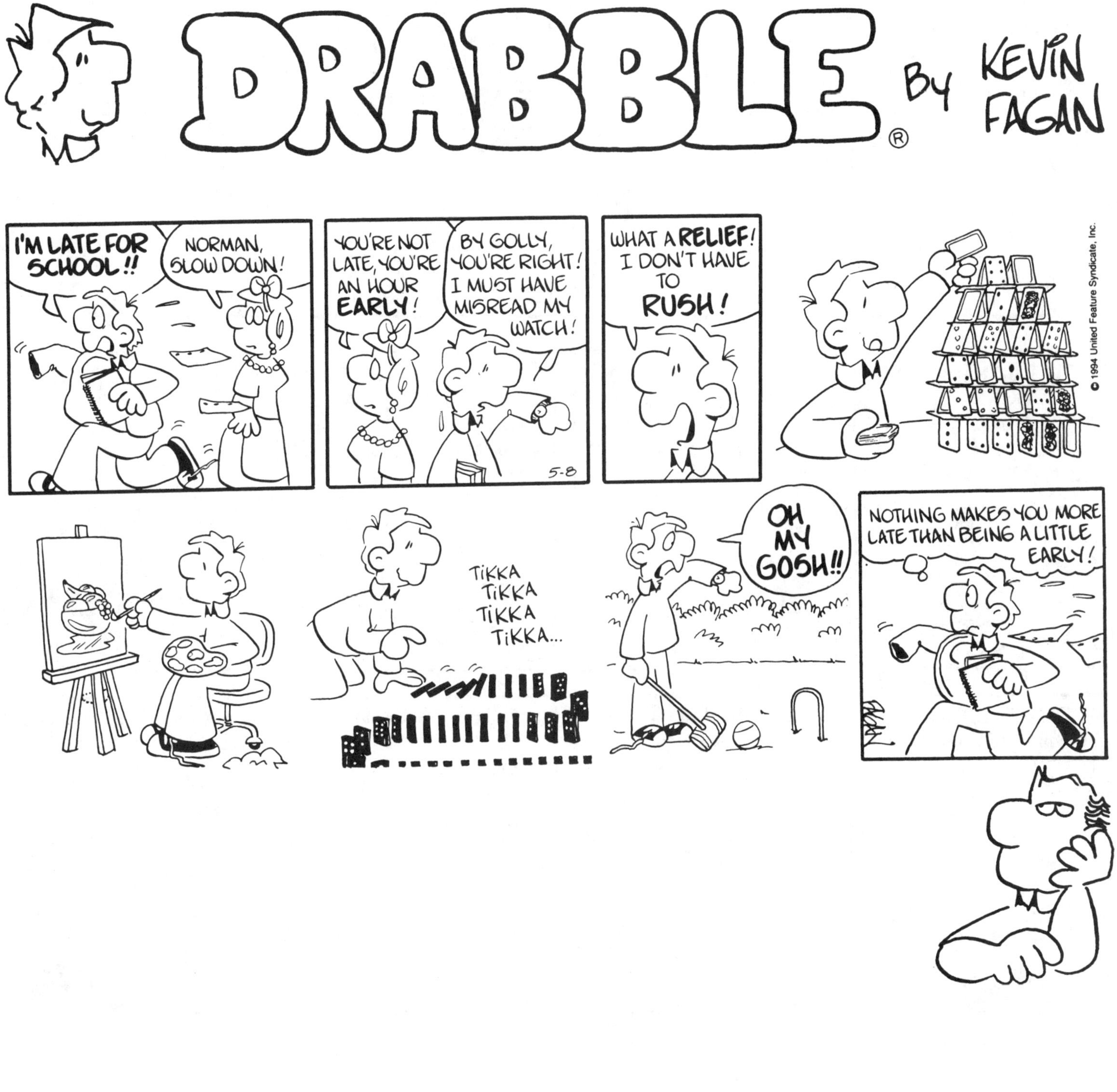
DRABBLE
By KEVIN FAGAN
I'M LATE FOR SCHOOL!!
NORMAN, SLOW DOWN!
YOU'RE NOT LATE, YOU'RE AN HOUR EARLY!
BY GOLLY, YOU'RE RIGHT! I MUST HAVE MISREAD MY WATCH!
5-8
WHAT A RELIEF! I DON'T HAVE TO RUSH!
© 1994 United Feature Syndicate, Inc.
TIKKA TIKKA TIKKA TIKKA...
OH MY GOSH!!
NOTHING MAKES YOU MORE LATE THAN BEING A LITTLE EARLY!

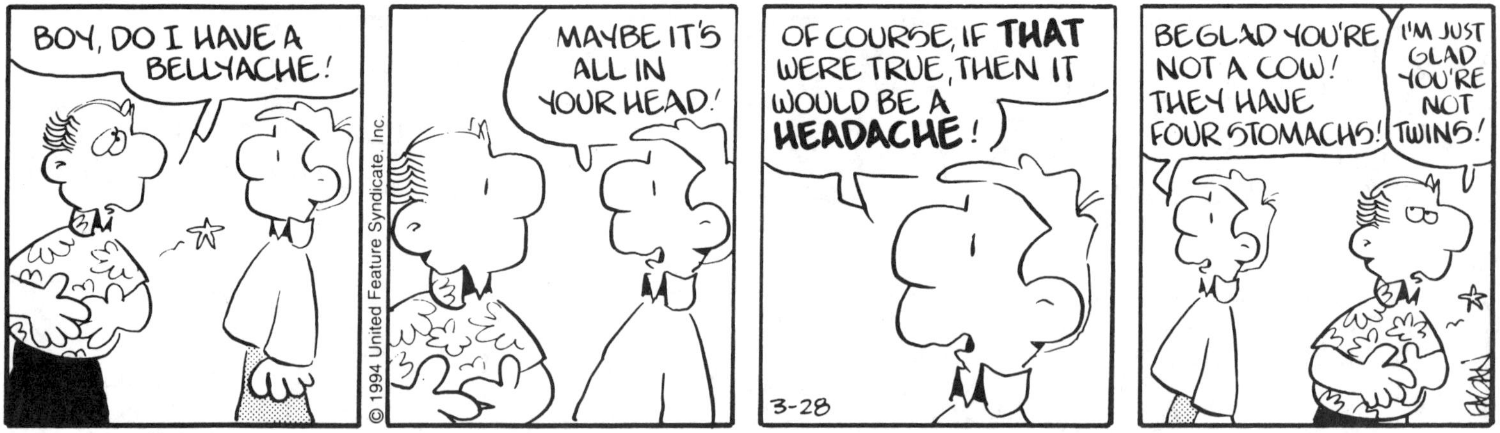
BOY, DO I HAVE A BELLYACHE!
MAYBE IT'S ALL IN YOUR HEAD!
© 1994 United Feature Syndicate, Inc.
OF COURSE, IF **THAT** WERE TRUE, THEN IT WOULD BE A **HEADACHE**!
3-28
BE GLAD YOU'RE NOT A COW! THEY HAVE FOUR STOMACHS!
I'M JUST GLAD YOU'RE NOT TWINS!

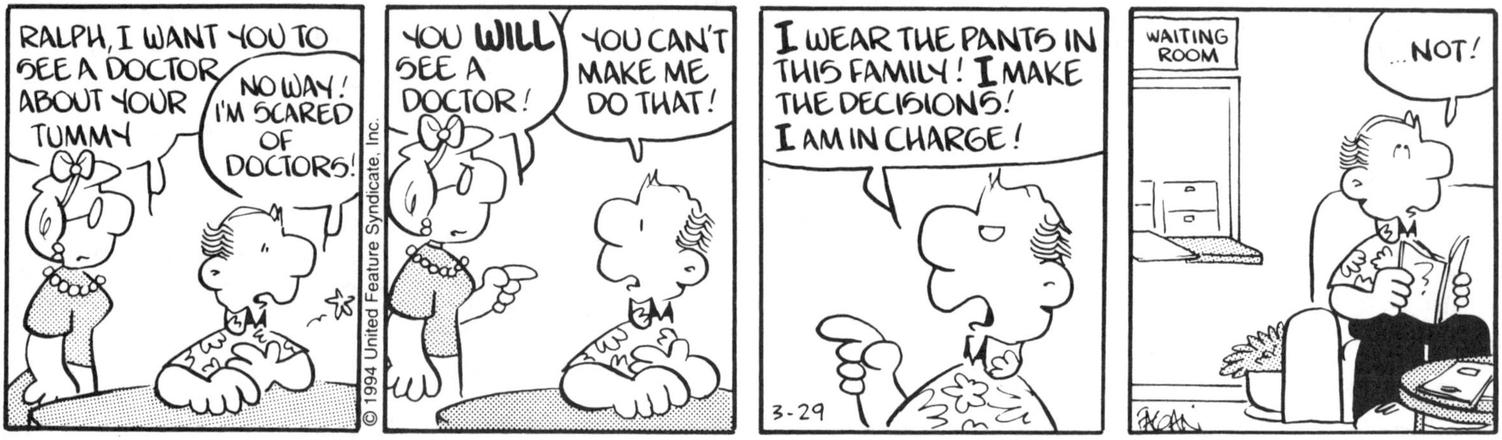
RALPH, I WANT YOU TO SEE A DOCTOR ABOUT YOUR TUMMY
NO WAY! I'M SCARED OF DOCTORS!
© 1994 United Feature Syndicate, Inc.
YOU **WILL** SEE A DOCTOR!
YOU CAN'T MAKE ME DO THAT!
I WEAR THE PANTS IN THIS FAMILY! **I** MAKE THE DECISIONS! **I** AM IN CHARGE!
3-29
WAITING ROOM
...NOT!

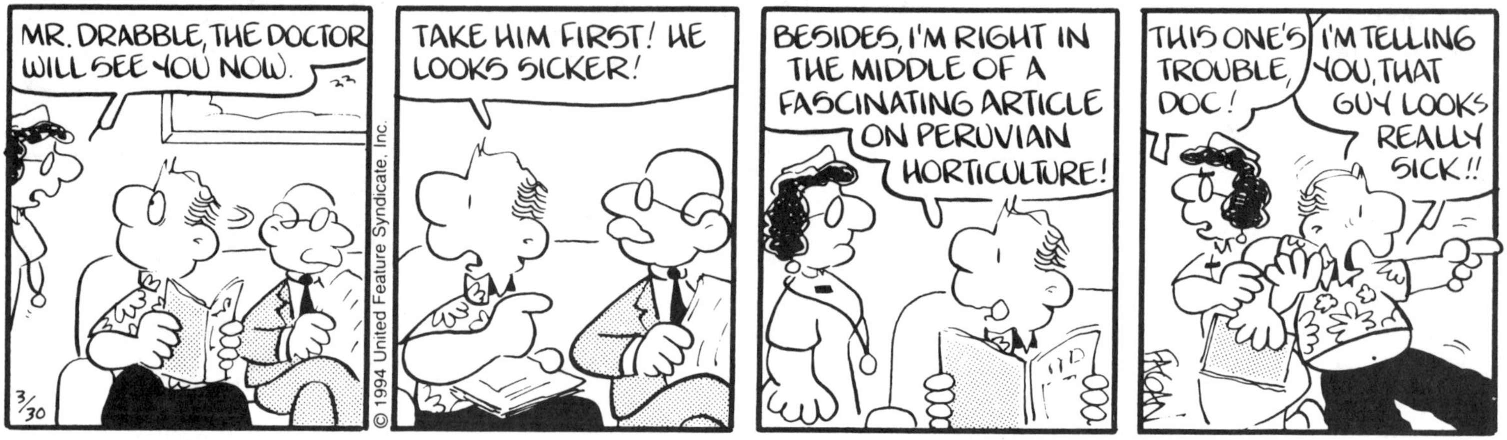
MR. DRABBLE, THE DOCTOR WILL SEE YOU NOW.
3/30
© 1994 United Feature Syndicate, Inc.
TAKE HIM FIRST! HE LOOKS SICKER!
BESIDES, I'M RIGHT IN THE MIDDLE OF A FASCINATING ARTICLE ON PERUVIAN HORTICULTURE!
THIS ONE'S TROUBLE, DOC!
I'M TELLING YOU, THAT GUY LOOKS REALLY SICK!!

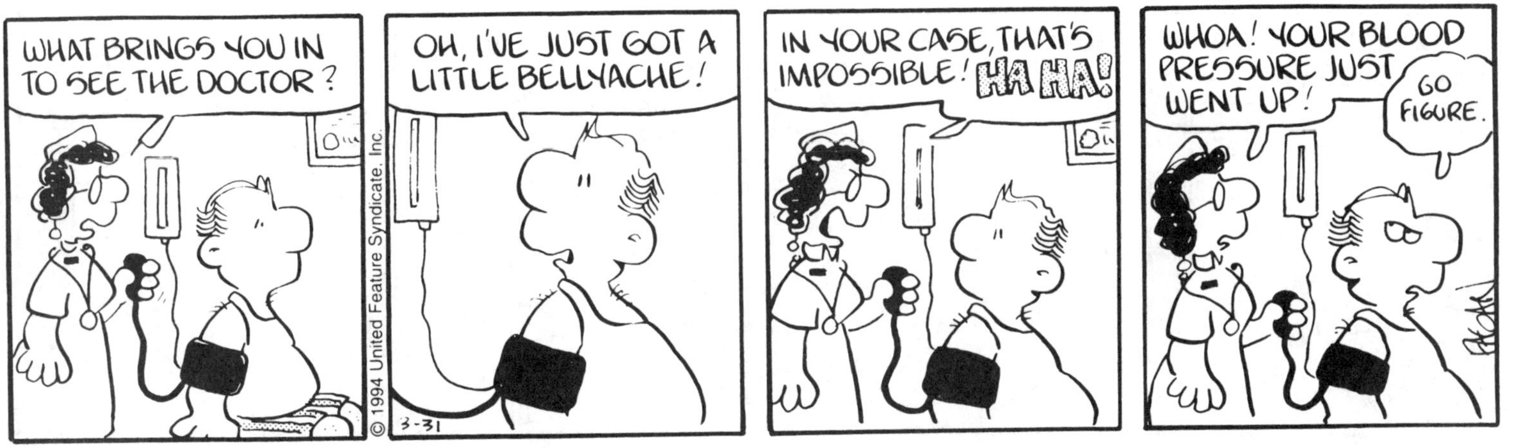
WHAT BRINGS YOU IN TO SEE THE DOCTOR?
OH, I'VE JUST GOT A LITTLE BELLYACHE!
IN YOUR CASE, THAT'S IMPOSSIBLE! HA HA!
WHOA! YOUR BLOOD PRESSURE JUST WENT UP!
GO FIGURE.
© 1994 United Feature Syndicate, Inc.
3-31

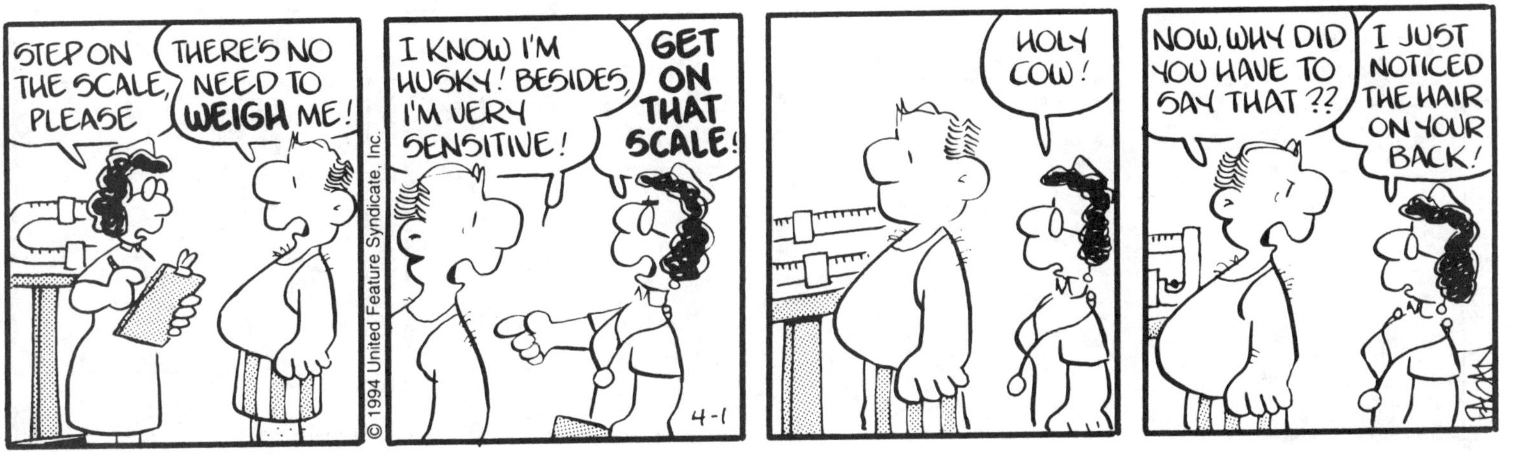
STEP ON THE SCALE, PLEASE
THERE'S NO NEED TO WEIGH ME!
I KNOW I'M HUSKY! BESIDES, I'M VERY SENSITIVE!
GET ON THAT SCALE!
HOLY COW!
NOW, WHY DID YOU HAVE TO SAY THAT??
I JUST NOTICED THE HAIR ON YOUR BACK!
© 1994 United Feature Syndicate, Inc.
4-1

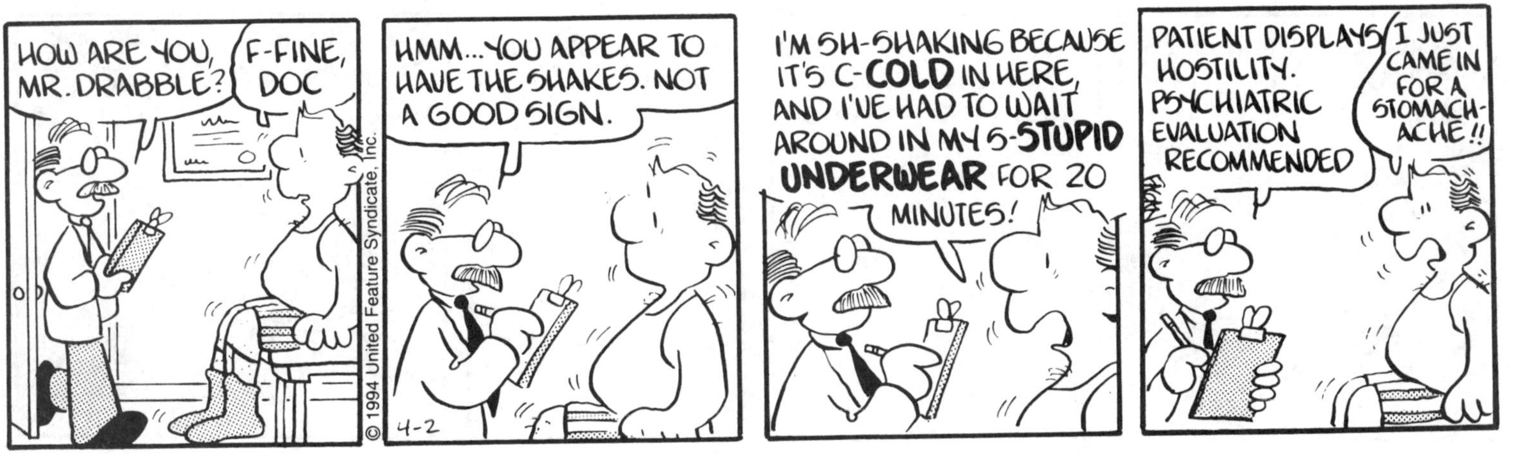
HOW ARE YOU, MR. DRABBLE?
F-FINE, DOC
HMM... YOU APPEAR TO HAVE THE SHAKES. NOT A GOOD SIGN.
I'M SH-SHAKING BECAUSE IT'S C-COLD IN HERE, AND I'VE HAD TO WAIT AROUND IN MY S-STUPID UNDERWEAR FOR 20 MINUTES!
PATIENT DISPLAYS HOSTILITY. PSYCHIATRIC EVALUATION RECOMMENDED
I JUST CAME IN FOR A STOMACH-ACHE!!
© 1994 United Feature Syndicate, Inc.
4-2

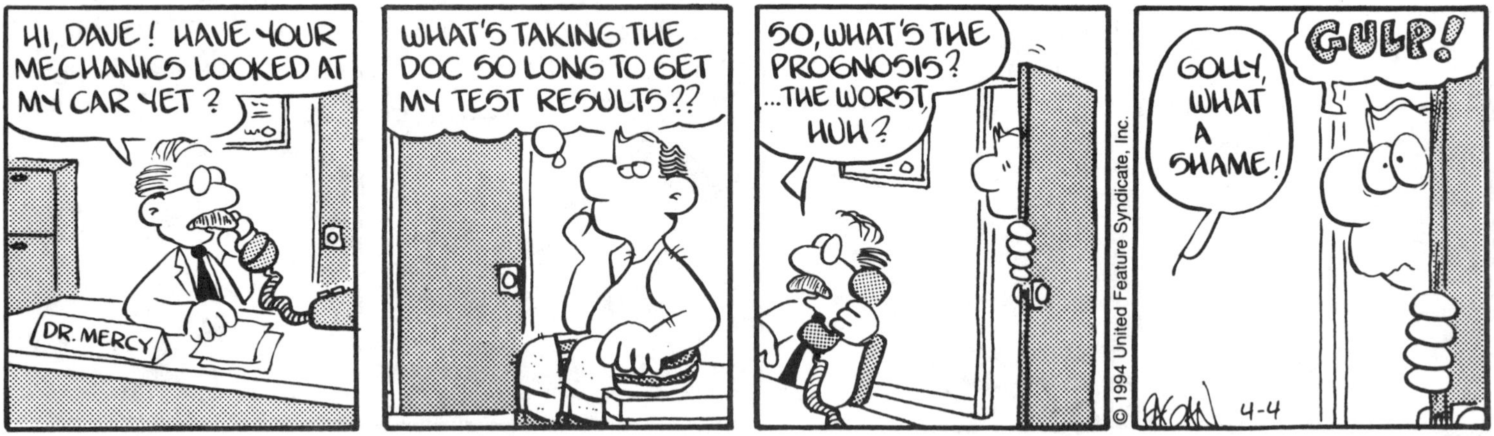
HI, DAVE! HAVE YOUR MECHANICS LOOKED AT MY CAR YET?
DR. MERCY
WHAT'S TAKING THE DOC SO LONG TO GET MY TEST RESULTS??
SO, WHAT'S THE PROGNOSIS? ...THE WORST, HUH?
GOLLY, WHAT A SHAME!
GULP!
© 1994 United Feature Syndicate, Inc.
4-4

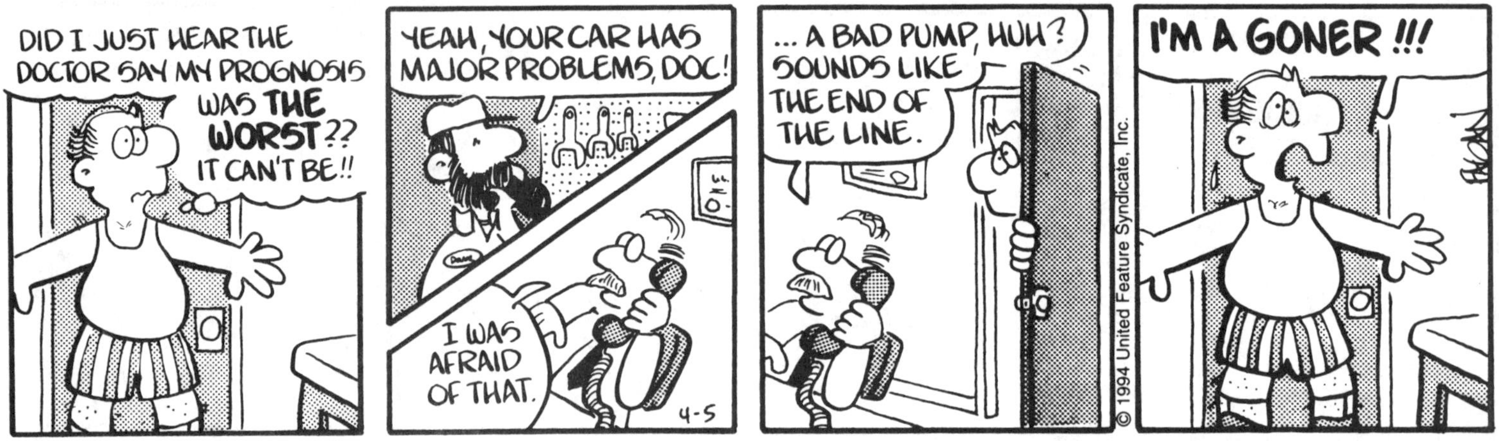
DID I JUST HEAR THE DOCTOR SAY MY PROGNOSIS WAS **THE WORST**?? IT CAN'T BE!!
YEAH, YOUR CAR HAS MAJOR PROBLEMS, DOC!
I WAS AFRAID OF THAT.
4-5
... A BAD PUMP, HUH? SOUNDS LIKE THE END OF THE LINE.
© 1994 United Feature Syndicate, Inc.
I'M A GONER!!!

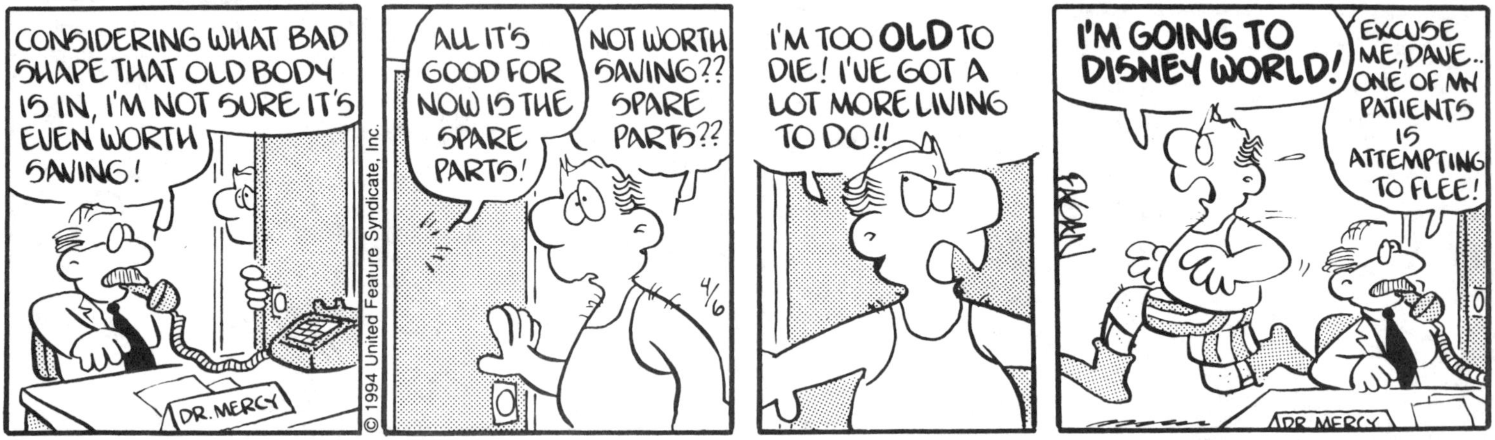
CONSIDERING WHAT BAD SHAPE THAT OLD BODY IS IN, I'M NOT SURE IT'S EVEN WORTH SAVING!
DR. MERCY
© 1994 United Feature Syndicate, Inc.
ALL IT'S GOOD FOR NOW IS THE SPARE PARTS!
NOT WORTH SAVING?? SPARE PARTS??
4/6
I'M TOO **OLD** TO DIE! I'VE GOT A LOT MORE LIVING TO DO!!
I'M GOING TO DISNEY WORLD!
EXCUSE ME, DAVE... ONE OF MY PATIENTS IS ATTEMPTING TO FLEE!

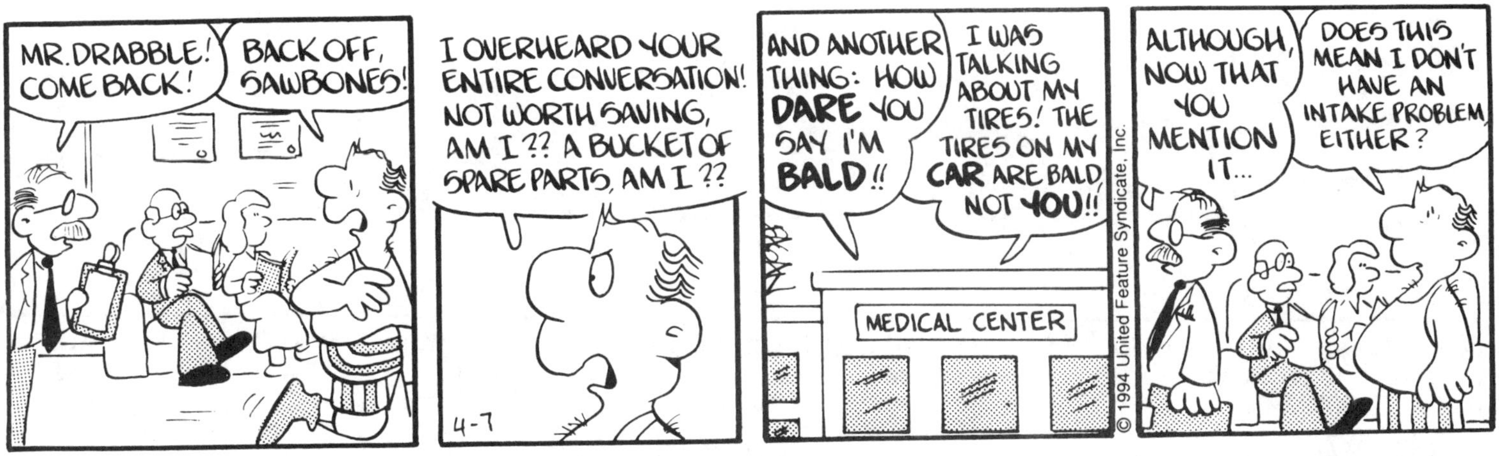
MR. DRABBLE! COME BACK!
BACK OFF, SAWBONES!
I OVERHEARD YOUR ENTIRE CONVERSATION! NOT WORTH SAVING, AM I?? A BUCKET OF SPARE PARTS, AM I??
4-7
AND ANOTHER THING: HOW DARE YOU SAY I'M BALD!!
I WAS TALKING ABOUT MY TIRES! THE TIRES ON MY CAR ARE BALD, NOT YOU!!
MEDICAL CENTER
© 1994 United Feature Syndicate, Inc.
ALTHOUGH, NOW THAT YOU MENTION IT...
DOES THIS MEAN I DON'T HAVE AN INTAKE PROBLEM, EITHER?

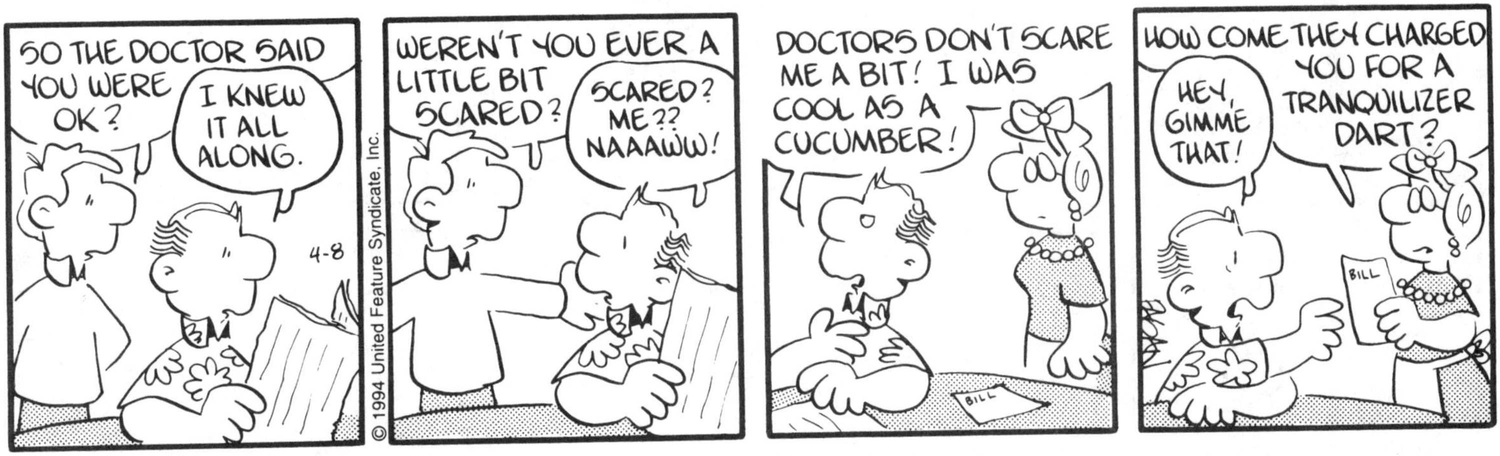
SO THE DOCTOR SAID YOU WERE OK?
I KNEW IT ALL ALONG.
4-8
© 1994 United Feature Syndicate, Inc.
WEREN'T YOU EVER A LITTLE BIT SCARED?
SCARED? ME?? NAAAWW!
DOCTORS DON'T SCARE ME A BIT! I WAS COOL AS A CUCUMBER!
BILL
HOW COME THEY CHARGED YOU FOR A TRANQUILIZER DART?
HEY, GIMME THAT!
BILL

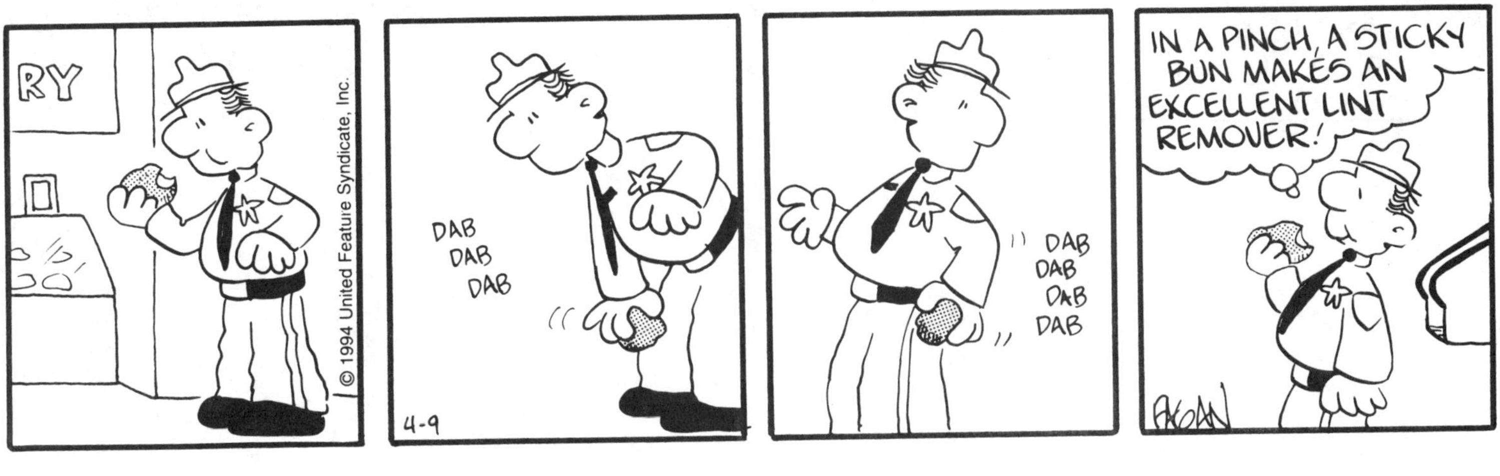
RY
© 1994 United Feature Syndicate, Inc.
DAB DAB DAB
4-9
DAB DAB DAB DAB
IN A PINCH, A STICKY BUN MAKES AN EXCELLENT LINT REMOVER!
FAGAN

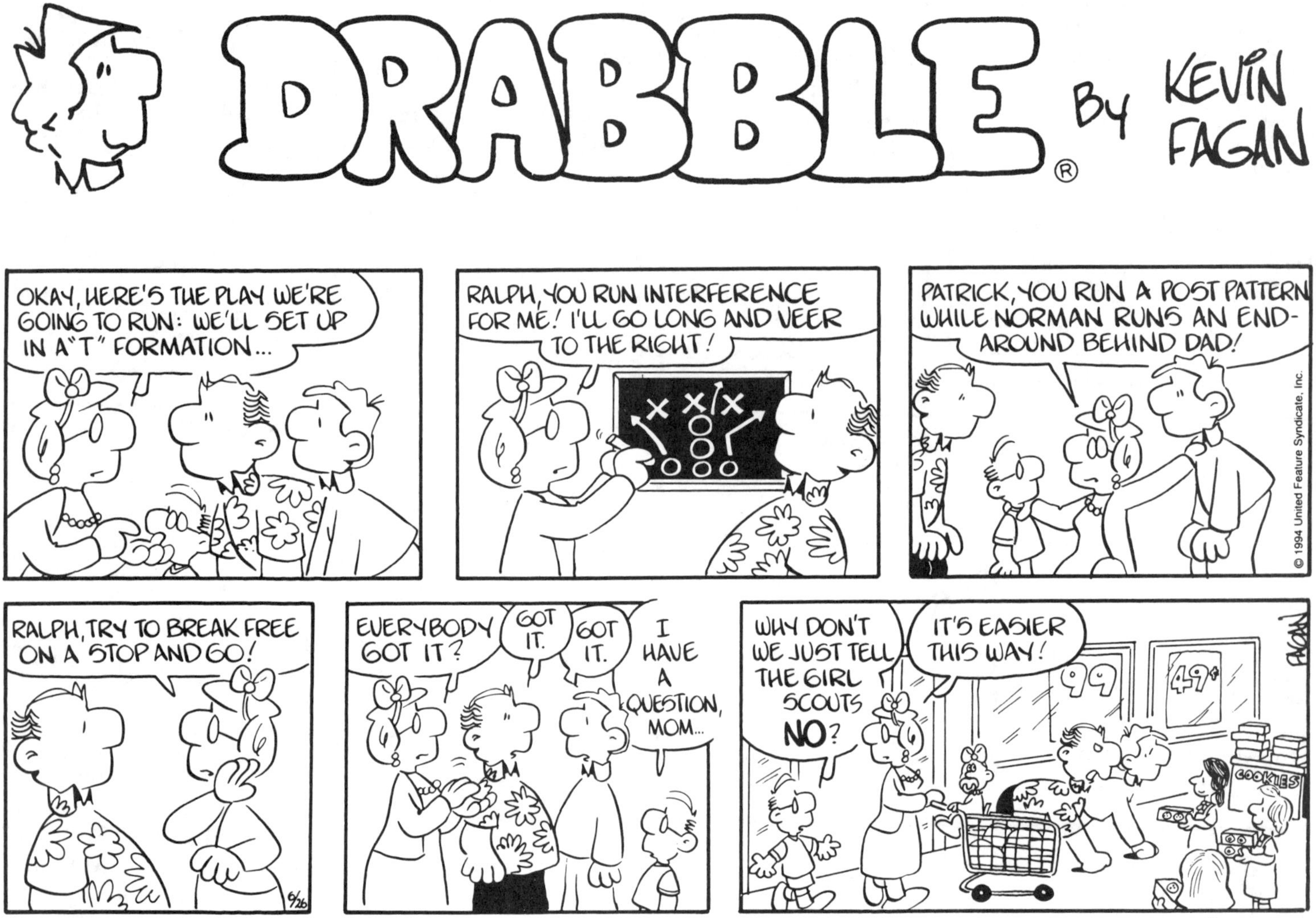
DRABBLE®
By KEVIN FAGAN
OKAY, HERE'S THE PLAY WE'RE GOING TO RUN: WE'LL SET UP IN A "T" FORMATION...
RALPH, YOU RUN INTERFERENCE FOR ME! I'LL GO LONG AND VEER TO THE RIGHT!
PATRICK, YOU RUN A POST PATTERN WHILE NORMAN RUNS AN END-AROUND BEHIND DAD!
© 1994 United Feature Syndicate, Inc.
RALPH, TRY TO BREAK FREE ON A STOP AND GO!
6/26
EVERYBODY GOT IT?
GOT IT.
GOT IT.
I HAVE A QUESTION, MOM...
FAGAN
WHY DON'T WE JUST TELL THE GIRL SCOUTS NO?
IT'S EASIER THIS WAY!
99
49¢
COOKIES

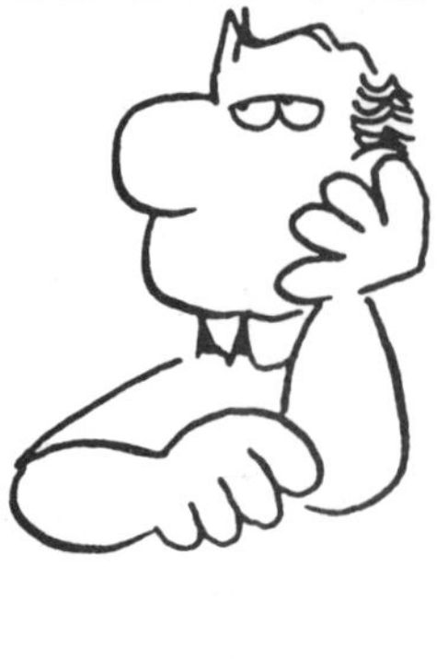

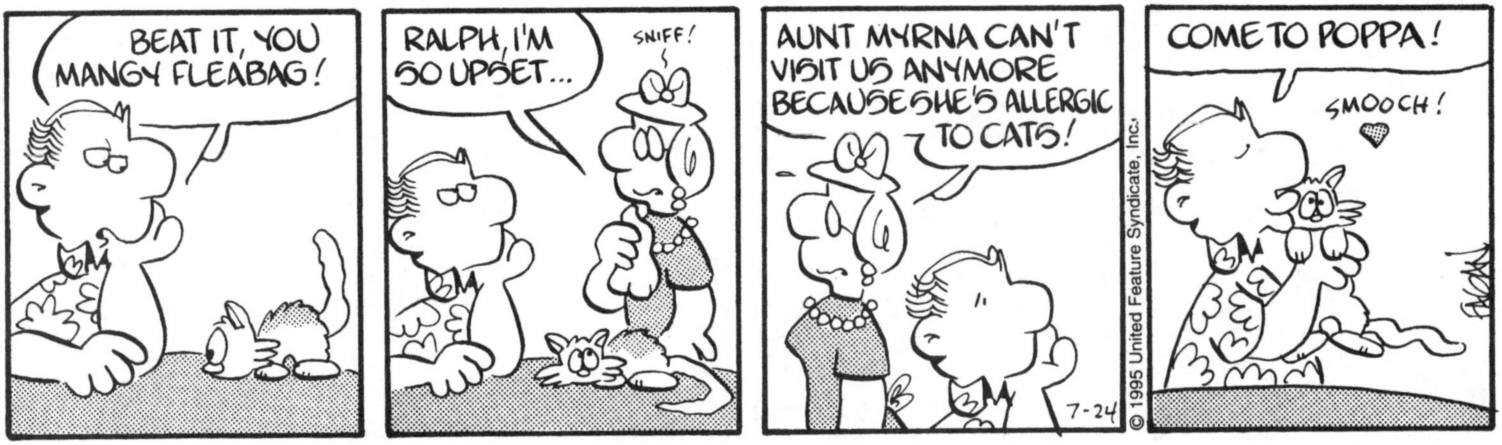
BEAT IT, YOU MANGY FLEABAG!
RALPH, I'M SO UPSET...
SNIFF!
AUNT MYRNA CAN'T VISIT US ANYMORE BECAUSE SHE'S ALLERGIC TO CATS!
7-24
© 1995 United Feature Syndicate, Inc.
COME TO POPPA!
SMOOCH!

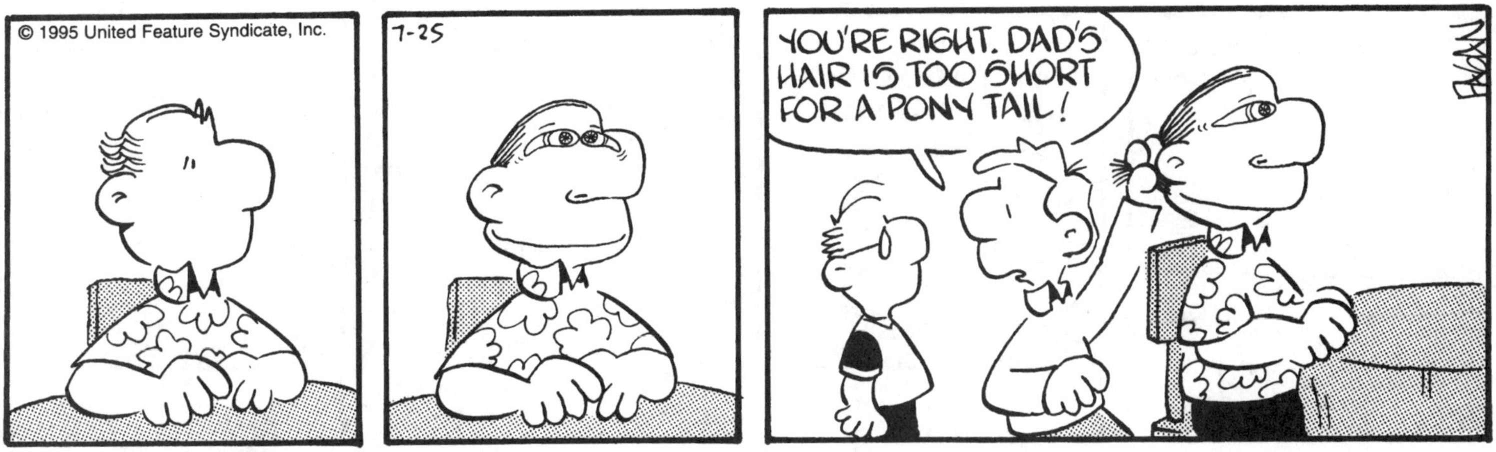
© 1995 United Feature Syndicate, Inc.
7-25
YOU'RE RIGHT. DAD'S HAIR IS TOO SHORT FOR A PONY TAIL!

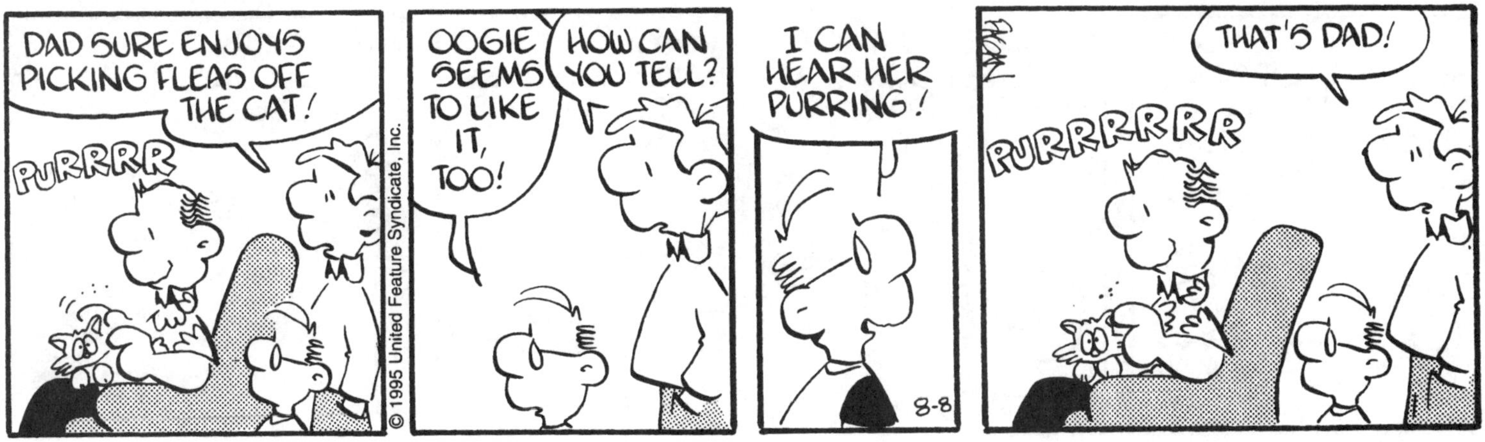
DAD SURE ENJOYS PICKING FLEAS OFF THE CAT!
PURRRR
© 1995 United Feature Syndicate, Inc.
OOGIE SEEMS TO LIKE IT, TOO!
HOW CAN YOU TELL?
I CAN HEAR HER PURRING!
8-8
PURRRRRRR
THAT'S DAD!

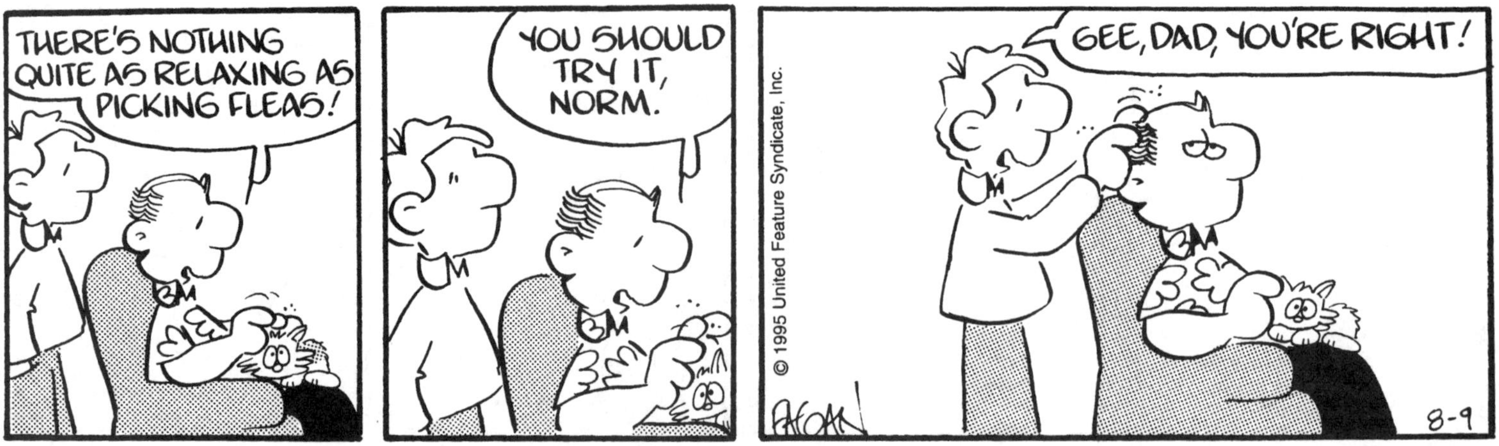
THERE'S NOTHING QUITE AS RELAXING AS PICKING FLEAS!
YOU SHOULD TRY IT, NORM.
© 1995 United Feature Syndicate, Inc.
GEE, DAD, YOU'RE RIGHT!
FAGAN
8-9

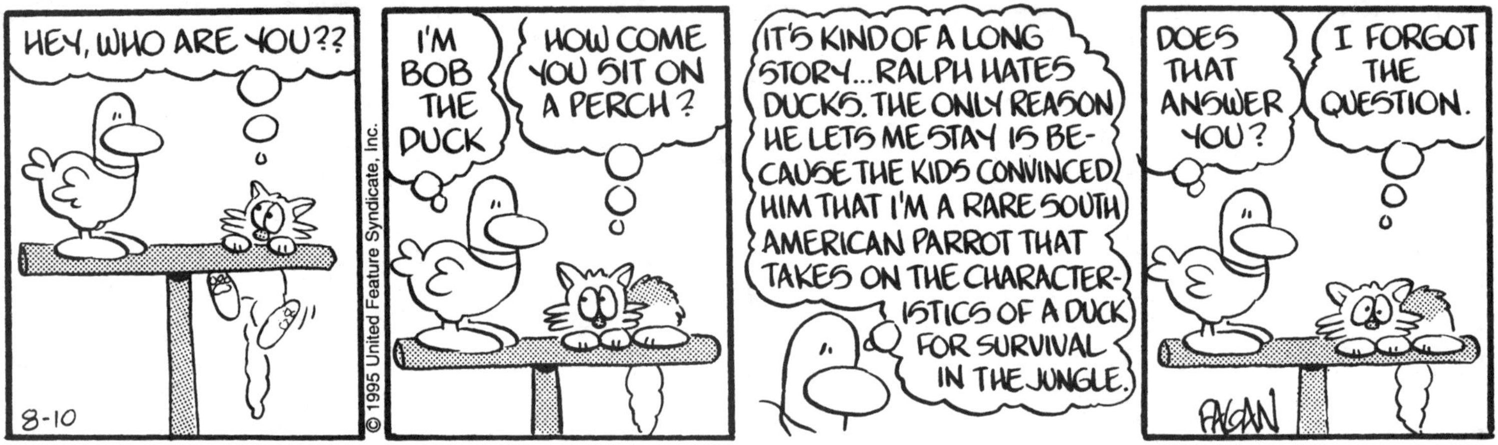
HEY, WHO ARE YOU??
8-10
© 1995 United Feature Syndicate, Inc.
I'M BOB THE DUCK
HOW COME YOU SIT ON A PERCH?
IT'S KIND OF A LONG STORY... RALPH HATES DUCKS. THE ONLY REASON HE LETS ME STAY IS BECAUSE THE KIDS CONVINCED HIM THAT I'M A RARE SOUTH AMERICAN PARROT THAT TAKES ON THE CHARACTERISTICS OF A DUCK FOR SURVIVAL IN THE JUNGLE.
DOES THAT ANSWER YOU?
I FORGOT THE QUESTION.
FAGAN

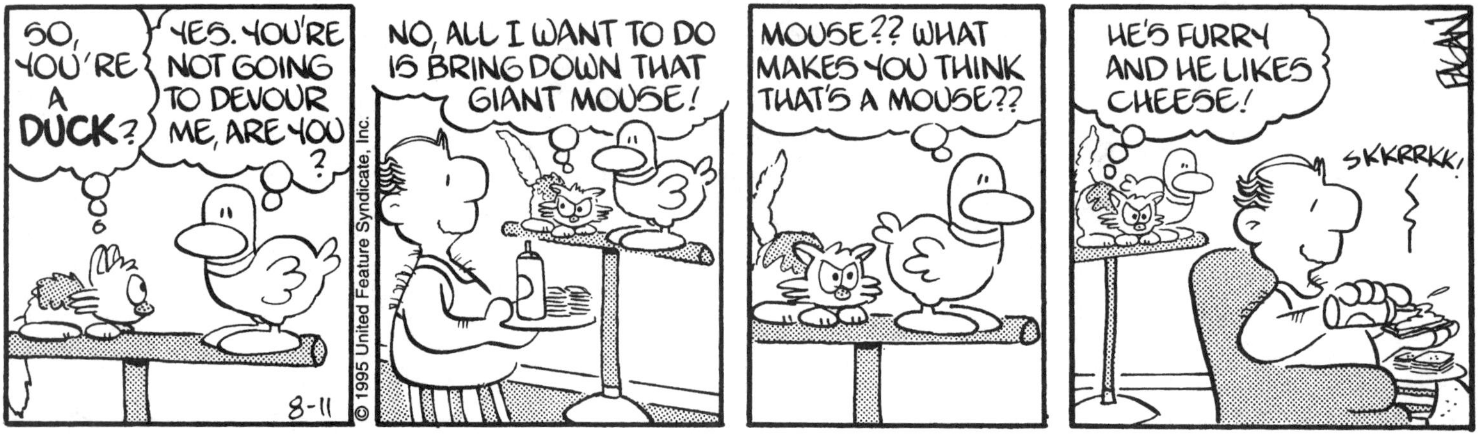
SO, YOU'RE A DUCK?
YES. YOU'RE NOT GOING TO DEVOUR ME, ARE YOU?
8-11
© 1995 United Feature Syndicate, Inc.
NO, ALL I WANT TO DO IS BRING DOWN THAT GIANT MOUSE!
MOUSE?? WHAT MAKES YOU THINK THAT'S A MOUSE??
HE'S FURRY AND HE LIKES CHEESE!
FAGAN
SKKRRKK!

DRABBLE®

By KEVIN FAGAN

YOU NEVER ASK ME OUT ANYMORE, RALPH. EVERY TIME WE GO OUT, IT'S BECAUSE I ASKED YOU!
IT SURE WOULD BE NICE IF YOU'D ASK ME OUT SOMETIME!
DON'T DO IT, RALPH! IT COULD BE A TRAP!!
DUMB RALPH
NONSENSE! ASK HER OUT FOR A DATE RIGHT NOW! YOU'LL BE GLAD YOU DID!
SMART RALPH
7-10
HONEYBUNCH, WHADDAYA SAY WE GO OUT ON THE TOWN TONIGHT?!
OH, FORGET IT, RALPH. YOU'RE ONLY ASKING BECAUSE I ASKED YOU TO!
HEY, JUST 'CAUSE I'M SMART DOESN'T MEAN I UNDERSTAND WOMEN!
SMART RALPH
© 1994 United Feature Syndicate, Inc.
FAGAN

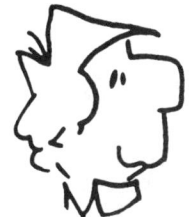

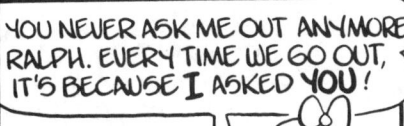

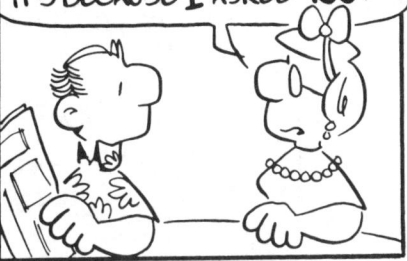

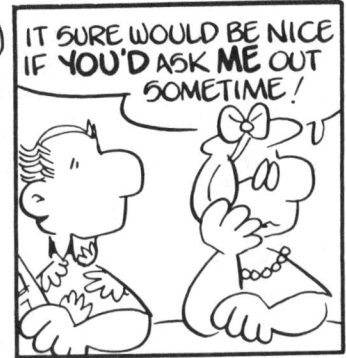

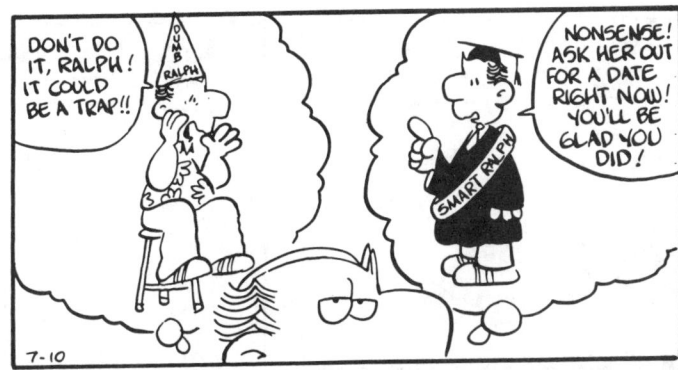

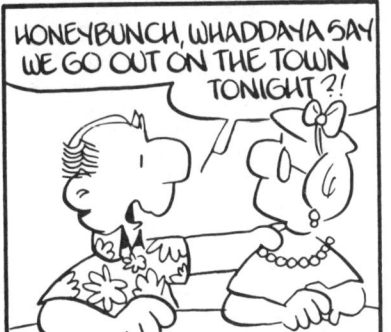

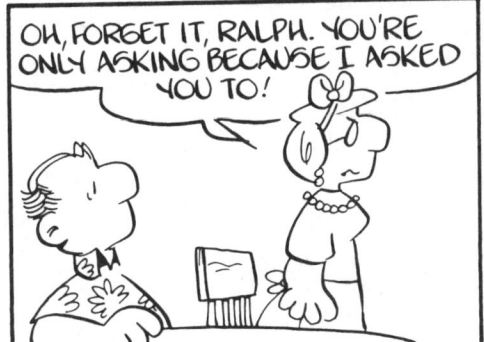

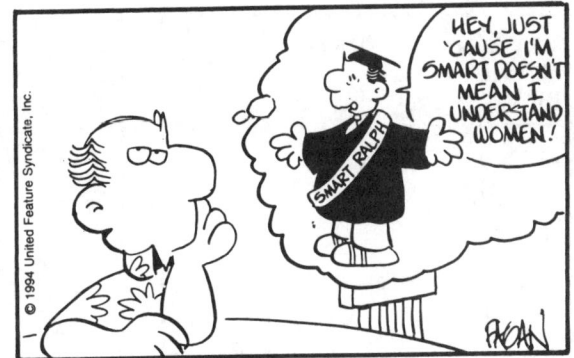

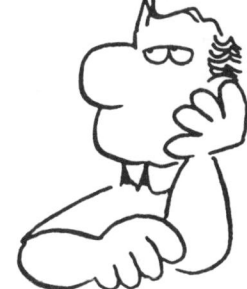

DRABBLE® By KEVIN FAGAN

WHAT'S WRONG, DAD? YOU LOOK GRUMPY THIS MORNING!
I'M NOT GRUMPY.
WHO'S GRUMPY?
DAD'S GRUMPY.
I'M NOT GRUMPY!!
© 1994 United Feature Syndicate, Inc.
THEN WHAT'S WRONG WITH YOU?
NOTHING IS WRONG!!
WHAT ARE YOU HOLLERING ABOUT, RALPH?
I'M NOT HOLLERING!!!
YOU ARE HOLLERING, SO TELL ME WHAT THE PROBLEM IS!!
I DON'T HAVE A PROBLEM!!!
FOR SOMEONE WHO DOESN'T HAVE A PROBLEM, YOU'RE SURE DOING A LOT OF HOLLERING!
YOU CERTAINLY ARE!
WHAT ARE YOU DOING HERE, RALPH? IT'S YOUR DAY OFF!
I CAME HERE TO UNWIND.
8-14
FAGAN

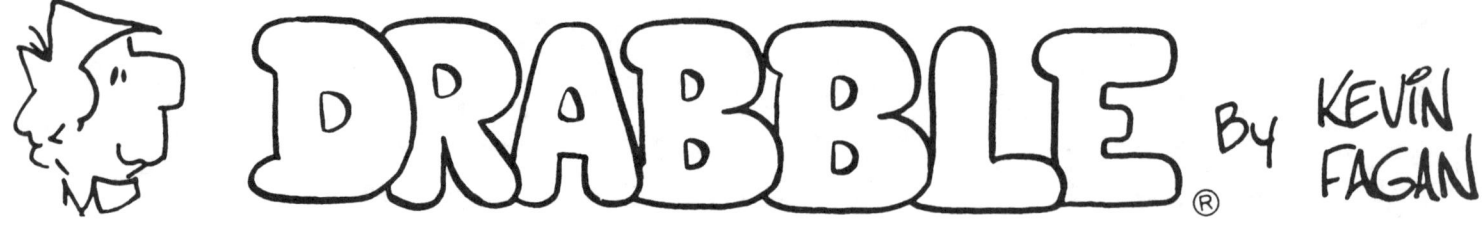

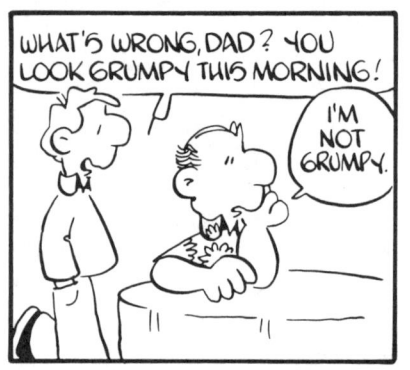

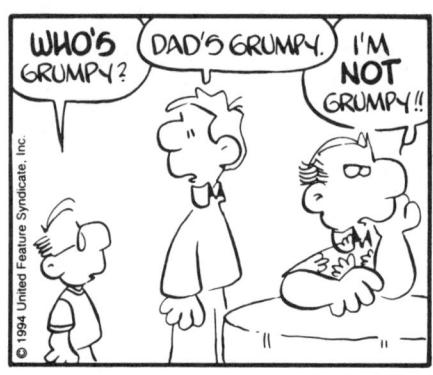

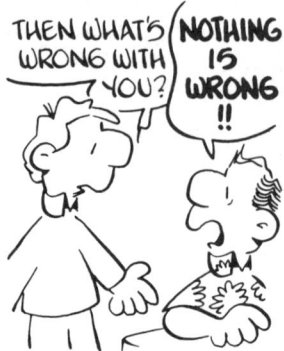

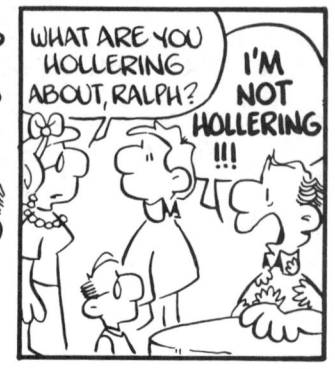

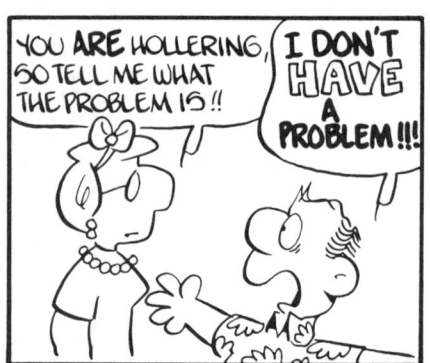

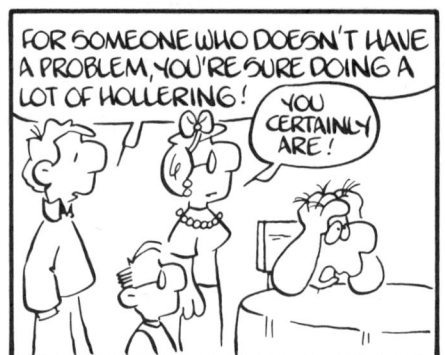

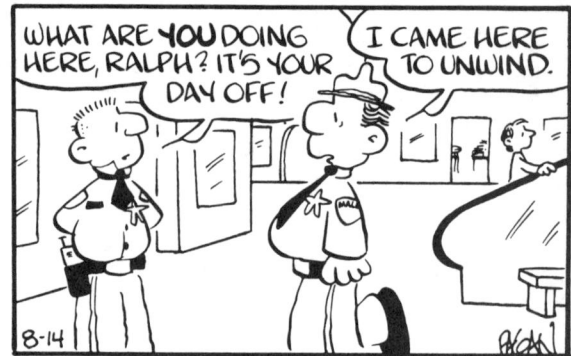

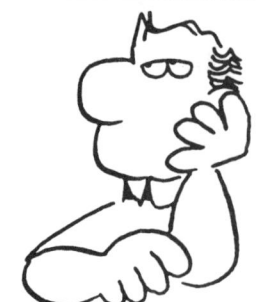

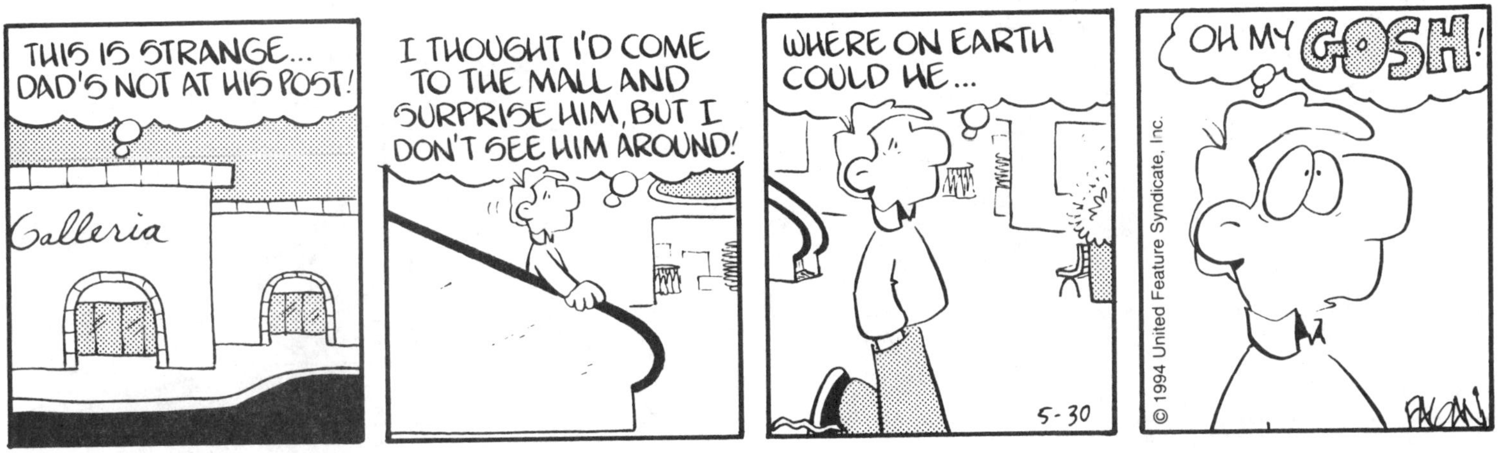
THIS IS STRANGE... DAD'S NOT AT HIS POST!
Galleria
I THOUGHT I'D COME TO THE MALL AND SURPRISE HIM, BUT I DON'T SEE HIM AROUND!
WHERE ON EARTH COULD HE...
5-30
OH MY GOSH!
© 1994 United Feature Syndicate, Inc.
FAGAN

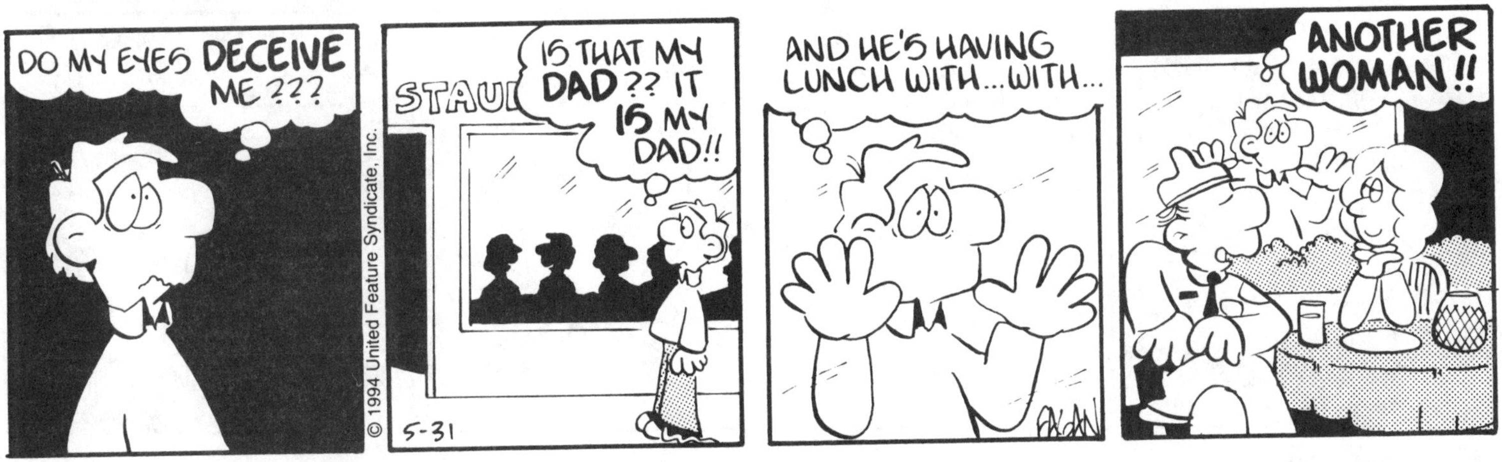
DO MY EYES DECEIVE ME???
© 1994 United Feature Syndicate, Inc.
STAU
IS THAT MY DAD?? IT IS MY DAD!!
5-31
AND HE'S HAVING LUNCH WITH...WITH...
FAGAN
ANOTHER WOMAN!!

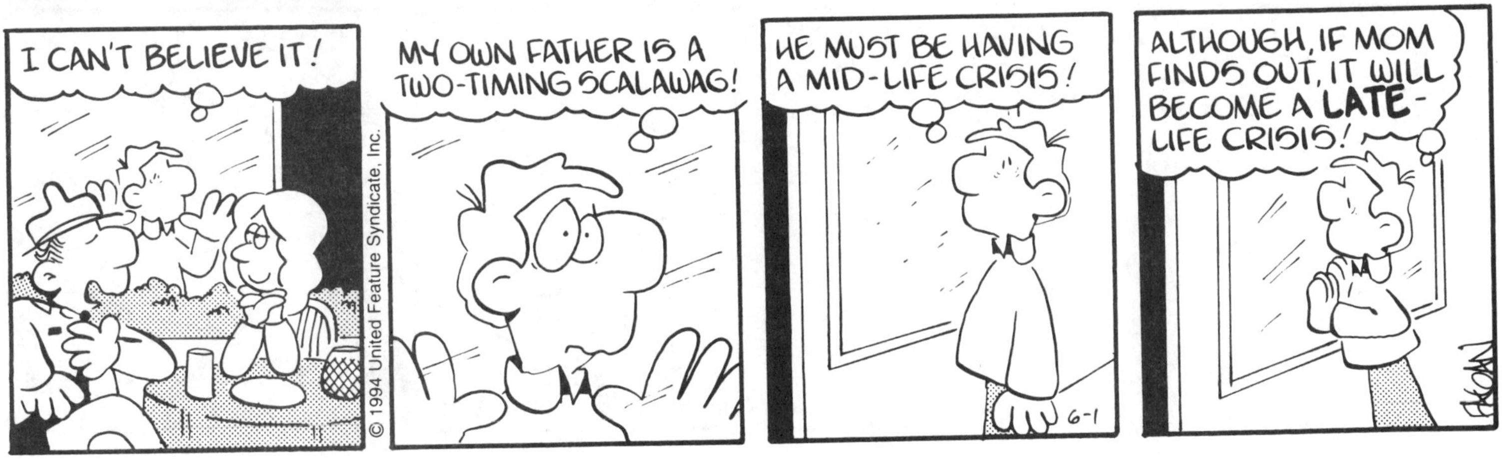
I CAN'T BELIEVE IT!
© 1994 United Feature Syndicate, Inc.
MY OWN FATHER IS A TWO-TIMING SCALAWAG!
HE MUST BE HAVING A MID-LIFE CRISIS!
6-1
ALTHOUGH, IF MOM FINDS OUT, IT WILL BECOME A LATE-LIFE CRISIS!
FAGAN

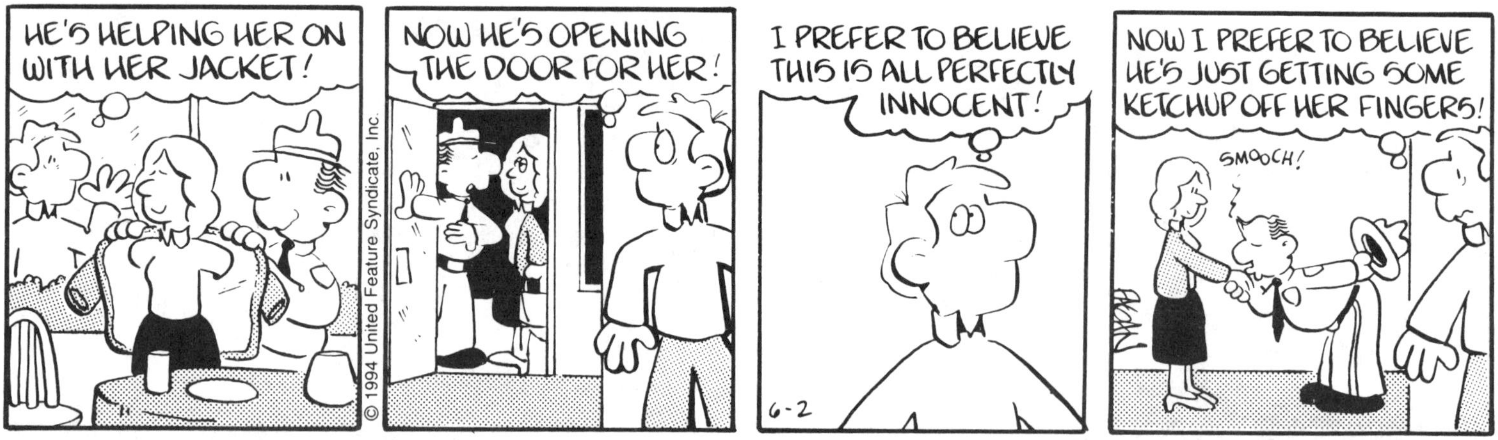
HE'S HELPING HER ON WITH HER JACKET!
© 1994 United Feature Syndicate, Inc.
NOW HE'S OPENING THE DOOR FOR HER!
I PREFER TO BELIEVE THIS IS ALL PERFECTLY INNOCENT!
6-2
NOW I PREFER TO BELIEVE HE'S JUST GETTING SOME KETCHUP OFF HER FINGERS!
SMOOCH!

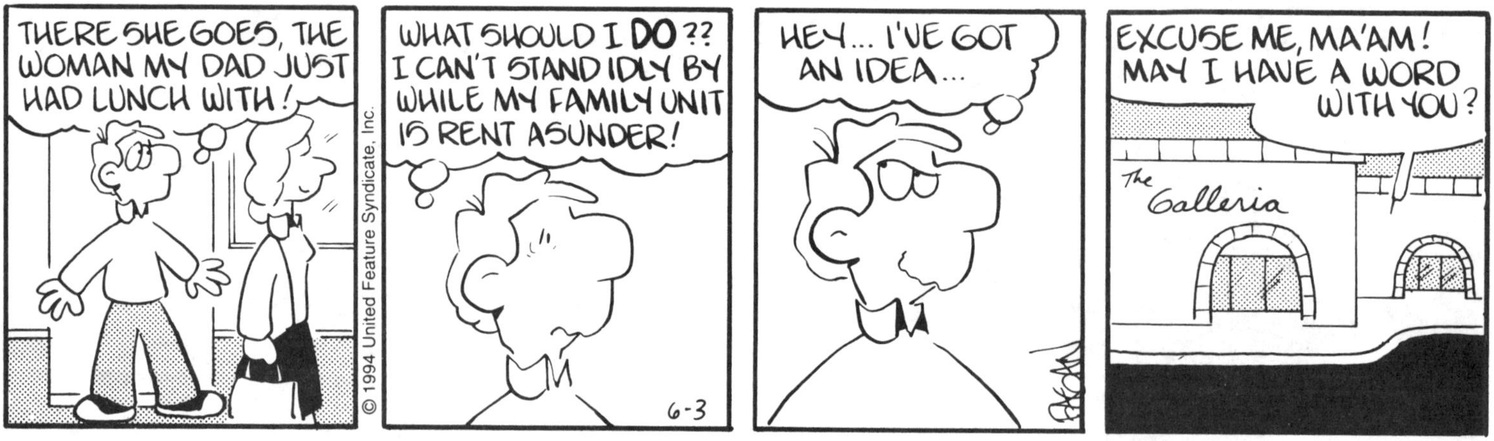
THERE SHE GOES, THE WOMAN MY DAD JUST HAD LUNCH WITH!
© 1994 United Feature Syndicate, Inc.
WHAT SHOULD I DO?? I CAN'T STAND IDLY BY WHILE MY FAMILY UNIT IS RENT ASUNDER!
6-3
HEY... I'VE GOT AN IDEA...
EXCUSE ME, MA'AM! MAY I HAVE A WORD WITH YOU?
The Galleria

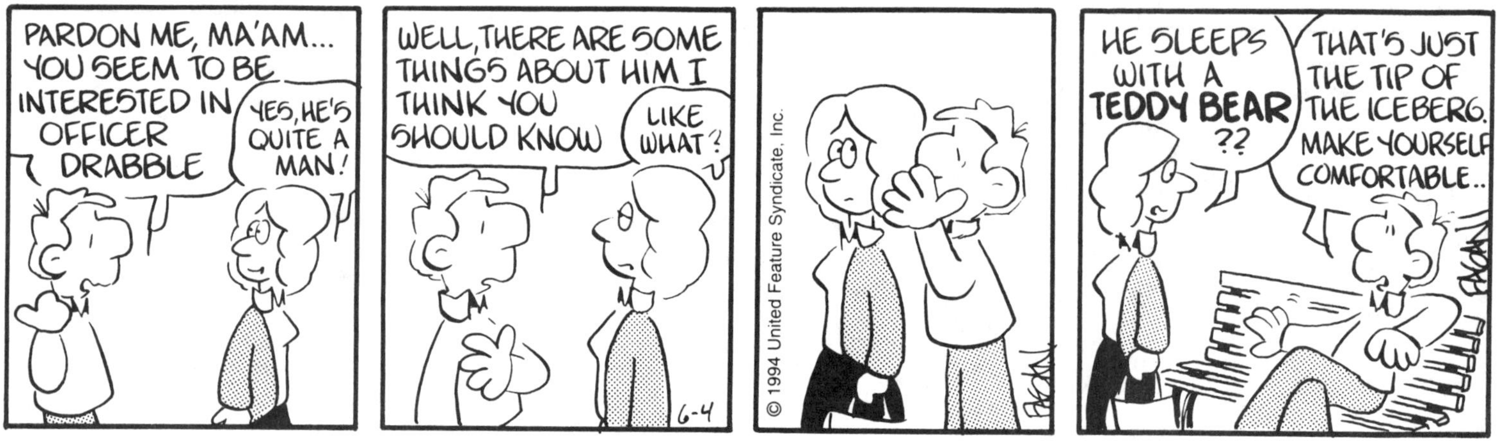
PARDON ME, MA'AM... YOU SEEM TO BE INTERESTED IN OFFICER DRABBLE
YES, HE'S QUITE A MAN!
WELL, THERE ARE SOME THINGS ABOUT HIM I THINK YOU SHOULD KNOW
LIKE WHAT?
6-4
© 1994 United Feature Syndicate, Inc.
HE SLEEPS WITH A TEDDY BEAR??
THAT'S JUST THE TIP OF THE ICEBERG. MAKE YOURSELF COMFORTABLE...

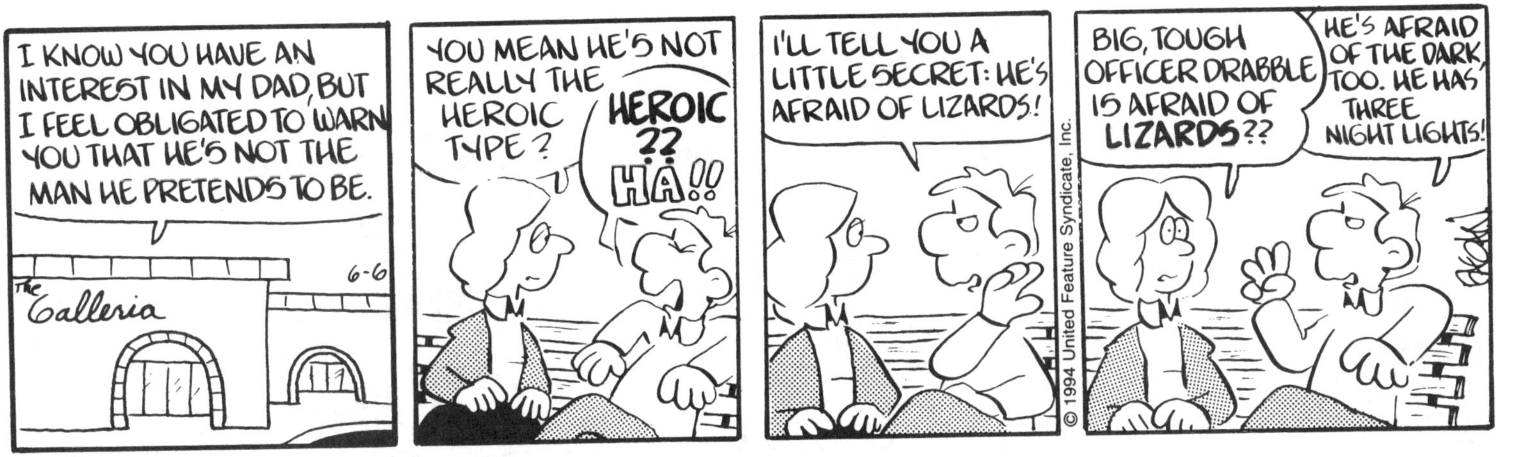
I KNOW YOU HAVE AN INTEREST IN MY DAD, BUT I FEEL OBLIGATED TO WARN YOU THAT HE'S NOT THE MAN HE PRETENDS TO BE.
The Galleria
6-6
YOU MEAN HE'S NOT REALLY THE HEROIC TYPE ?
HEROIC ?? HA!!
I'LL TELL YOU A LITTLE SECRET: HE'S AFRAID OF LIZARDS!
© 1994 United Feature Syndicate, Inc.
BIG, TOUGH OFFICER DRABBLE IS AFRAID OF LIZARDS??
HE'S AFRAID OF THE DARK, TOO. HE HAS THREE NIGHT LIGHTS!

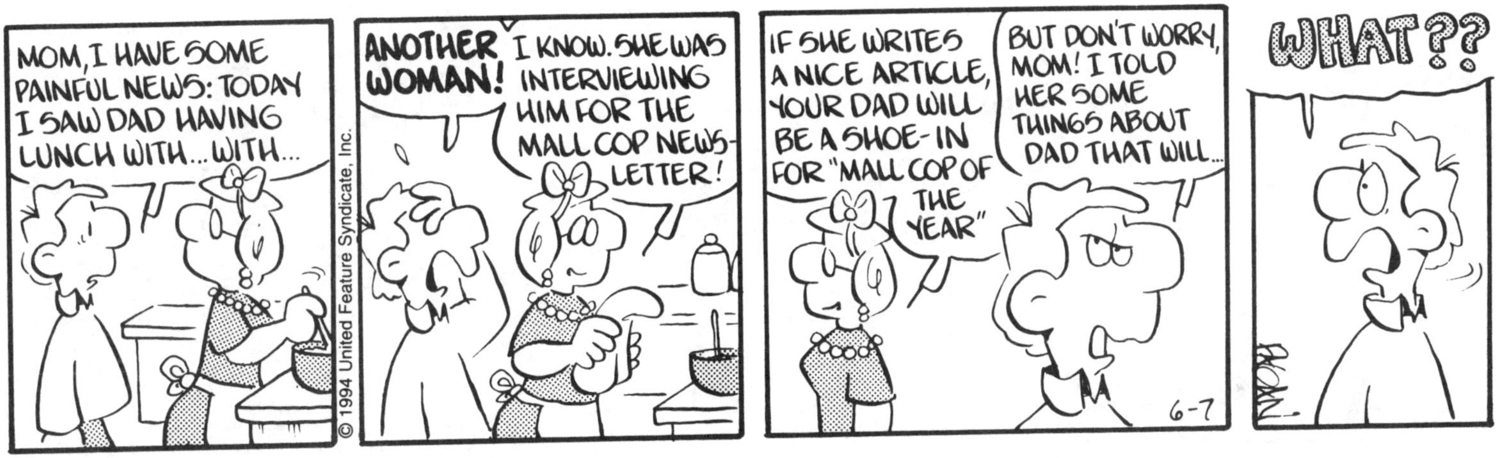
MOM, I HAVE SOME PAINFUL NEWS: TODAY I SAW DAD HAVING LUNCH WITH... WITH...
© 1994 United Feature Syndicate, Inc.
ANOTHER WOMAN!
I KNOW. SHE WAS INTERVIEWING HIM FOR THE MALL COP NEWS-LETTER!
IF SHE WRITES A NICE ARTICLE, YOUR DAD WILL BE A SHOE-IN FOR "MALL COP OF THE YEAR"
BUT DON'T WORRY, MOM! I TOLD HER SOME THINGS ABOUT DAD THAT WILL...
6-7
WHAT??

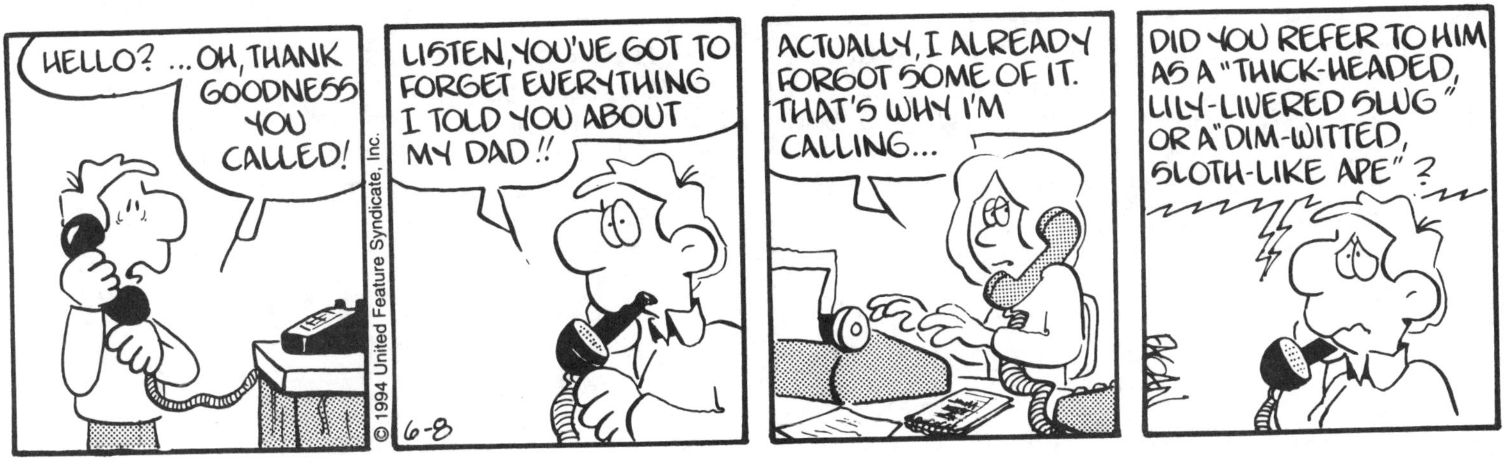
HELLO? ...OH, THANK GOODNESS YOU CALLED!
© 1994 United Feature Syndicate, Inc.
LISTEN, YOU'VE GOT TO FORGET EVERYTHING I TOLD YOU ABOUT MY DAD!!
6-8
ACTUALLY, I ALREADY FORGOT SOME OF IT. THAT'S WHY I'M CALLING...
DID YOU REFER TO HIM AS A "THICK-HEADED, LILY-LIVERED SLUG" OR A "DIM-WITTED, SLOTH-LIKE APE"?

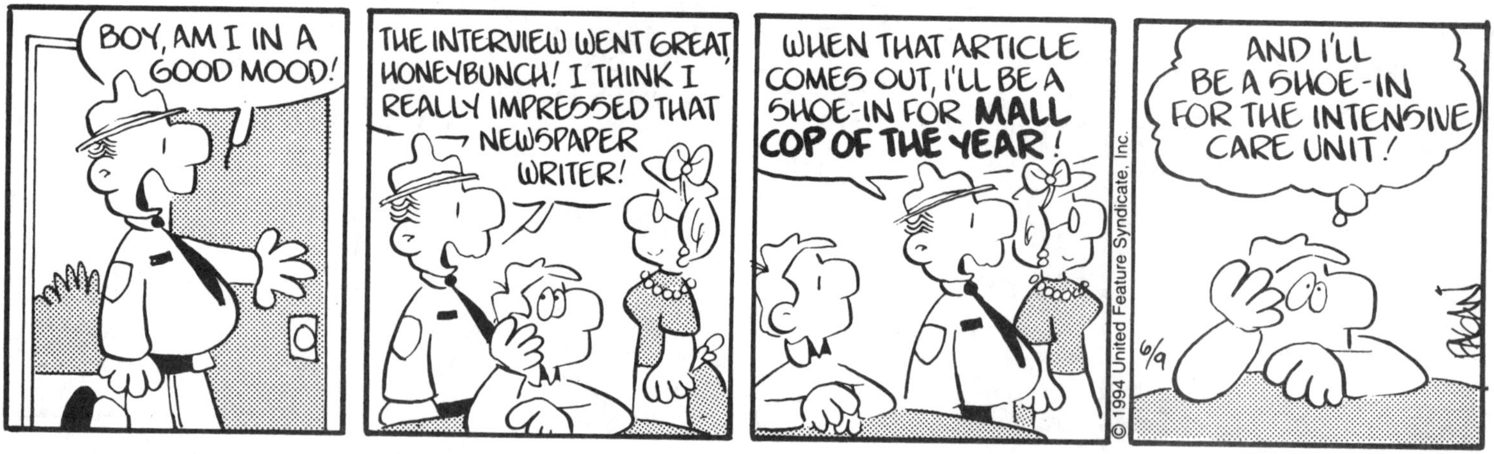

BOY, AM I IN A GOOD MOOD!
THE INTERVIEW WENT GREAT, HONEYBUNCH! I THINK I REALLY IMPRESSED THAT NEWSPAPER WRITER!
WHEN THAT ARTICLE COMES OUT, I'LL BE A SHOE-IN FOR **MALL COP OF THE YEAR**!
AND I'LL BE A SHOE-IN FOR THE INTENSIVE CARE UNIT!
© 1994 United Feature Syndicate, Inc.
6/9

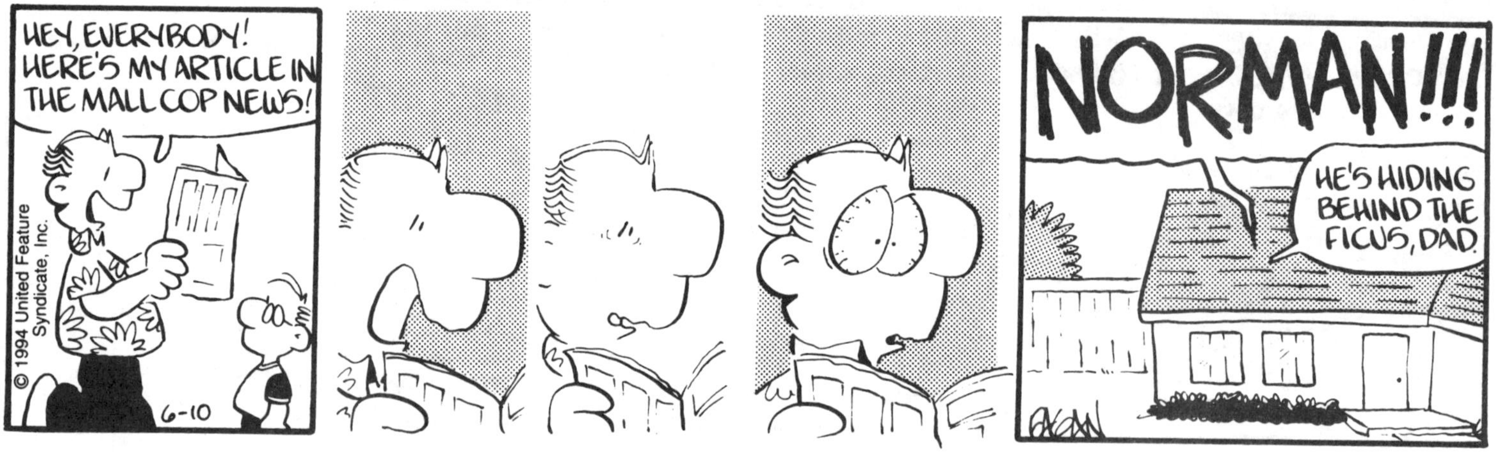

HEY, EVERYBODY! HERE'S MY ARTICLE IN THE MALL COP NEWS!
© 1994 United Feature Syndicate, Inc.
6-10
NORMAN!!!
HE'S HIDING BEHIND THE FICUS, DAD.

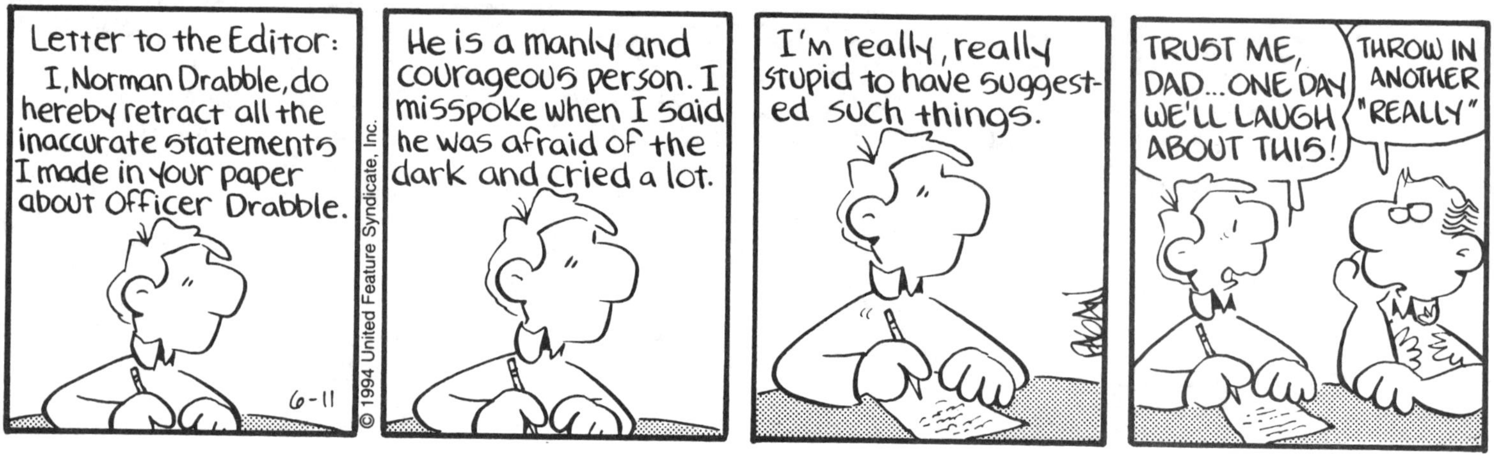

Letter to the Editor: I, Norman Drabble, do hereby retract all the inaccurate statements I made in your paper about Officer Drabble.
6-11
© 1994 United Feature Syndicate, Inc.
He is a manly and courageous person. I misspoke when I said he was afraid of the dark and cried a lot.
I'm really, really stupid to have suggested such things.
TRUST ME, DAD... ONE DAY WE'LL LAUGH ABOUT THIS!
THROW IN ANOTHER "REALLY"

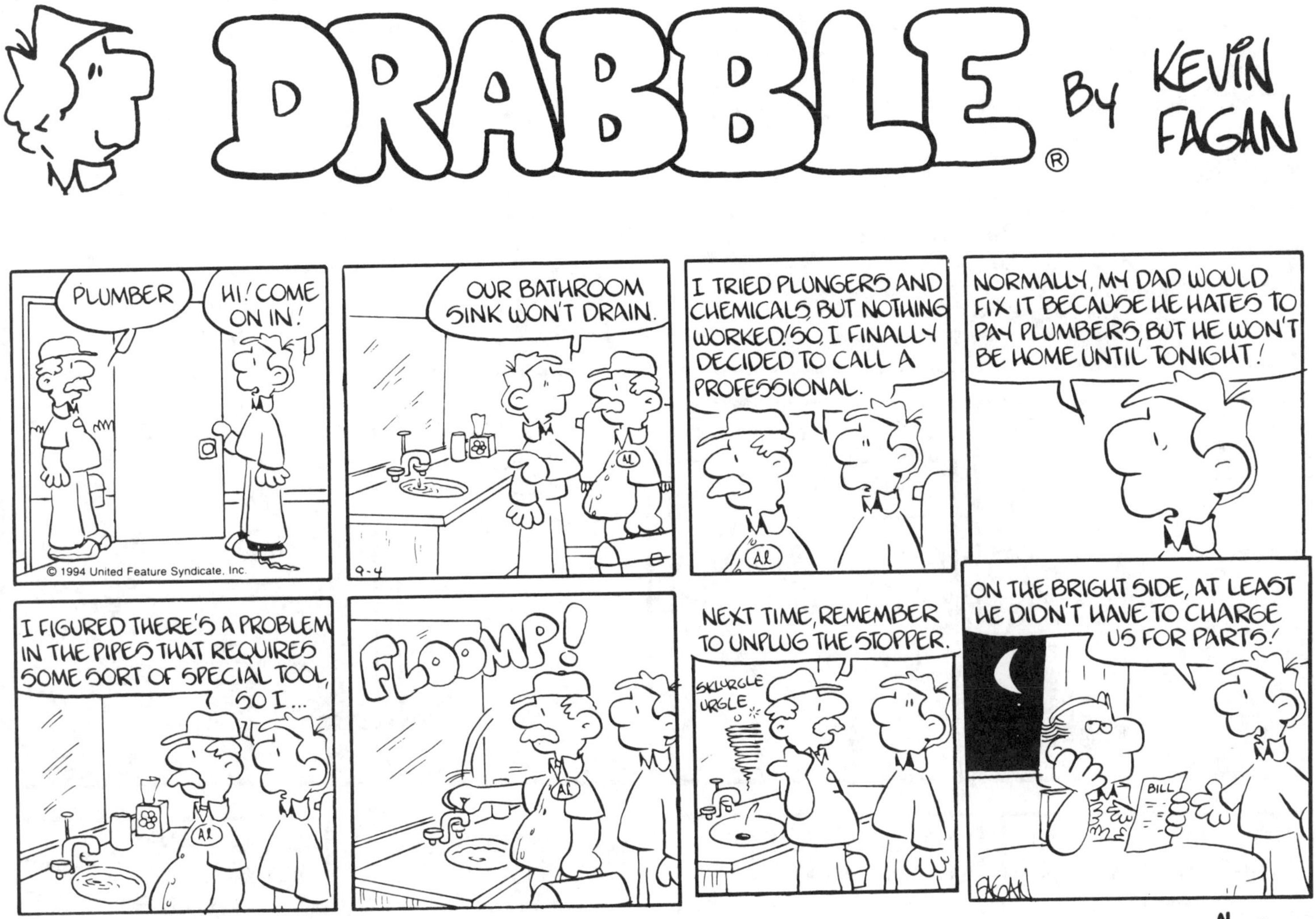
DRABBLE
By KEVIN FAGAN
PLUMBER
HI! COME ON IN!
© 1994 United Feature Syndicate, Inc.
OUR BATHROOM SINK WON'T DRAIN.
9-4
I TRIED PLUNGERS AND CHEMICALS, BUT NOTHING WORKED! SO I FINALLY DECIDED TO CALL A PROFESSIONAL.
NORMALLY, MY DAD WOULD FIX IT BECAUSE HE HATES TO PAY PLUMBERS, BUT HE WON'T BE HOME UNTIL TONIGHT!
AL
I FIGURED THERE'S A PROBLEM IN THE PIPES THAT REQUIRES SOME SORT OF SPECIAL TOOL, SO I...
FLOOMP!
NEXT TIME, REMEMBER TO UNPLUG THE STOPPER.
SKLURGLE URGLE
ON THE BRIGHT SIDE, AT LEAST HE DIDN'T HAVE TO CHARGE US FOR PARTS!
BILL
FAGAN

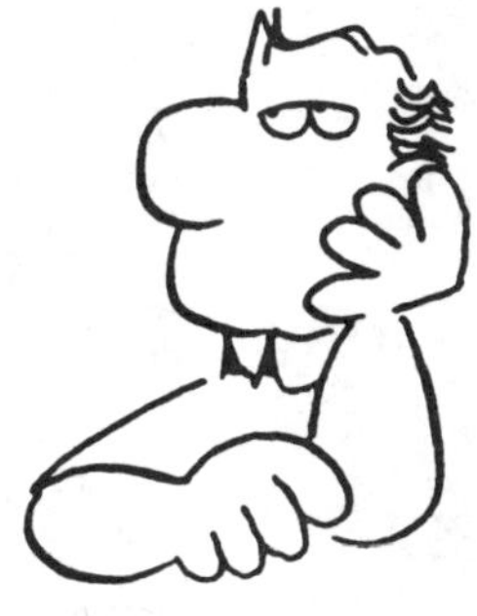

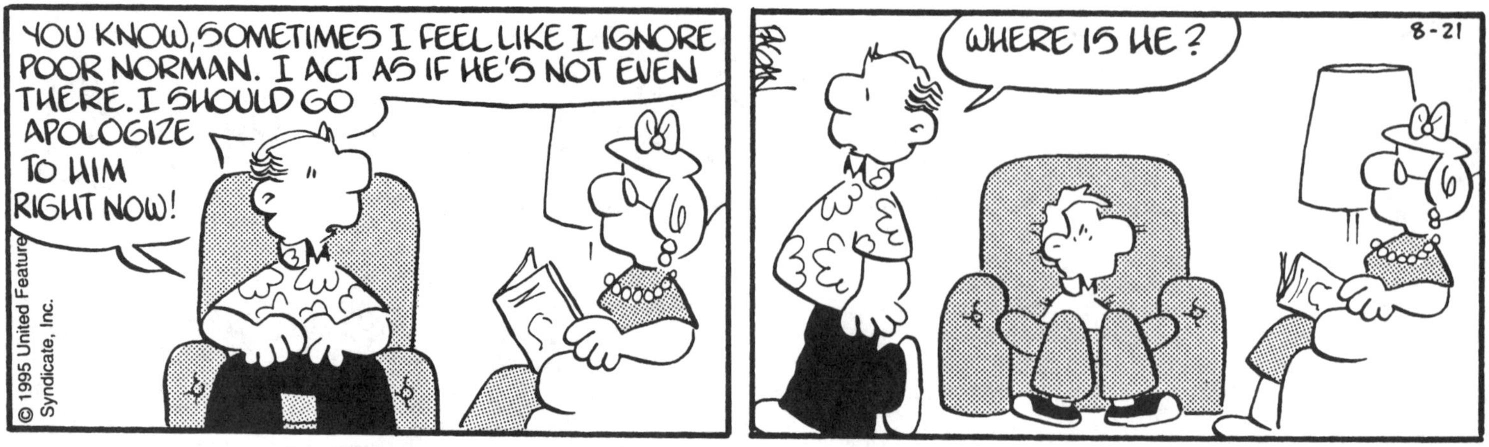
YOU KNOW, SOMETIMES I FEEL LIKE I IGNORE POOR NORMAN. I ACT AS IF HE'S NOT EVEN THERE. I SHOULD GO APOLOGIZE TO HIM RIGHT NOW!
© 1995 United Feature Syndicate, Inc.
8-21
WHERE IS HE?

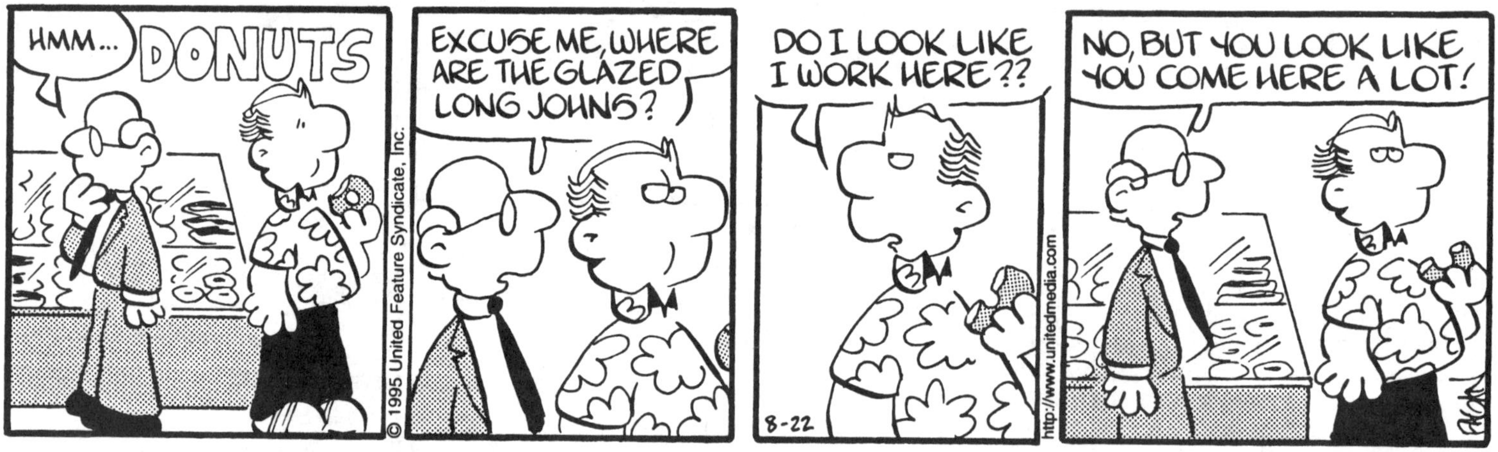
HMM...
DONUTS
EXCUSE ME, WHERE ARE THE GLAZED LONG JOHNS?
© 1995 United Feature Syndicate, Inc.
DO I LOOK LIKE I WORK HERE??
8-22
http://www.unitedmedia.com
NO, BUT YOU LOOK LIKE YOU COME HERE A LOT!

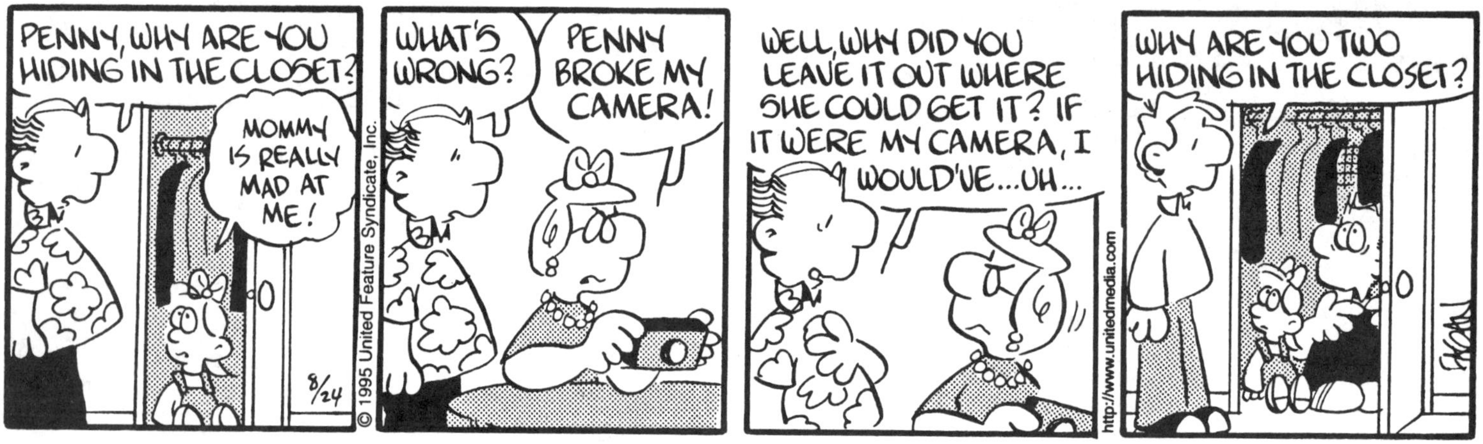
PENNY, WHY ARE YOU HIDING IN THE CLOSET?
MOMMY IS REALLY MAD AT ME!
8/24
© 1995 United Feature Syndicate, Inc.
WHAT'S WRONG?
PENNY BROKE MY CAMERA!
WELL, WHY DID YOU LEAVE IT OUT WHERE SHE COULD GET IT? IF IT WERE MY CAMERA, I WOULD'VE...UH...
http://www.unitedmedia.com
WHY ARE YOU TWO HIDING IN THE CLOSET?

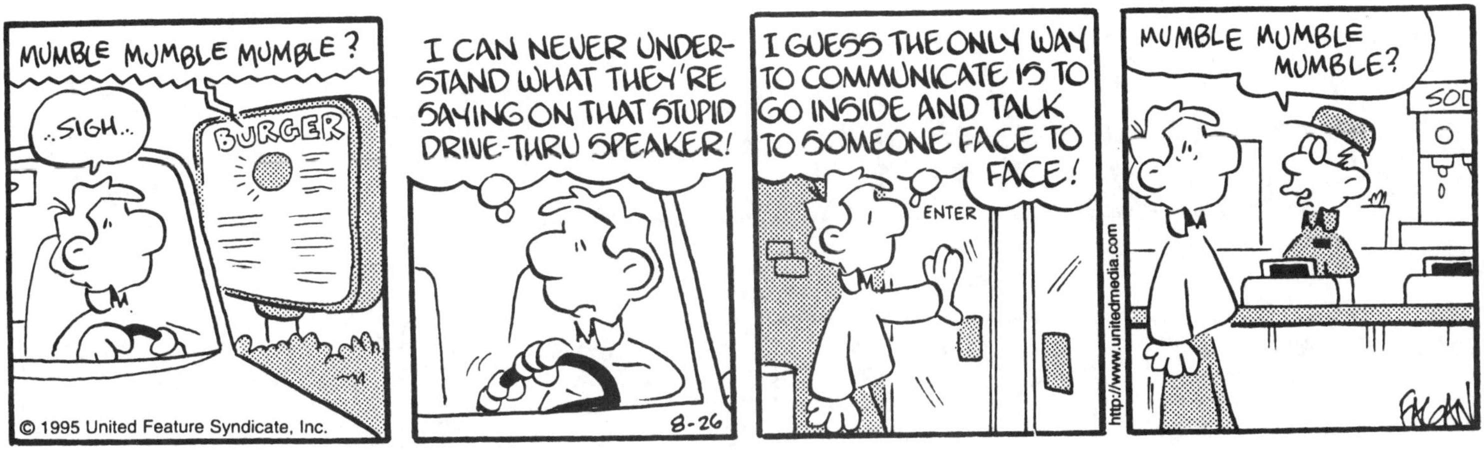
MUMBLE MUMBLE MUMBLE ?
..SIGH..
BURGER
© 1995 United Feature Syndicate, Inc.
I CAN NEVER UNDERSTAND WHAT THEY'RE SAYING ON THAT STUPID DRIVE-THRU SPEAKER!
8-26
I GUESS THE ONLY WAY TO COMMUNICATE IS TO GO INSIDE AND TALK TO SOMEONE FACE TO FACE!
ENTER
http://www.unitedmedia.com
MUMBLE MUMBLE MUMBLE?

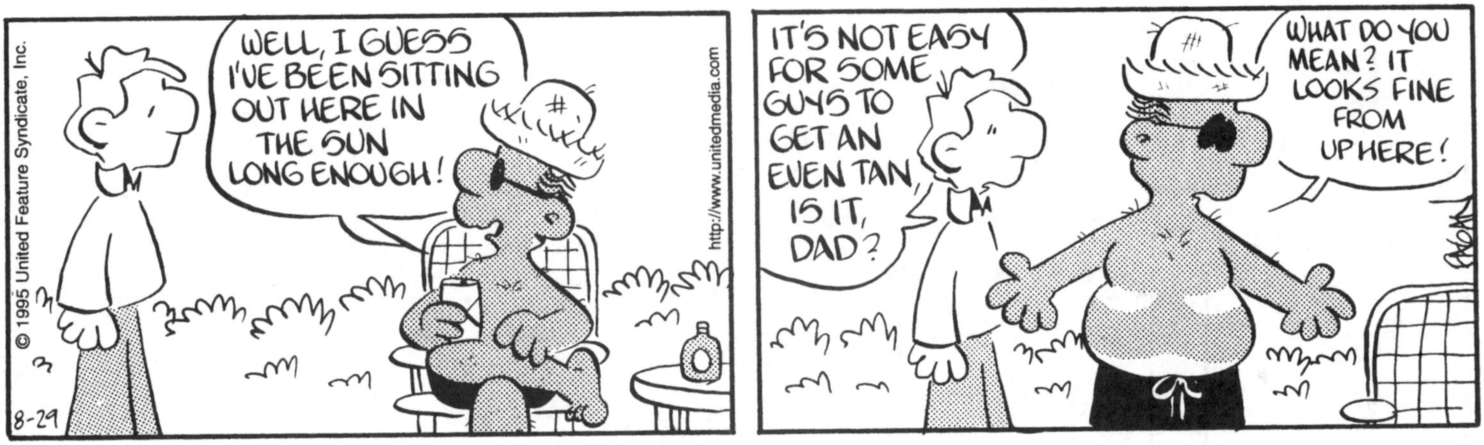
© 1995 United Feature Syndicate, Inc.
8-29
WELL, I GUESS I'VE BEEN SITTING OUT HERE IN THE SUN LONG ENOUGH!
http://www.unitedmedia.com
IT'S NOT EASY FOR SOME GUYS TO GET AN EVEN TAN, IS IT, DAD?
WHAT DO YOU MEAN? IT LOOKS FINE FROM UP HERE!

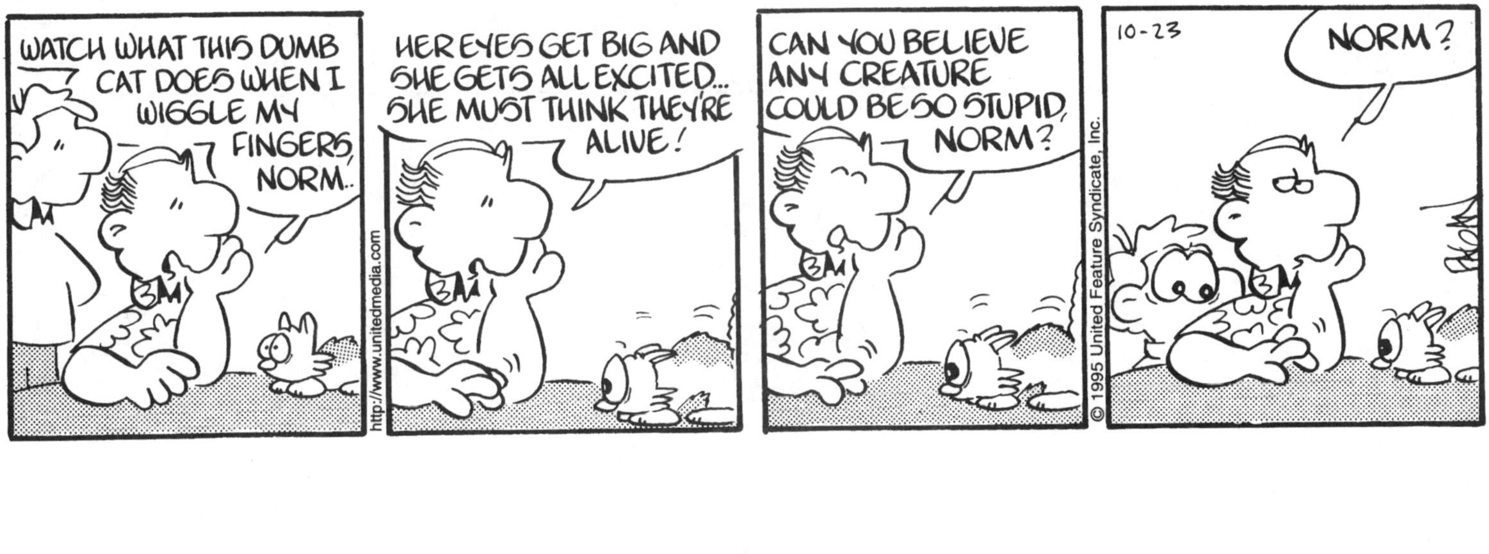
WATCH WHAT THIS DUMB CAT DOES WHEN I WIGGLE MY FINGERS, NORM..
http://www.unitedmedia.com
HER EYES GET BIG AND SHE GETS ALL EXCITED... SHE MUST THINK THEY'RE ALIVE!
CAN YOU BELIEVE ANY CREATURE COULD BE SO STUPID, NORM?
© 1995 United Feature Syndicate, Inc.
10-23
NORM?

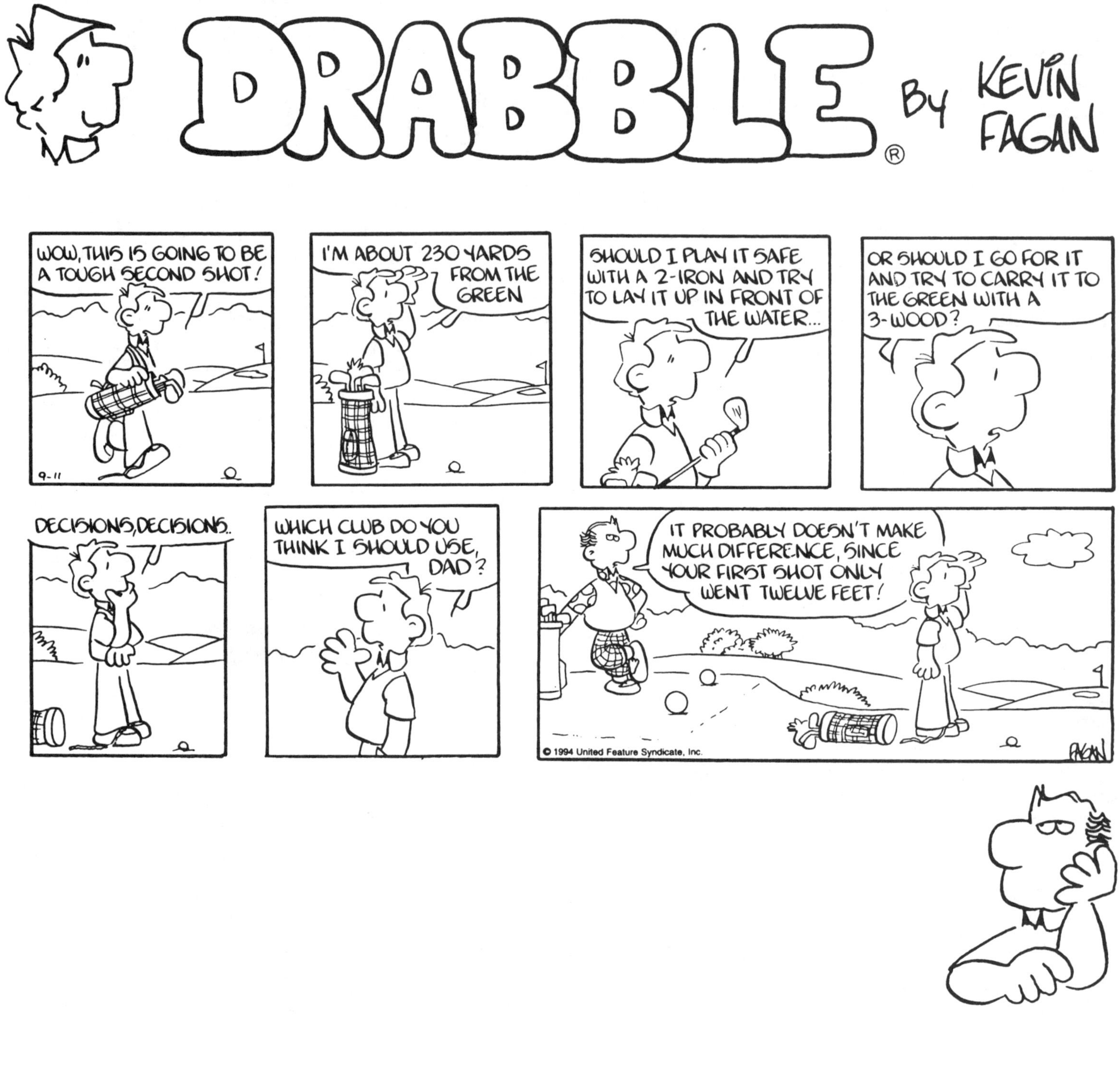
DRABBLE® By KEVIN FAGAN
WOW, THIS IS GOING TO BE A TOUGH SECOND SHOT!
9-11
I'M ABOUT 230 YARDS FROM THE GREEN
SHOULD I PLAY IT SAFE WITH A 2-IRON AND TRY TO LAY IT UP IN FRONT OF THE WATER...
OR SHOULD I GO FOR IT AND TRY TO CARRY IT TO THE GREEN WITH A 3-WOOD?
DECISIONS, DECISIONS..
WHICH CLUB DO YOU THINK I SHOULD USE, DAD?
IT PROBABLY DOESN'T MAKE MUCH DIFFERENCE, SINCE YOUR FIRST SHOT ONLY WENT TWELVE FEET!
© 1994 United Feature Syndicate, Inc.
FAGAN

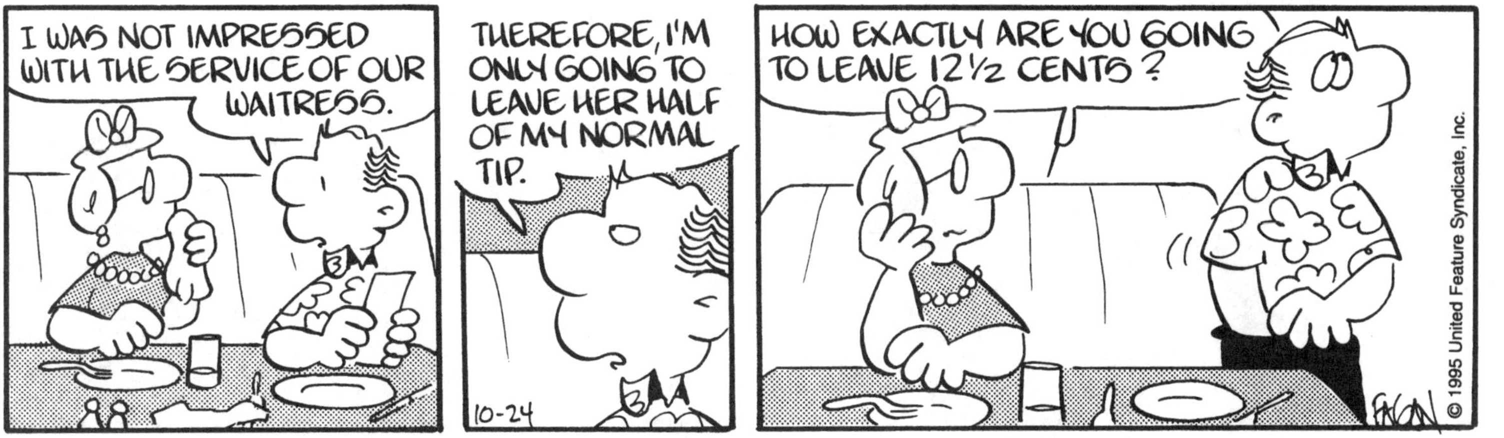
I WAS NOT IMPRESSED WITH THE SERVICE OF OUR WAITRESS.
THEREFORE, I'M ONLY GOING TO LEAVE HER HALF OF MY NORMAL TIP.
10-24
HOW EXACTLY ARE YOU GOING TO LEAVE 12½ CENTS?
FAGAN
© 1995 United Feature Syndicate, Inc.

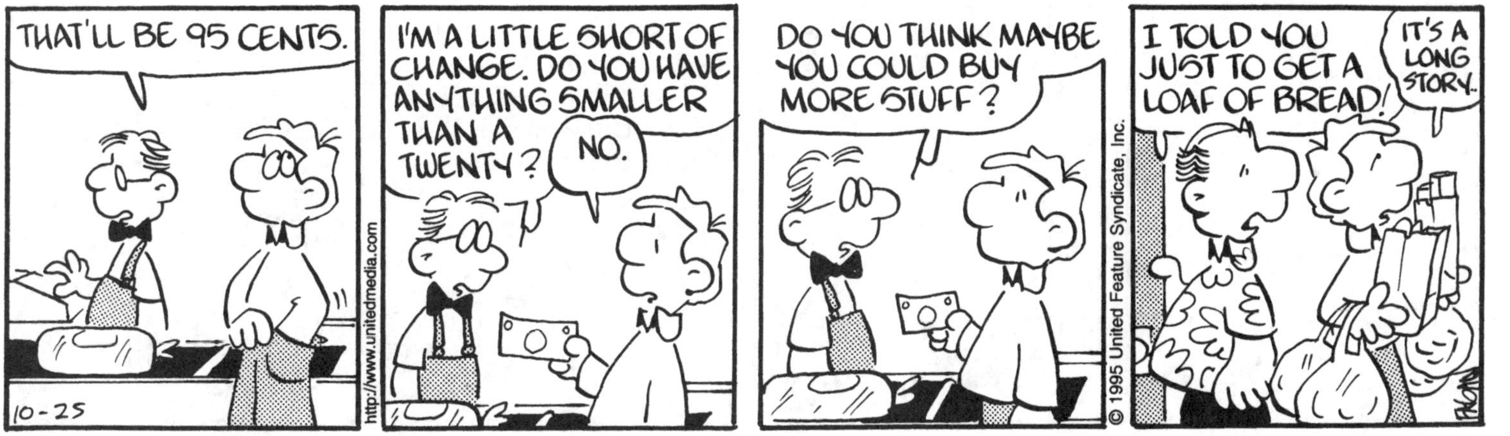
THAT'LL BE 95 CENTS.
10-25
http://www.unitedmedia.com
I'M A LITTLE SHORT OF CHANGE. DO YOU HAVE ANYTHING SMALLER THAN A TWENTY?
NO.
DO YOU THINK MAYBE YOU COULD BUY MORE STUFF?
© 1995 United Feature Syndicate, Inc.
I TOLD YOU JUST TO GET A LOAF OF BREAD!
IT'S A LONG STORY..
FAGAN

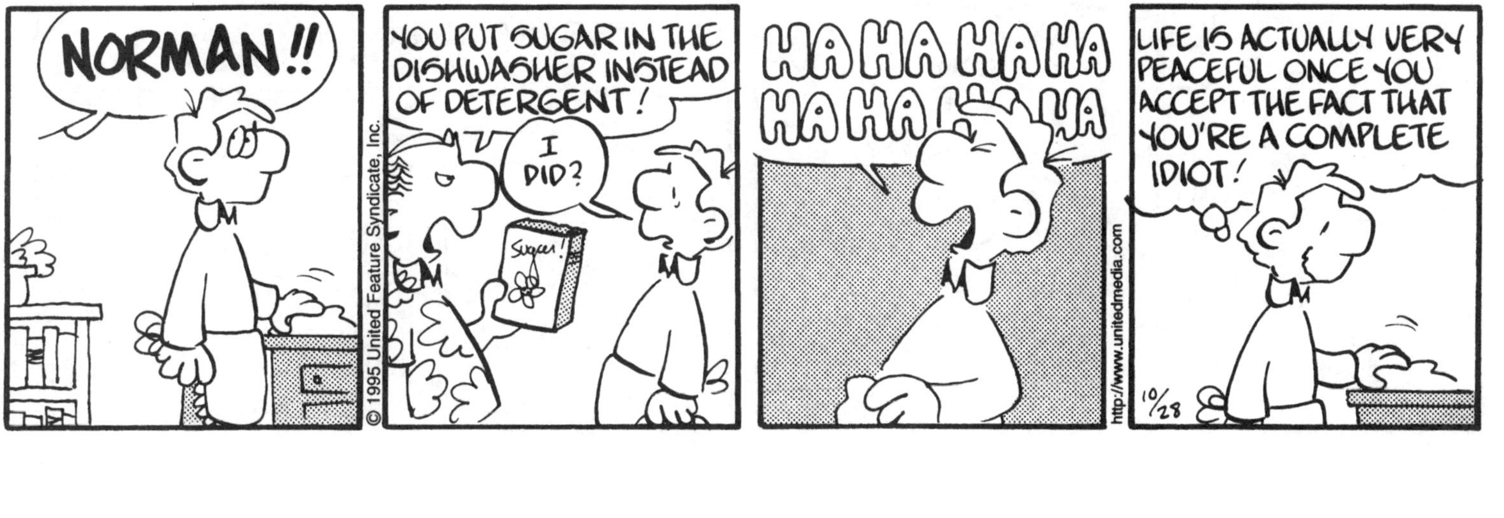
NORMAN!!
© 1995 United Feature Syndicate, Inc.
YOU PUT SUGAR IN THE DISHWASHER INSTEAD OF DETERGENT!
I DID?
Sugar!
HA HA HA HA
HA HA HA
http://www.unitedmedia.com
LIFE IS ACTUALLY VERY PEACEFUL ONCE YOU ACCEPT THE FACT THAT YOU'RE A COMPLETE IDIOT!
10/28

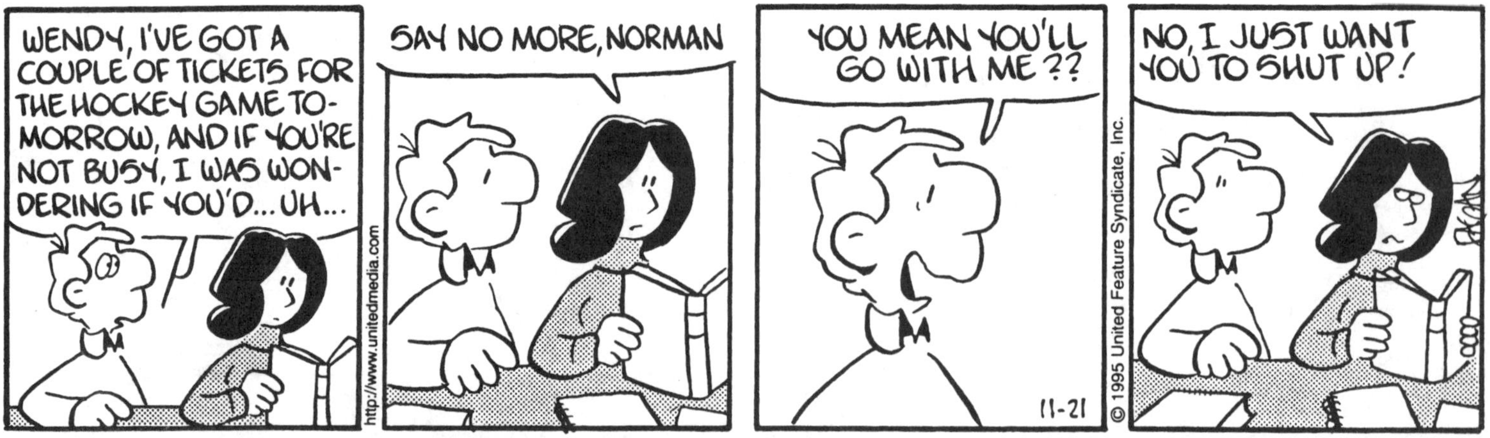
WENDY, I'VE GOT A COUPLE OF TICKETS FOR THE HOCKEY GAME TOMORROW, AND IF YOU'RE NOT BUSY, I WAS WONDERING IF YOU'D... UH...
http://www.unitedmedia.com
SAY NO MORE, NORMAN
YOU MEAN YOU'LL GO WITH ME??
11-21
© 1995 United Feature Syndicate, Inc.
NO, I JUST WANT YOU TO SHUT UP!

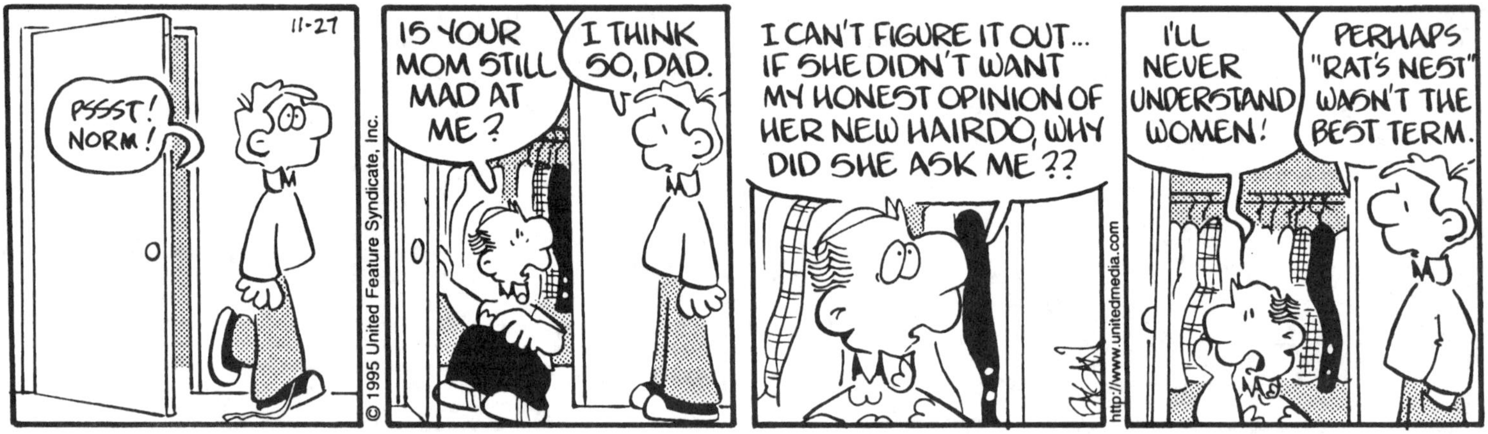
11-27
PSSST! NORM!
© 1995 United Feature Syndicate, Inc.
IS YOUR MOM STILL MAD AT ME?
I THINK SO, DAD.
I CAN'T FIGURE IT OUT... IF SHE DIDN'T WANT MY HONEST OPINION OF HER NEW HAIRDO, WHY DID SHE ASK ME??
http://www.unitedmedia.com
I'LL NEVER UNDERSTAND WOMEN!
PERHAPS "RAT'S NEST" WASN'T THE BEST TERM.

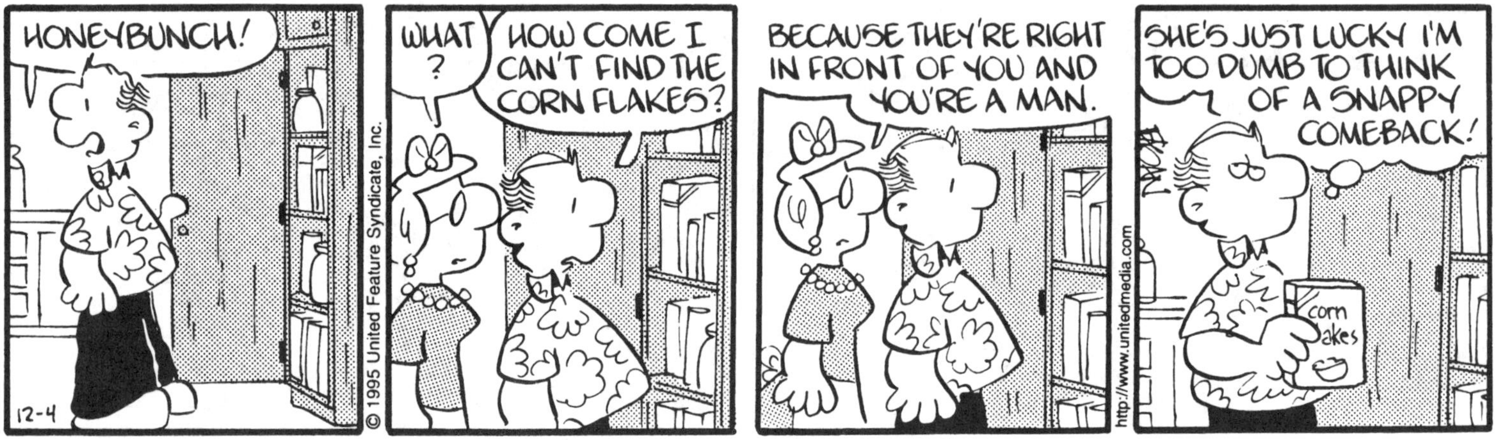
HONEYBUNCH!
12-4
© 1995 United Feature Syndicate, Inc.
WHAT?
HOW COME I CAN'T FIND THE CORN FLAKES?
BECAUSE THEY'RE RIGHT IN FRONT OF YOU AND YOU'RE A MAN.
http://www.unitedmedia.com
SHE'S JUST LUCKY I'M TOO DUMB TO THINK OF A SNAPPY COMEBACK!
corn flakes

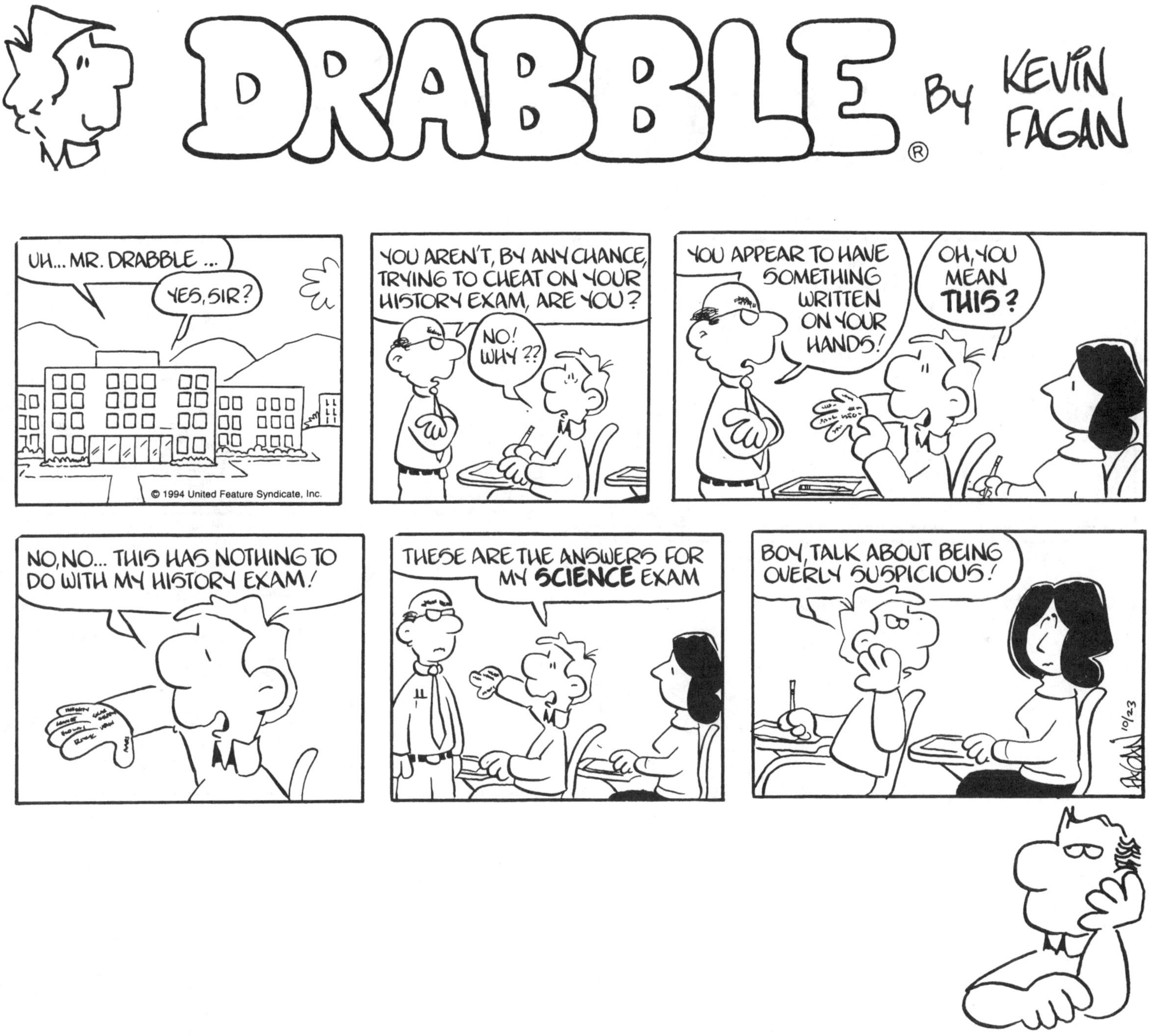
DRABBLE®
By KEVIN FAGAN
UH... MR. DRABBLE ...
YES, SIR?
© 1994 United Feature Syndicate, Inc.
YOU AREN'T, BY ANY CHANCE, TRYING TO CHEAT ON YOUR HISTORY EXAM, ARE YOU?
NO! WHY??
YOU APPEAR TO HAVE SOMETHING WRITTEN ON YOUR HANDS!
OH, YOU MEAN **THIS**?
NO, NO... THIS HAS NOTHING TO DO WITH MY HISTORY EXAM!
THESE ARE THE ANSWERS FOR MY **SCIENCE** EXAM
BOY, TALK ABOUT BEING OVERLY SUSPICIOUS!
10/23
FAGAN

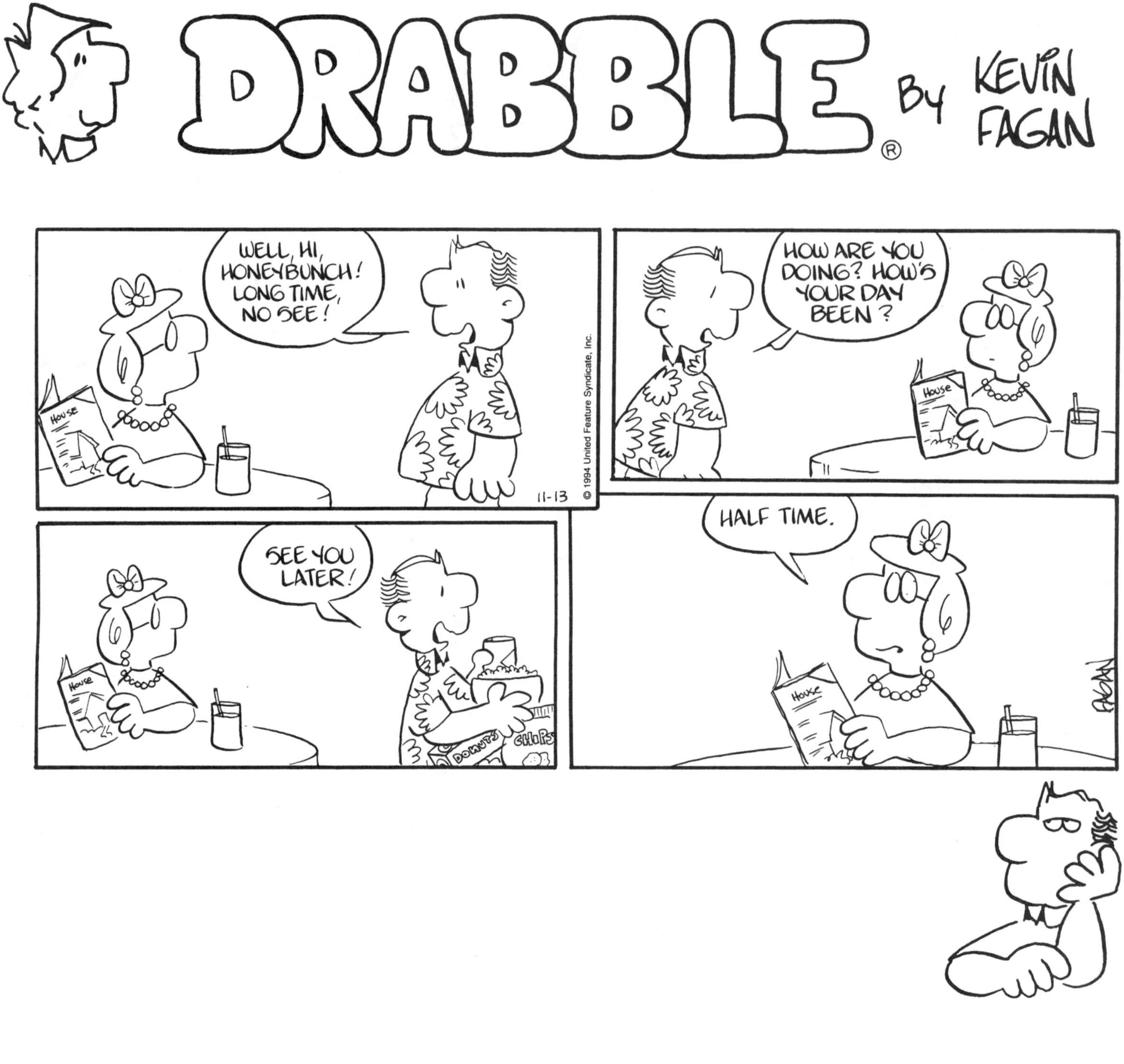
DRABBLE
By KEVIN FAGAN
WELL, HI, HONEYBUNCH! LONG TIME, NO SEE!
© 1994 United Feature Syndicate, Inc.
11-13
HOW ARE YOU DOING? HOW'S YOUR DAY BEEN?
SEE YOU LATER!
DONUTS
CHIPS
HALF TIME.
FAGAN

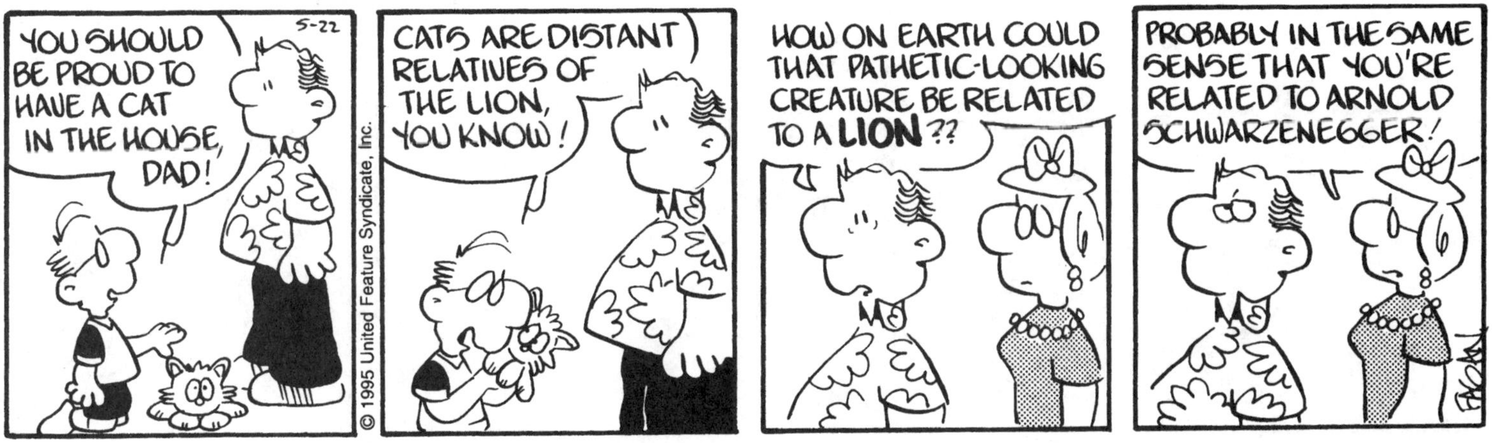
5-22
YOU SHOULD BE PROUD TO HAVE A CAT IN THE HOUSE, DAD!
CATS ARE DISTANT RELATIVES OF THE LION, YOU KNOW!
HOW ON EARTH COULD THAT PATHETIC-LOOKING CREATURE BE RELATED TO A **LION**??
PROBABLY IN THE SAME SENSE THAT YOU'RE RELATED TO ARNOLD SCHWARZENEGGER!
© 1995 United Feature Syndicate, Inc.

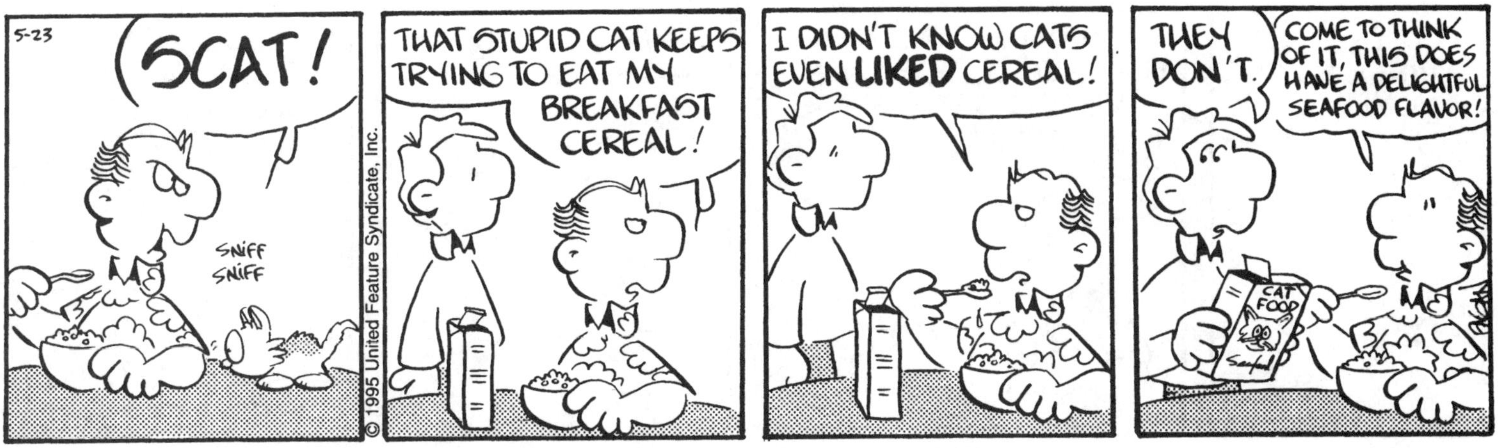
5-23
SCAT!
SNIFF SNIFF
THAT STUPID CAT KEEPS TRYING TO EAT MY BREAKFAST CEREAL!
I DIDN'T KNOW CATS EVEN **LIKED** CEREAL!
THEY DON'T.
COME TO THINK OF IT, THIS DOES HAVE A DELIGHTFUL SEAFOOD FLAVOR!
CAT FOOD
© 1995 United Feature Syndicate, Inc.

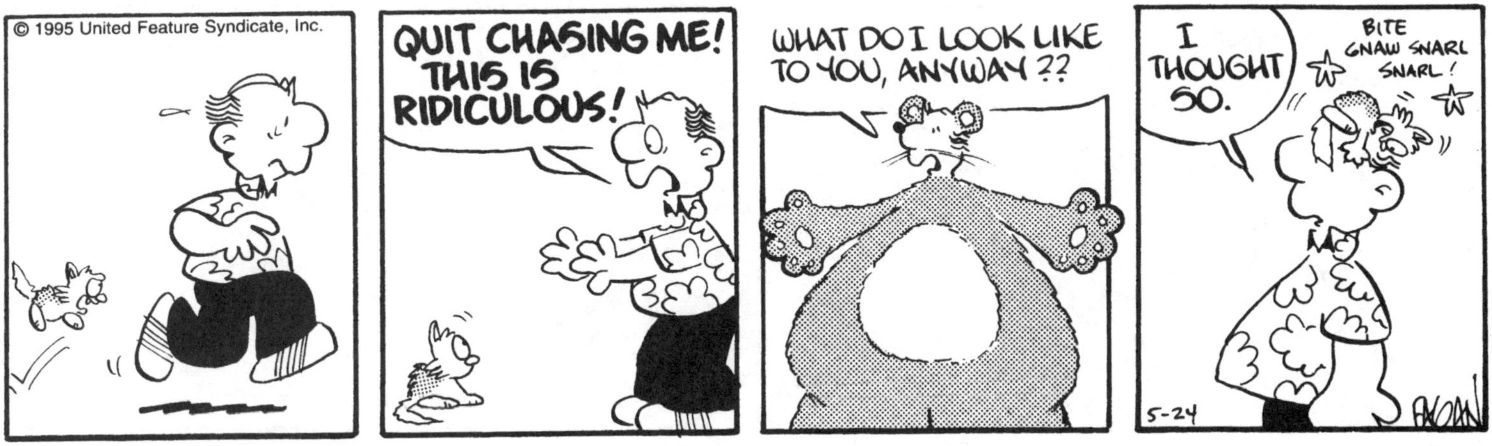
© 1995 United Feature Syndicate, Inc.
QUIT CHASING ME! THIS IS RIDICULOUS!
WHAT DO I LOOK LIKE TO YOU, ANYWAY??
I THOUGHT SO.
BITE GNAW SNARL SNARL!
5-24

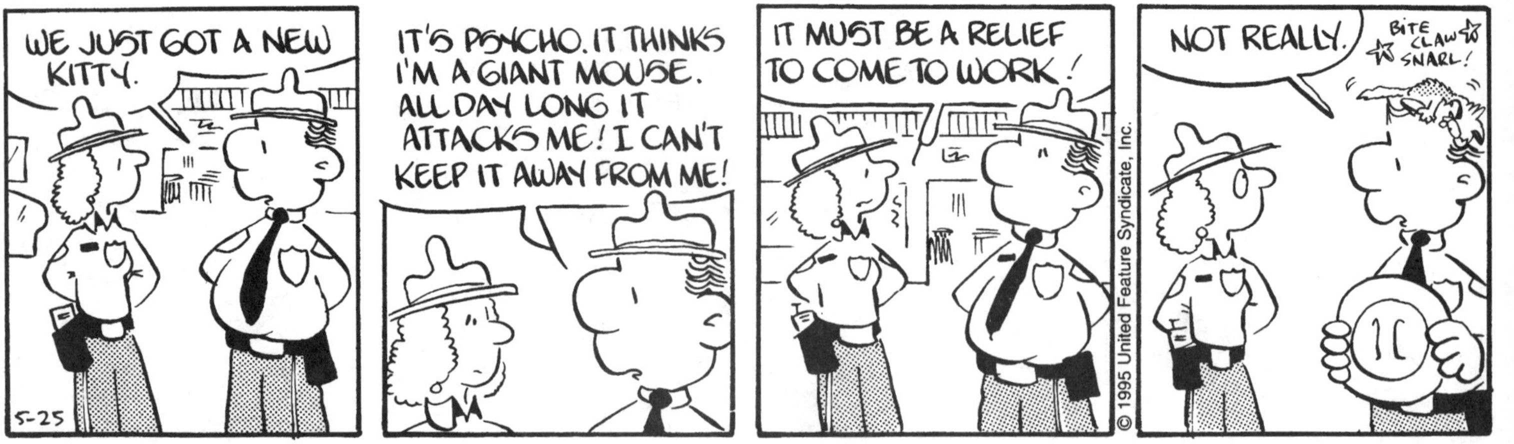
WE JUST GOT A NEW KITTY.
IT'S PSYCHO. IT THINKS I'M A GIANT MOUSE. ALL DAY LONG IT ATTACKS ME! I CAN'T KEEP IT AWAY FROM ME!
IT MUST BE A RELIEF TO COME TO WORK!
NOT REALLY.
BITE CLAW SNARL!
5-25
© 1995 United Feature Syndicate, Inc.

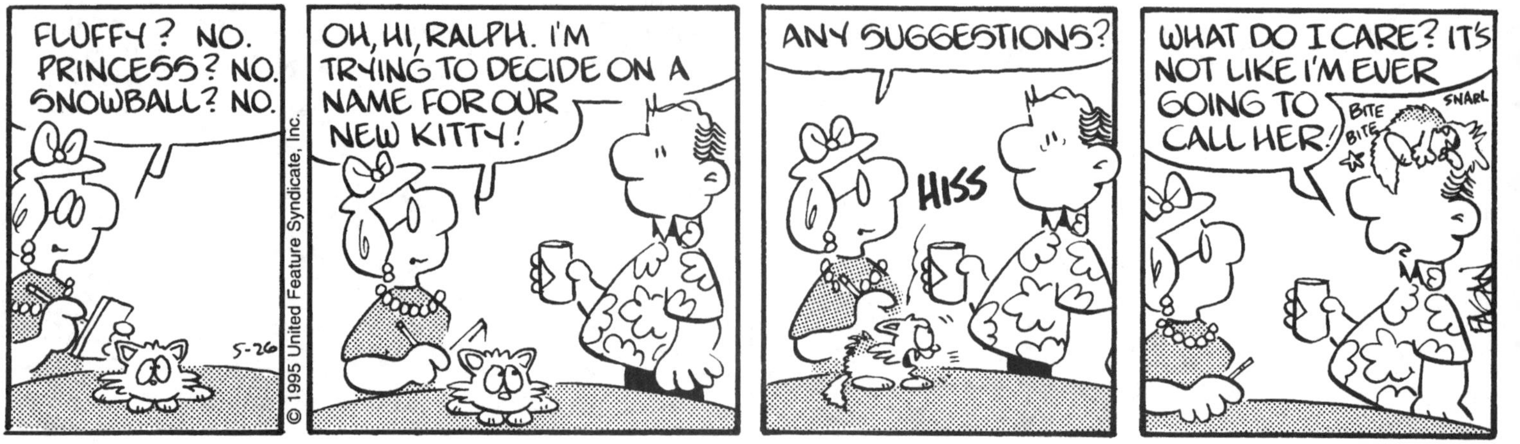
FLUFFY? NO. PRINCESS? NO. SNOWBALL? NO.
5-26
© 1995 United Feature Syndicate, Inc.
OH, HI, RALPH. I'M TRYING TO DECIDE ON A NAME FOR OUR NEW KITTY!
ANY SUGGESTIONS?
HISS
WHAT DO I CARE? IT'S NOT LIKE I'M EVER GOING TO CALL HER!
BITE BITE SNARL

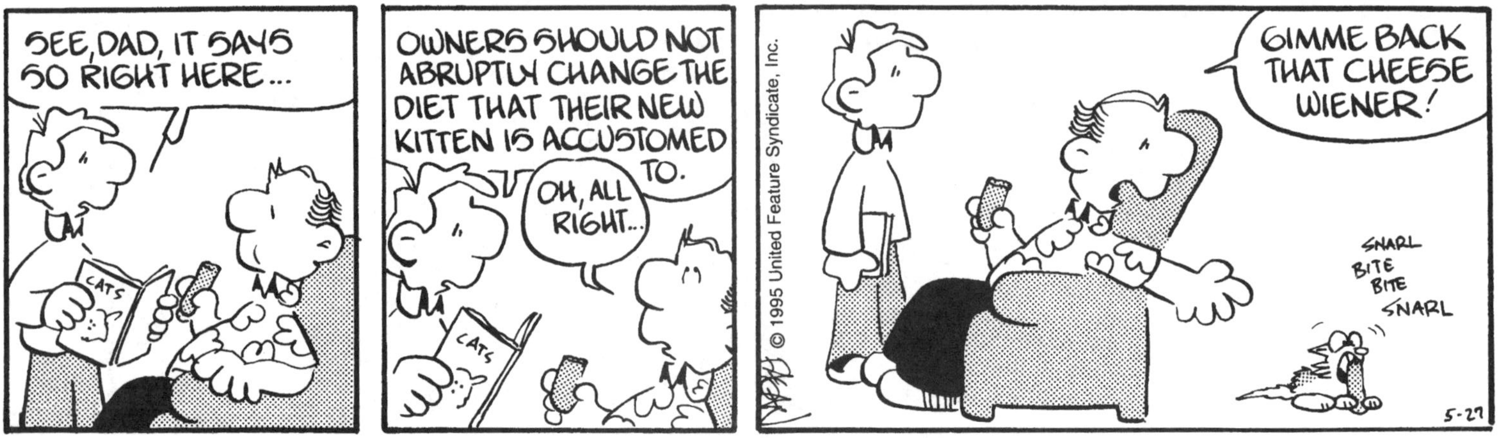
SEE, DAD, IT SAYS SO RIGHT HERE...
CATS
OWNERS SHOULD NOT ABRUPTLY CHANGE THE DIET THAT THEIR NEW KITTEN IS ACCUSTOMED TO.
OH, ALL RIGHT...
CATS
© 1995 United Feature Syndicate, Inc.
GIMME BACK THAT CHEESE WIENER!
SNARL BITE BITE SNARL
5-27

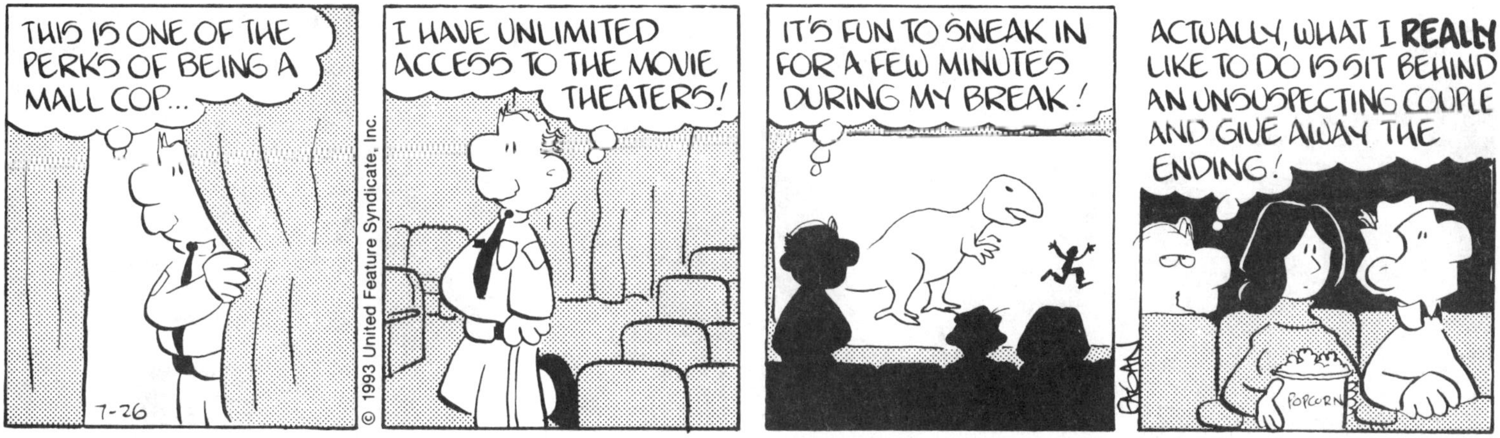
THIS IS ONE OF THE PERKS OF BEING A MALL COP...
7-26
I HAVE UNLIMITED ACCESS TO THE MOVIE THEATERS!
© 1993 United Feature Syndicate, Inc.
IT'S FUN TO SNEAK IN FOR A FEW MINUTES DURING MY BREAK!
ACTUALLY, WHAT I REALLY LIKE TO DO IS SIT BEHIND AN UNSUSPECTING COUPLE AND GIVE AWAY THE ENDING!
POPCORN

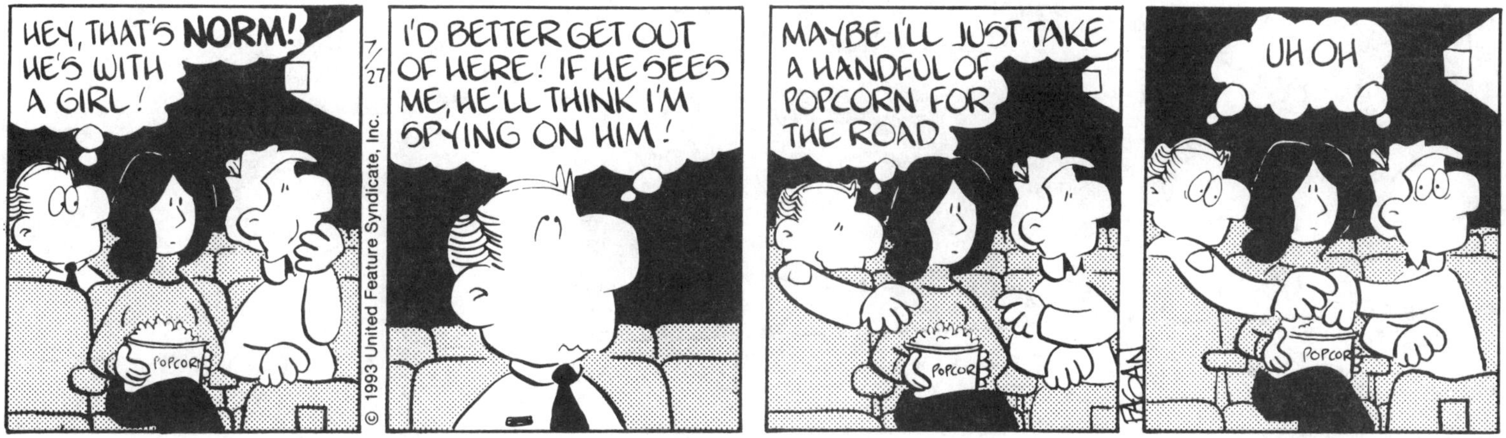
HEY, THAT'S NORM! HE'S WITH A GIRL!
POPCORN
7/27
© 1993 United Feature Syndicate, Inc.
I'D BETTER GET OUT OF HERE! IF HE SEES ME, HE'LL THINK I'M SPYING ON HIM!
MAYBE I'LL JUST TAKE A HANDFUL OF POPCORN FOR THE ROAD
POPCOR
UH OH
POPCOR

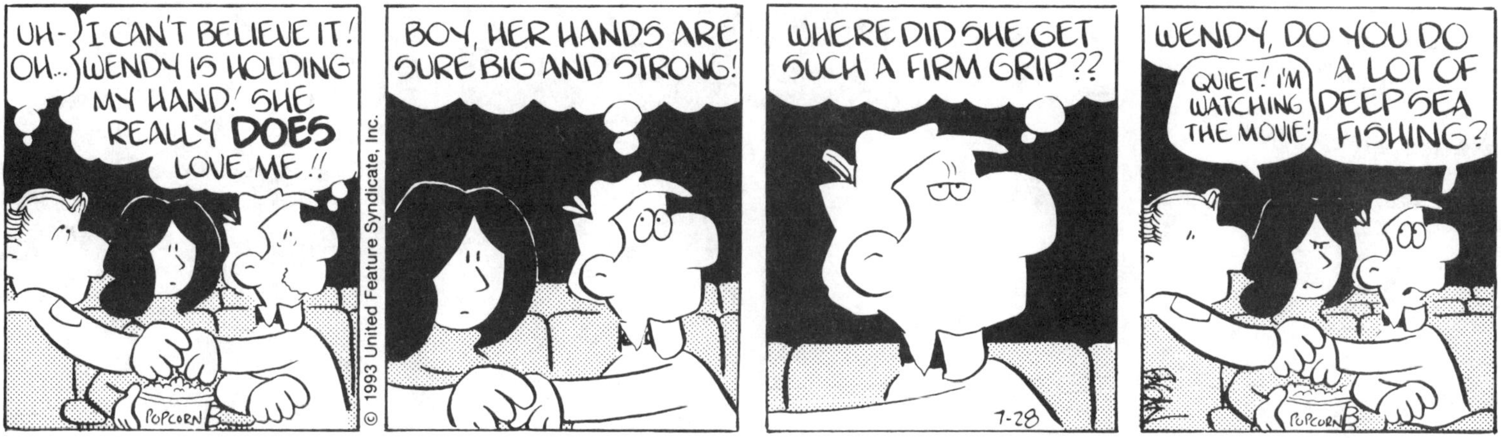
UH-OH...
I CAN'T BELIEVE IT! WENDY IS HOLDING MY HAND! SHE REALLY DOES LOVE ME!!
POPCORN
© 1993 United Feature Syndicate, Inc.
BOY, HER HANDS ARE SURE BIG AND STRONG!
WHERE DID SHE GET SUCH A FIRM GRIP??
7-28
WENDY, DO YOU DO A LOT OF DEEP SEA FISHING?
QUIET! I'M WATCHING THE MOVIE!
POPCORN

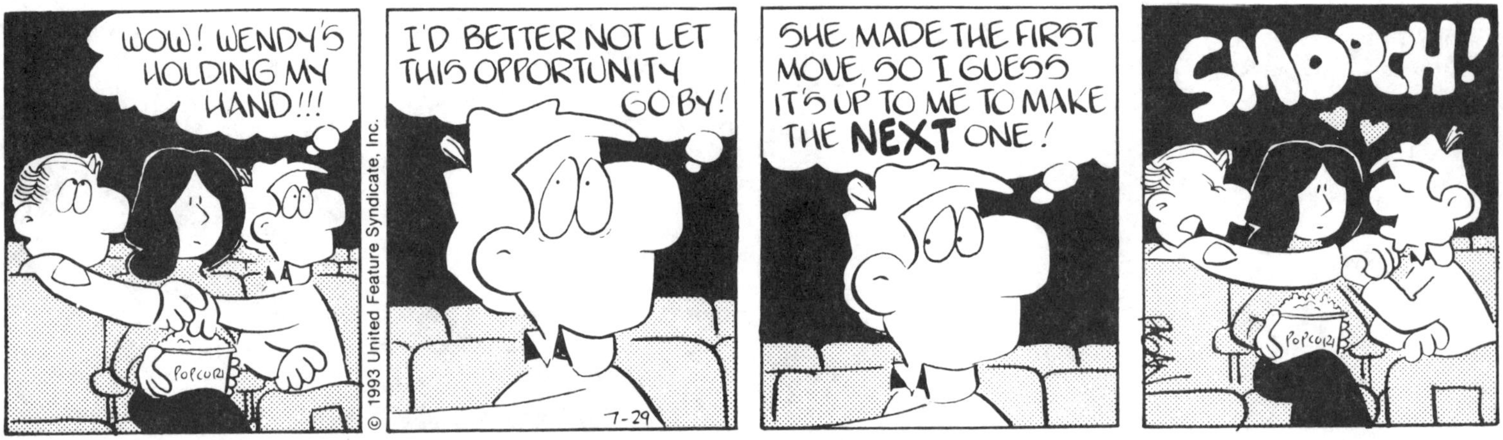
WOW! WENDY'S HOLDING MY HAND!!!
© 1993 United Feature Syndicate, Inc.
I'D BETTER NOT LET THIS OPPORTUNITY GO BY!
7-29
SHE MADE THE FIRST MOVE, SO I GUESS IT'S UP TO ME TO MAKE THE NEXT ONE!
SMOOCH!
POPCORN

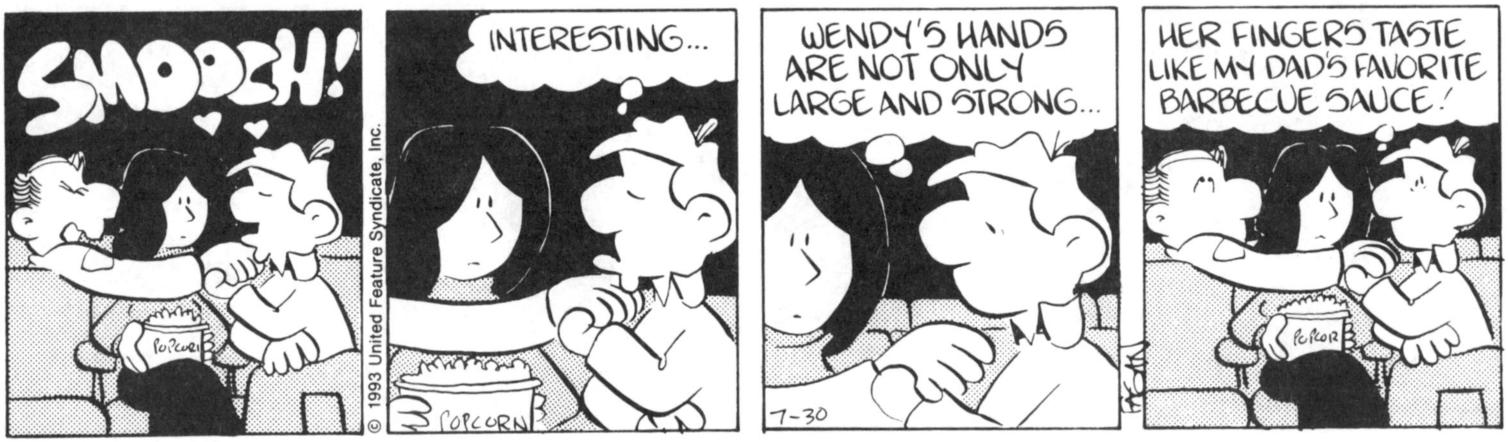
SMOOCH!
POPCORN
© 1993 United Feature Syndicate, Inc.
INTERESTING...
POPCORN
WENDY'S HANDS ARE NOT ONLY LARGE AND STRONG...
7-30
HER FINGERS TASTE LIKE MY DAD'S FAVORITE BARBECUE SAUCE!
POPCORN

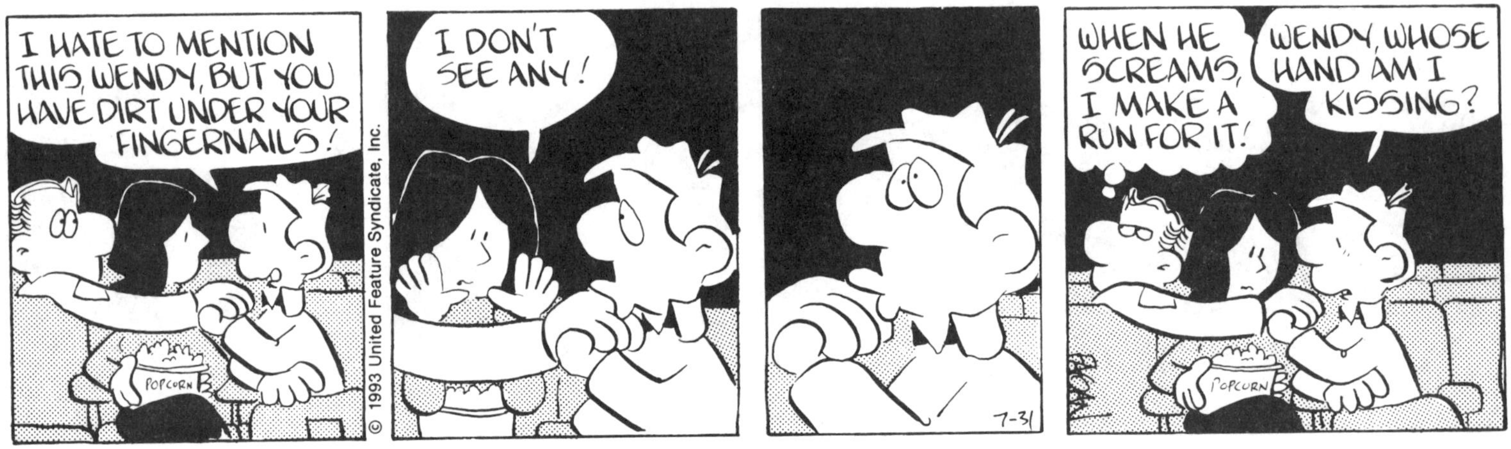
I HATE TO MENTION THIS, WENDY, BUT YOU HAVE DIRT UNDER YOUR FINGERNAILS!
POPCORN
© 1993 United Feature Syndicate, Inc.
I DON'T SEE ANY!
7-31
WHEN HE SCREAMS, I MAKE A RUN FOR IT!
WENDY, WHOSE HAND AM I KISSING?
POPCORN

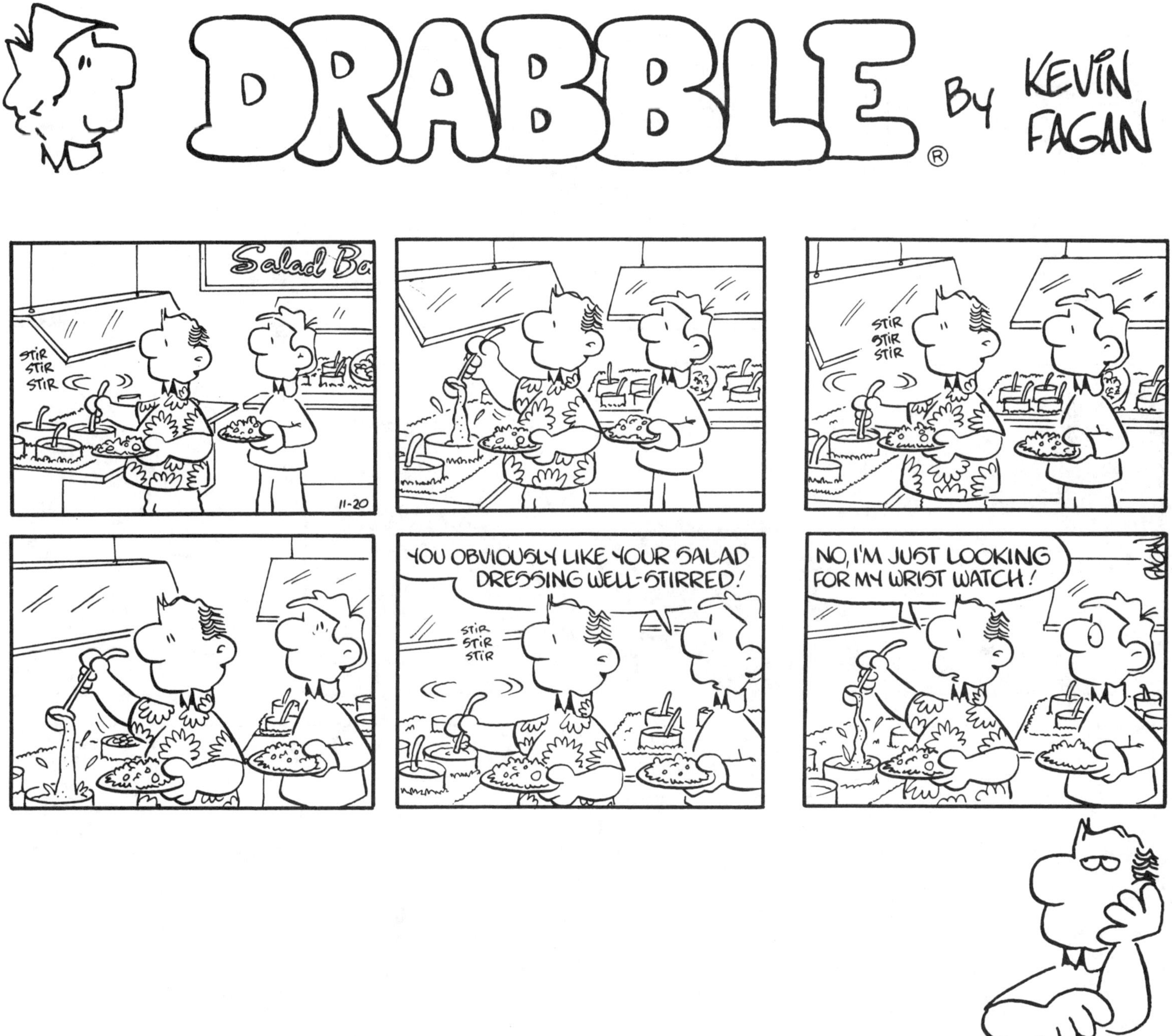
DRABBLE®
By KEVIN FAGAN
Salad Ba
STIR STIR STIR
11-20
STIR STIR STIR
STIR STIR STIR
YOU OBVIOUSLY LIKE YOUR SALAD DRESSING WELL-STIRRED!
NO, I'M JUST LOOKING FOR MY WRIST WATCH!

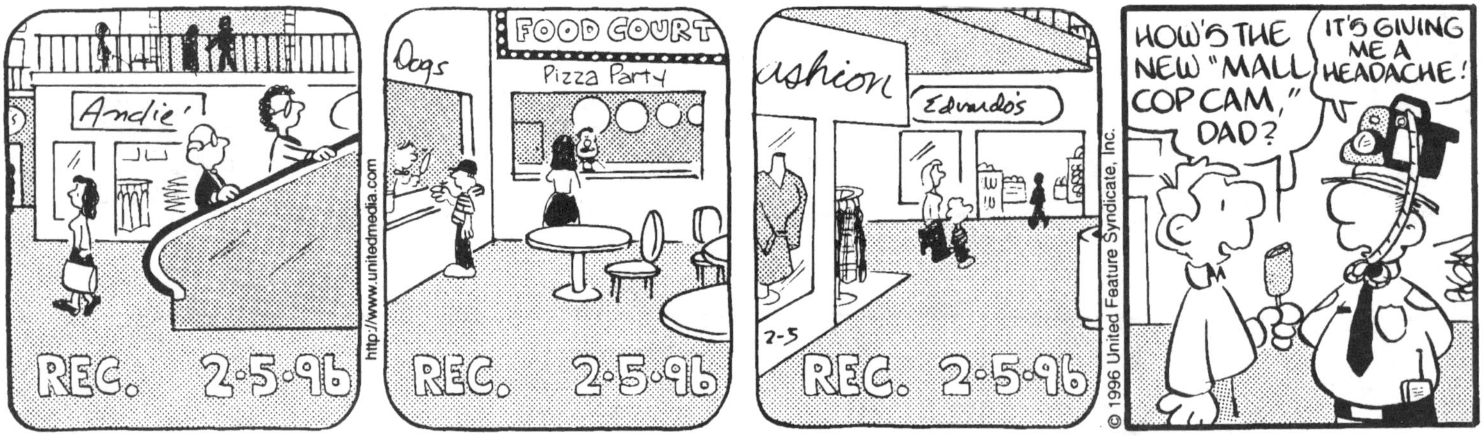
Andie'
REC. 2-5-96
http://www.unitedmedia.com
Dogs
FOOD COURT
Pizza Party
REC. 2-5-96
ushion
Eduardo's
2-5
REC. 2-5-96
© 1996 United Feature Syndicate, Inc.
HOW'S THE NEW "MALL COP CAM," DAD?
IT'S GIVING ME A HEADACHE!

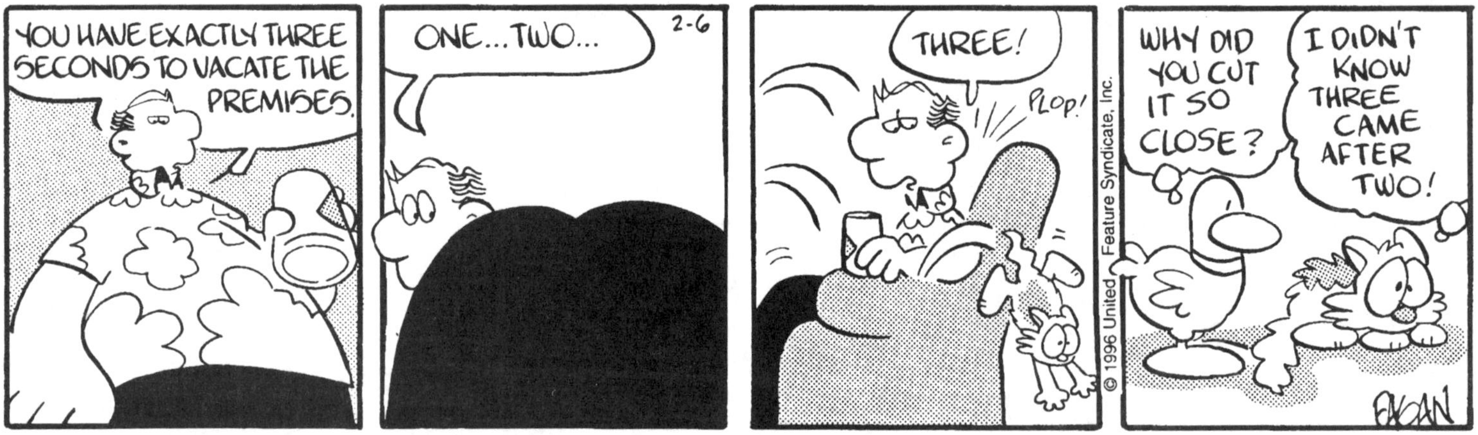
YOU HAVE EXACTLY THREE SECONDS TO VACATE THE PREMISES.
2-6
ONE... TWO...
THREE!
PLOP!
© 1996 United Feature Syndicate, Inc.
WHY DID YOU CUT IT SO CLOSE?
I DIDN'T KNOW THREE CAME AFTER TWO!
FAGAN

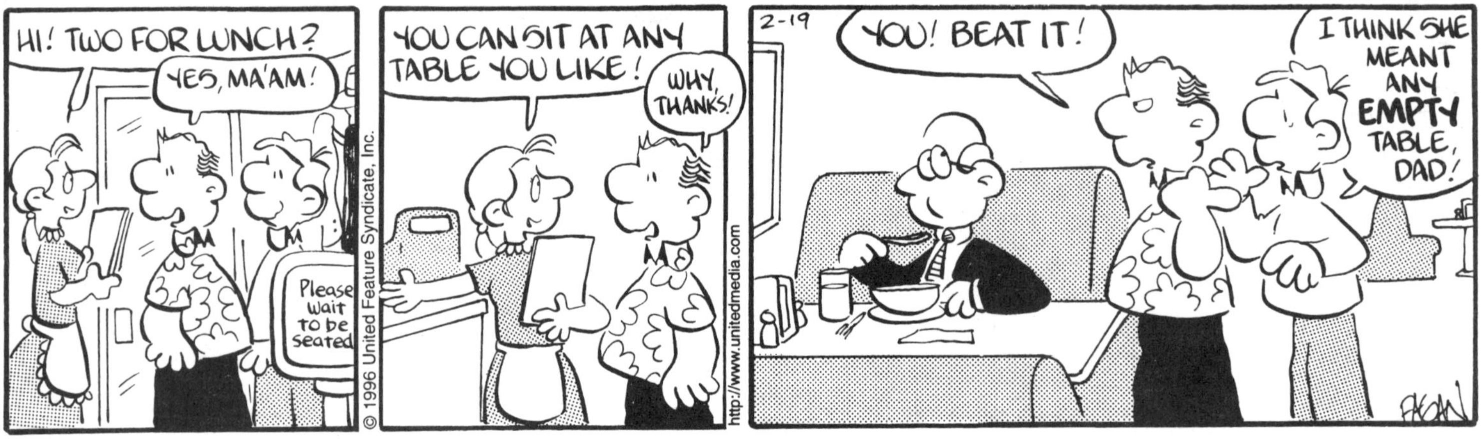
HI! TWO FOR LUNCH?
YES, MA'AM!
Please wait to be seated
© 1996 United Feature Syndicate, Inc.
YOU CAN SIT AT ANY TABLE YOU LIKE!
WHY, THANKS!
http://www.unitedmedia.com
2-19
YOU! BEAT IT!
I THINK SHE MEANT ANY **EMPTY** TABLE, DAD!
FAGAN

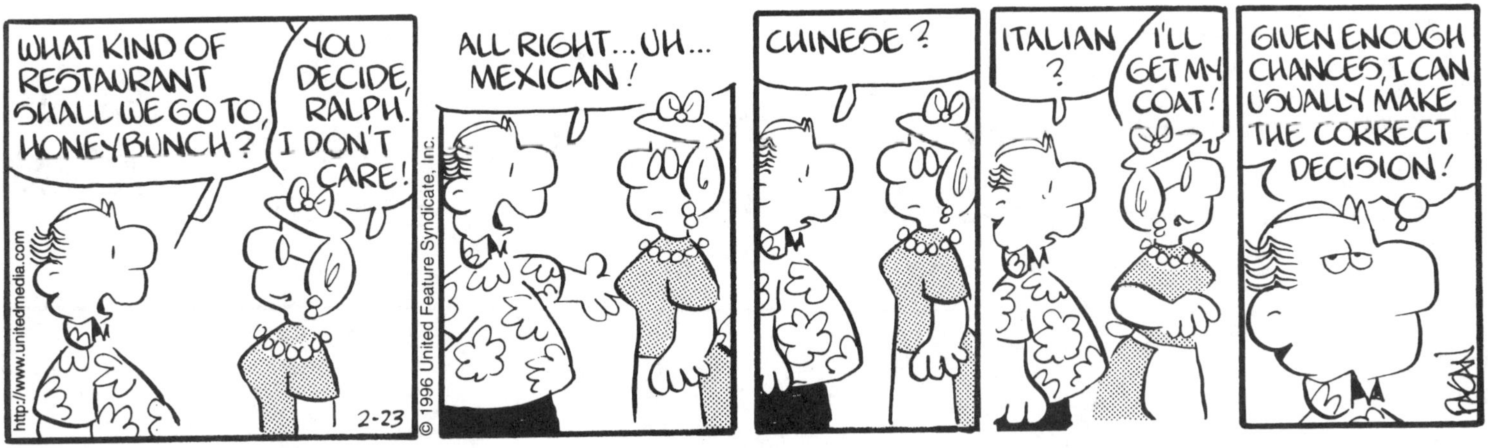
WHAT KIND OF RESTAURANT SHALL WE GO TO, HONEYBUNCH?
YOU DECIDE, RALPH. I DON'T CARE!
http://www.unitedmedia.com
2-23
© 1996 United Feature Syndicate, Inc.
ALL RIGHT... UH... MEXICAN!
CHINESE?
ITALIAN?
I'LL GET MY COAT!
GIVEN ENOUGH CHANCES, I CAN USUALLY MAKE THE CORRECT DECISION!
FAGAN

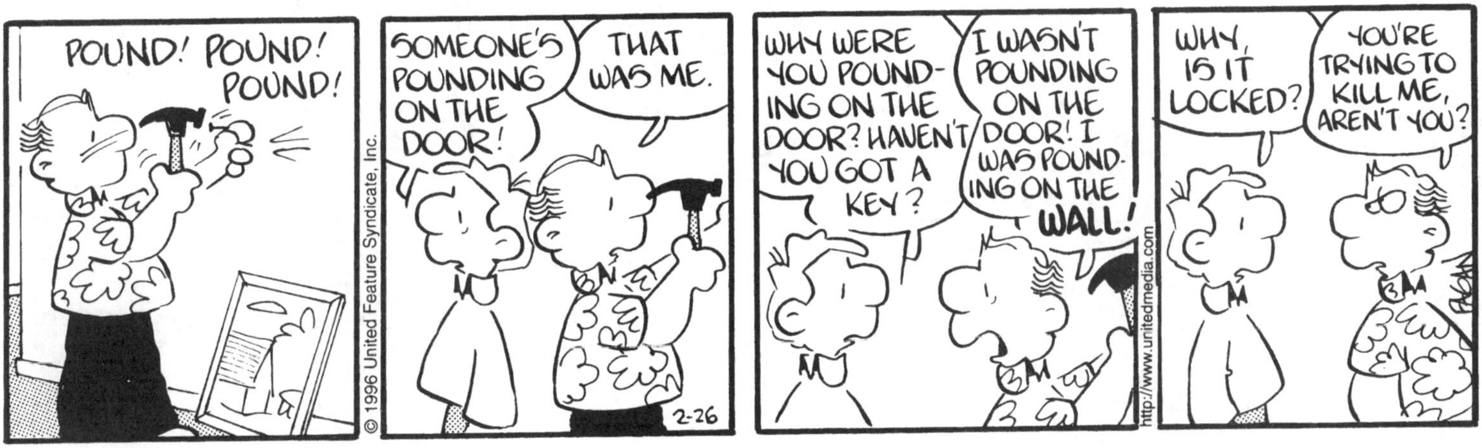
POUND! POUND! POUND! POUND!
© 1996 United Feature Syndicate, Inc.
SOMEONE'S POUNDING ON THE DOOR!
THAT WAS ME.
2-26
WHY WERE YOU POUNDING ON THE DOOR? HAVEN'T YOU GOT A KEY?
I WASN'T POUNDING ON THE DOOR! I WAS POUNDING ON THE WALL!
http://www.unitedmedia.com
WHY, IS IT LOCKED?
YOU'RE TRYING TO KILL ME, AREN'T YOU?
FAGAN

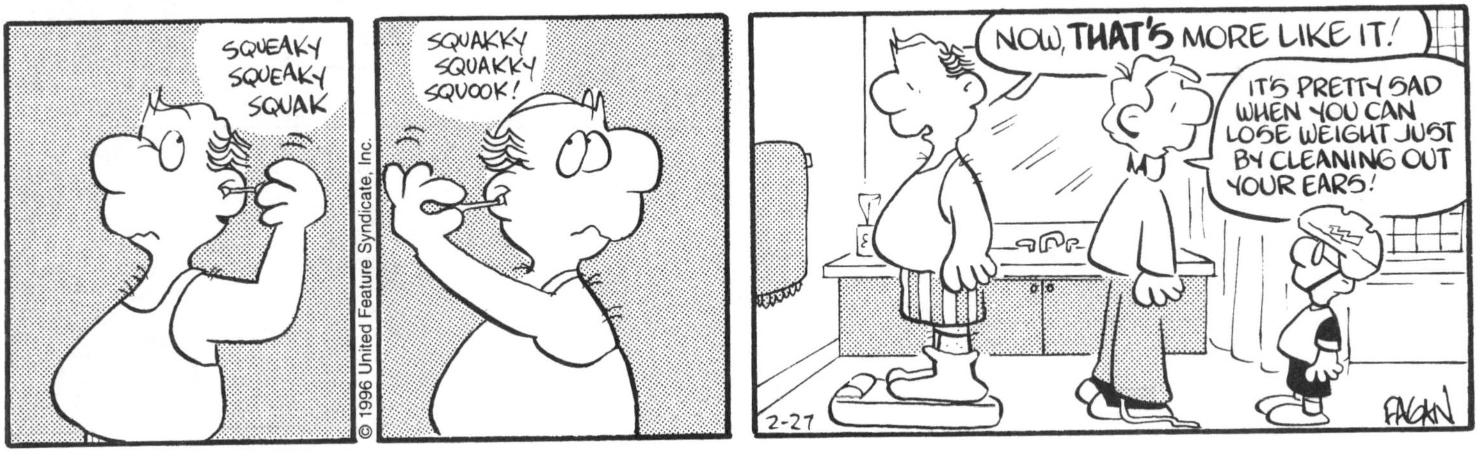
SQUEAKY SQUEAKY SQUAK
© 1996 United Feature Syndicate, Inc.
SQUAKKY SQUAKKY SQUOOK!
NOW, THAT'S MORE LIKE IT!
IT'S PRETTY SAD WHEN YOU CAN LOSE WEIGHT JUST BY CLEANING OUT YOUR EARS!
2-27
FAGAN

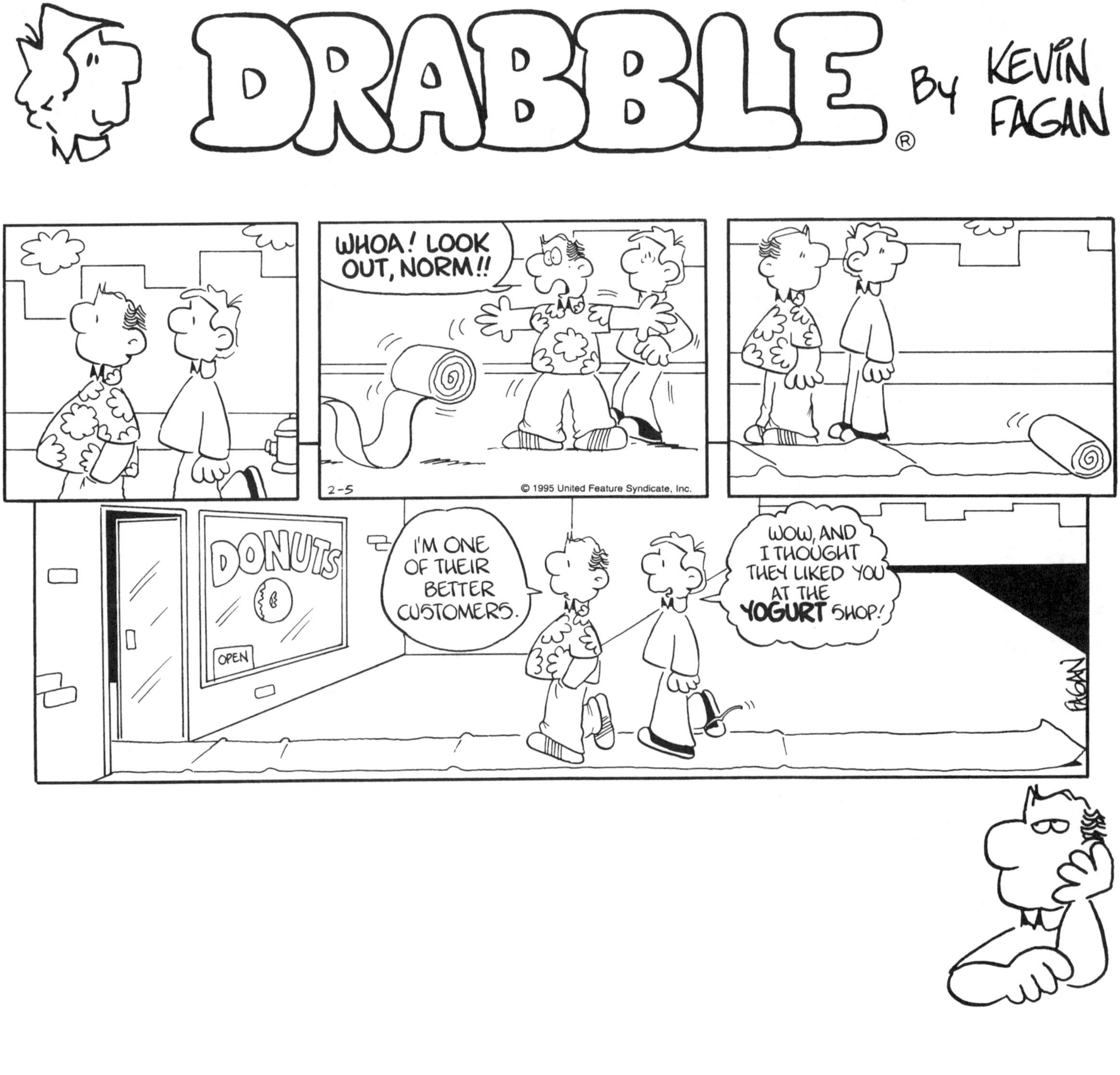
DRABBLE® By KEVIN FAGAN
WHOA! LOOK OUT, NORM!!
2-5
© 1995 United Feature Syndicate, Inc.
DONUTS
OPEN
I'M ONE OF THEIR BETTER CUSTOMERS.
WOW, AND I THOUGHT THEY LIKED YOU AT THE YOGURT SHOP!
FAGAN

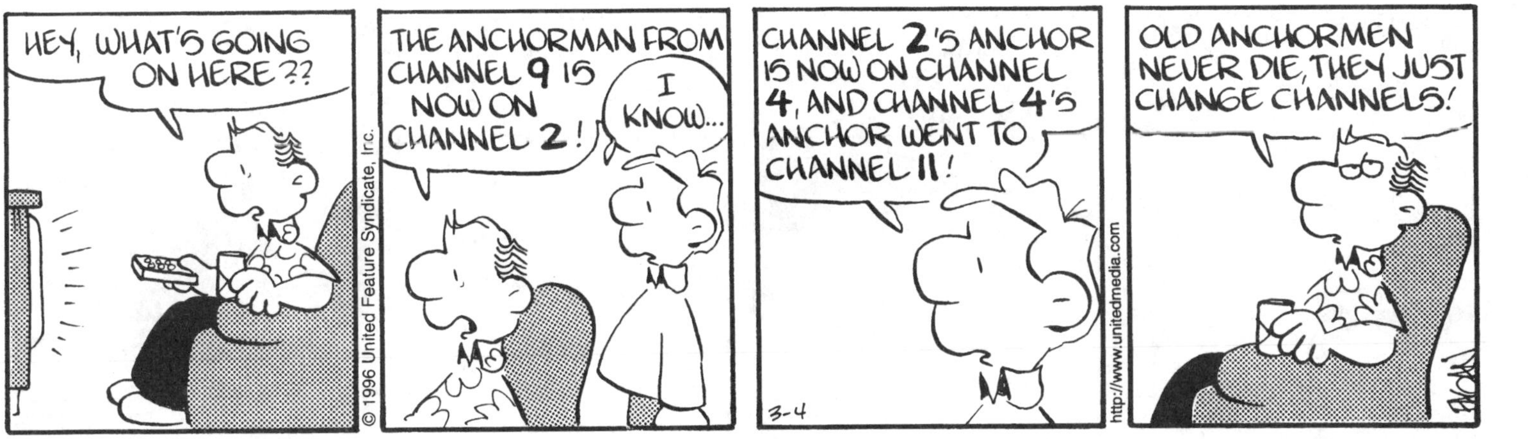
HEY, WHAT'S GOING ON HERE??
THE ANCHORMAN FROM CHANNEL 9 IS NOW ON CHANNEL 2!
I KNOW...
CHANNEL 2'S ANCHOR IS NOW ON CHANNEL 4, AND CHANNEL 4'S ANCHOR WENT TO CHANNEL 11!
OLD ANCHORMEN NEVER DIE, THEY JUST CHANGE CHANNELS!
© 1996 United Feature Syndicate, Inc.
http://www.unitedmedia.com
3-4

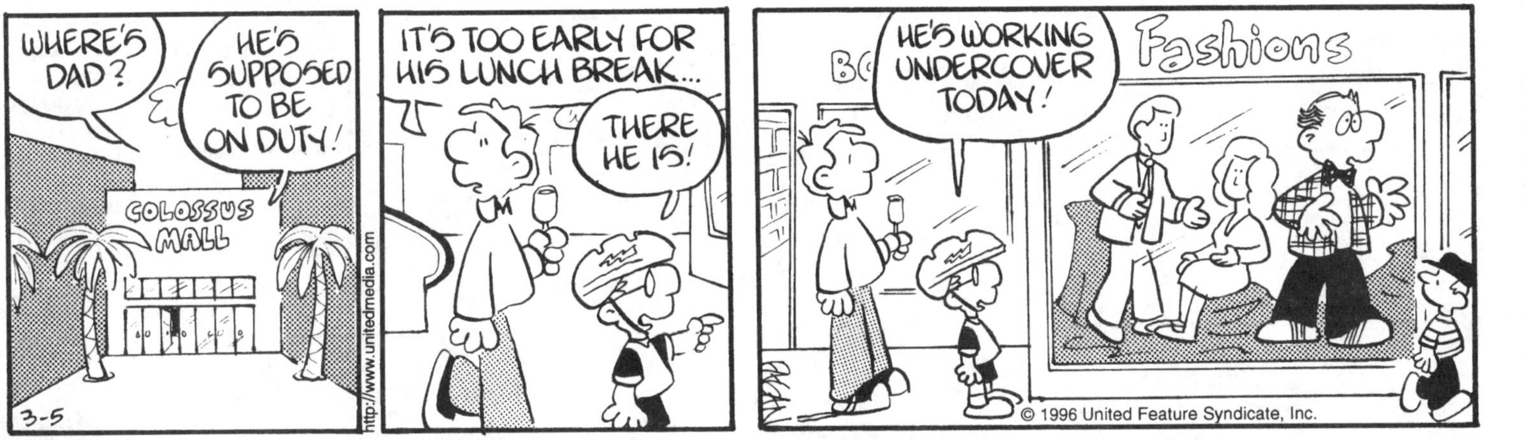
WHERE'S DAD?
HE'S SUPPOSED TO BE ON DUTY!
COLOSSUS MALL
3-5
http://www.unitedmedia.com
IT'S TOO EARLY FOR HIS LUNCH BREAK...
THERE HE IS!
HE'S WORKING UNDERCOVER TODAY!
Fashions
© 1996 United Feature Syndicate, Inc.

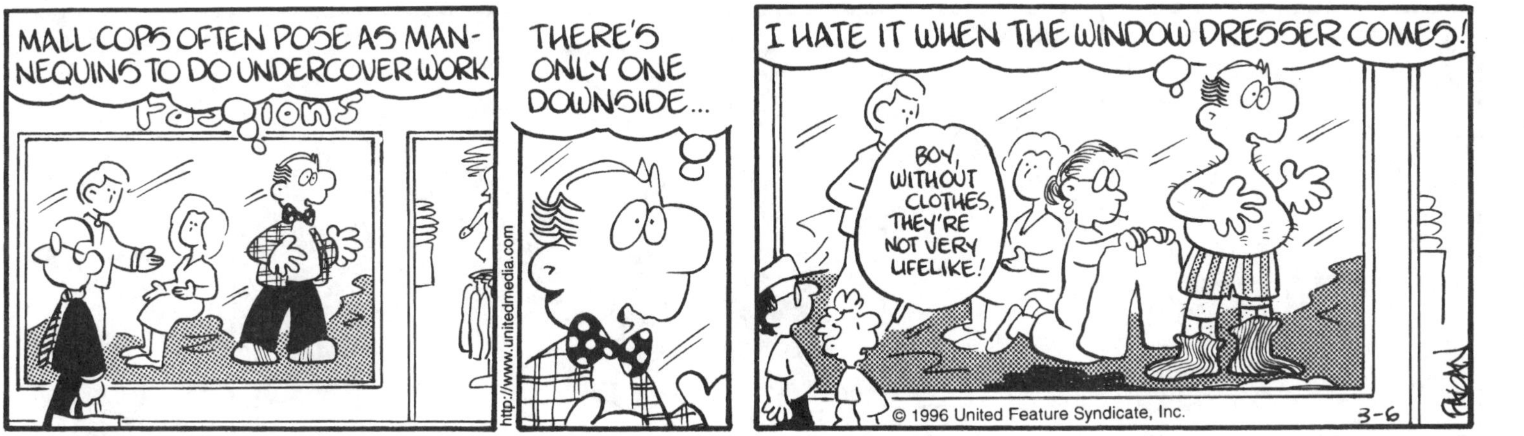
MALL COPS OFTEN POSE AS MANNEQUINS TO DO UNDERCOVER WORK.
THERE'S ONLY ONE DOWNSIDE...
http://www.unitedmedia.com
I HATE IT WHEN THE WINDOW DRESSER COMES!
BOY, WITHOUT CLOTHES, THEY'RE NOT VERY LIFELIKE!
© 1996 United Feature Syndicate, Inc.
3-6

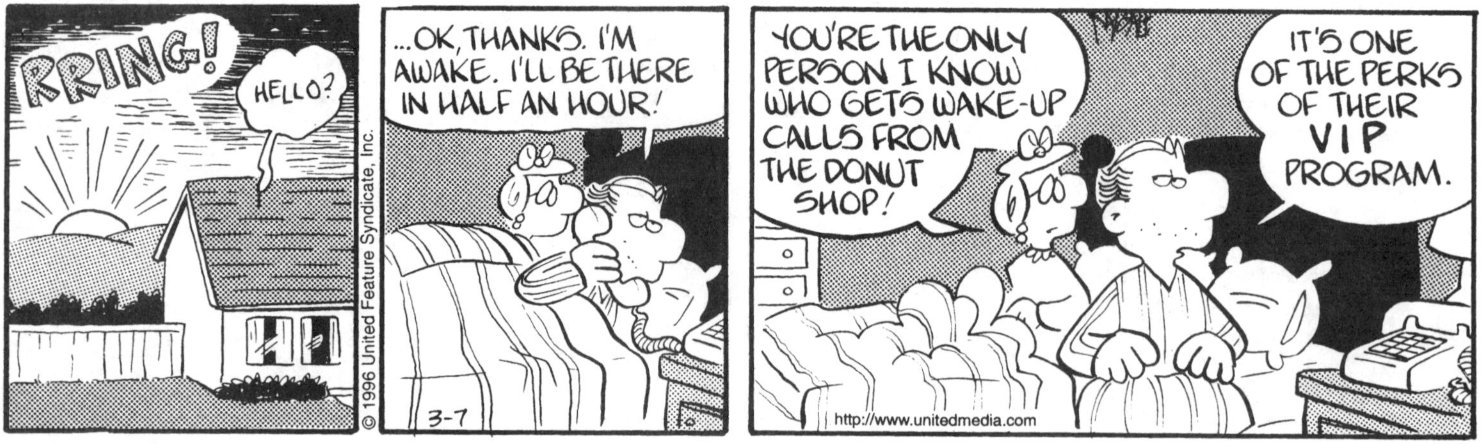
RRING!
HELLO?
© 1996 United Feature Syndicate, Inc.
...OK, THANKS. I'M AWAKE. I'LL BE THERE IN HALF AN HOUR!
3-7
YOU'RE THE ONLY PERSON I KNOW WHO GETS WAKE-UP CALLS FROM THE DONUT SHOP!
IT'S ONE OF THE PERKS OF THEIR VIP PROGRAM.
http://www.unitedmedia.com

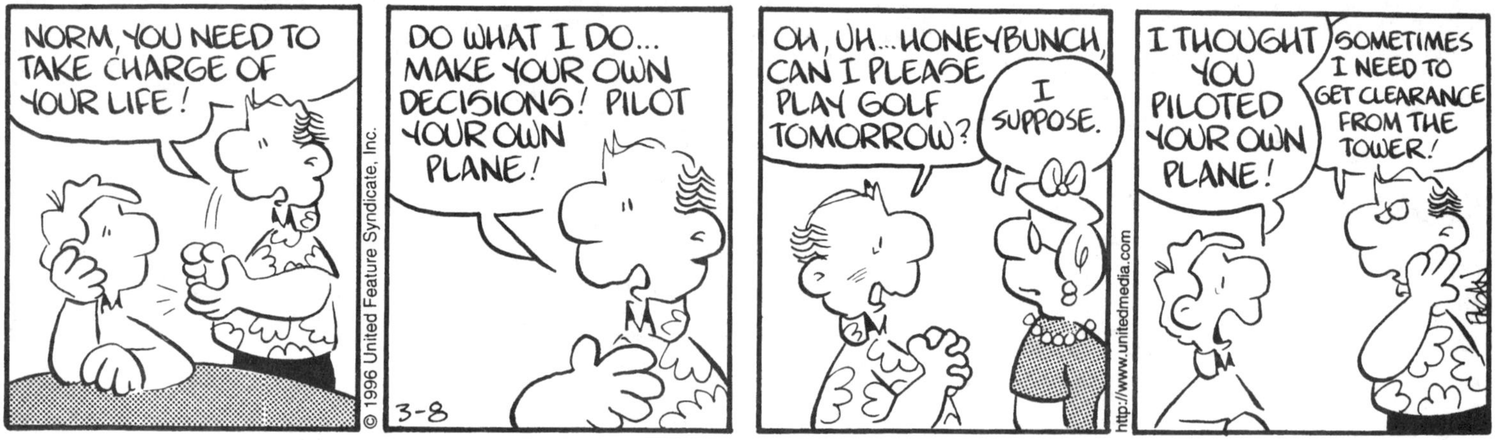
NORM, YOU NEED TO TAKE CHARGE OF YOUR LIFE!
© 1996 United Feature Syndicate, Inc.
DO WHAT I DO... MAKE YOUR OWN DECISIONS! PILOT YOUR OWN PLANE!
3-8
OH, UH... HONEYBUNCH, CAN I PLEASE PLAY GOLF TOMORROW?
I SUPPOSE.
http://www.unitedmedia.com
I THOUGHT YOU PILOTED YOUR OWN PLANE!
SOMETIMES I NEED TO GET CLEARANCE FROM THE TOWER!

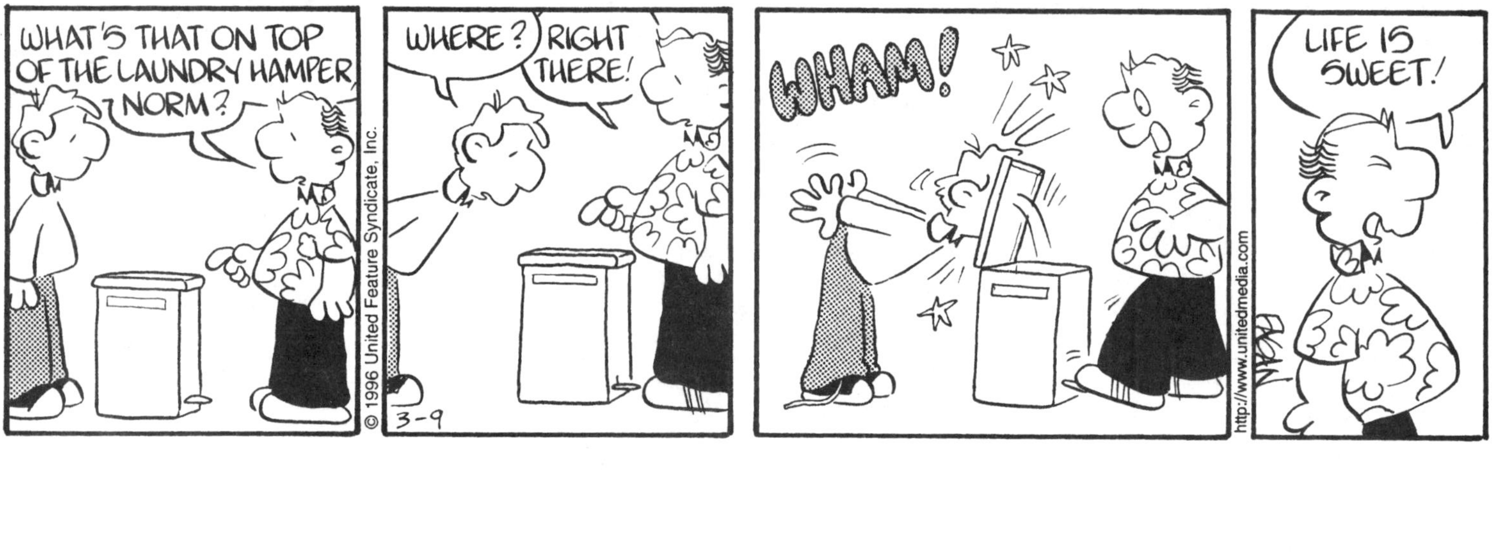
WHAT'S THAT ON TOP OF THE LAUNDRY HAMPER, NORM?
© 1996 United Feature Syndicate, Inc.
WHERE?
RIGHT THERE!
3-9
WHAM!
http://www.unitedmedia.com
LIFE IS SWEET!

DRABBLE® By KEVIN FAGAN

HONEYBUNCH, YOU'VE BEEN DOING HOUSEWORK ALL DAY.
2-26
YOU NEED A BREAK!
HOW WOULD YOU LIKE TO TAKE A NICE, SCENIC DRIVE... WATCH THE SUNSET...
© 1995 United Feature Syndicate, Inc.
THEN MAYBE GO HAVE A RELAXING, CANDLELIGHT DINNER AT THAT NICE RESTAURANT THAT OVERLOOKS THE HARBOR!
RALPH, THAT SOUNDS WONDERFUL! I'D **LOVE** TO DO THAT!
GREAT!
REMEMBER TO PUT GAS IN THE CAR ON YOUR WAY HOME!
FAGAN

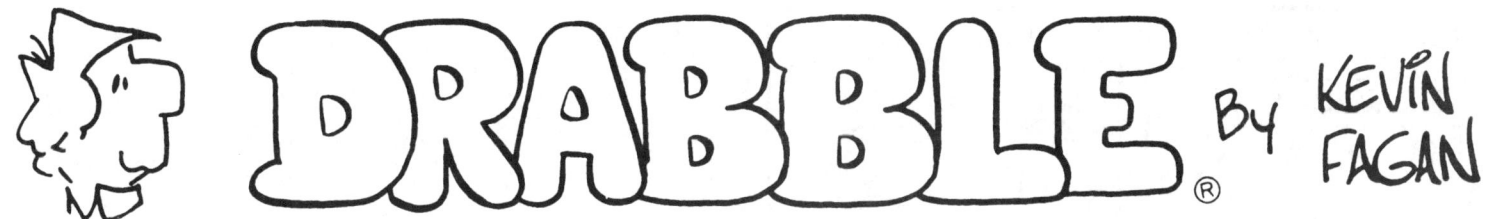

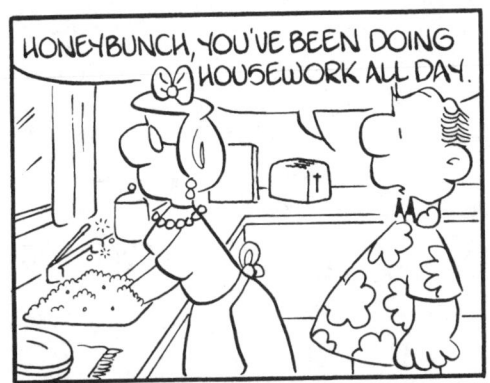

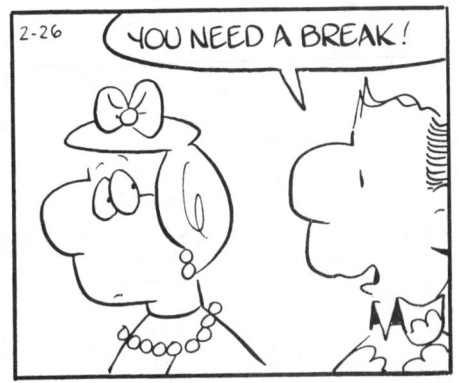

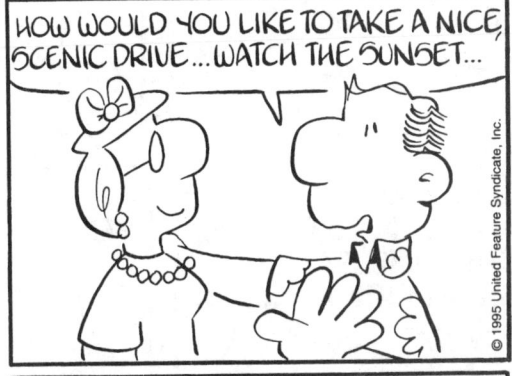

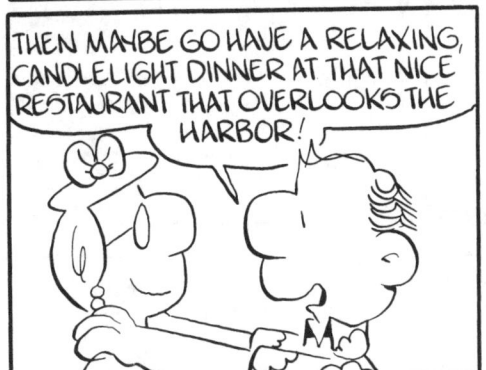

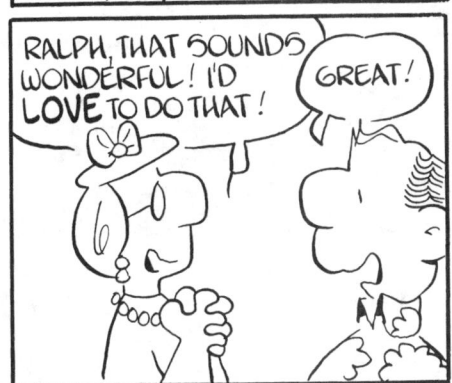

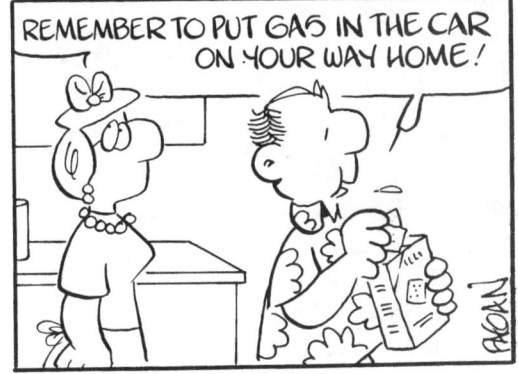

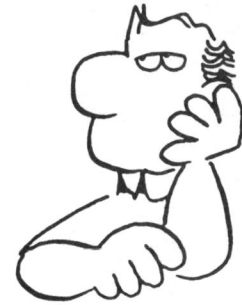

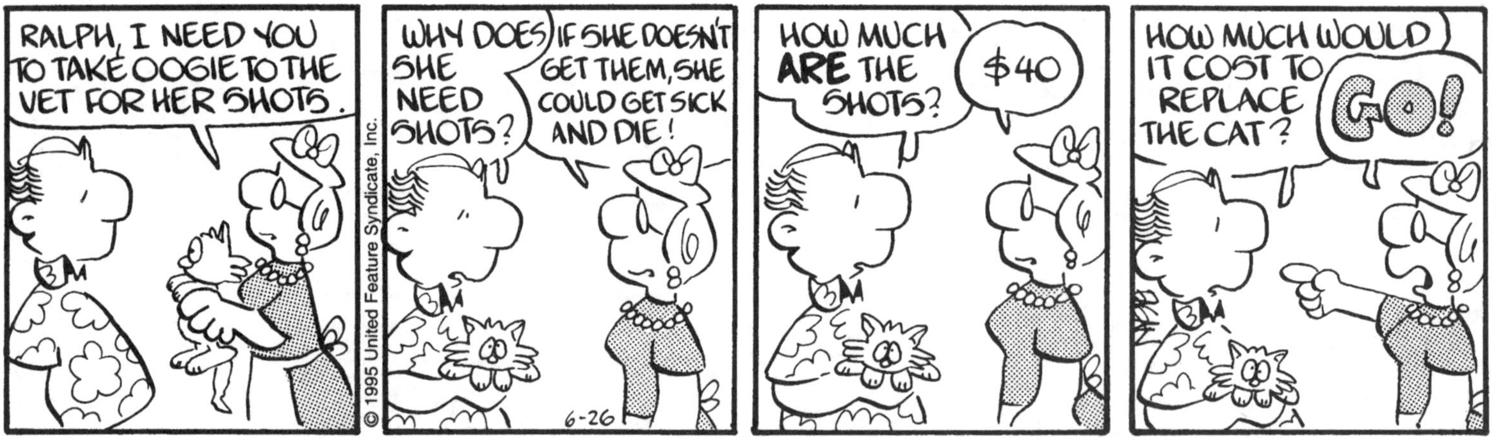
RALPH, I NEED YOU TO TAKE OOGIE TO THE VET FOR HER SHOTS.
WHY DOES SHE NEED SHOTS?
IF SHE DOESN'T GET THEM, SHE COULD GET SICK AND DIE!
© 1995 United Feature Syndicate, Inc.
6-26
HOW MUCH **ARE** THE SHOTS?
$40
HOW MUCH WOULD IT COST TO REPLACE THE CAT?
GO!

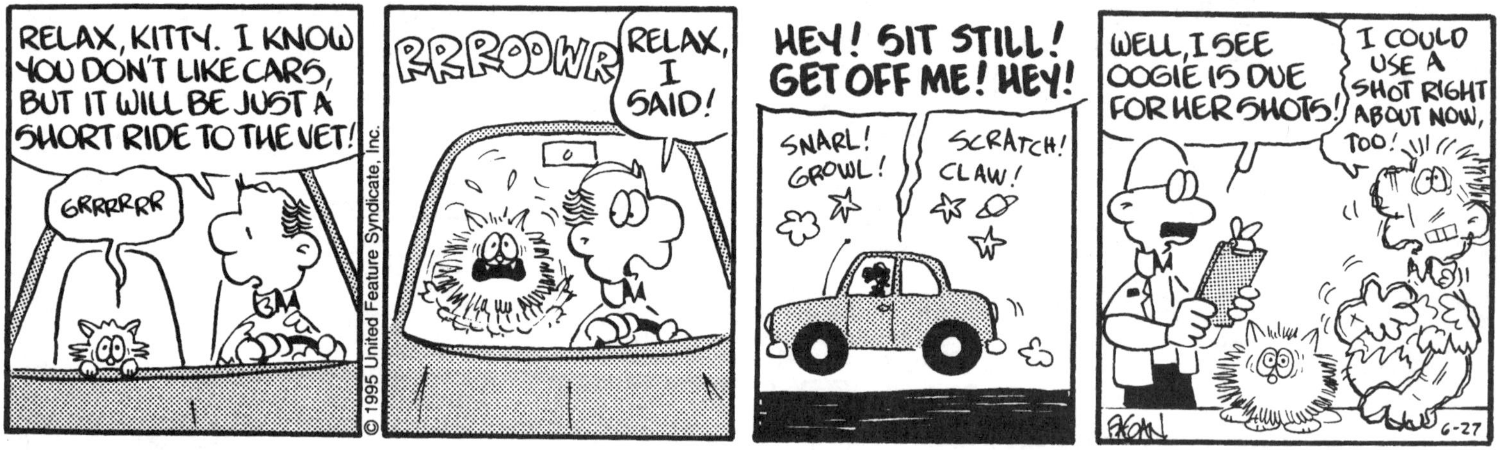
RELAX, KITTY. I KNOW YOU DON'T LIKE CARS, BUT IT WILL BE JUST A SHORT RIDE TO THE VET!
GRRRRRR
© 1995 United Feature Syndicate, Inc.
RRROOWR
RELAX, I SAID!
HEY! SIT STILL! GET OFF ME! HEY!
SNARL! GROWL!
SCRATCH! CLAW!
WELL, I SEE OOGIE IS DUE FOR HER SHOTS!
I COULD USE A SHOT RIGHT ABOUT NOW, TOO!
FAGAN
6-27

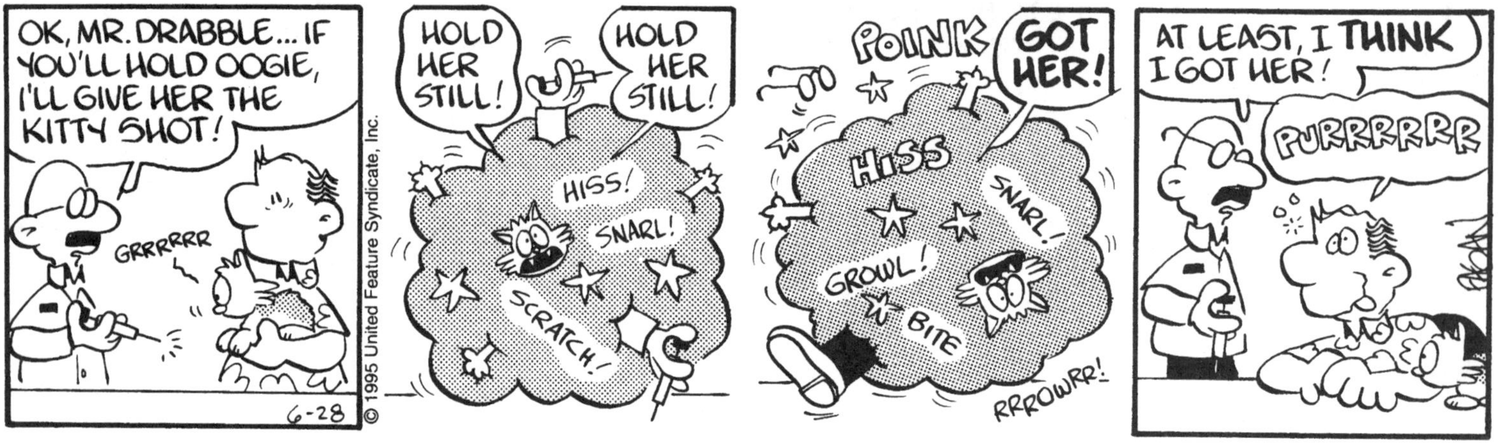
OK, MR. DRABBLE... IF YOU'LL HOLD OOGIE, I'LL GIVE HER THE KITTY SHOT!
GRRRRRR
6-28
© 1995 United Feature Syndicate, Inc.
HOLD HER STILL!
HOLD HER STILL!
HISS!
SNARL!
SCRATCH!
POINK
GOT HER!
HISS
SNARL!
GROWL!
BITE
RRROWRR!
AT LEAST, I **THINK** I GOT HER!
PURRRRRR

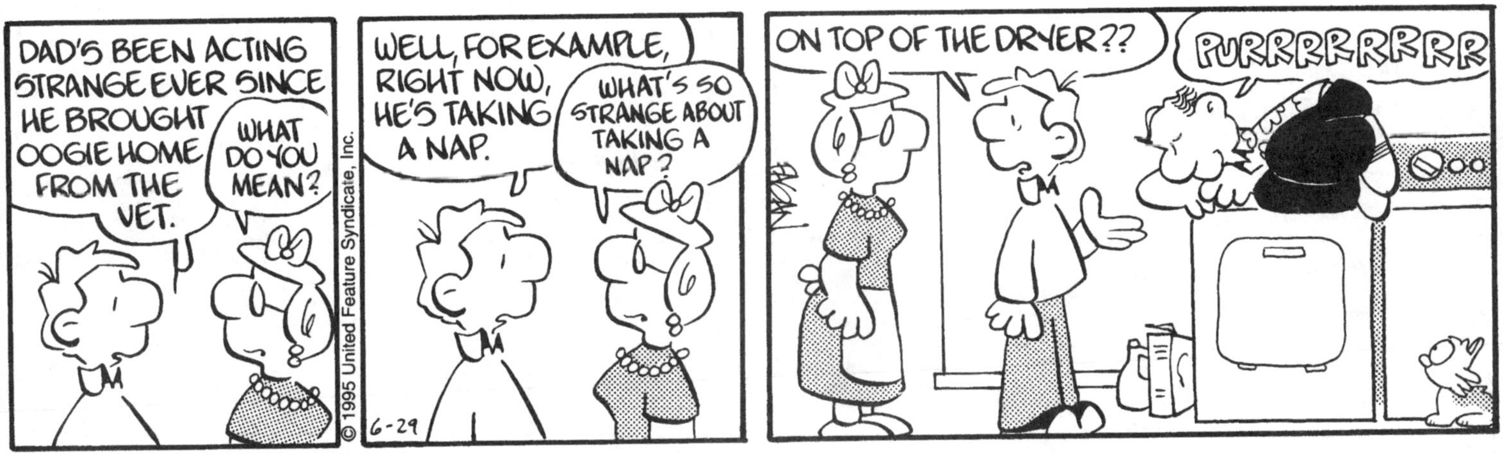
DAD'S BEEN ACTING STRANGE EVER SINCE HE BROUGHT OOGIE HOME FROM THE VET.
WHAT DO YOU MEAN?
© 1995 United Feature Syndicate, Inc.
WELL, FOR EXAMPLE, RIGHT NOW, HE'S TAKING A NAP.
WHAT'S SO STRANGE ABOUT TAKING A NAP?
6-29
ON TOP OF THE DRYER??
PURRRRRRRR

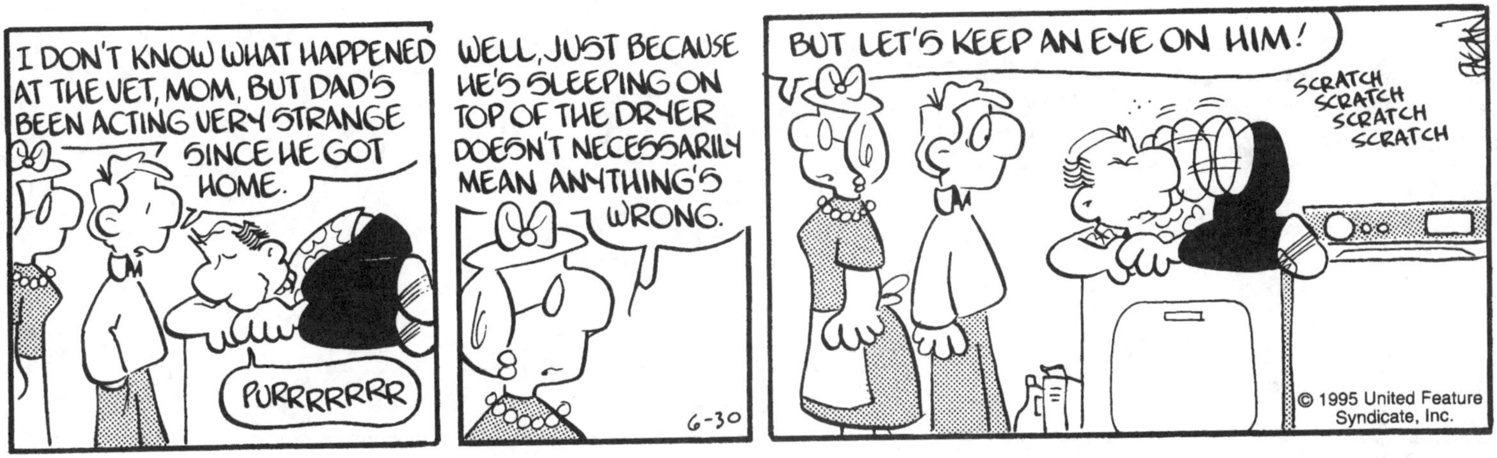
I DON'T KNOW WHAT HAPPENED AT THE VET, MOM, BUT DAD'S BEEN ACTING VERY STRANGE SINCE HE GOT HOME.
PURRRRRRR
WELL, JUST BECAUSE HE'S SLEEPING ON TOP OF THE DRYER DOESN'T NECESSARILY MEAN ANYTHING'S WRONG.
6-30
BUT LET'S KEEP AN EYE ON HIM!
SCRATCH SCRATCH SCRATCH SCRATCH
© 1995 United Feature Syndicate, Inc.

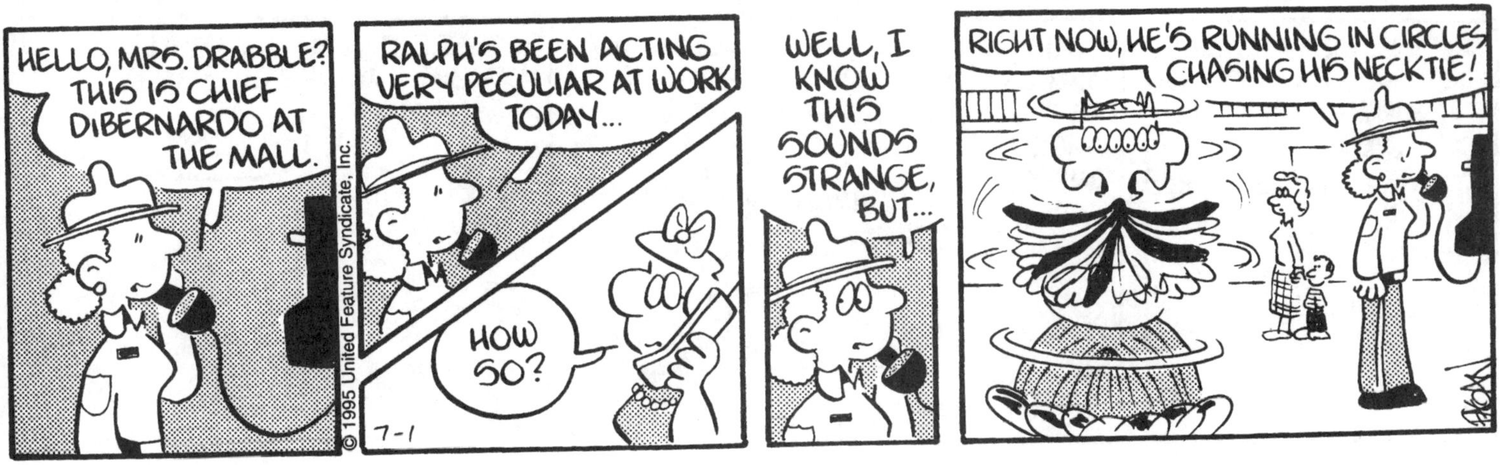
HELLO, MRS. DRABBLE? THIS IS CHIEF DIBERNARDO AT THE MALL.
© 1995 United Feature Syndicate, Inc.
RALPH'S BEEN ACTING VERY PECULIAR AT WORK TODAY...
HOW SO?
7-1
WELL, I KNOW THIS SOUNDS STRANGE, BUT...
RIGHT NOW, HE'S RUNNING IN CIRCLES CHASING HIS NECKTIE!

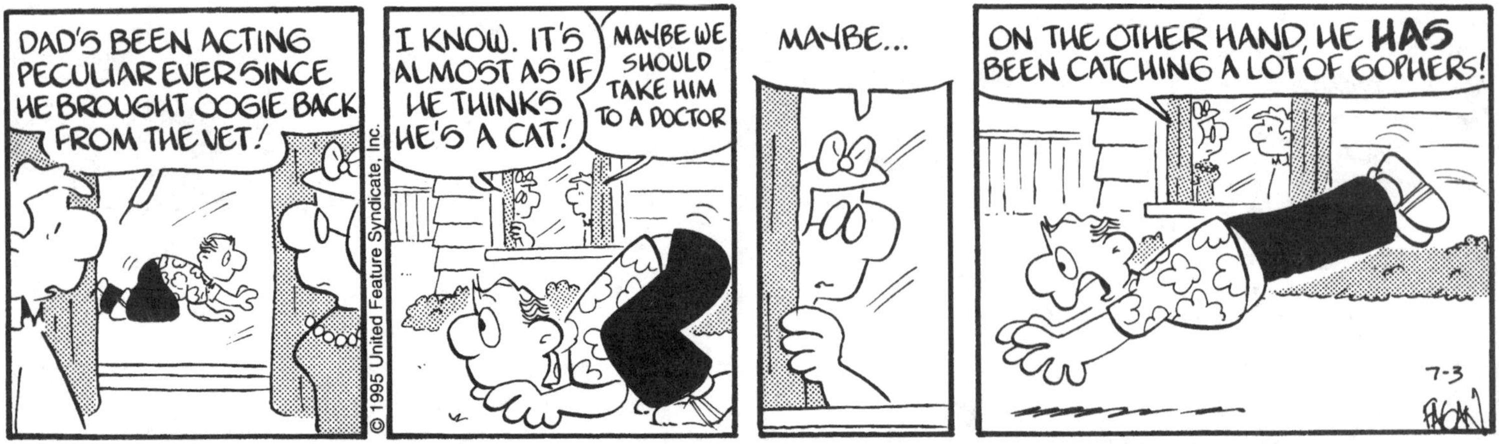
DAD'S BEEN ACTING PECULIAR EVER SINCE HE BROUGHT OOGIE BACK FROM THE VET!
© 1995 United Feature Syndicate, Inc.
I KNOW. IT'S ALMOST AS IF HE THINKS HE'S A CAT!
MAYBE WE SHOULD TAKE HIM TO A DOCTOR
MAYBE...
ON THE OTHER HAND, HE **HAS** BEEN CATCHING A LOT OF GOPHERS!
7-3

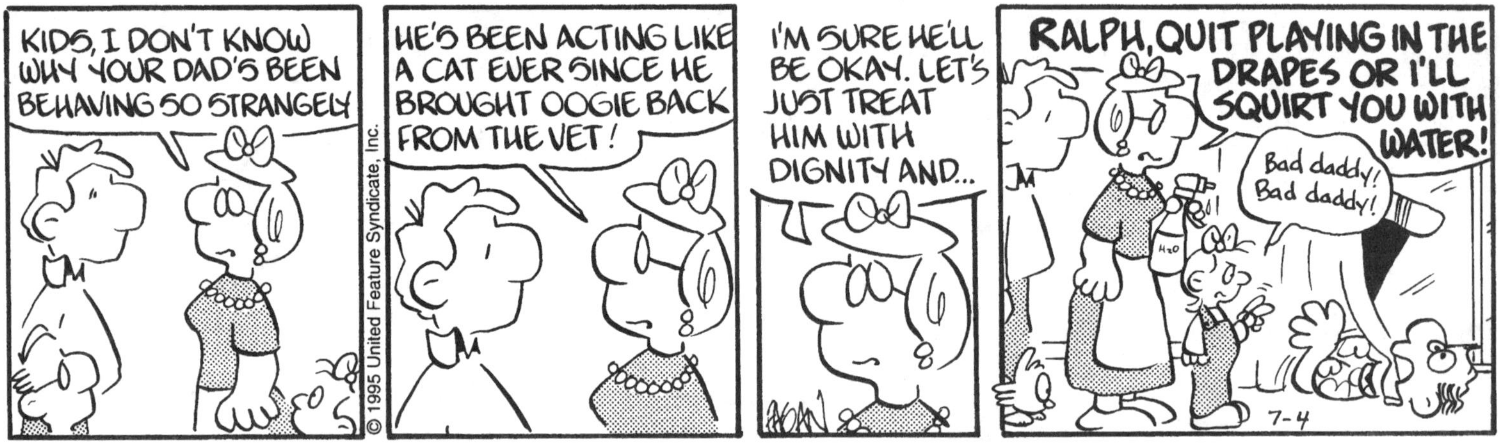
KIDS, I DON'T KNOW WHY YOUR DAD'S BEEN BEHAVING SO STRANGELY
© 1995 United Feature Syndicate, Inc.
HE'S BEEN ACTING LIKE A CAT EVER SINCE HE BROUGHT OOGIE BACK FROM THE VET!
I'M SURE HE'LL BE OKAY. LET'S JUST TREAT HIM WITH DIGNITY AND...
RALPH, QUIT PLAYING IN THE DRAPES OR I'LL SQUIRT YOU WITH WATER!
Bad daddy! Bad daddy!
7-4

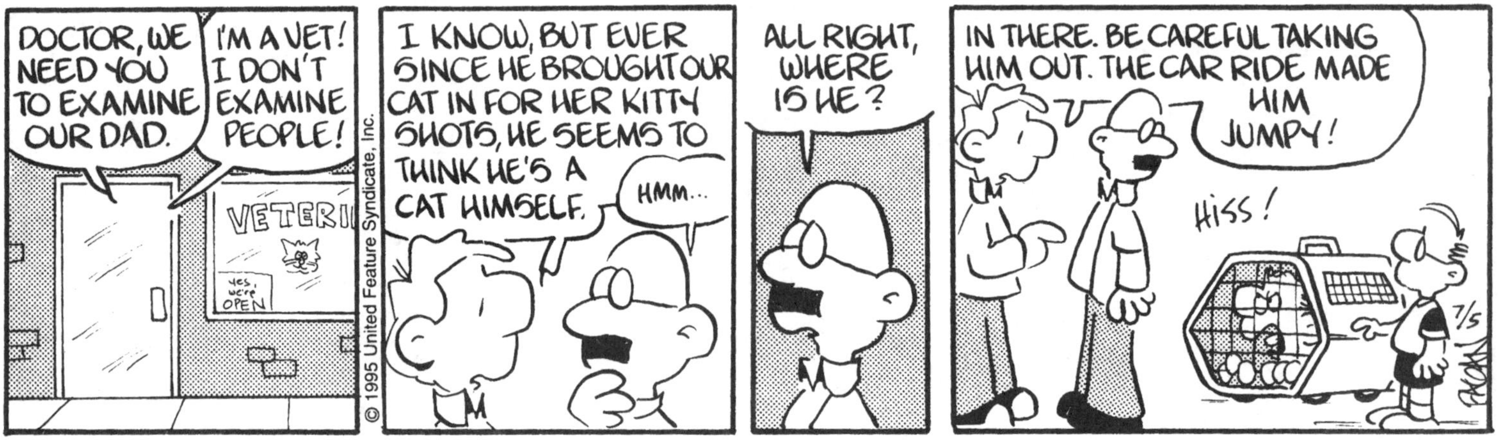
DOCTOR, WE NEED YOU TO EXAMINE OUR DAD.
I'M A VET! I DON'T EXAMINE PEOPLE!
VETERI
yes, we're OPEN
© 1995 United Feature Syndicate, Inc.
I KNOW, BUT EVER SINCE HE BROUGHT OUR CAT IN FOR HER KITTY SHOTS, HE SEEMS TO THINK HE'S A CAT HIMSELF.
HMM...
ALL RIGHT, WHERE IS HE?
IN THERE. BE CAREFUL TAKING HIM OUT. THE CAR RIDE MADE HIM JUMPY!
HISS!
7/5

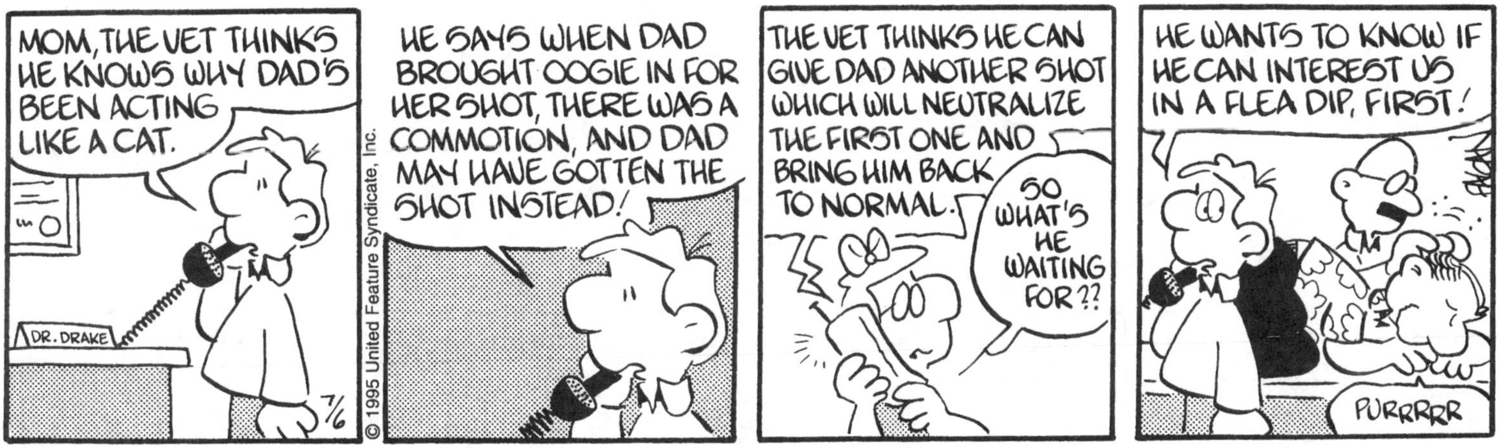
MOM, THE VET THINKS HE KNOWS WHY DAD'S BEEN ACTING LIKE A CAT.
DR. DRAKE
7/6
© 1995 United Feature Syndicate, Inc.
HE SAYS WHEN DAD BROUGHT OOGIE IN FOR HER SHOT, THERE WAS A COMMOTION, AND DAD MAY HAVE GOTTEN THE SHOT INSTEAD!
THE VET THINKS HE CAN GIVE DAD ANOTHER SHOT WHICH WILL NEUTRALIZE THE FIRST ONE AND BRING HIM BACK TO NORMAL.
SO WHAT'S HE WAITING FOR??
HE WANTS TO KNOW IF HE CAN INTEREST US IN A FLEA DIP, FIRST!
PURRRRR

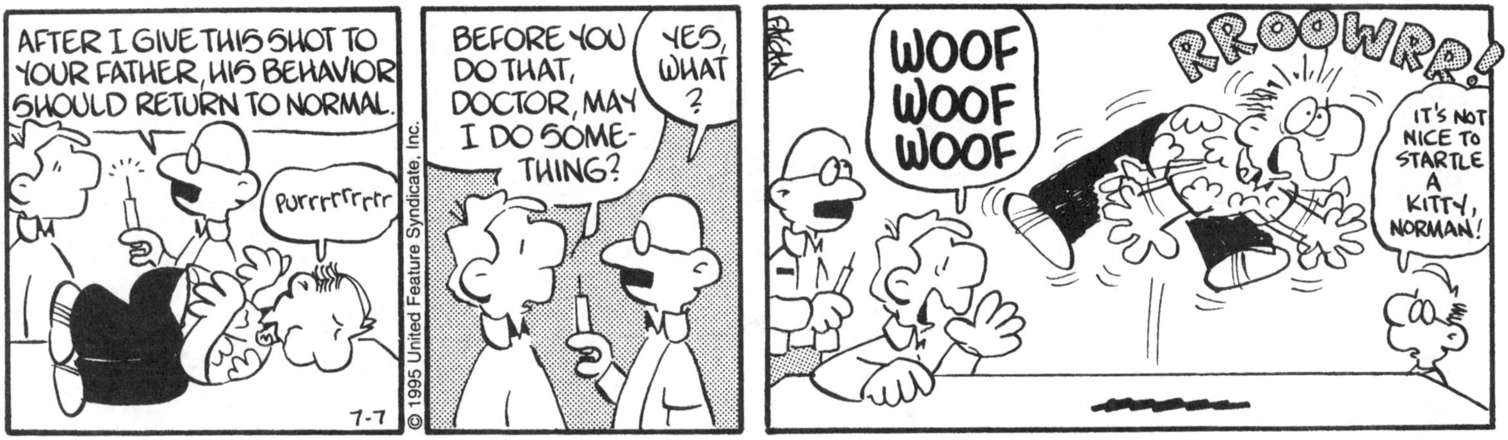
AFTER I GIVE THIS SHOT TO YOUR FATHER, HIS BEHAVIOR SHOULD RETURN TO NORMAL.
Purrrrrrrrr
7-7
© 1995 United Feature Syndicate, Inc.
BEFORE YOU DO THAT, DOCTOR, MAY I DO SOMETHING?
YES, WHAT?
WOOF WOOF WOOF
RROOWRR!
IT'S NOT NICE TO STARTLE A KITTY, NORMAN!

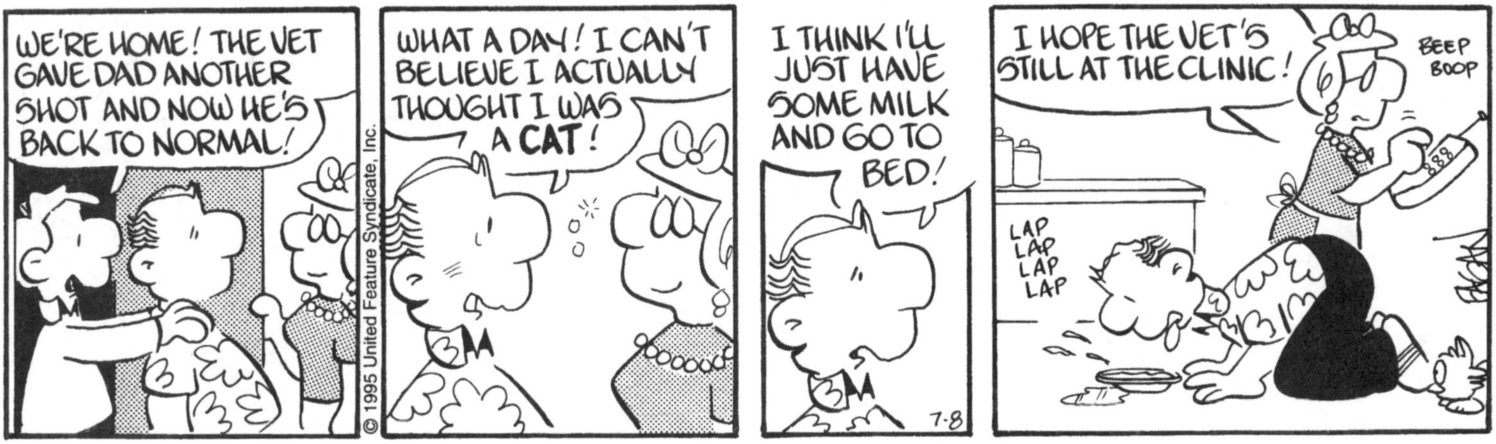
WE'RE HOME! THE VET GAVE DAD ANOTHER SHOT AND NOW HE'S BACK TO NORMAL!
© 1995 United Feature Syndicate, Inc.
WHAT A DAY! I CAN'T BELIEVE I ACTUALLY THOUGHT I WAS A CAT!
I THINK I'LL JUST HAVE SOME MILK AND GO TO BED!
7-8
I HOPE THE VET'S STILL AT THE CLINIC!
BEEP BOOP
LAP LAP LAP LAP

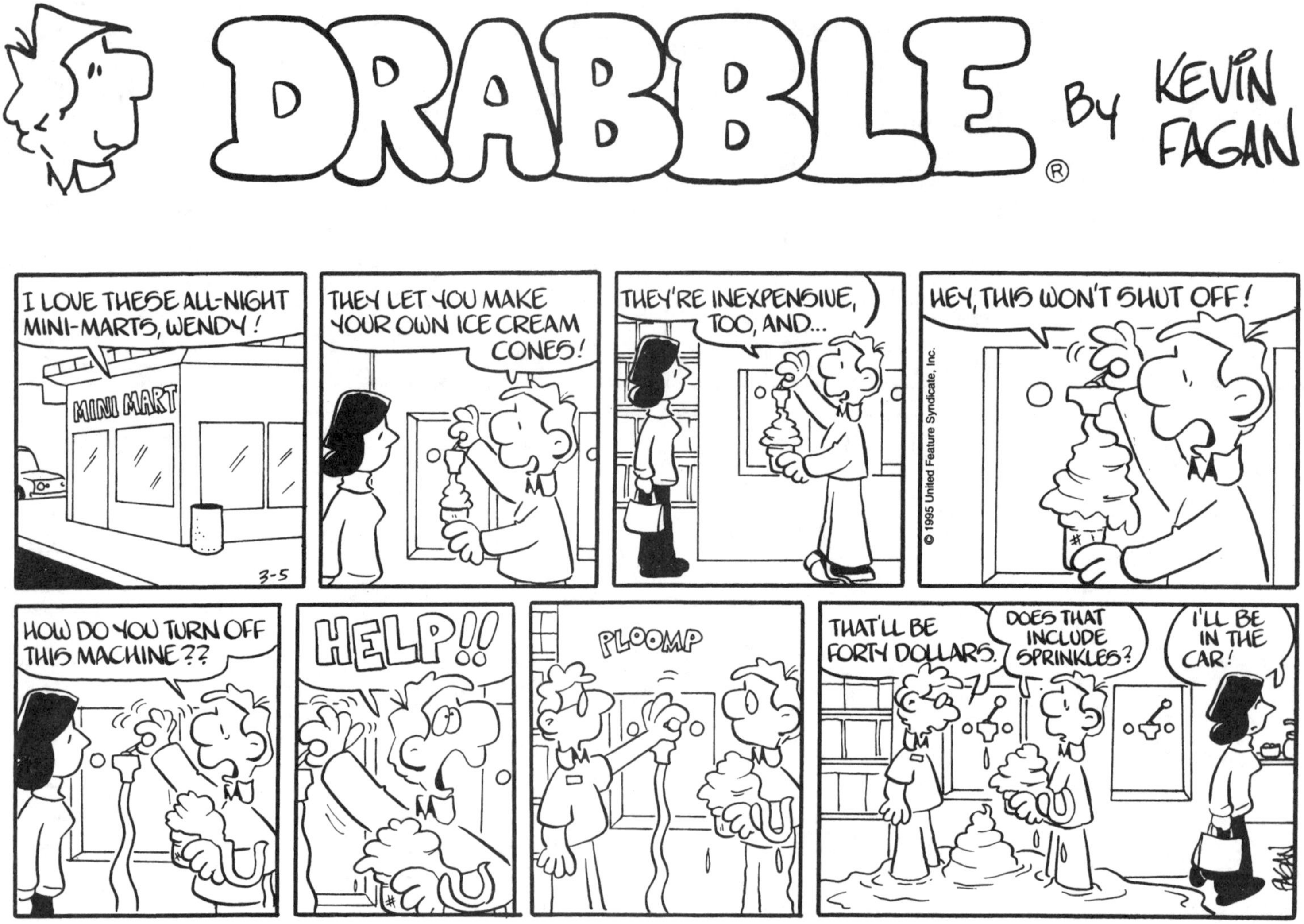
DRABBLE® By KEVIN FAGAN
I LOVE THESE ALL-NIGHT MINI-MARTS, WENDY!
MINI MART
3-5
THEY LET YOU MAKE YOUR OWN ICE CREAM CONES!
THEY'RE INEXPENSIVE, TOO, AND...
HEY, THIS WON'T SHUT OFF!
© 1995 United Feature Syndicate, Inc.
HOW DO YOU TURN OFF THIS MACHINE??
HELP!!
PLOOMP
THAT'LL BE FORTY DOLLARS.
DOES THAT INCLUDE SPRINKLES?
I'LL BE IN THE CAR!

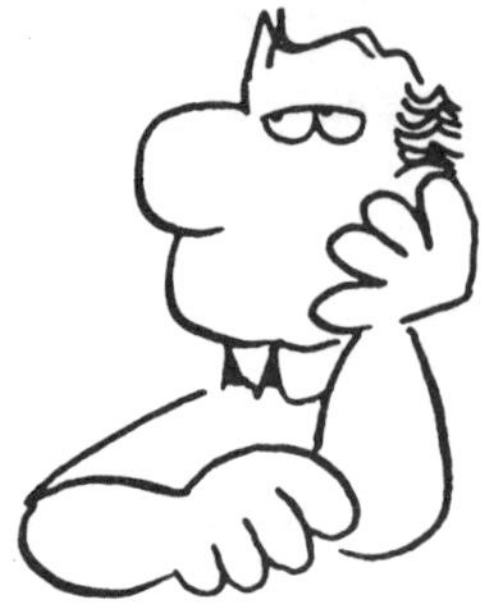

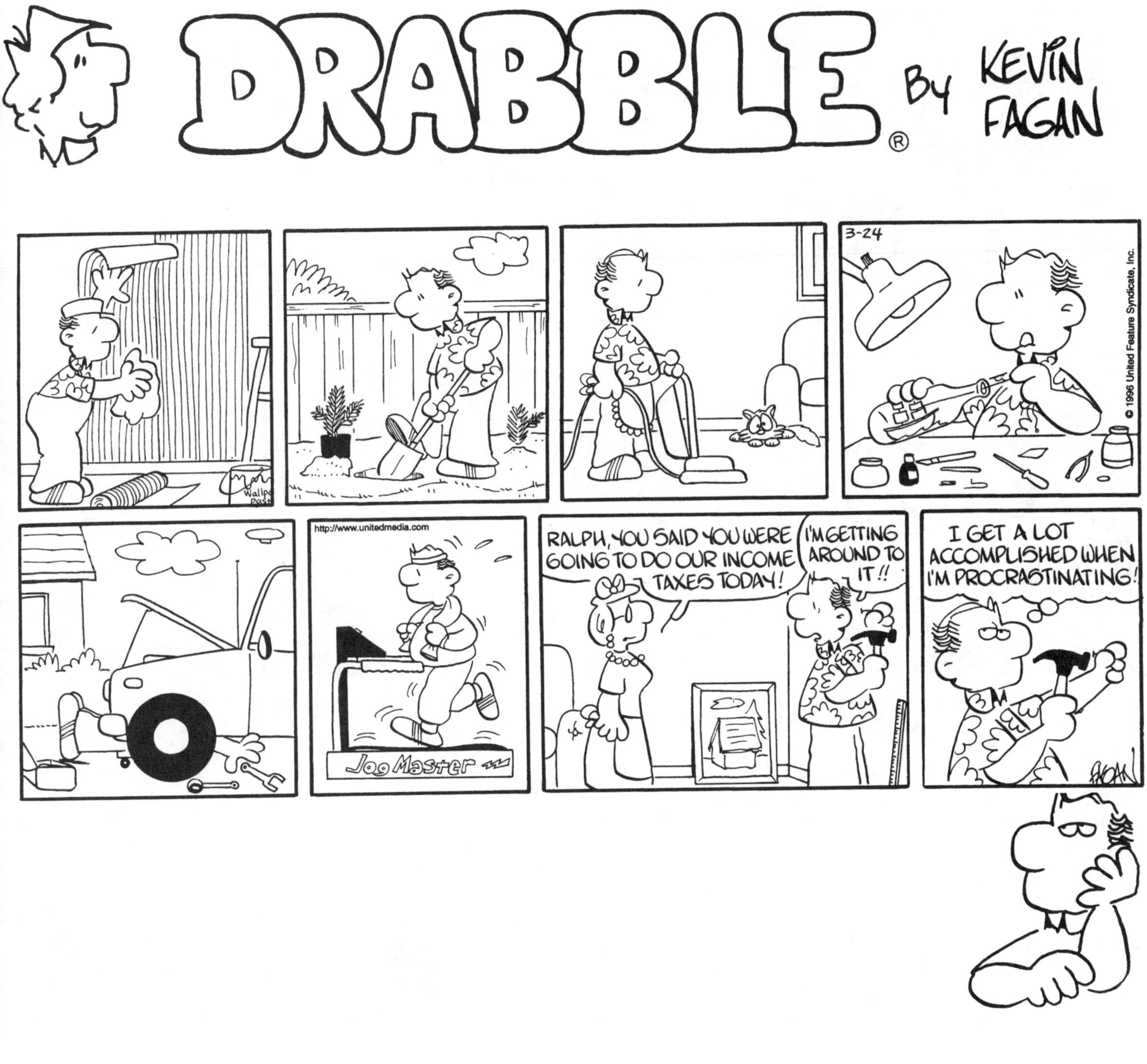
DRABBLE
By KEVIN FAGAN
3-24
© 1996 United Feature Syndicate, Inc.
http://www.unitedmedia.com
Jog Master
RALPH, YOU SAID YOU WERE GOING TO DO OUR INCOME TAXES TODAY!
I'M GETTING AROUND TO IT!!
I GET A LOT ACCOMPLISHED WHEN I'M PROCRASTINATING!
FAGAN

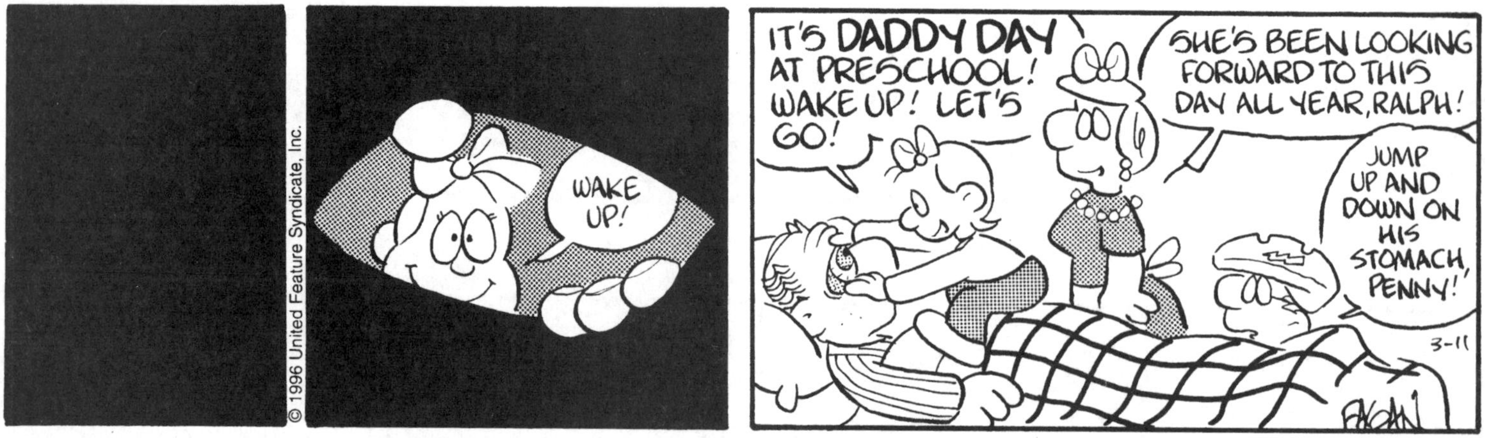
© 1996 United Feature Syndicate, Inc.
WAKE UP!
IT'S DADDY DAY AT PRESCHOOL! WAKE UP! LET'S GO!
SHE'S BEEN LOOKING FORWARD TO THIS DAY ALL YEAR, RALPH!
JUMP UP AND DOWN ON HIS STOMACH, PENNY!
3-11
FAGAN

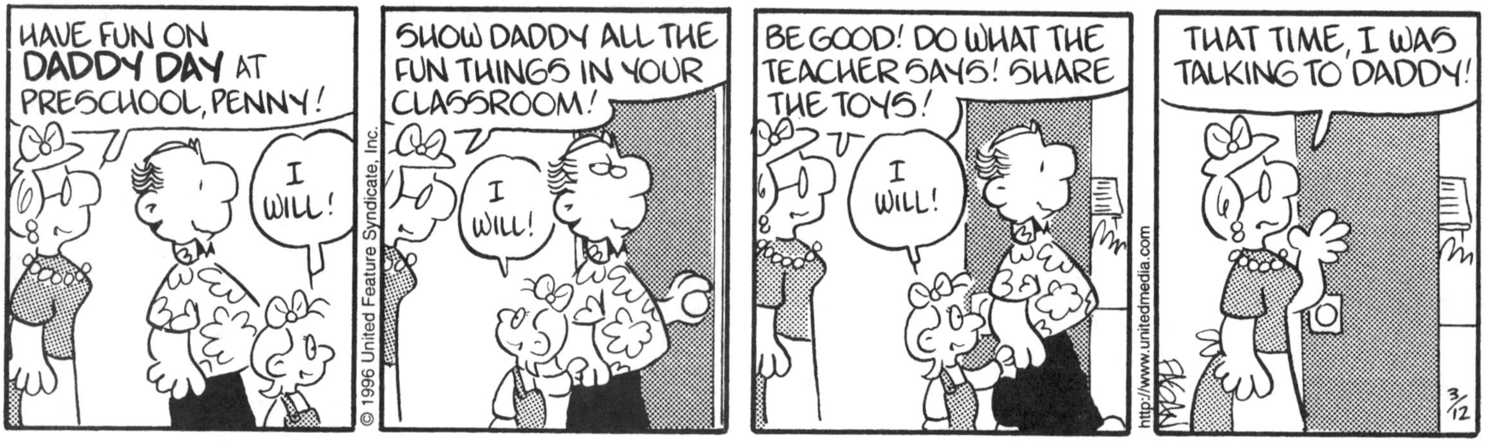
HAVE FUN ON DADDY DAY AT PRESCHOOL, PENNY!
I WILL!
© 1996 United Feature Syndicate, Inc.
SHOW DADDY ALL THE FUN THINGS IN YOUR CLASSROOM!
I WILL!
BE GOOD! DO WHAT THE TEACHER SAYS! SHARE THE TOYS!
I WILL!
http://www.unitedmedia.com
THAT TIME, I WAS TALKING TO DADDY!
3/12

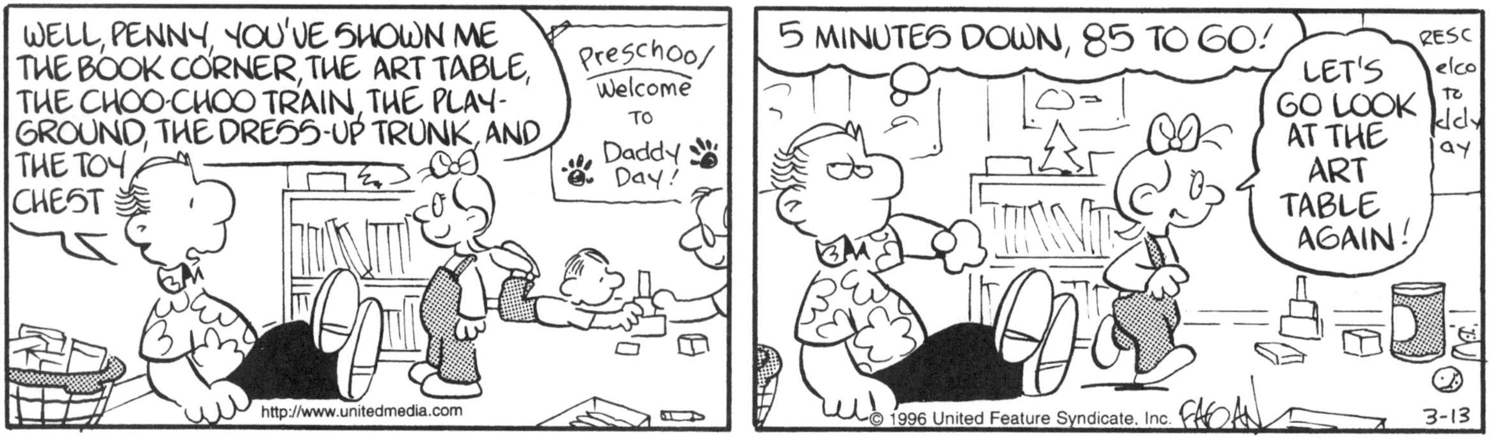
WELL, PENNY, YOU'VE SHOWN ME THE BOOK CORNER, THE ART TABLE, THE CHOO-CHOO TRAIN, THE PLAYGROUND, THE DRESS-UP TRUNK, AND THE TOY CHEST
Preschool
Welcome to Daddy Day!
http://www.unitedmedia.com
5 MINUTES DOWN, 85 TO GO!
LET'S GO LOOK AT THE ART TABLE AGAIN!
© 1996 United Feature Syndicate, Inc.
FAGAN
3-13

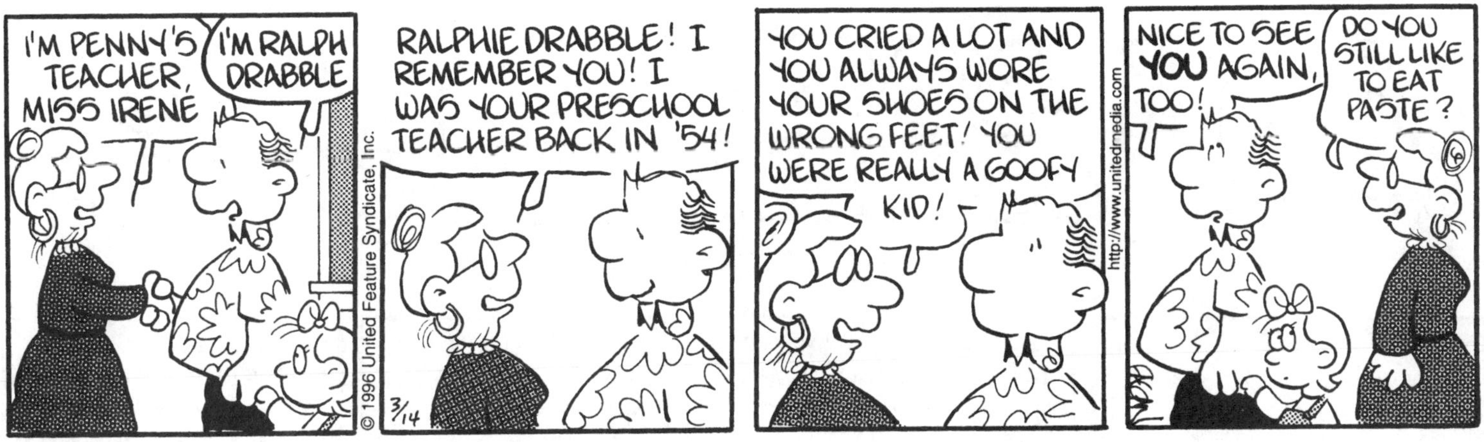
I'M PENNY'S TEACHER, MISS IRENE
I'M RALPH DRABBLE
© 1996 United Feature Syndicate, Inc.
3/14
RALPHIE DRABBLE! I REMEMBER YOU! I WAS YOUR PRESCHOOL TEACHER BACK IN '54!
YOU CRIED A LOT AND YOU ALWAYS WORE YOUR SHOES ON THE WRONG FEET! YOU WERE REALLY A GOOFY KID!
http://www.unitedmedia.com
NICE TO SEE **YOU** AGAIN, TOO!
DO YOU STILL LIKE TO EAT PASTE?

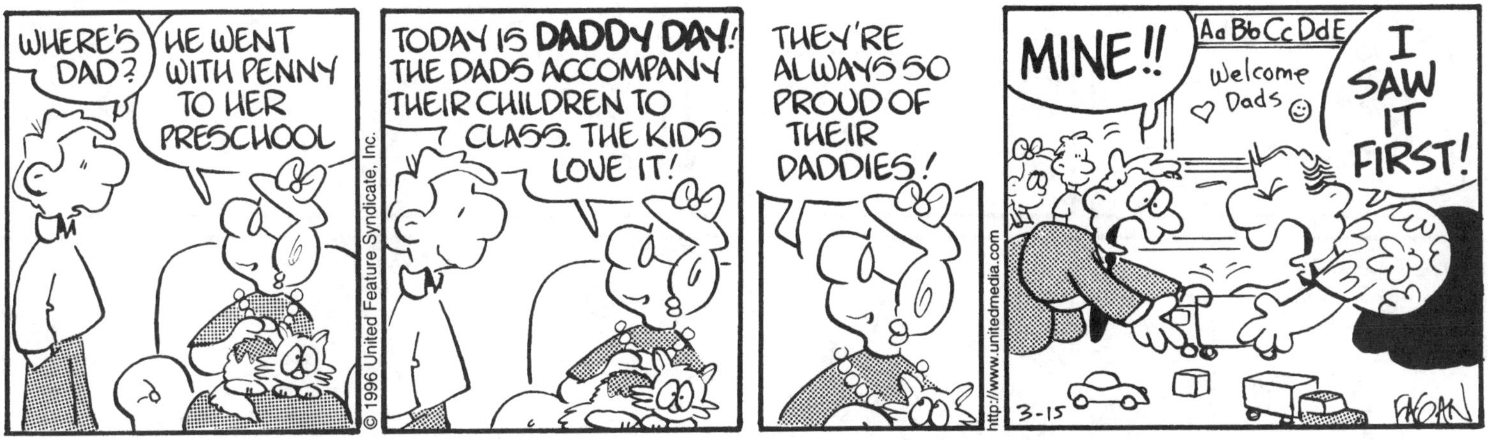
WHERE'S DAD?
HE WENT WITH PENNY TO HER PRESCHOOL
© 1996 United Feature Syndicate, Inc.
TODAY IS **DADDY DAY**! THE DADS ACCOMPANY THEIR CHILDREN TO CLASS. THE KIDS LOVE IT!
THEY'RE ALWAYS SO PROUD OF THEIR DADDIES!
http://www.unitedmedia.com
Aa Bb Cc Dd E
Welcome Dads
MINE!!
I SAW IT FIRST!
3-15
FAGAN

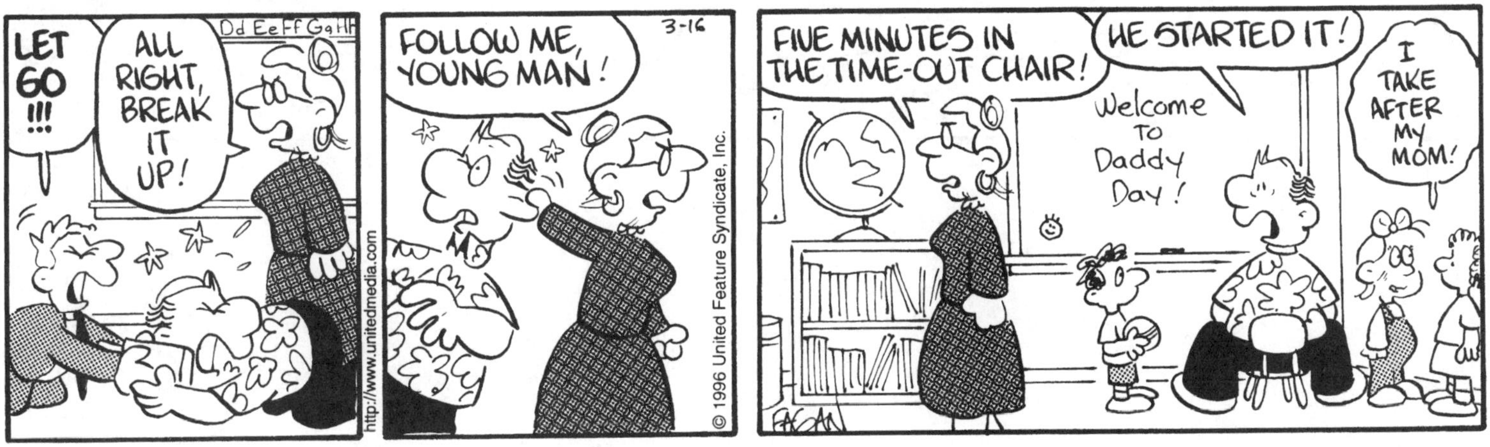
Dd Ee Ff Gg H
LET GO!!!
ALL RIGHT, BREAK IT UP!
http://www.unitedmedia.com
3-16
FOLLOW ME, YOUNG MAN!
© 1996 United Feature Syndicate, Inc.
FIVE MINUTES IN THE TIME-OUT CHAIR!
HE STARTED IT!
Welcome To Daddy Day!
I TAKE AFTER MY MOM!
FAGAN

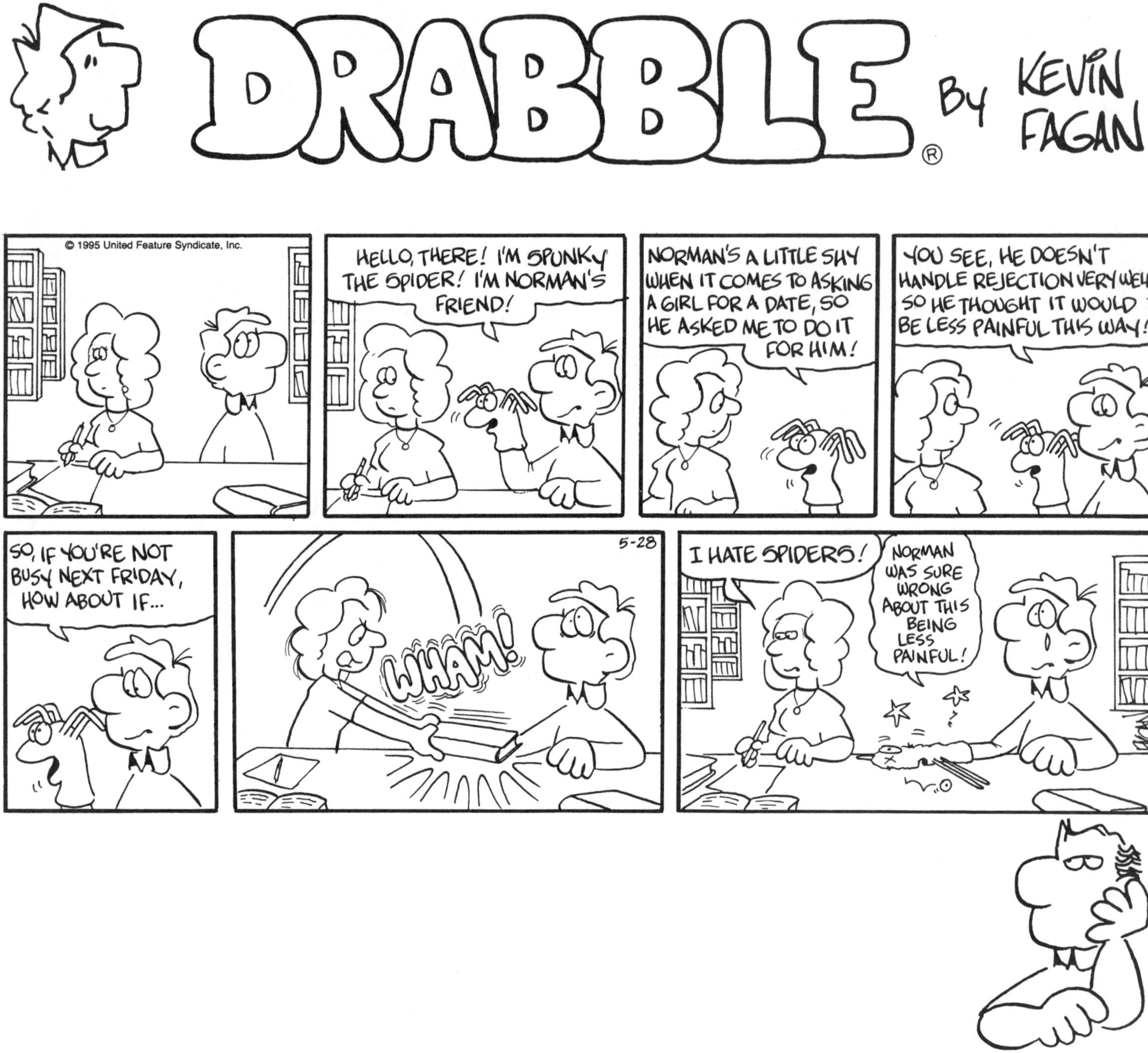

DRABBLE
By KEVIN FAGAN
© 1995 United Feature Syndicate, Inc.
HELLO, THERE! I'M SPUNKY THE SPIDER! I'M NORMAN'S FRIEND!
NORMAN'S A LITTLE SHY WHEN IT COMES TO ASKING A GIRL FOR A DATE, SO HE ASKED ME TO DO IT FOR HIM!
YOU SEE, HE DOESN'T HANDLE REJECTION VERY WELL, SO HE THOUGHT IT WOULD BE LESS PAINFUL THIS WAY!
SO, IF YOU'RE NOT BUSY NEXT FRIDAY, HOW ABOUT IF...
5-28
WHAM!
I HATE SPIDERS!
NORMAN WAS SURE WRONG ABOUT THIS BEING LESS PAINFUL!

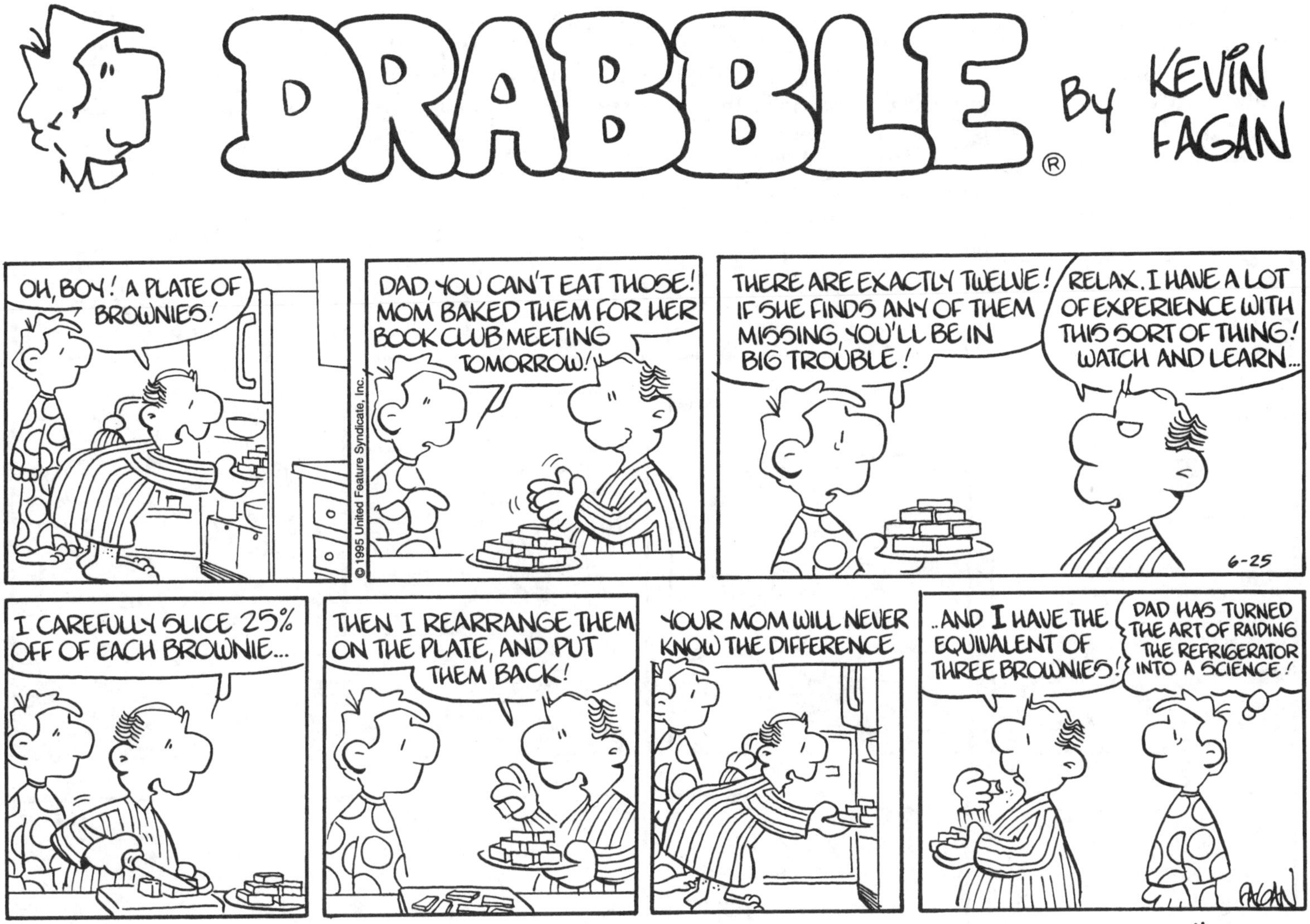
DRABBLE®
By KEVIN FAGAN
OH, BOY! A PLATE OF BROWNIES!
DAD, YOU CAN'T EAT THOSE! MOM BAKED THEM FOR HER BOOK CLUB MEETING TOMORROW!
© 1995 United Feature Syndicate, Inc.
THERE ARE EXACTLY TWELVE! IF SHE FINDS ANY OF THEM MISSING, YOU'LL BE IN BIG TROUBLE!
RELAX. I HAVE A LOT OF EXPERIENCE WITH THIS SORT OF THING! WATCH AND LEARN...
6-25
I CAREFULLY SLICE 25% OFF OF EACH BROWNIE...
THEN I REARRANGE THEM ON THE PLATE, AND PUT THEM BACK!
YOUR MOM WILL NEVER KNOW THE DIFFERENCE
..AND I HAVE THE EQUIVALENT OF THREE BROWNIES!
DAD HAS TURNED THE ART OF RAIDING THE REFRIGERATOR INTO A SCIENCE!
FAGAN

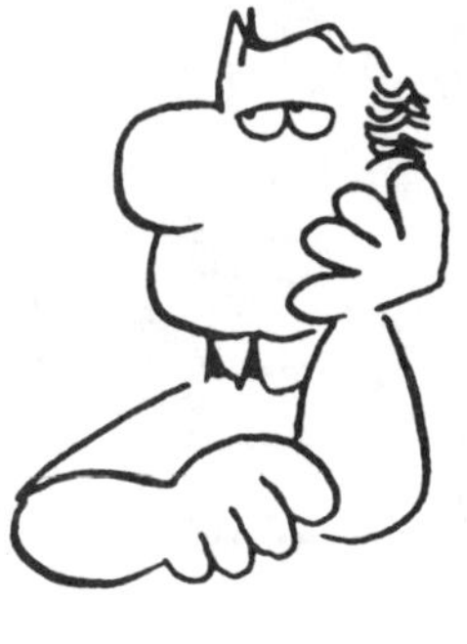

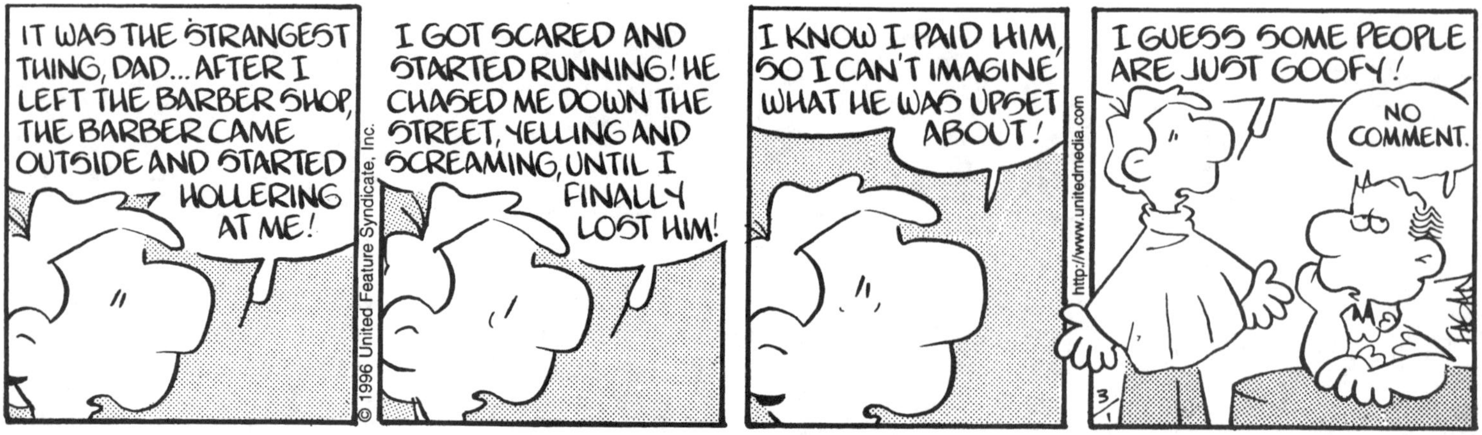
IT WAS THE STRANGEST THING, DAD... AFTER I LEFT THE BARBER SHOP, THE BARBER CAME OUTSIDE AND STARTED HOLLERING AT ME!
© 1996 United Feature Syndicate, Inc.
I GOT SCARED AND STARTED RUNNING! HE CHASED ME DOWN THE STREET, YELLING AND SCREAMING, UNTIL I FINALLY LOST HIM!
I KNOW I PAID HIM, SO I CAN'T IMAGINE WHAT HE WAS UPSET ABOUT!
http://www.unitedmedia.com
I GUESS SOME PEOPLE ARE JUST GOOFY!
NO COMMENT.
FAGAN

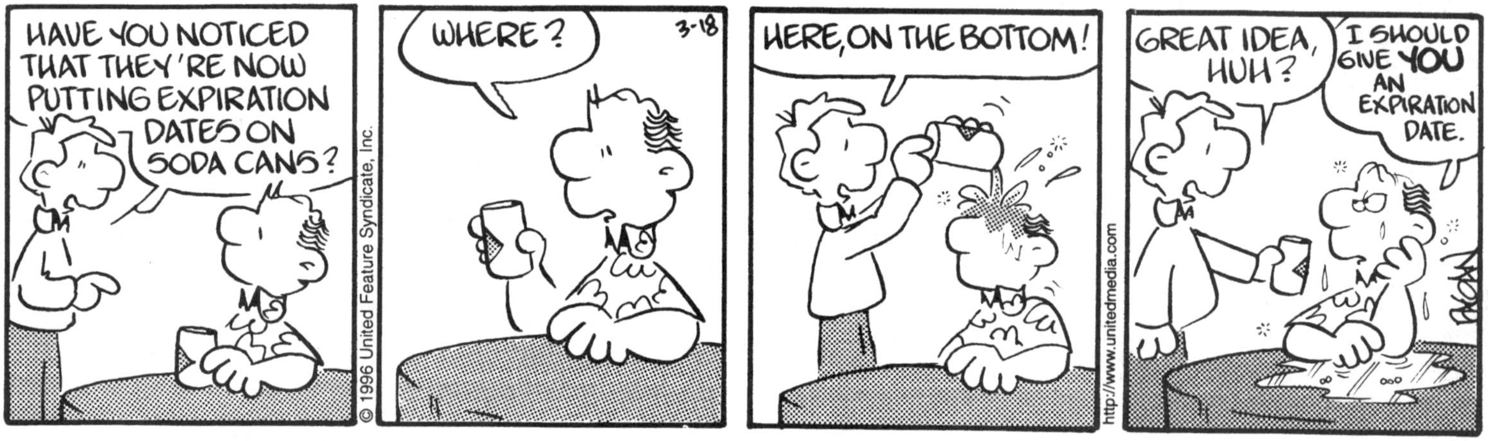
HAVE YOU NOTICED THAT THEY'RE NOW PUTTING EXPIRATION DATES ON SODA CANS?
© 1996 United Feature Syndicate, Inc.
3-18
WHERE?
HERE, ON THE BOTTOM!
http://www.unitedmedia.com
GREAT IDEA, HUH?
I SHOULD GIVE YOU AN EXPIRATION DATE.
FAGAN

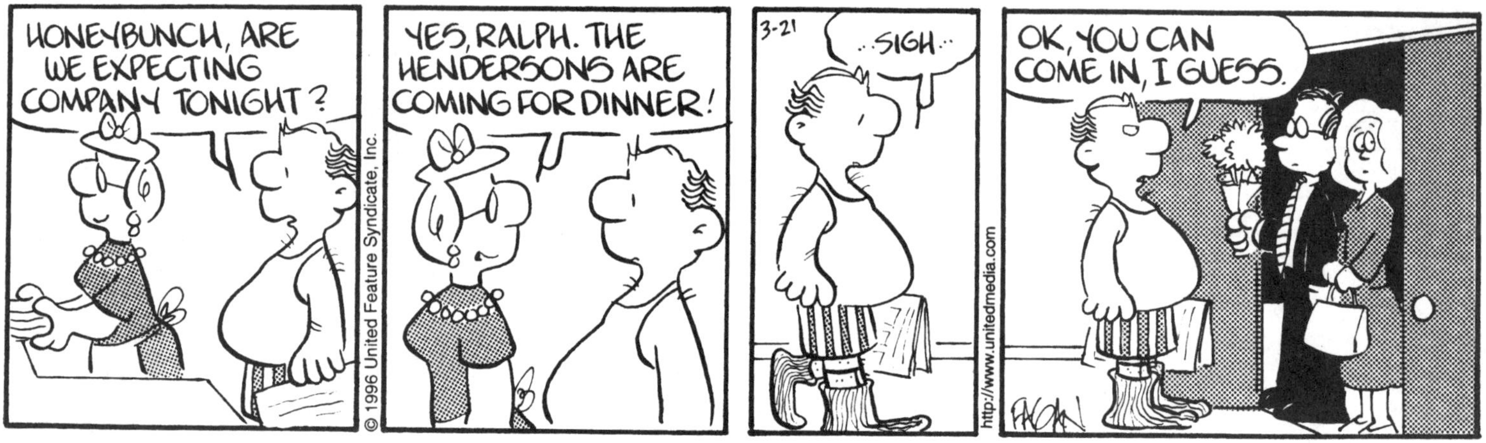
HONEYBUNCH, ARE WE EXPECTING COMPANY TONIGHT?
© 1996 United Feature Syndicate, Inc.
YES, RALPH. THE HENDERSONS ARE COMING FOR DINNER!
3-21
...SIGH...
http://www.unitedmedia.com
OK, YOU CAN COME IN, I GUESS.
FAGAN

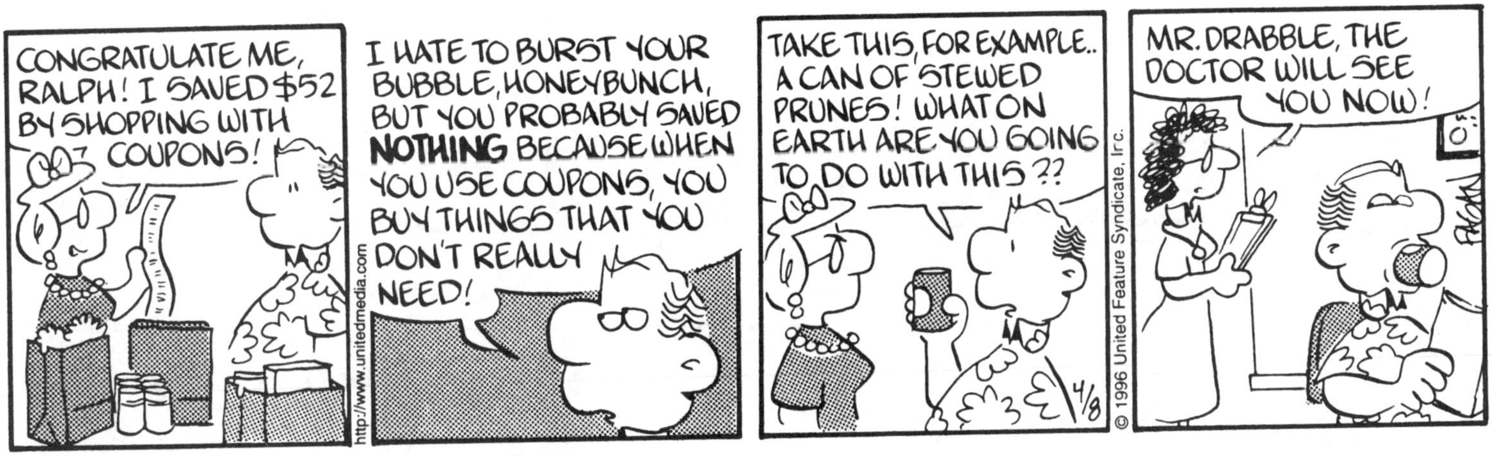
CONGRATULATE ME, RALPH! I SAVED $52 BY SHOPPING WITH COUPONS!
I HATE TO BURST YOUR BUBBLE, HONEYBUNCH, BUT YOU PROBABLY SAVED NOTHING BECAUSE WHEN YOU USE COUPONS, YOU BUY THINGS THAT YOU DON'T REALLY NEED!
http://www.unitedmedia.com
TAKE THIS, FOR EXAMPLE.. A CAN OF STEWED PRUNES! WHAT ON EARTH ARE YOU GOING TO DO WITH THIS??
4/8
© 1996 United Feature Syndicate, Inc.
MR. DRABBLE, THE DOCTOR WILL SEE YOU NOW!
FAGAN

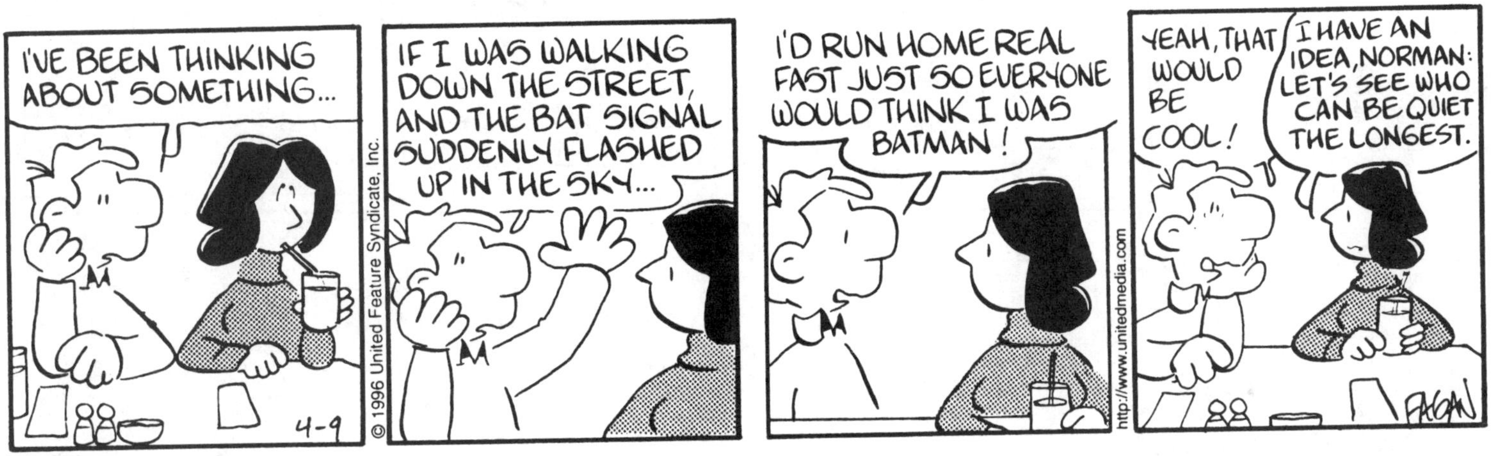
I'VE BEEN THINKING ABOUT SOMETHING...
4-9
© 1996 United Feature Syndicate, Inc.
IF I WAS WALKING DOWN THE STREET, AND THE BAT SIGNAL SUDDENLY FLASHED UP IN THE SKY...
I'D RUN HOME REAL FAST JUST SO EVERYONE WOULD THINK I WAS BATMAN!
http://www.unitedmedia.com
YEAH, THAT WOULD BE COOL!
I HAVE AN IDEA, NORMAN: LET'S SEE WHO CAN BE QUIET THE LONGEST.
FAGAN

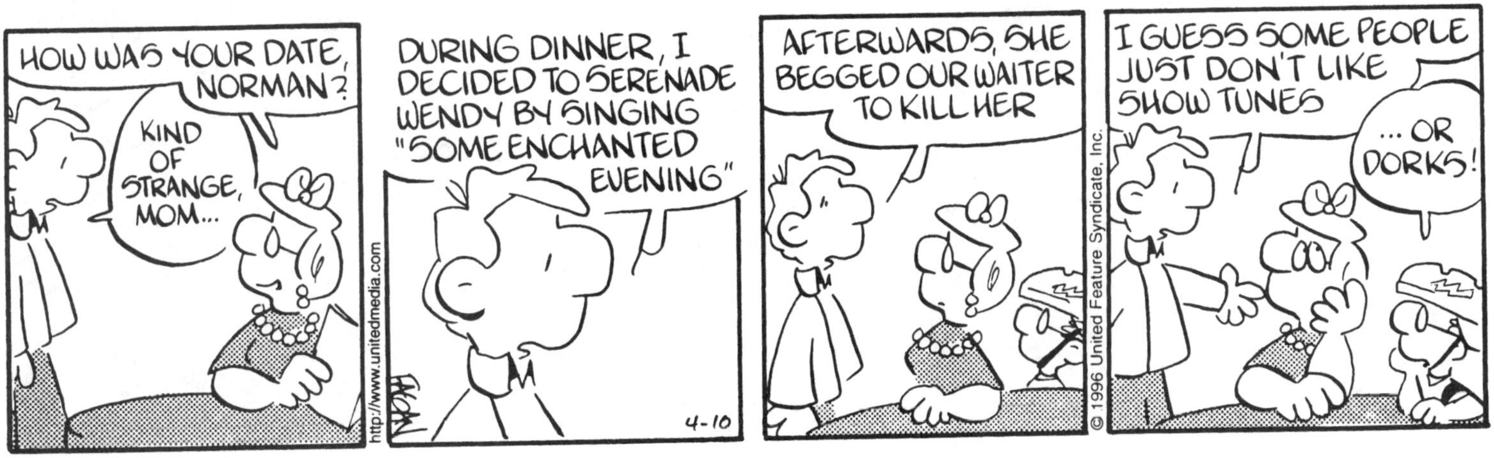
HOW WAS YOUR DATE, NORMAN?
KIND OF STRANGE, MOM...
http://www.unitedmedia.com
FAGAN
DURING DINNER, I DECIDED TO SERENADE WENDY BY SINGING "SOME ENCHANTED EVENING"
4-10
AFTERWARDS, SHE BEGGED OUR WAITER TO KILL HER
© 1996 United Feature Syndicate, Inc.
I GUESS SOME PEOPLE JUST DON'T LIKE SHOW TUNES
...OR DORKS!

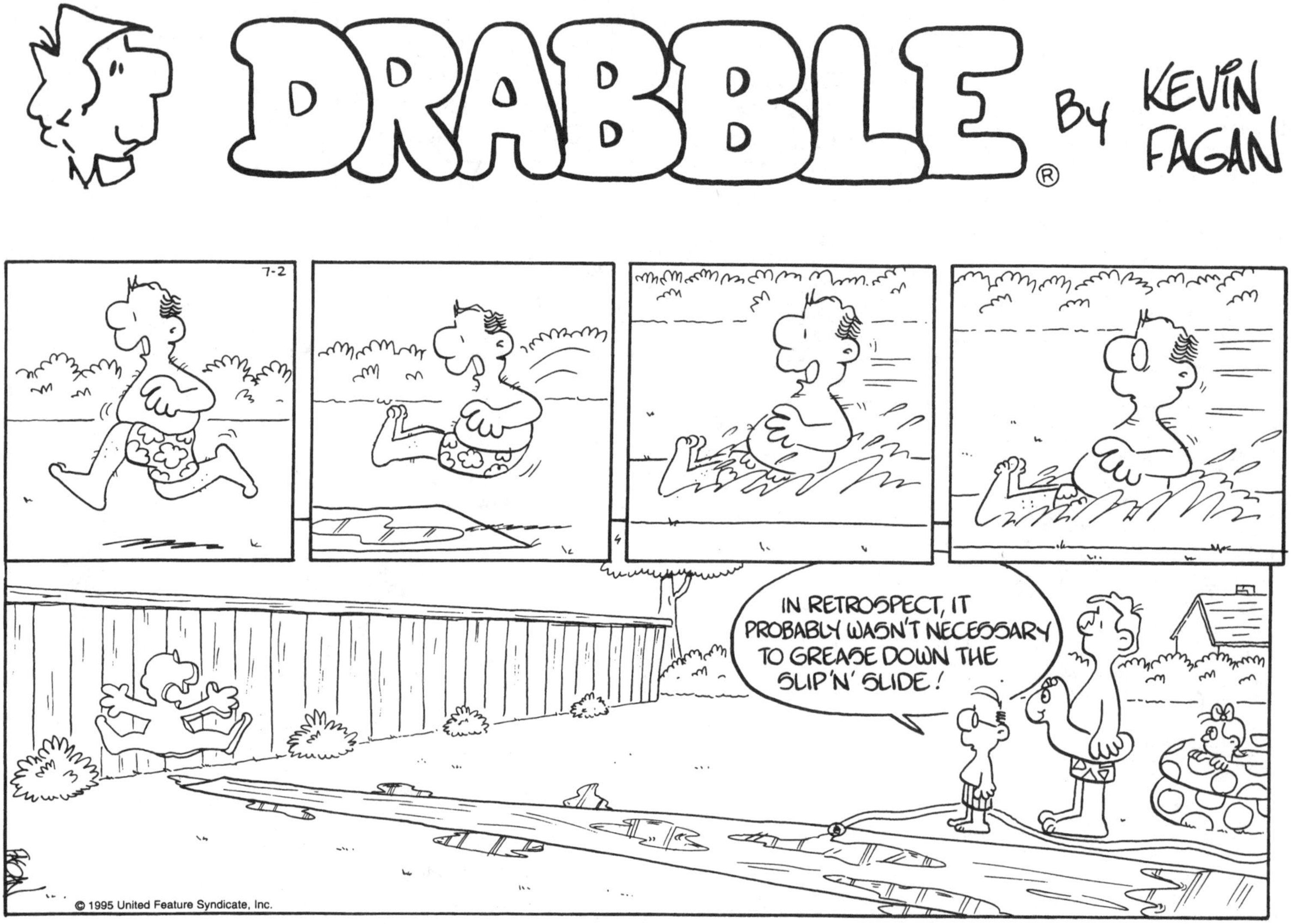
DRABBLE
By KEVIN FAGAN
7-2
IN RETROSPECT, IT PROBABLY WASN'T NECESSARY TO GREASE DOWN THE SLIP'N' SLIDE!
© 1995 United Feature Syndicate, Inc.

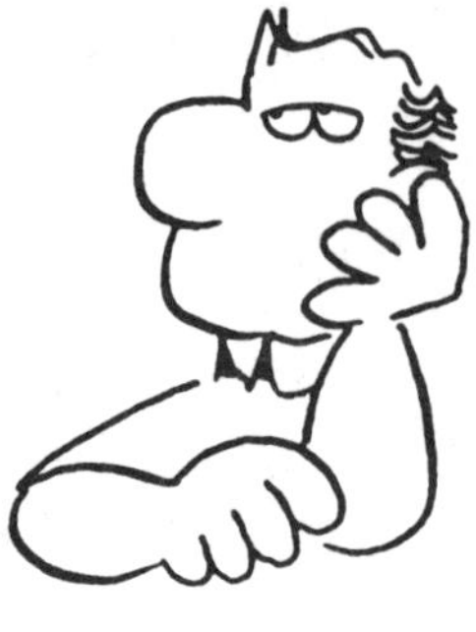

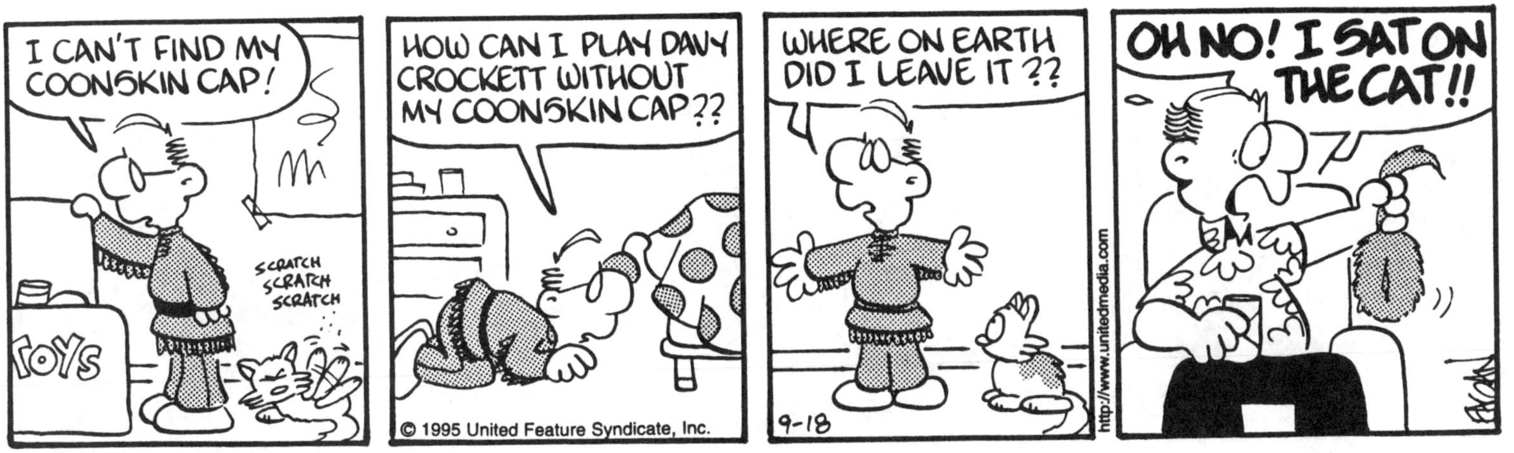
I CAN'T FIND MY COONSKIN CAP!
TOYS
SCRATCH SCRATCH SCRATCH
HOW CAN I PLAY DAVY CROCKETT WITHOUT MY COONSKIN CAP??
© 1995 United Feature Syndicate, Inc.
WHERE ON EARTH DID I LEAVE IT??
9-18
http://www.unitedmedia.com
OH NO! I SAT ON THE CAT!!

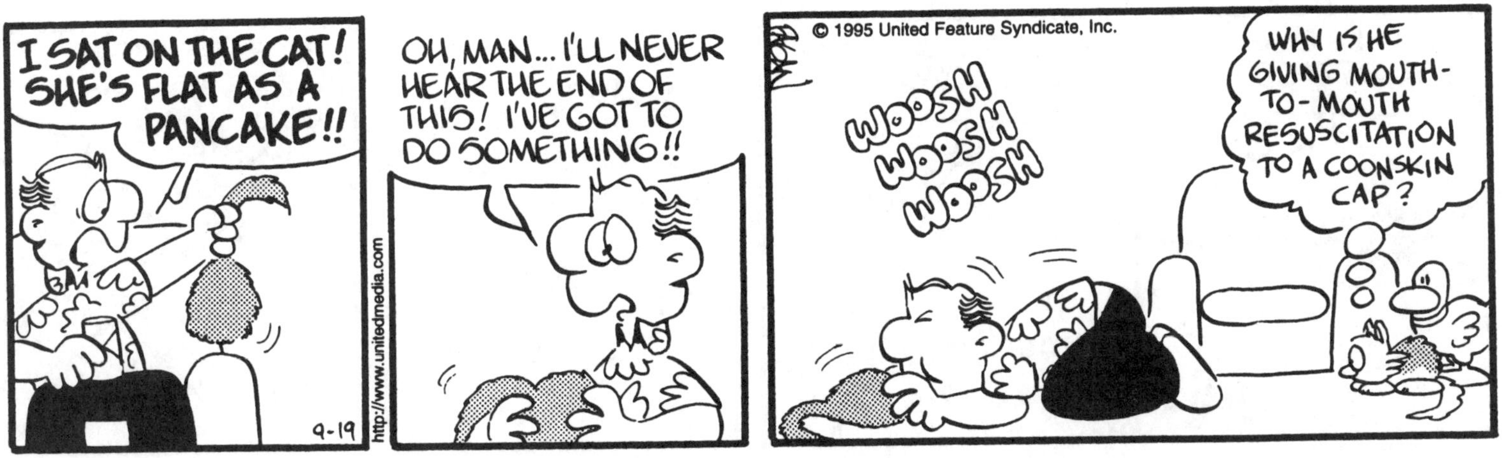
I SAT ON THE CAT! SHE'S FLAT AS A PANCAKE!!
9-19
http://www.unitedmedia.com
OH, MAN... I'LL NEVER HEAR THE END OF THIS! I'VE GOT TO DO SOMETHING!!
© 1995 United Feature Syndicate, Inc.
WOOSH WOOSH WOOSH
WHY IS HE GIVING MOUTH-TO-MOUTH RESUSCITATION TO A COONSKIN CAP?

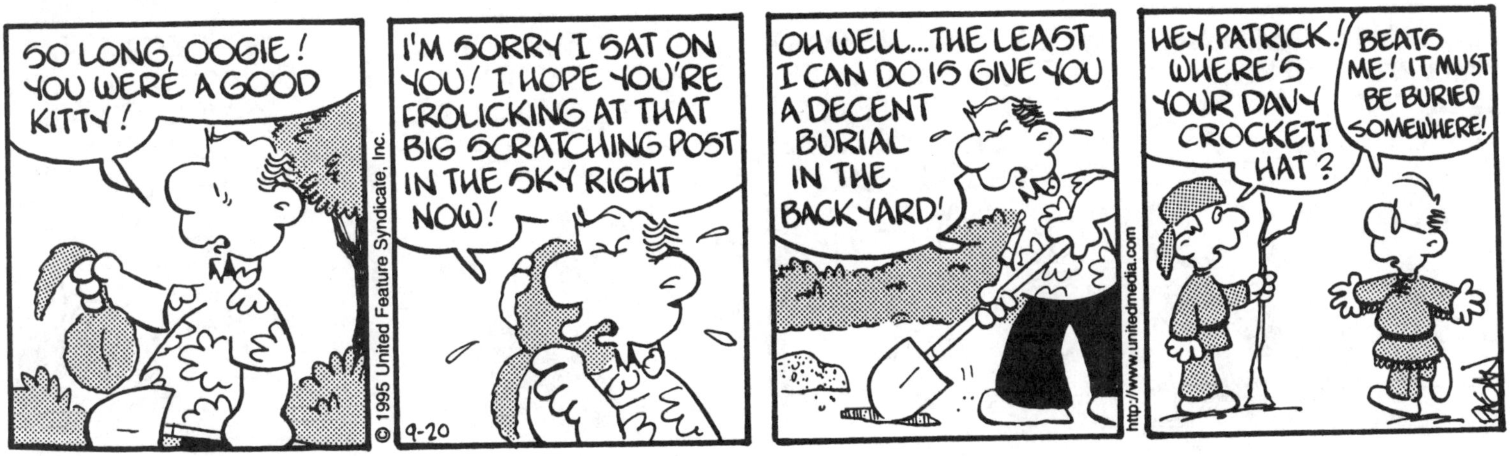
SO LONG, OOGIE! YOU WERE A GOOD KITTY!
© 1995 United Feature Syndicate, Inc.
I'M SORRY I SAT ON YOU! I HOPE YOU'RE FROLICKING AT THAT BIG SCRATCHING POST IN THE SKY RIGHT NOW!
9-20
OH WELL... THE LEAST I CAN DO IS GIVE YOU A DECENT BURIAL IN THE BACKYARD!
http://www.unitedmedia.com
HEY, PATRICK! WHERE'S YOUR DAVY CROCKETT HAT?
BEATS ME! IT MUST BE BURIED SOMEWHERE!

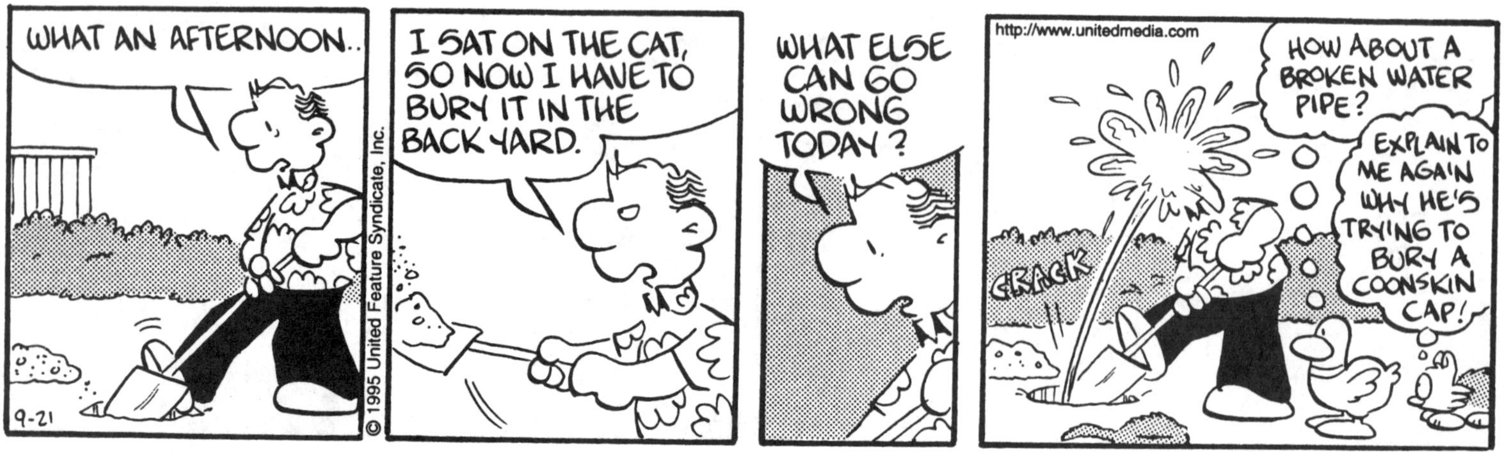
WHAT AN AFTERNOON..
9-21
© 1995 United Feature Syndicate, Inc.
I SAT ON THE CAT, SO NOW I HAVE TO BURY IT IN THE BACK YARD.
WHAT ELSE CAN GO WRONG TODAY?
http://www.unitedmedia.com
HOW ABOUT A BROKEN WATER PIPE?
CRACK
EXPLAIN TO ME AGAIN WHY HE'S TRYING TO BURY A COONSKIN CAP!

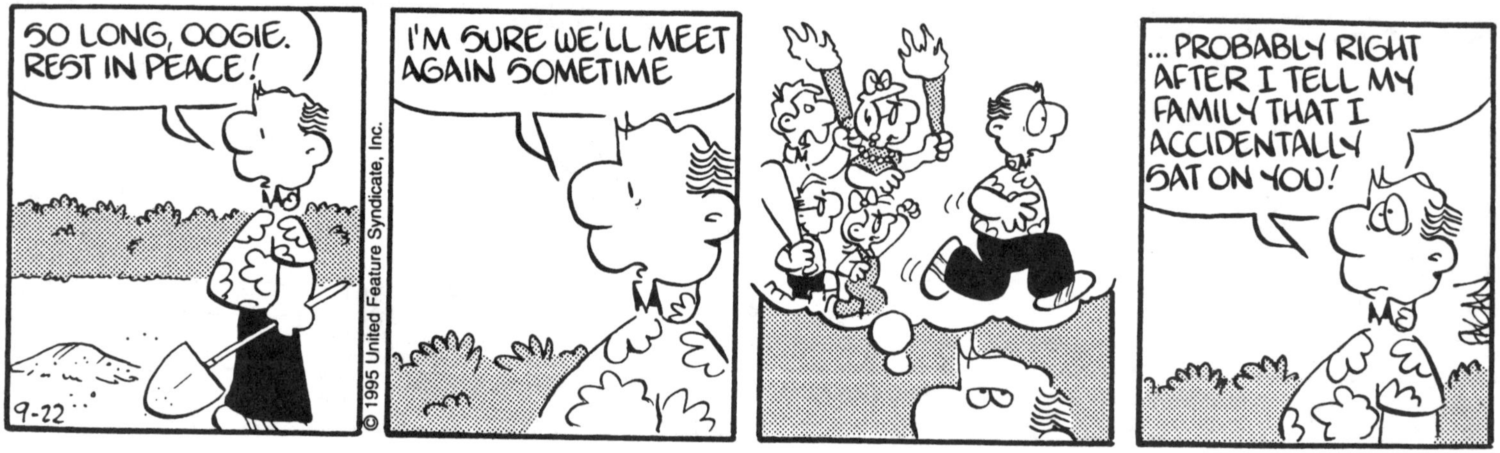
SO LONG, OOGIE. REST IN PEACE!
9-22
© 1995 United Feature Syndicate, Inc.
I'M SURE WE'LL MEET AGAIN SOMETIME
...PROBABLY RIGHT AFTER I TELL MY FAMILY THAT I ACCIDENTALLY SAT ON YOU!

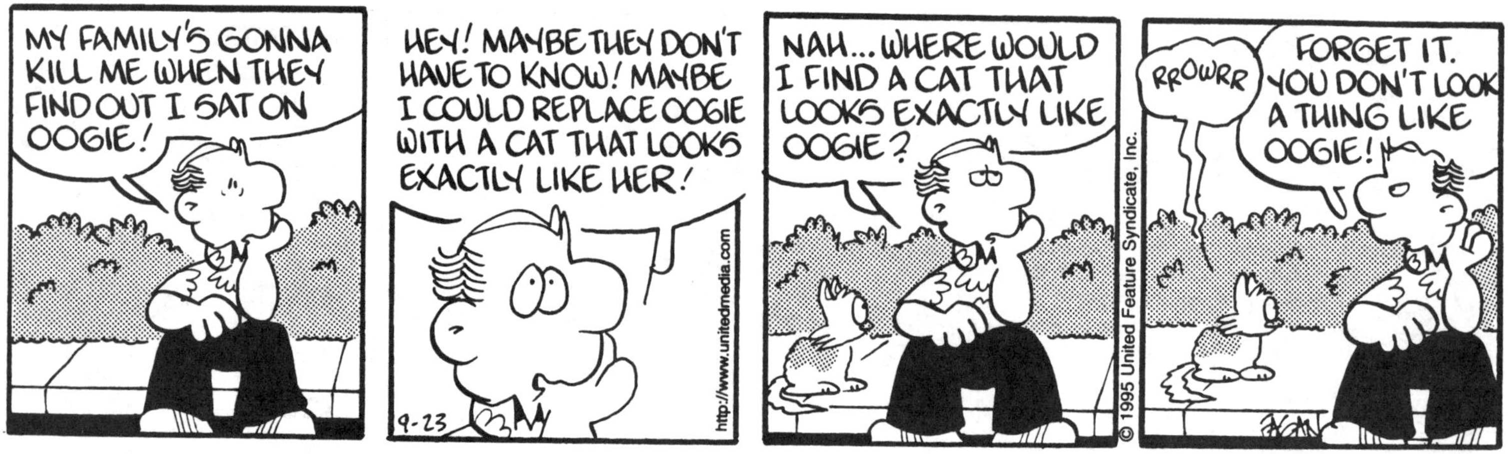
MY FAMILY'S GONNA KILL ME WHEN THEY FIND OUT I SAT ON OOGIE!
HEY! MAYBE THEY DON'T HAVE TO KNOW! MAYBE I COULD REPLACE OOGIE WITH A CAT THAT LOOKS EXACTLY LIKE HER!
9-23
http://www.unitedmedia.com
NAH... WHERE WOULD I FIND A CAT THAT LOOKS EXACTLY LIKE OOGIE?
© 1995 United Feature Syndicate, Inc.
RROWRR
FORGET IT. YOU DON'T LOOK A THING LIKE OOGIE!

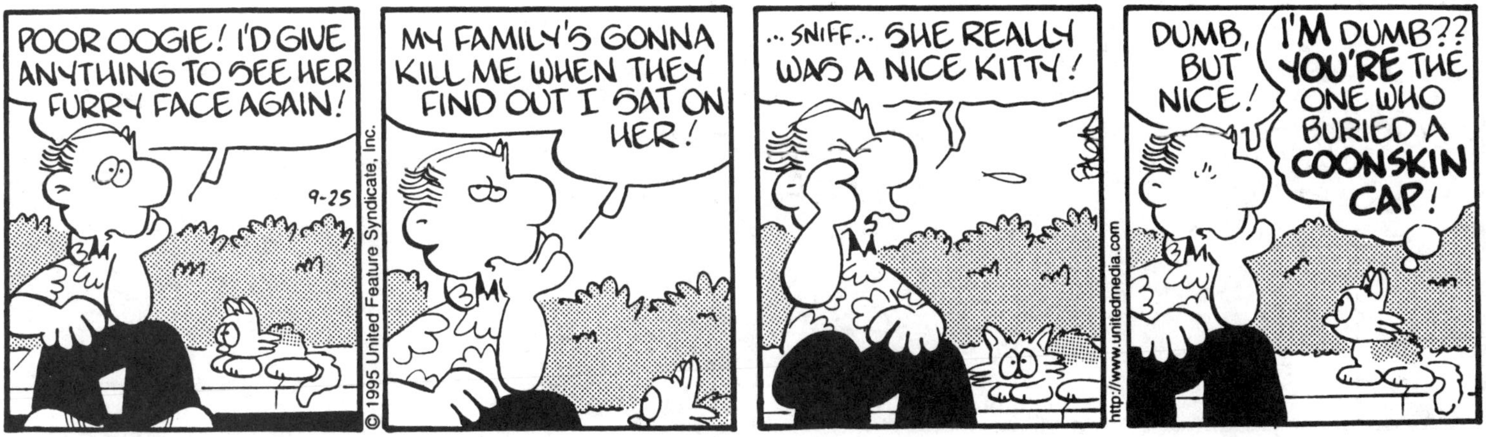
POOR OOGIE! I'D GIVE ANYTHING TO SEE HER FURRY FACE AGAIN!
9-25
© 1995 United Feature Syndicate, Inc.
MY FAMILY'S GONNA KILL ME WHEN THEY FIND OUT I SAT ON HER!
... SNIFF... SHE REALLY WAS A NICE KITTY!
http://www.unitedmedia.com
DUMB, BUT NICE!
I'M DUMB?? YOU'RE THE ONE WHO BURIED A COONSKIN CAP!

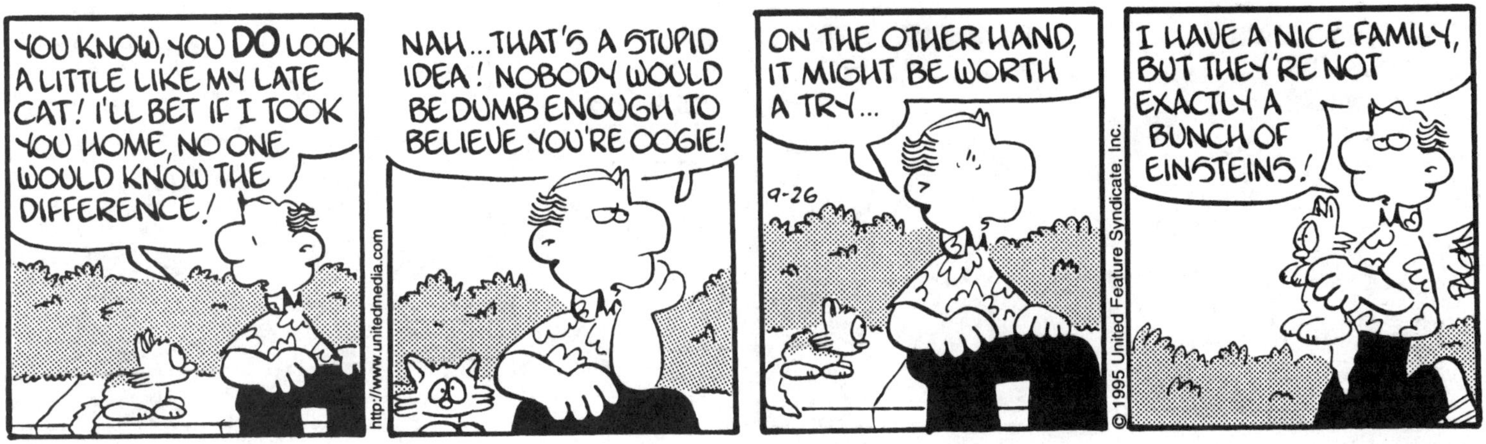
YOU KNOW, YOU DO LOOK A LITTLE LIKE MY LATE CAT! I'LL BET IF I TOOK YOU HOME, NO ONE WOULD KNOW THE DIFFERENCE!
http://www.unitedmedia.com
NAH... THAT'S A STUPID IDEA! NOBODY WOULD BE DUMB ENOUGH TO BELIEVE YOU'RE OOGIE!
ON THE OTHER HAND, IT MIGHT BE WORTH A TRY...
9-26
© 1995 United Feature Syndicate, Inc.
I HAVE A NICE FAMILY, BUT THEY'RE NOT EXACTLY A BUNCH OF EINSTEINS!

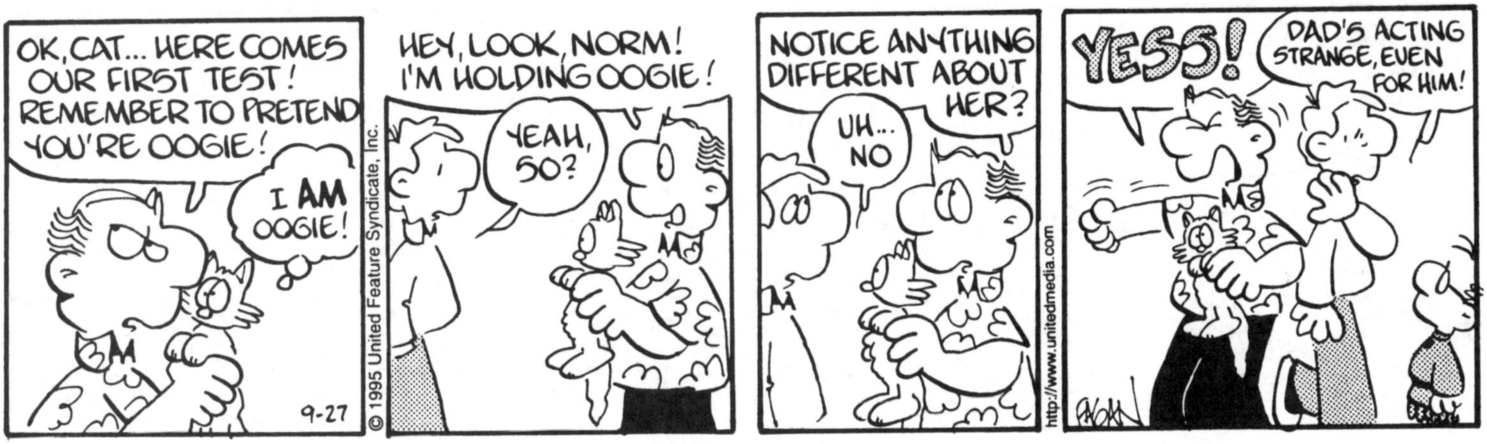
OK, CAT... HERE COMES OUR FIRST TEST! REMEMBER TO PRETEND YOU'RE OOGIE!
I AM OOGIE!
9-27
© 1995 United Feature Syndicate, Inc.
HEY, LOOK, NORM! I'M HOLDING OOGIE!
YEAH, SO?
NOTICE ANYTHING DIFFERENT ABOUT HER?
UH... NO
http://www.unitedmedia.com
YESS!
DAD'S ACTING STRANGE, EVEN FOR HIM!

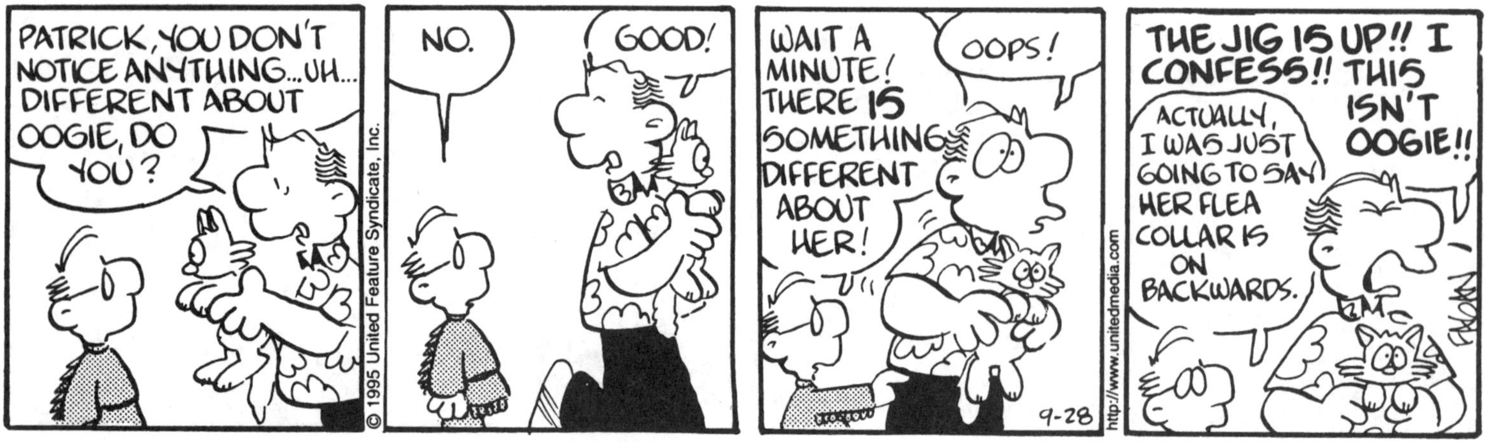
PATRICK, YOU DON'T NOTICE ANYTHING...UH... DIFFERENT ABOUT OOGIE, DO YOU?
© 1995 United Feature Syndicate, Inc.
NO.
GOOD!
WAIT A MINUTE! THERE IS SOMETHING DIFFERENT ABOUT HER!
OOPS!
9-28
http://www.unitedmedia.com
THE JIG IS UP!! I CONFESS!! THIS ISN'T OOGIE!!
ACTUALLY, I WAS JUST GOING TO SAY HER FLEA COLLAR IS ON BACKWARDS.

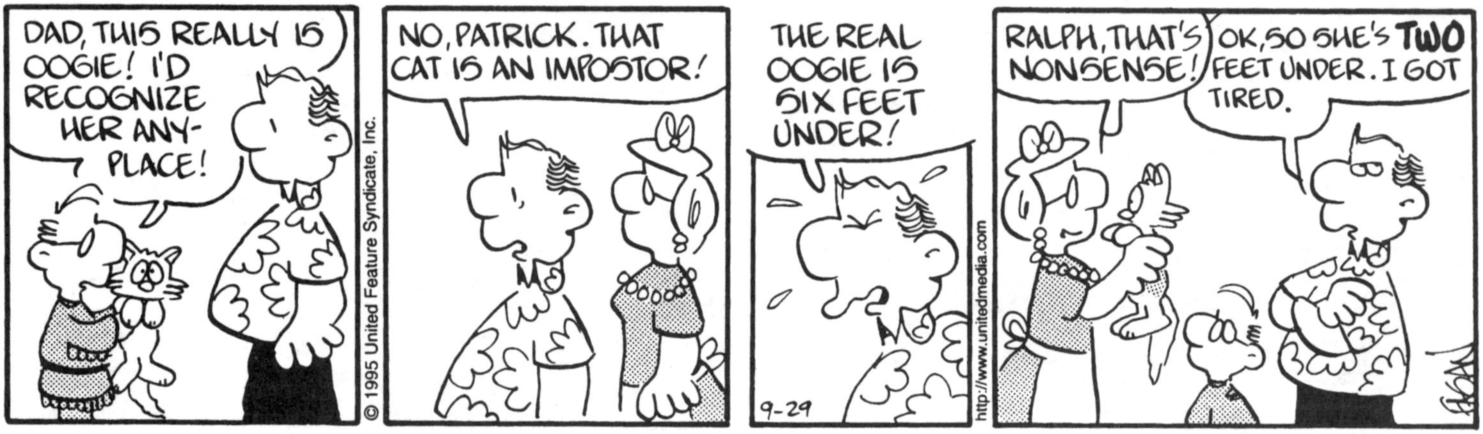
DAD, THIS REALLY IS OOGIE! I'D RECOGNIZE HER ANY-PLACE!
© 1995 United Feature Syndicate, Inc.
NO, PATRICK. THAT CAT IS AN IMPOSTOR!
THE REAL OOGIE IS SIX FEET UNDER!
9-29
http://www.unitedmedia.com
RALPH, THAT'S NONSENSE!
OK, SO SHE'S TWO FEET UNDER. I GOT TIRED.

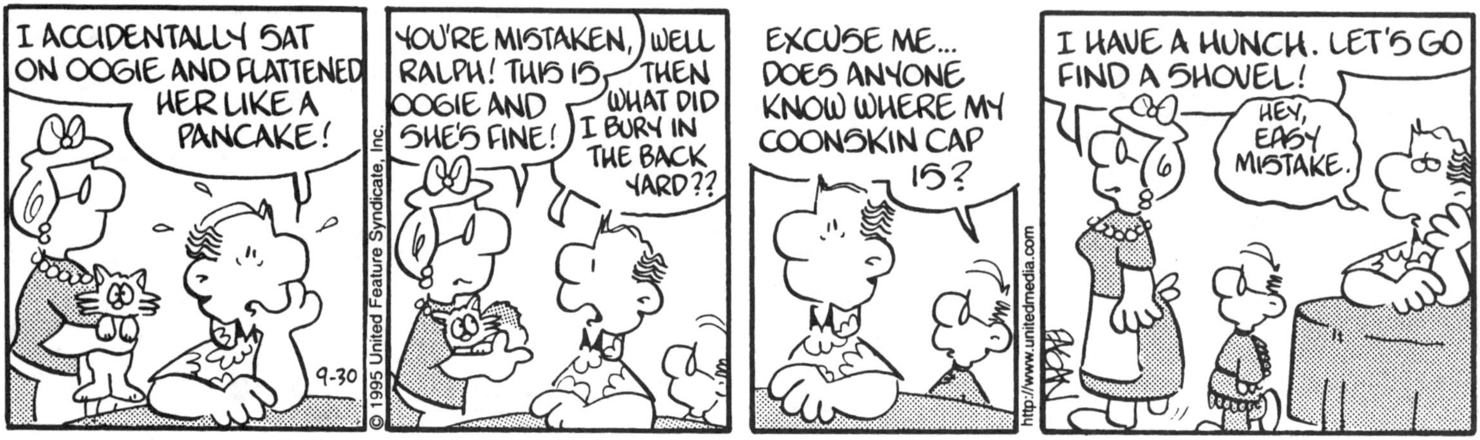
I ACCIDENTALLY SAT ON OOGIE AND FLATTENED HER LIKE A PANCAKE!
9-30
© 1995 United Feature Syndicate, Inc.
YOU'RE MISTAKEN, RALPH! THIS IS OOGIE AND SHE'S FINE!
WELL THEN WHAT DID I BURY IN THE BACK YARD??
EXCUSE ME... DOES ANYONE KNOW WHERE MY COONSKIN CAP IS?
http://www.unitedmedia.com
I HAVE A HUNCH. LET'S GO FIND A SHOVEL!
HEY, EASY MISTAKE.

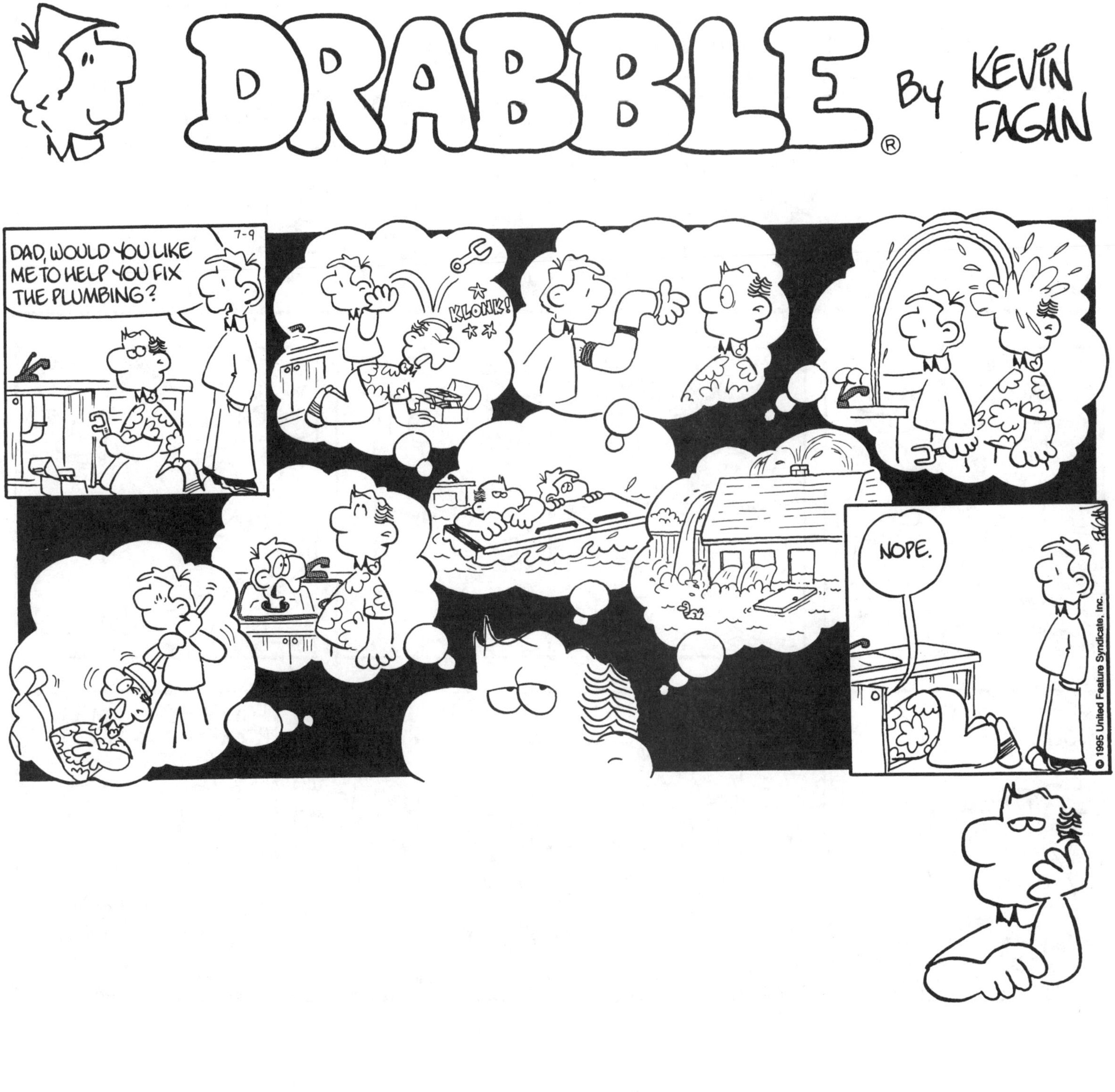
DRABBLE
By KEVIN FAGAN
7-9
DAD, WOULD YOU LIKE ME TO HELP YOU FIX THE PLUMBING?
KLONK!
NOPE.
© 1995 United Feature Syndicate, Inc.

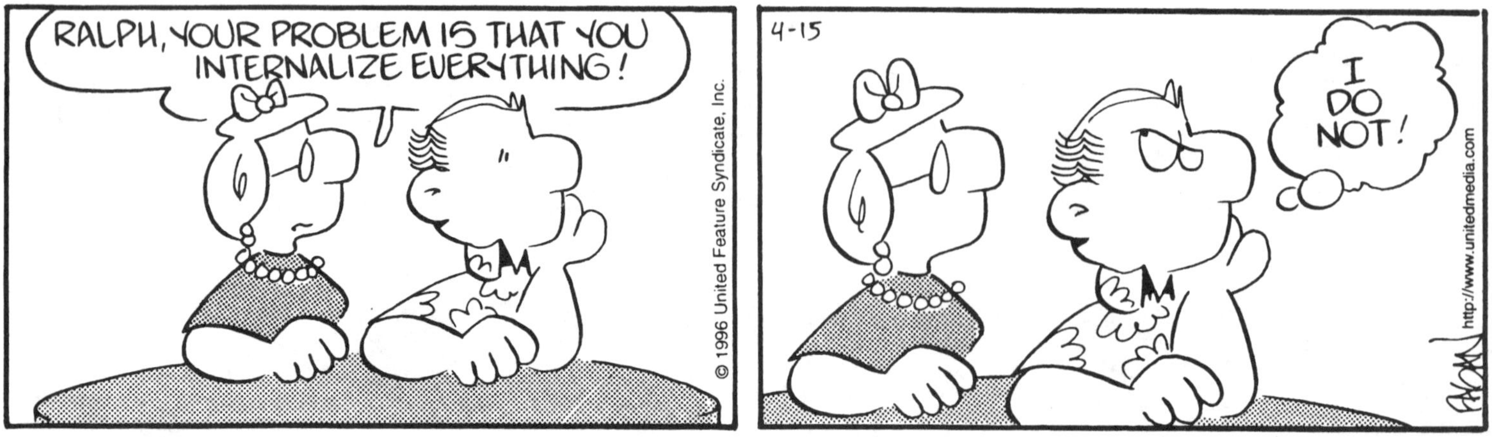
RALPH, YOUR PROBLEM IS THAT YOU INTERNALIZE EVERYTHING!
© 1996 United Feature Syndicate, Inc.
4-15
I DO NOT!
http://www.unitedmedia.com

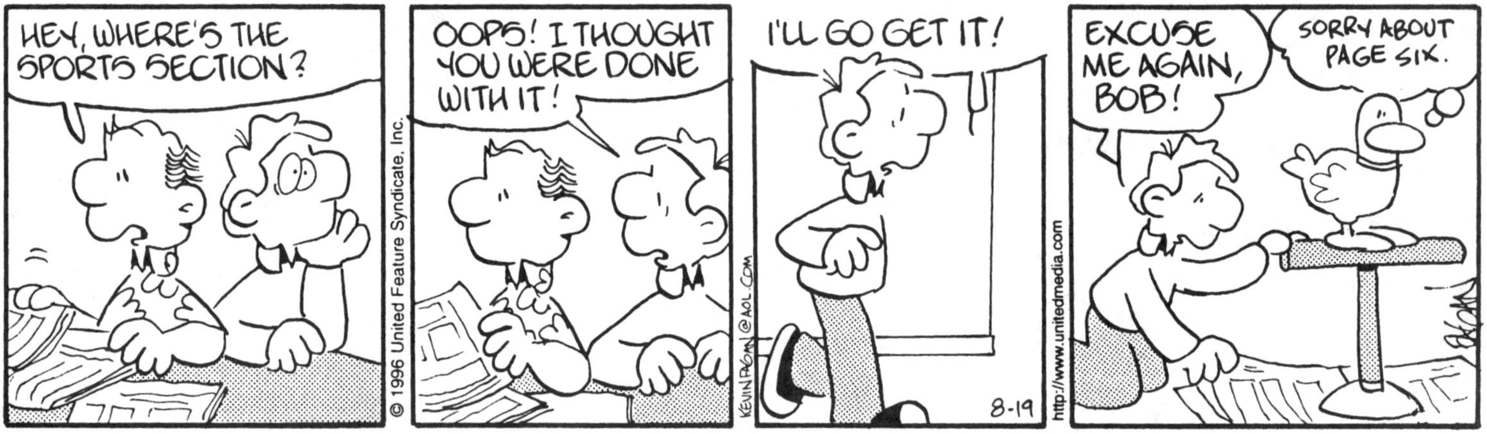
HEY, WHERE'S THE SPORTS SECTION?
© 1996 United Feature Syndicate, Inc.
OOPS! I THOUGHT YOU WERE DONE WITH IT!
KEVIN FAGAN @AOL.COM
I'LL GO GET IT!
8-19
http://www.unitedmedia.com
EXCUSE ME AGAIN, BOB!
SORRY ABOUT PAGE SIX.

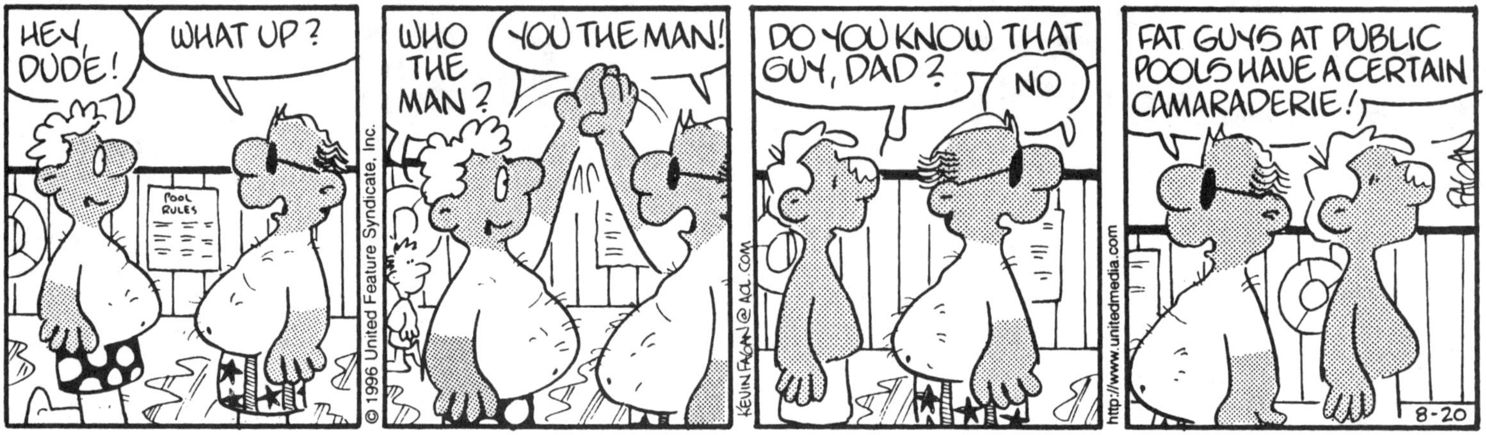
HEY, DUDE!
WHAT UP?
POOL RULES
© 1996 United Feature Syndicate, Inc.
WHO THE MAN?
YOU THE MAN!
KEVIN FAGAN @AOL.COM
DO YOU KNOW THAT GUY, DAD?
NO
http://www.unitedmedia.com
FAT GUYS AT PUBLIC POOLS HAVE A CERTAIN CAMARADERIE!
8-20

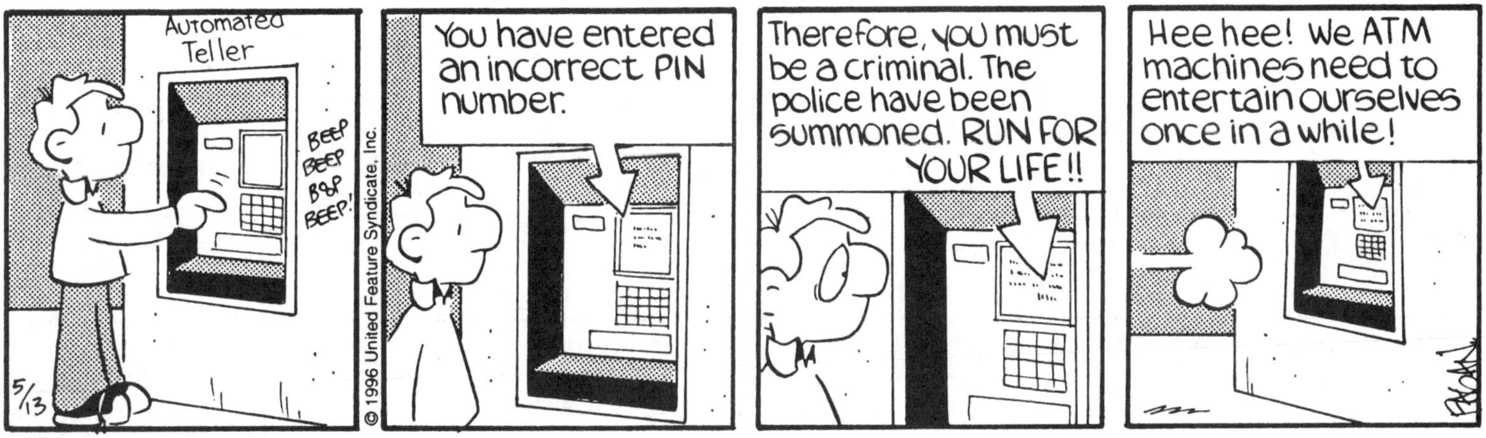
Automated Teller
BEEP BEEP B&P BEEP!
5/13
© 1996 United Feature Syndicate, Inc.
You have entered an incorrect PIN number.
Therefore, you must be a criminal. The police have been summoned. RUN FOR YOUR LIFE!!
Hee hee! We ATM machines need to entertain ourselves once in a while!

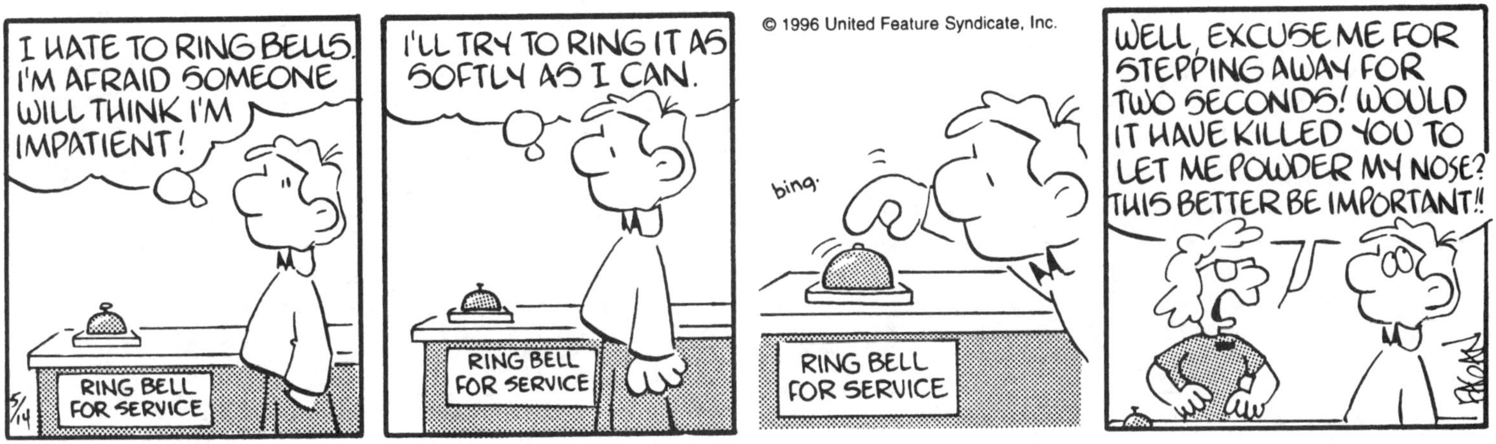
I HATE TO RING BELLS. I'M AFRAID SOMEONE WILL THINK I'M IMPATIENT!
RING BELL FOR SERVICE
5/14
I'LL TRY TO RING IT AS SOFTLY AS I CAN.
RING BELL FOR SERVICE
© 1996 United Feature Syndicate, Inc.
bing.
RING BELL FOR SERVICE
WELL, EXCUSE ME FOR STEPPING AWAY FOR TWO SECONDS! WOULD IT HAVE KILLED YOU TO LET ME POWDER MY NOSE? THIS BETTER BE IMPORTANT!!

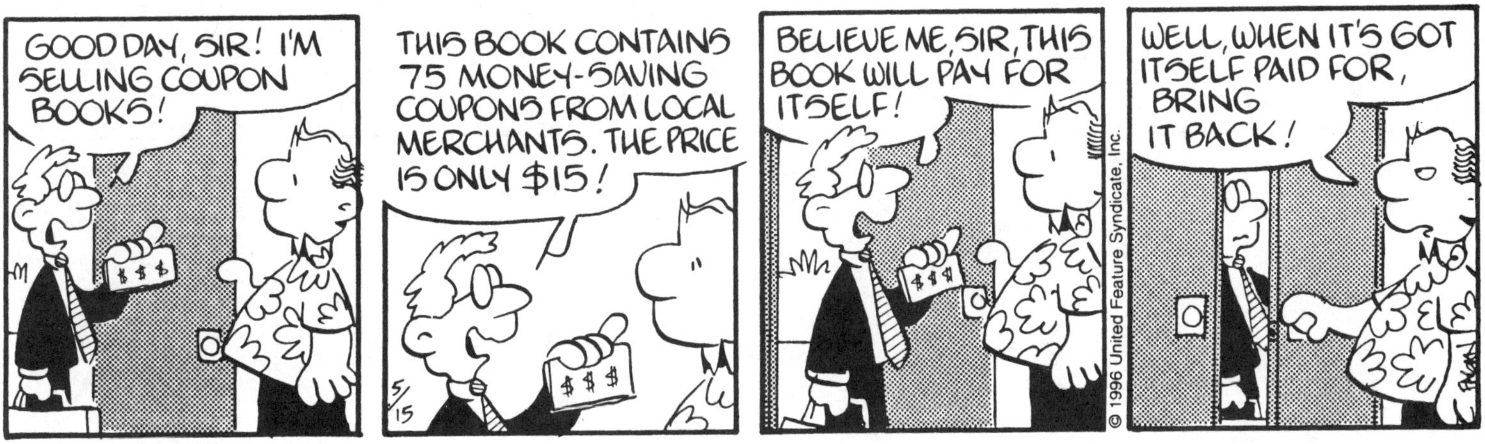
GOOD DAY, SIR! I'M SELLING COUPON BOOKS!
$ $ $
THIS BOOK CONTAINS 75 MONEY-SAVING COUPONS FROM LOCAL MERCHANTS. THE PRICE IS ONLY $15!
5/15
$ $ $
BELIEVE ME, SIR, THIS BOOK WILL PAY FOR ITSELF!
$ $ $
© 1996 United Feature Syndicate, Inc.
WELL, WHEN IT'S GOT ITSELF PAID FOR, BRING IT BACK!

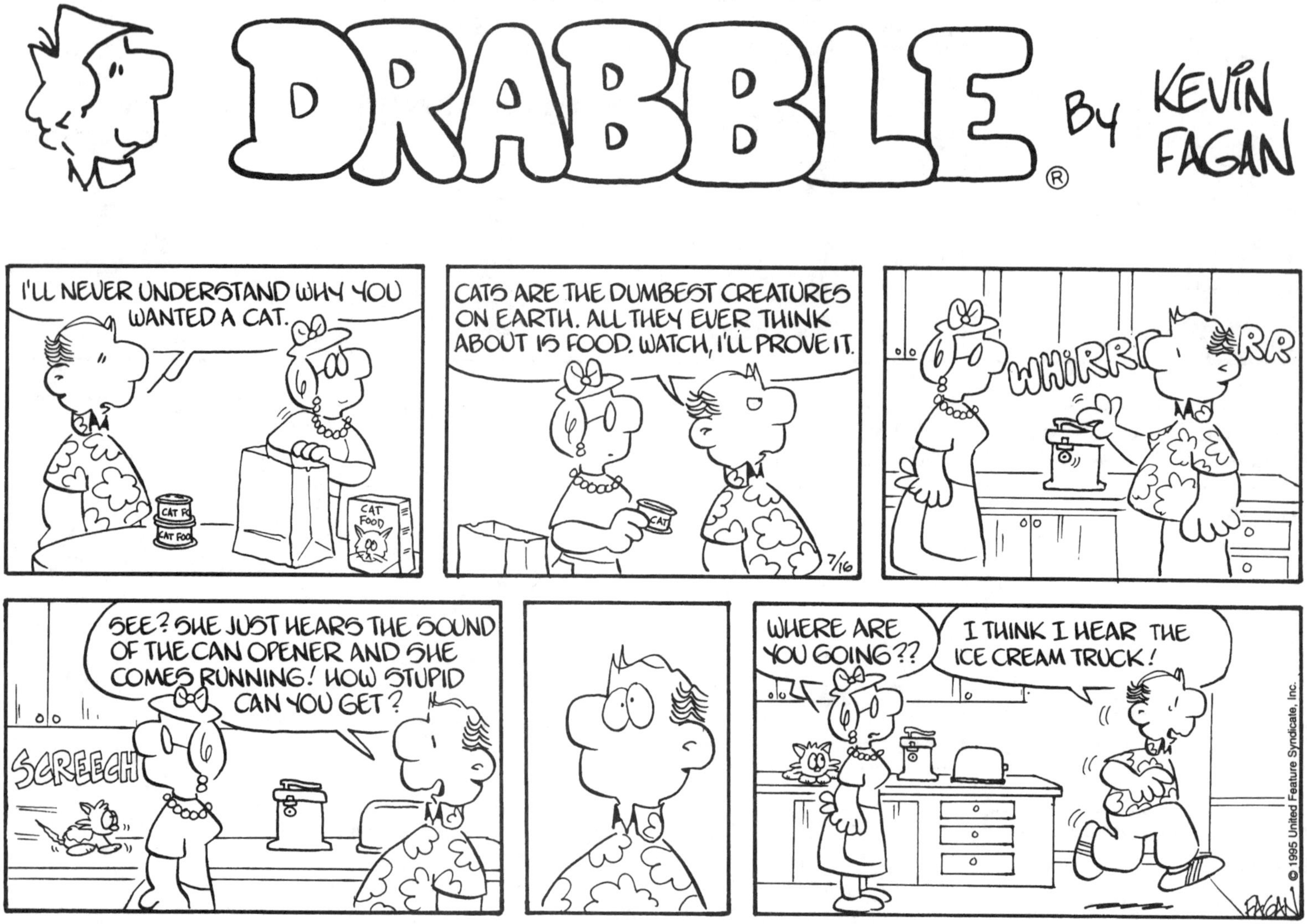
DRABBLE®
By KEVIN FAGAN
I'LL NEVER UNDERSTAND WHY YOU WANTED A CAT.
CAT FOOD
CAT FOOD
CAT FOOD
CATS ARE THE DUMBEST CREATURES ON EARTH. ALL THEY EVER THINK ABOUT IS FOOD. WATCH, I'LL PROVE IT.
CAT
7/16
WHIRR
RR
SEE? SHE JUST HEARS THE SOUND OF THE CAN OPENER AND SHE COMES RUNNING! HOW STUPID CAN YOU GET?
SCREECH
WHERE ARE YOU GOING??
I THINK I HEAR THE ICE CREAM TRUCK!
© 1995 United Feature Syndicate, Inc.
FAGAN

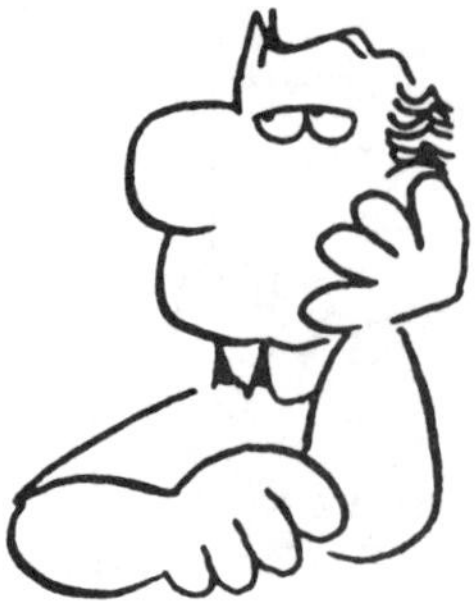

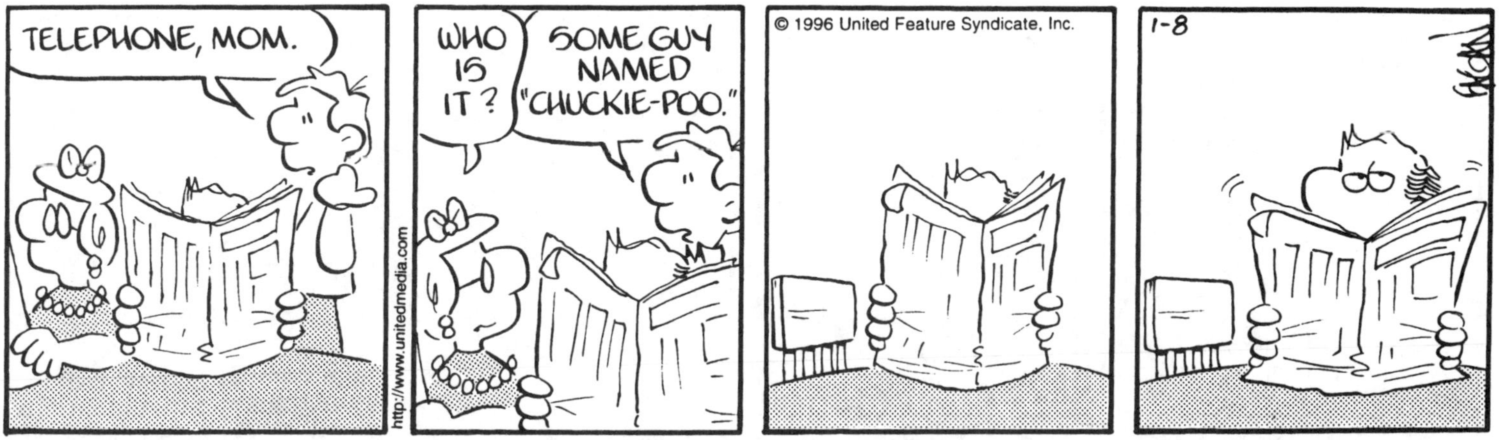
TELEPHONE, MOM.
WHO IS IT?
SOME GUY NAMED "CHUCKIE-POO."
http://www.unitedmedia.com
© 1996 United Feature Syndicate, Inc.
1-8

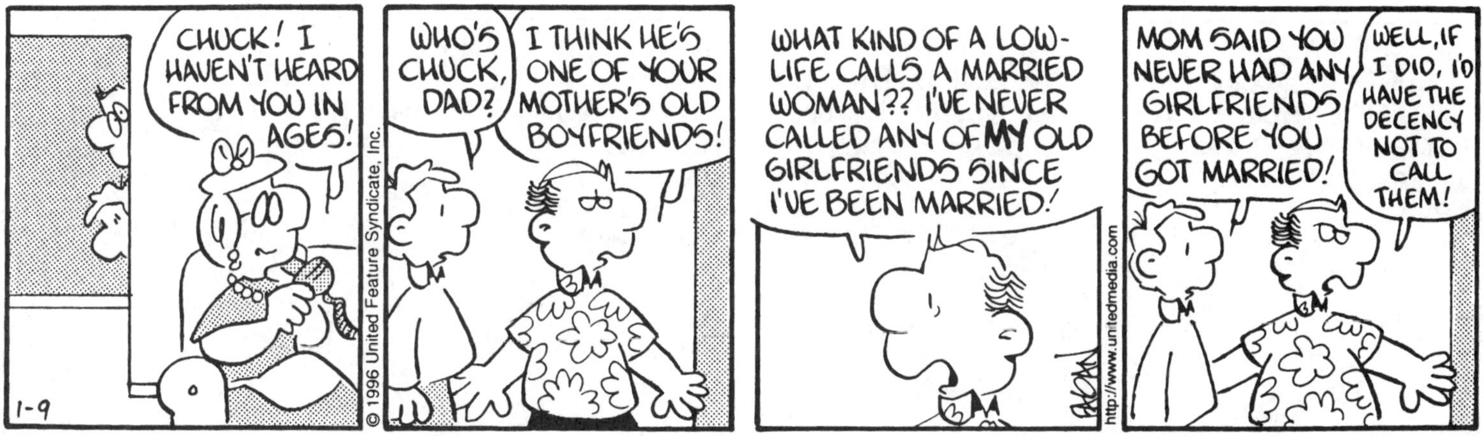
CHUCK! I HAVEN'T HEARD FROM YOU IN AGES!
1-9
© 1996 United Feature Syndicate, Inc.
WHO'S CHUCK, DAD?
I THINK HE'S ONE OF YOUR MOTHER'S OLD BOYFRIENDS!
WHAT KIND OF A LOW-LIFE CALLS A MARRIED WOMAN?? I'VE NEVER CALLED ANY OF MY OLD GIRLFRIENDS SINCE I'VE BEEN MARRIED!
http://www.unitedmedia.com
MOM SAID YOU NEVER HAD ANY GIRLFRIENDS BEFORE YOU GOT MARRIED!
WELL, IF I DID, I'D HAVE THE DECENCY NOT TO CALL THEM!

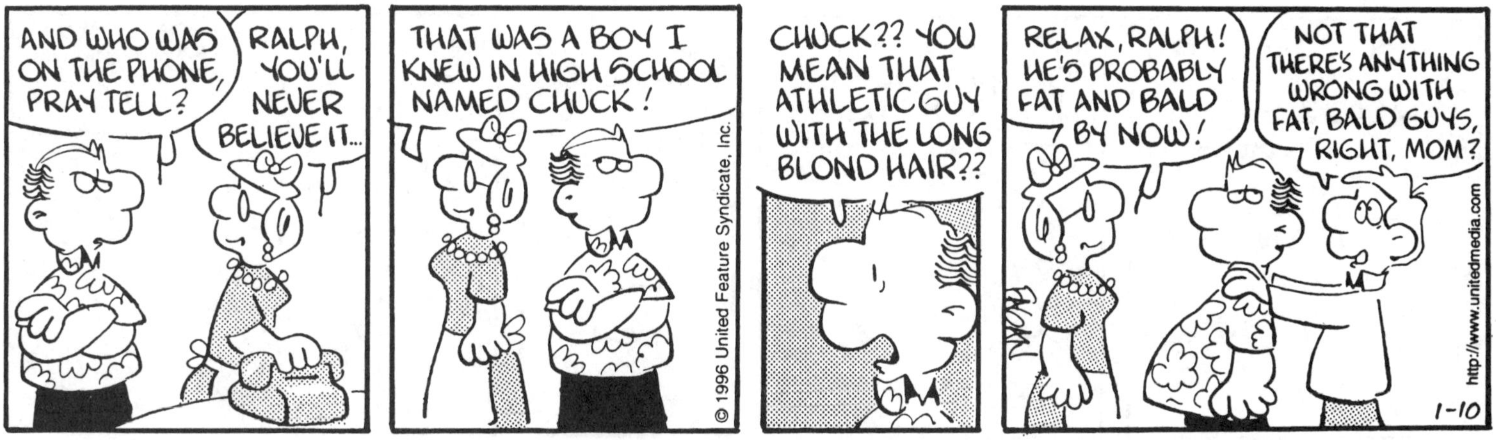
AND WHO WAS ON THE PHONE, PRAY TELL?
RALPH, YOU'LL NEVER BELIEVE IT...
THAT WAS A BOY I KNEW IN HIGH SCHOOL NAMED CHUCK!
© 1996 United Feature Syndicate, Inc.
CHUCK?? YOU MEAN THAT ATHLETIC GUY WITH THE LONG BLOND HAIR??
RELAX, RALPH! HE'S PROBABLY FAT AND BALD BY NOW!
NOT THAT THERE'S ANYTHING WRONG WITH FAT, BALD GUYS, RIGHT, MOM?
http://www.unitedmedia.com
1-10

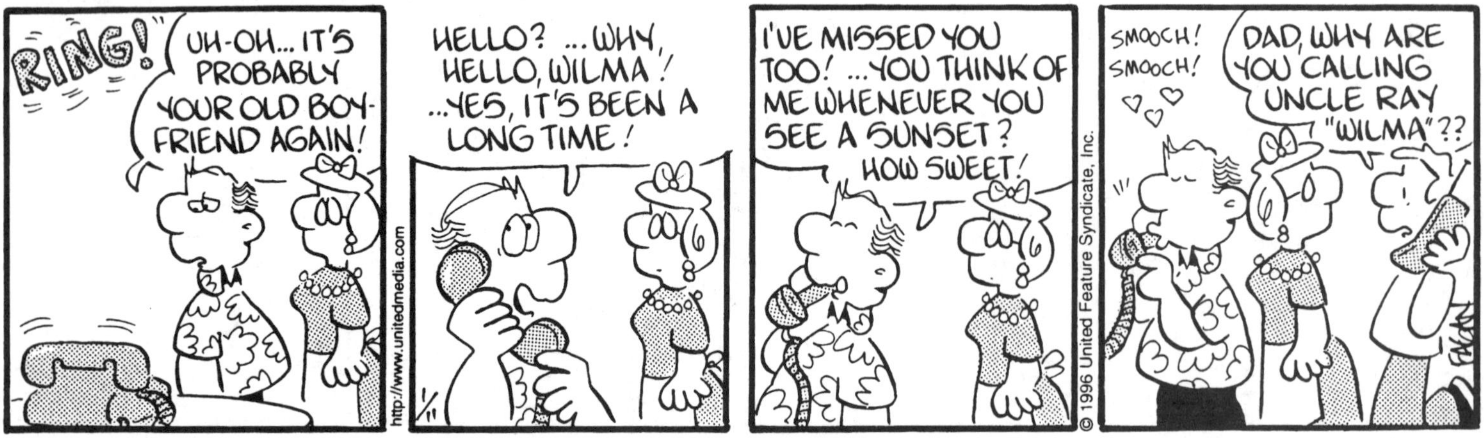
RING!
UH-OH... IT'S PROBABLY YOUR OLD BOY-FRIEND AGAIN!
HELLO? ...WHY, HELLO, WILMA! ...YES, IT'S BEEN A LONG TIME!
1-11
http://www.unitedmedia.com
I'VE MISSED YOU TOO! ...YOU THINK OF ME WHENEVER YOU SEE A SUNSET? HOW SWEET!
© 1996 United Feature Syndicate, Inc.
SMOOCH! SMOOCH!
DAD, WHY ARE YOU CALLING UNCLE RAY "WILMA"??
FAGAN

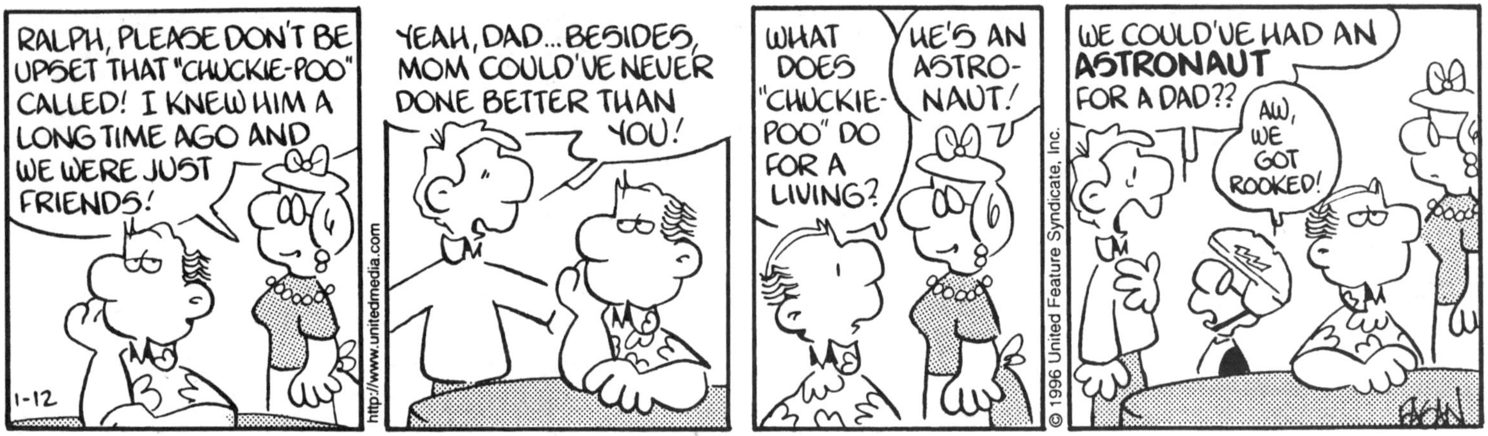
RALPH, PLEASE DON'T BE UPSET THAT "CHUCKIE-POO" CALLED! I KNEW HIM A LONG TIME AGO AND WE WERE JUST FRIENDS!
1-12
http://www.unitedmedia.com
YEAH, DAD... BESIDES, MOM COULD'VE NEVER DONE BETTER THAN YOU!
WHAT DOES "CHUCKIE-POO" DO FOR A LIVING?
HE'S AN ASTRONAUT!
© 1996 United Feature Syndicate, Inc.
WE COULD'VE HAD AN **ASTRONAUT** FOR A DAD??
AW, WE GOT ROOKED!
FAGAN

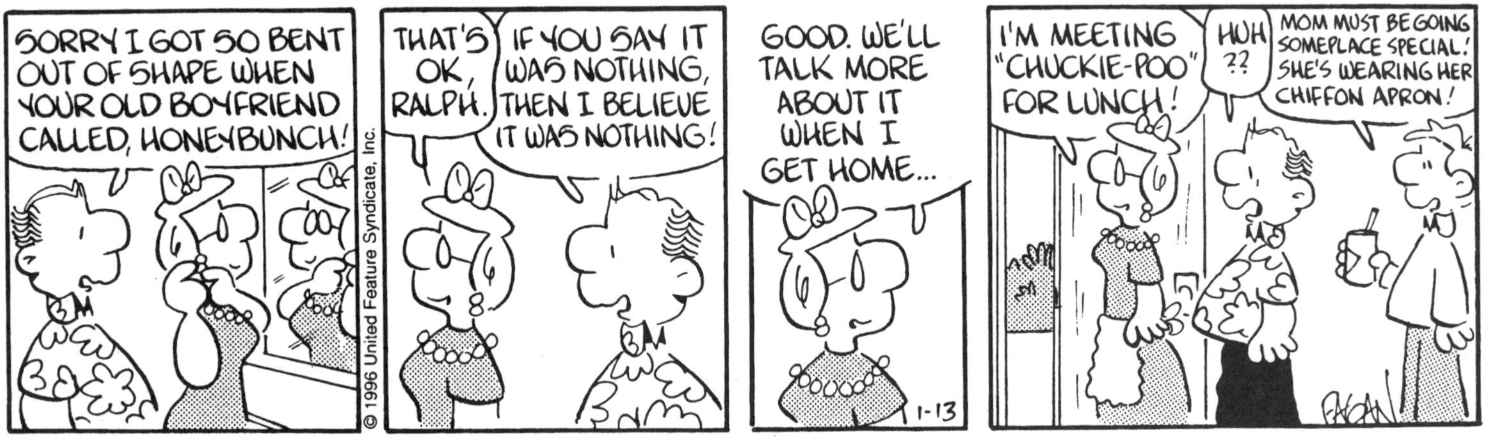
SORRY I GOT SO BENT OUT OF SHAPE WHEN YOUR OLD BOYFRIEND CALLED, HONEYBUNCH!
© 1996 United Feature Syndicate, Inc.
THAT'S OK, RALPH.
IF YOU SAY IT WAS NOTHING, THEN I BELIEVE IT WAS NOTHING!
GOOD. WE'LL TALK MORE ABOUT IT WHEN I GET HOME...
1-13
I'M MEETING "CHUCKIE-POO" FOR LUNCH!
HUH??
MOM MUST BE GOING SOMEPLACE SPECIAL! SHE'S WEARING HER CHIFFON APRON!
FAGAN

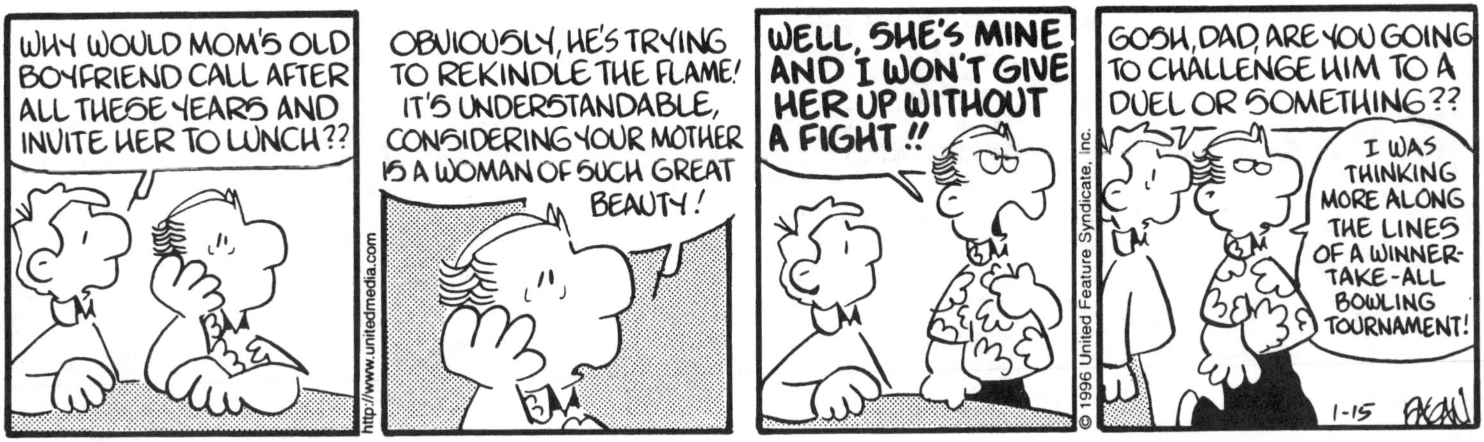
WHY WOULD MOM'S OLD BOYFRIEND CALL AFTER ALL THESE YEARS AND INVITE HER TO LUNCH??
OBVIOUSLY, HE'S TRYING TO REKINDLE THE FLAME! IT'S UNDERSTANDABLE, CONSIDERING YOUR MOTHER IS A WOMAN OF SUCH GREAT BEAUTY!
WELL, SHE'S MINE AND I WON'T GIVE HER UP WITHOUT A FIGHT!!
GOSH, DAD, ARE YOU GOING TO CHALLENGE HIM TO A DUEL OR SOMETHING??
I WAS THINKING MORE ALONG THE LINES OF A WINNER-TAKE-ALL BOWLING TOURNAMENT!
http://www.unitedmedia.com
© 1996 United Feature Syndicate, Inc.
1-15
FAGAN

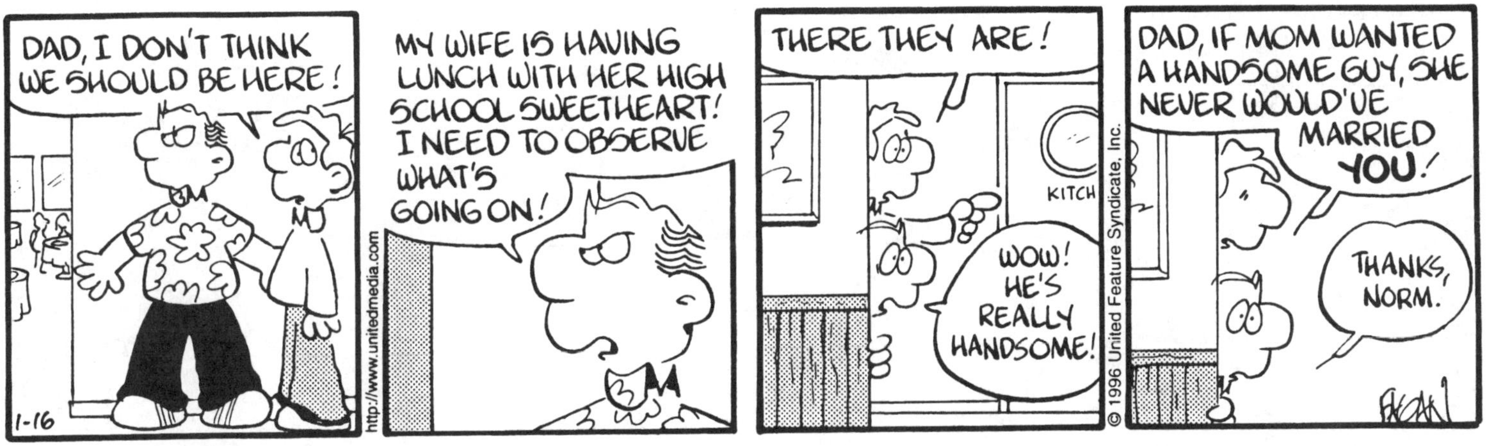
DAD, I DON'T THINK WE SHOULD BE HERE!
1-16
MY WIFE IS HAVING LUNCH WITH HER HIGH SCHOOL SWEETHEART! I NEED TO OBSERVE WHAT'S GOING ON!
THERE THEY ARE!
KITCH
WOW! HE'S REALLY HANDSOME!
DAD, IF MOM WANTED A HANDSOME GUY, SHE NEVER WOULD'VE MARRIED YOU!
THANKS, NORM.
http://www.unitedmedia.com
© 1996 United Feature Syndicate, Inc.
FAGAN

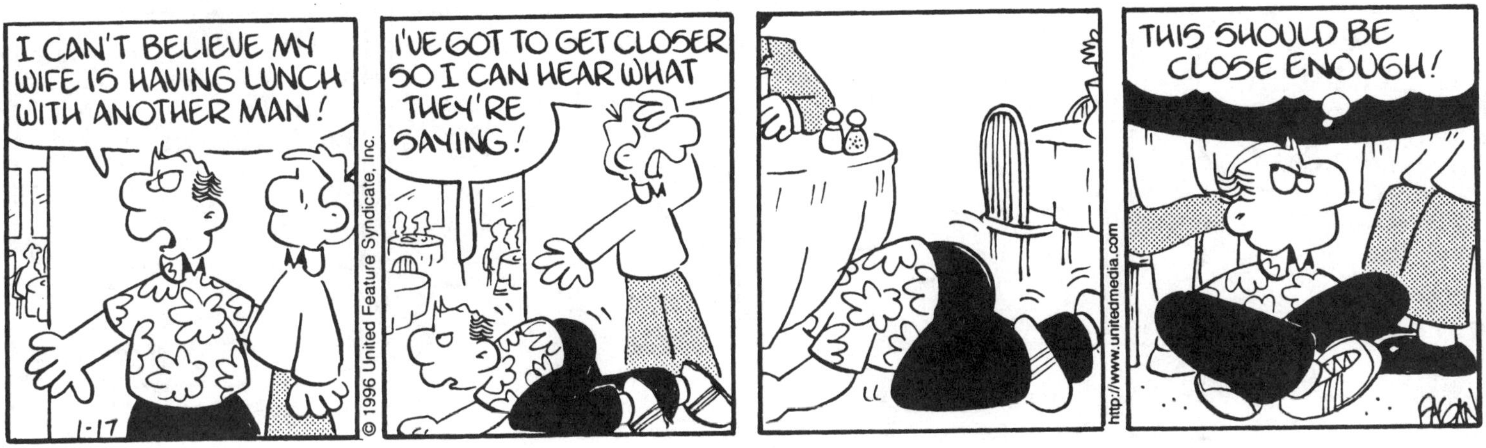
I CAN'T BELIEVE MY WIFE IS HAVING LUNCH WITH ANOTHER MAN!
1-17
I'VE GOT TO GET CLOSER SO I CAN HEAR WHAT THEY'RE SAYING!
THIS SHOULD BE CLOSE ENOUGH!
© 1996 United Feature Syndicate, Inc.
http://www.unitedmedia.com
FAGAN

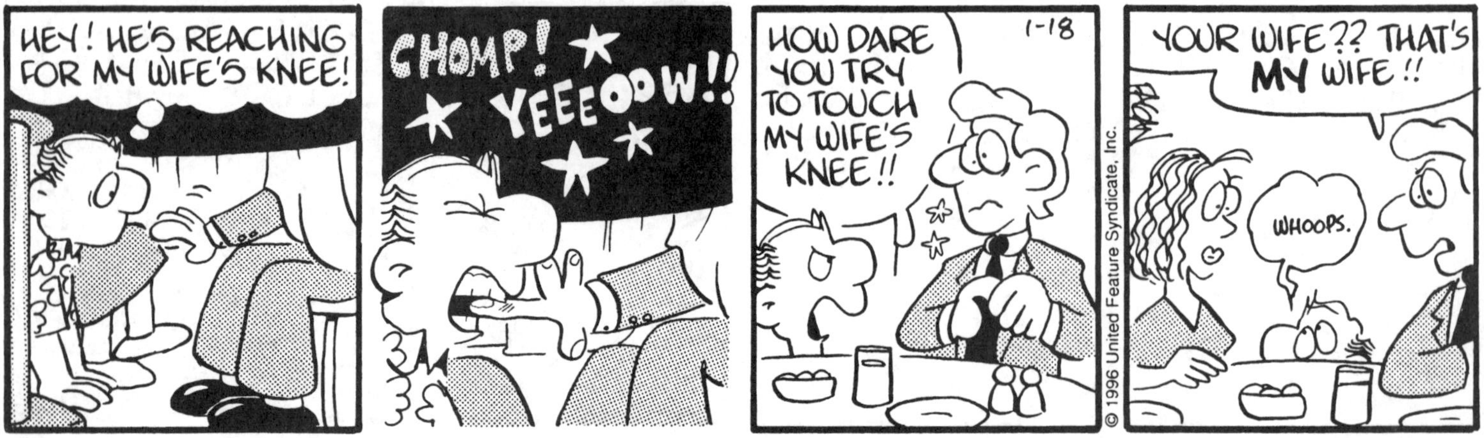
HEY! HE'S REACHING FOR MY WIFE'S KNEE!
CHOMP!
YEEEOOW!!
HOW DARE YOU TRY TO TOUCH MY WIFE'S KNEE!!
1-18
YOUR WIFE?? THAT'S MY WIFE!!
WHOOPS.
© 1996 United Feature Syndicate, Inc.

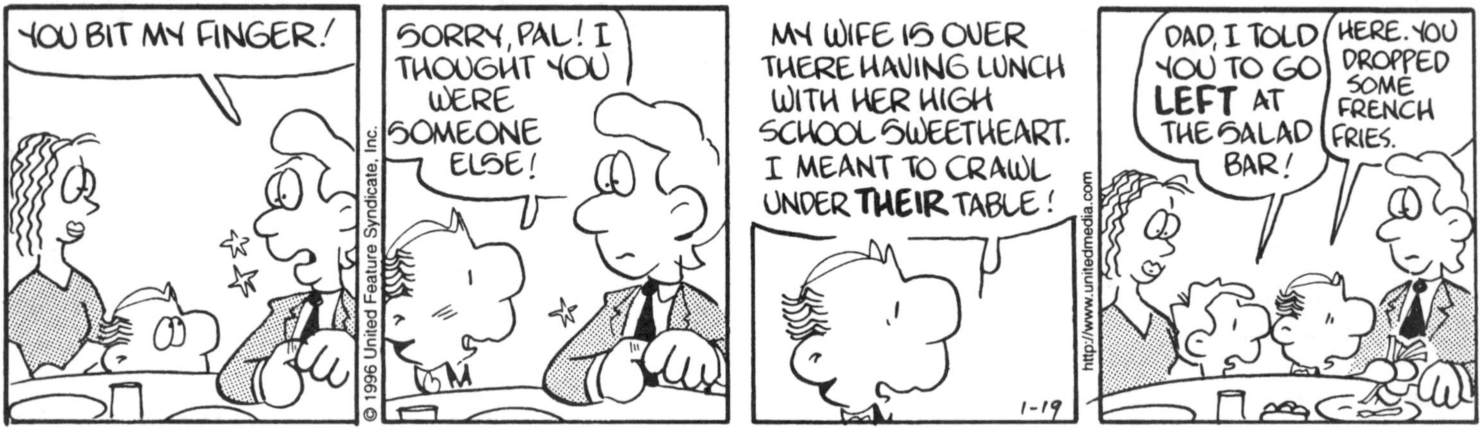
YOU BIT MY FINGER!
© 1996 United Feature Syndicate, Inc.
SORRY, PAL! I THOUGHT YOU WERE SOMEONE ELSE!
MY WIFE IS OVER THERE HAVING LUNCH WITH HER HIGH SCHOOL SWEETHEART. I MEANT TO CRAWL UNDER THEIR TABLE!
1-19
http://www.unitedmedia.com
DAD, I TOLD YOU TO GO LEFT AT THE SALAD BAR!
HERE. YOU DROPPED SOME FRENCH FRIES.

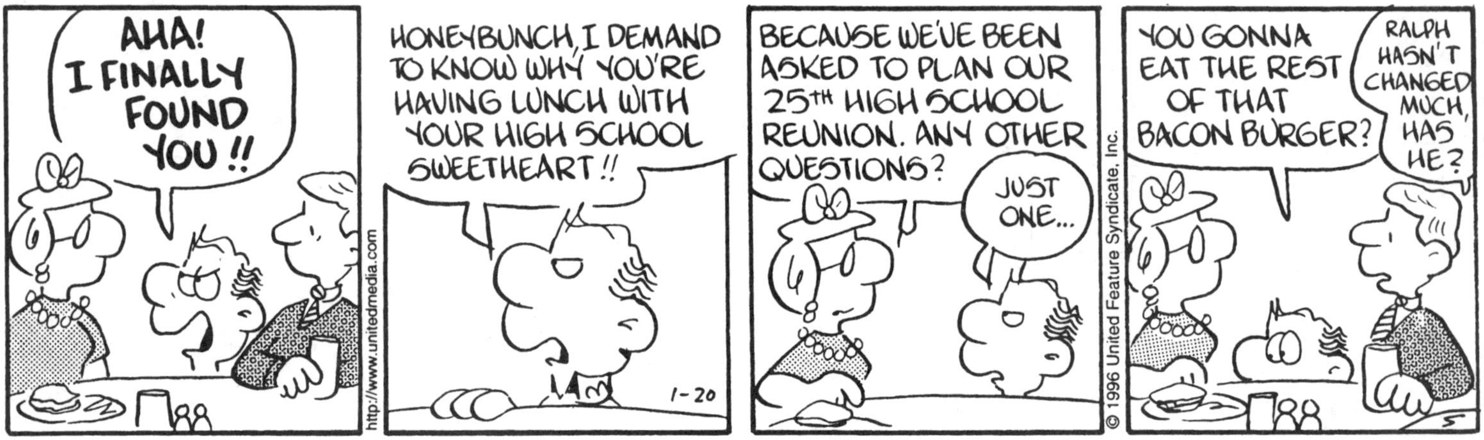
AHA! I FINALLY FOUND YOU!!
http://www.unitedmedia.com
HONEYBUNCH, I DEMAND TO KNOW WHY YOU'RE HAVING LUNCH WITH YOUR HIGH SCHOOL SWEETHEART!!
1-20
BECAUSE WE'VE BEEN ASKED TO PLAN OUR 25TH HIGH SCHOOL REUNION. ANY OTHER QUESTIONS?
JUST ONE...
© 1996 United Feature Syndicate, Inc.
YOU GONNA EAT THE REST OF THAT BACON BURGER?
RALPH HASN'T CHANGED MUCH, HAS HE?

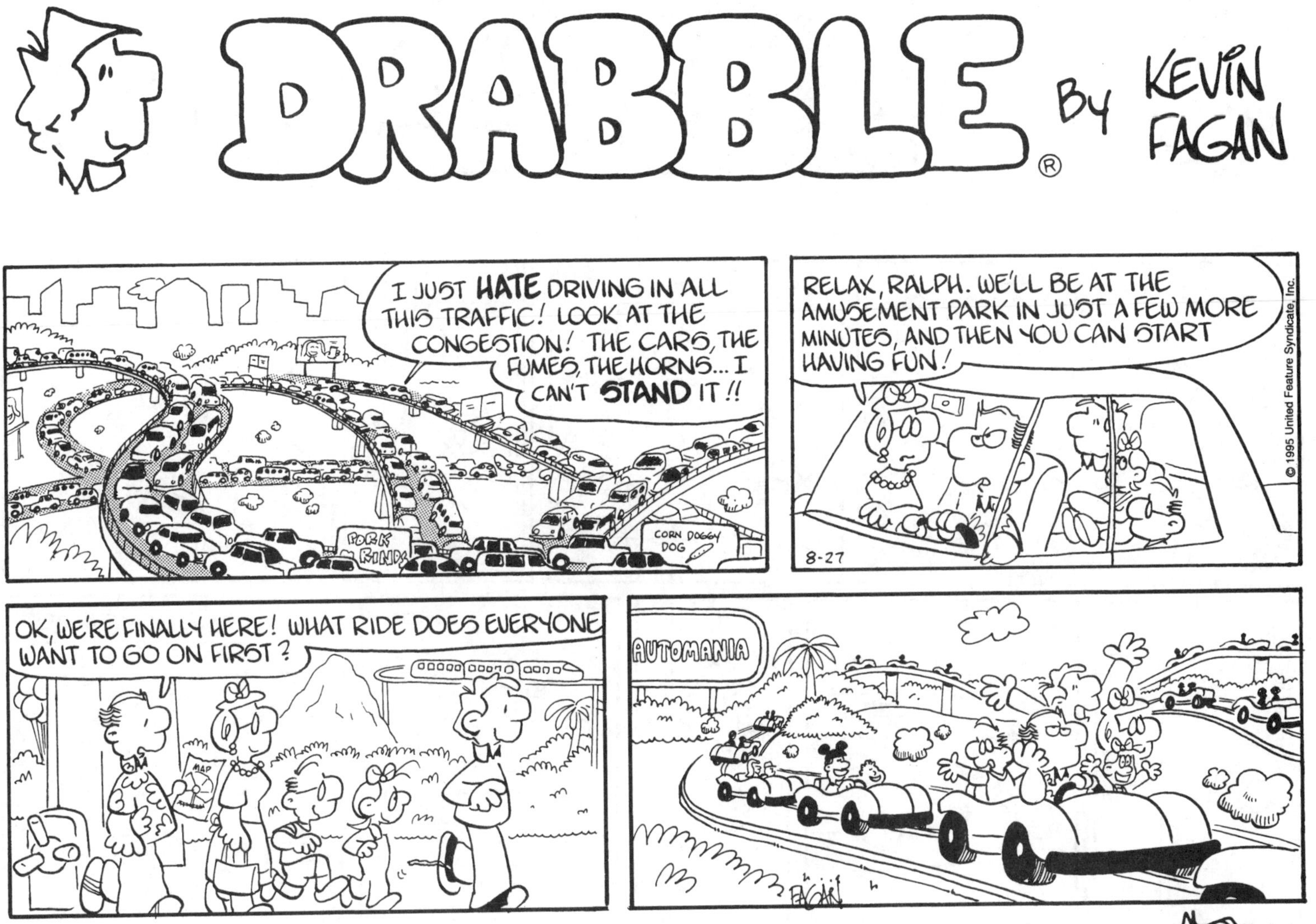
DRABBLE®
By KEVIN FAGAN
I JUST HATE DRIVING IN ALL THIS TRAFFIC! LOOK AT THE CONGESTION! THE CARS, THE FUMES, THE HORNS... I CAN'T STAND IT!!
PORK RINDS
CORN DOGGY DOG
RELAX, RALPH. WE'LL BE AT THE AMUSEMENT PARK IN JUST A FEW MORE MINUTES, AND THEN YOU CAN START HAVING FUN!
© 1995 United Feature Syndicate, Inc.
8-27
OK, WE'RE FINALLY HERE! WHAT RIDE DOES EVERYONE WANT TO GO ON FIRST?
MAP
AUTOMANIA
FAGAN

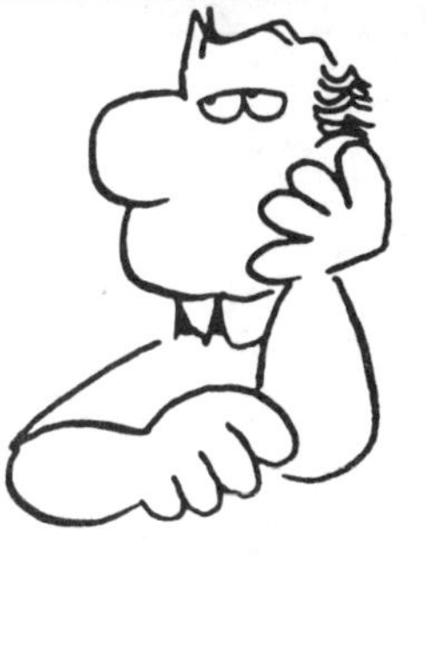

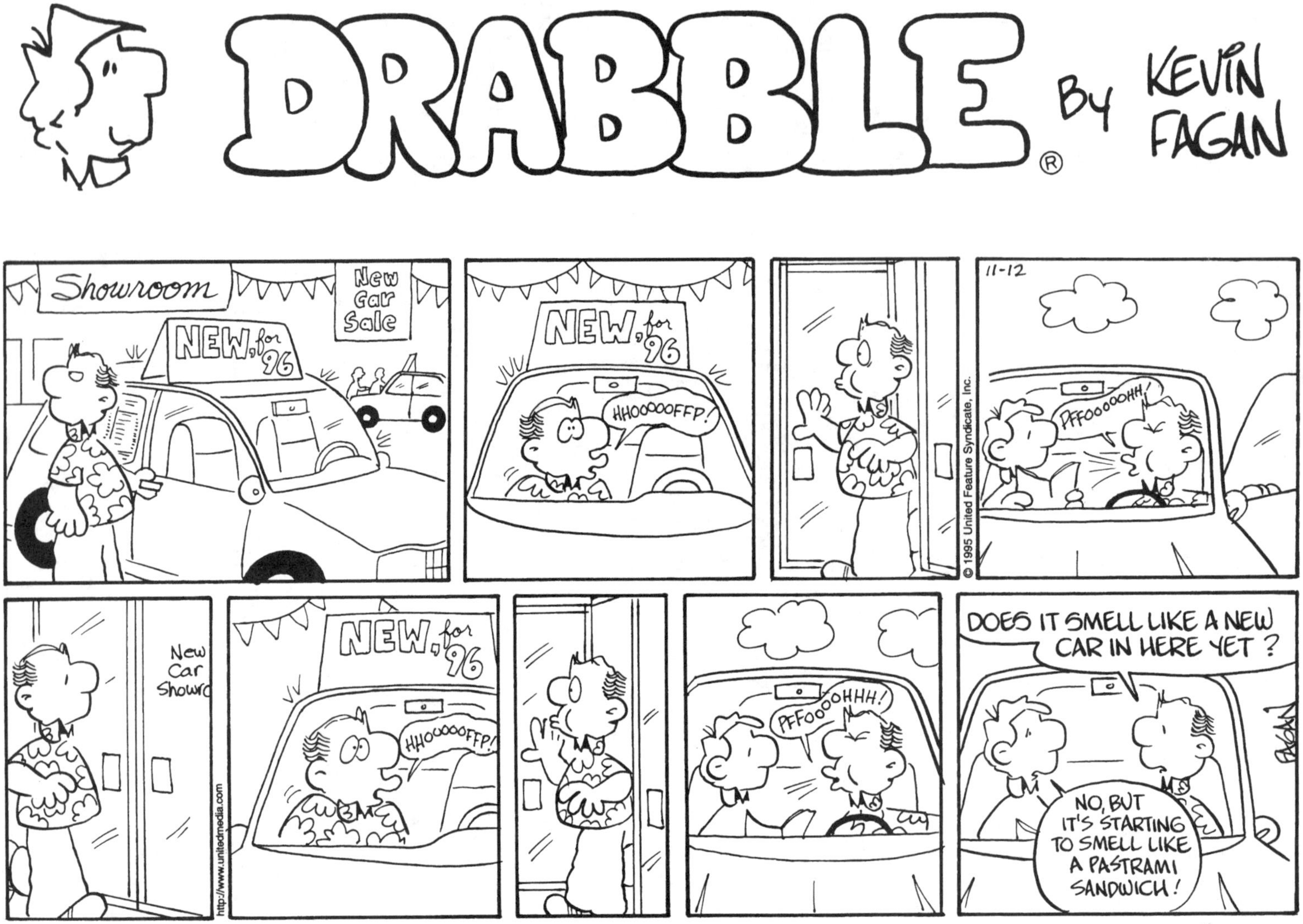
DRABBLE
By KEVIN FAGAN
Showroom
New Car Sale
NEW, for 96
HHOOOOOFFP!
© 1995 United Feature Syndicate, Inc.
11-12
PFFOOOOOOHH!
New Car Showro
http://www.unitedmedia.com
NEW, for 96
HHOOOOOFFP!
PFFOOOOHHH!
DOES IT SMELL LIKE A NEW CAR IN HERE YET ?
NO, BUT IT'S STARTING TO SMELL LIKE A PASTRAMI SANDWICH !
FAGAN

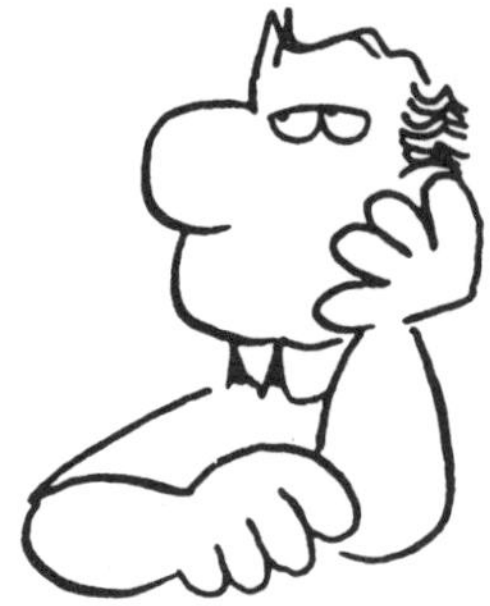

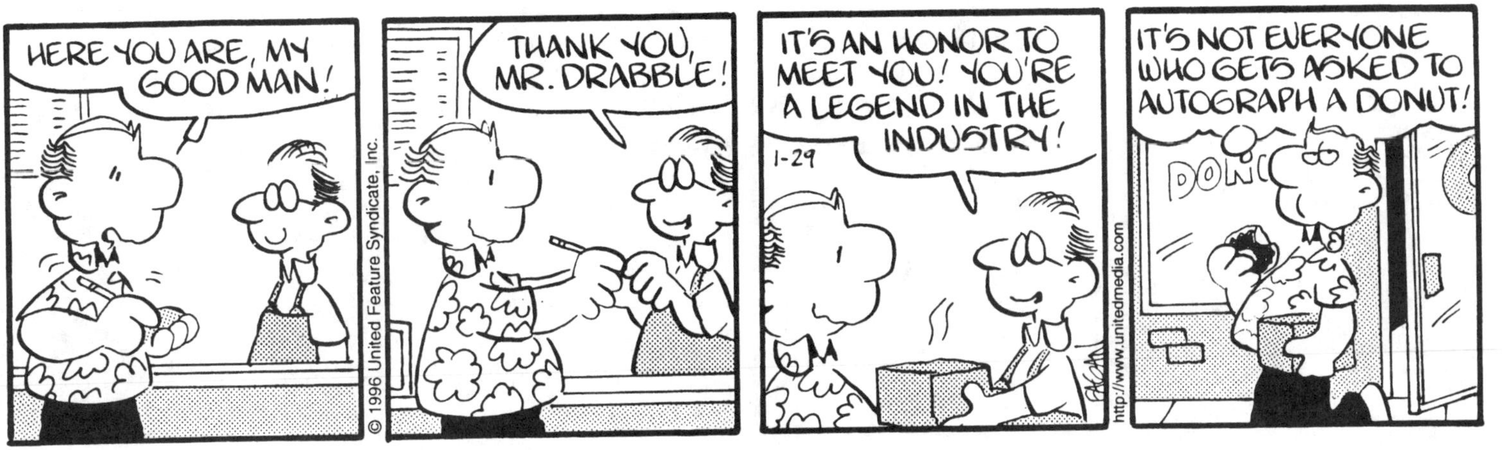
HERE YOU ARE, MY GOOD MAN!
THANK YOU, MR. DRABBLE!
IT'S AN HONOR TO MEET YOU! YOU'RE A LEGEND IN THE INDUSTRY!
1-29
IT'S NOT EVERYONE WHO GETS ASKED TO AUTOGRAPH A DONUT!
DON
© 1996 United Feature Syndicate, Inc.
http://www.unitedmedia.com

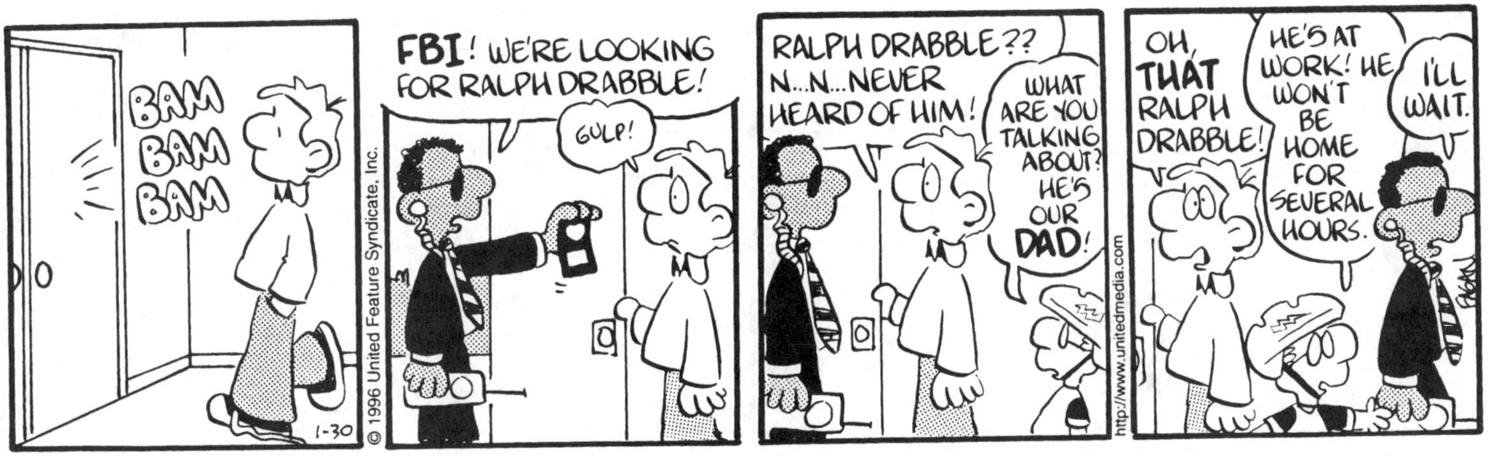
BAM BAM BAM
1-30
FBI! WE'RE LOOKING FOR RALPH DRABBLE!
GULP!
RALPH DRABBLE?? N...N...NEVER HEARD OF HIM!
WHAT ARE YOU TALKING ABOUT? HE'S OUR DAD!
OH, THAT RALPH DRABBLE!
HE'S AT WORK! HE WON'T BE HOME FOR SEVERAL HOURS.
I'LL WAIT.
© 1996 United Feature Syndicate, Inc.
http://www.unitedmedia.com

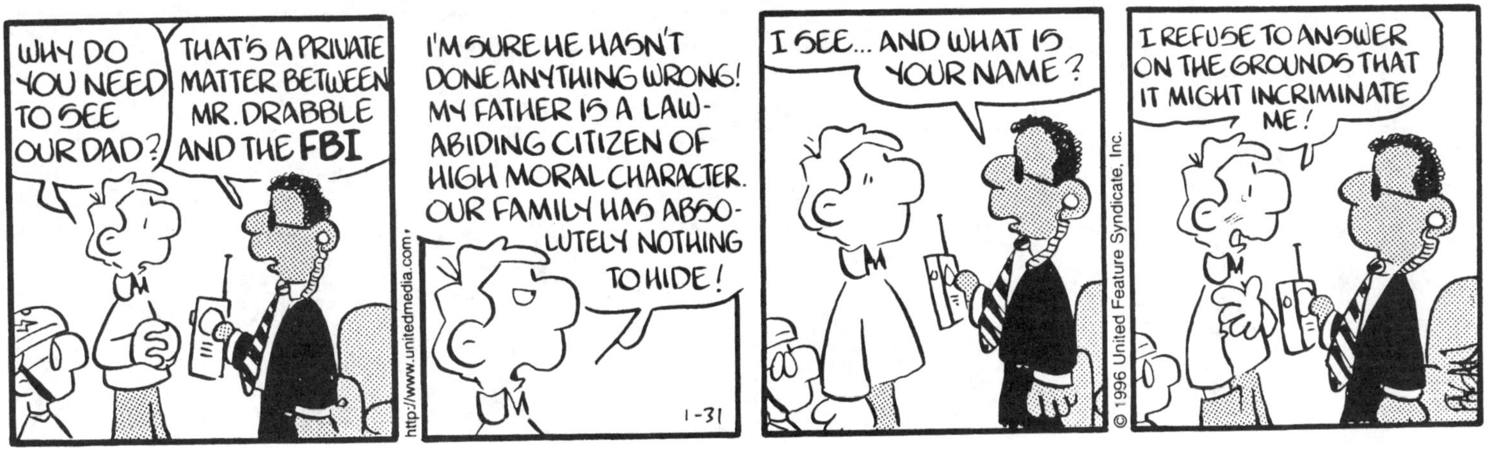
WHY DO YOU NEED TO SEE OUR DAD?
THAT'S A PRIVATE MATTER BETWEEN MR. DRABBLE AND THE FBI
I'M SURE HE HASN'T DONE ANYTHING WRONG! MY FATHER IS A LAW-ABIDING CITIZEN OF HIGH MORAL CHARACTER. OUR FAMILY HAS ABSOLUTELY NOTHING TO HIDE!
1-31
I SEE... AND WHAT IS YOUR NAME?
I REFUSE TO ANSWER ON THE GROUNDS THAT IT MIGHT INCRIMINATE ME!
http://www.unitedmedia.com
© 1996 United Feature Syndicate, Inc.

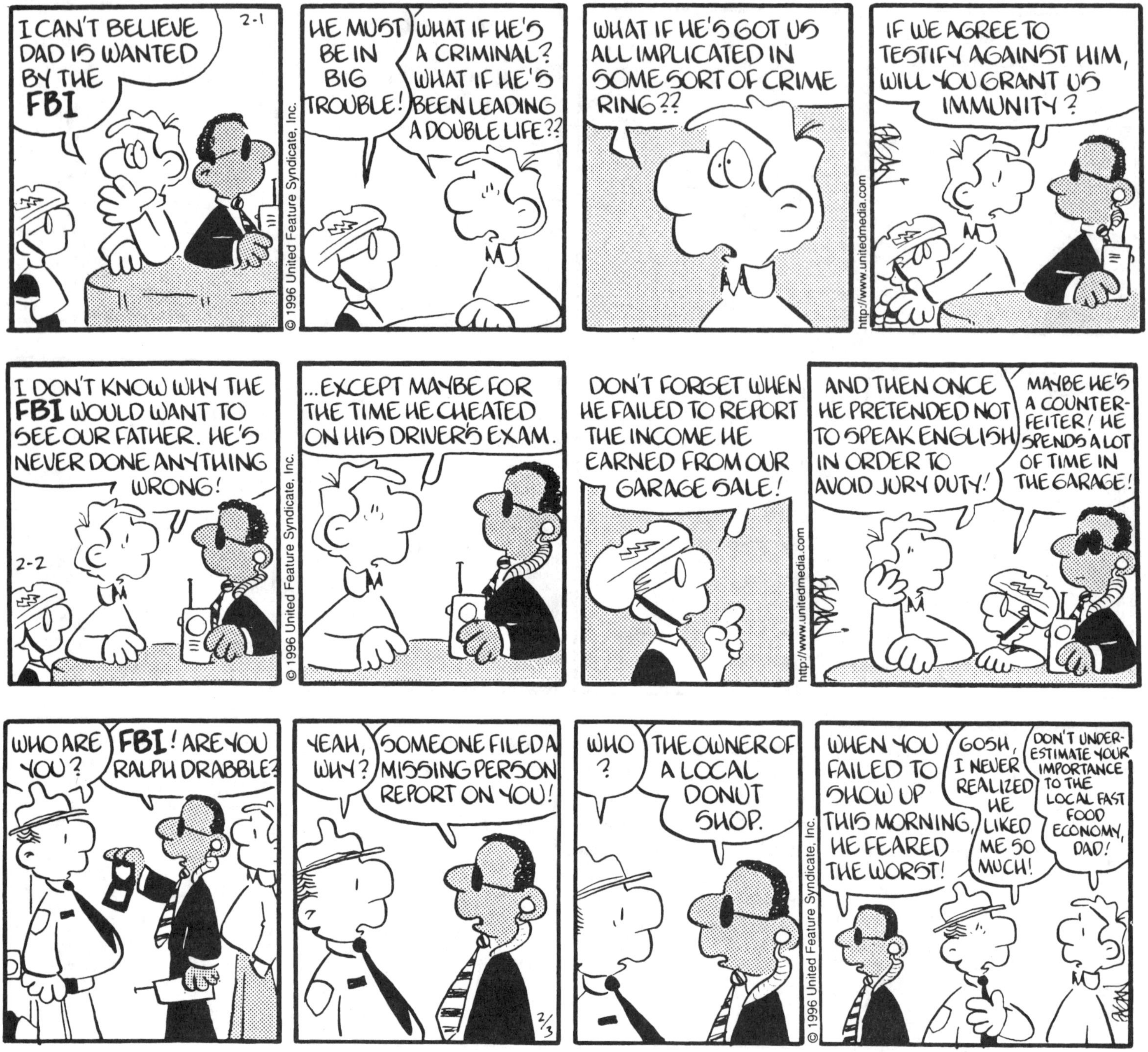
2-1
I CAN'T BELIEVE DAD IS WANTED BY THE FBI
HE MUST BE IN BIG TROUBLE!
WHAT IF HE'S A CRIMINAL? WHAT IF HE'S BEEN LEADING A DOUBLE LIFE??
© 1996 United Feature Syndicate, Inc.
WHAT IF HE'S GOT US ALL IMPLICATED IN SOME SORT OF CRIME RING??
IF WE AGREE TO TESTIFY AGAINST HIM, WILL YOU GRANT US IMMUNITY?
http://www.unitedmedia.com
I DON'T KNOW WHY THE FBI WOULD WANT TO SEE OUR FATHER. HE'S NEVER DONE ANYTHING WRONG!
2-2
...EXCEPT MAYBE FOR THE TIME HE CHEATED ON HIS DRIVER'S EXAM.
© 1996 United Feature Syndicate, Inc.
DON'T FORGET WHEN HE FAILED TO REPORT THE INCOME HE EARNED FROM OUR GARAGE SALE!
http://www.unitedmedia.com
AND THEN ONCE HE PRETENDED NOT TO SPEAK ENGLISH IN ORDER TO AVOID JURY DUTY!
MAYBE HE'S A COUNTERFEITER! HE SPENDS A LOT OF TIME IN THE GARAGE!
WHO ARE YOU?
FBI! ARE YOU RALPH DRABBLE?
YEAH, WHY?
SOMEONE FILED A MISSING PERSON REPORT ON YOU!
2/3
WHO?
THE OWNER OF A LOCAL DONUT SHOP.
© 1996 United Feature Syndicate, Inc.
WHEN YOU FAILED TO SHOW UP THIS MORNING, HE FEARED THE WORST!
GOSH, I NEVER REALIZED HE LIKED ME SO MUCH!
DON'T UNDERESTIMATE YOUR IMPORTANCE TO THE LOCAL FAST FOOD ECONOMY, DAD!

DRABBLE® By KEVIN FAGAN

RALPH! HOW ARE YOU?
HEL
HELLO, JIM! IT'S GOOD TO SEE YOU AGAIN!
IT'S BEEN A LONG TIME, HASN'T IT, RALPH?
YE
AT LEAST FIVE YEARS!
HOW'S THE FAMILY?
TH
THEY'RE FINE! GROWING UP FAST!
HOW'S THE GOLF GAME?
I SH
HE SHOT A 79 LAST WEEK!
WELL, IT WAS GOOD TO SEE YOU AGAIN, RALPH!
GOOD TO SEE YOU AGAIN, JIM! KEEP IN TOUCH!
ISN'T IT NICE TO TALK TO OLD FRIENDS AGAIN, RALPH?
HOW THE HECK WOULD I KNOW??
http://www.unitedmedia.com
1-28
© 1996 United Feature Syndicate, Inc.

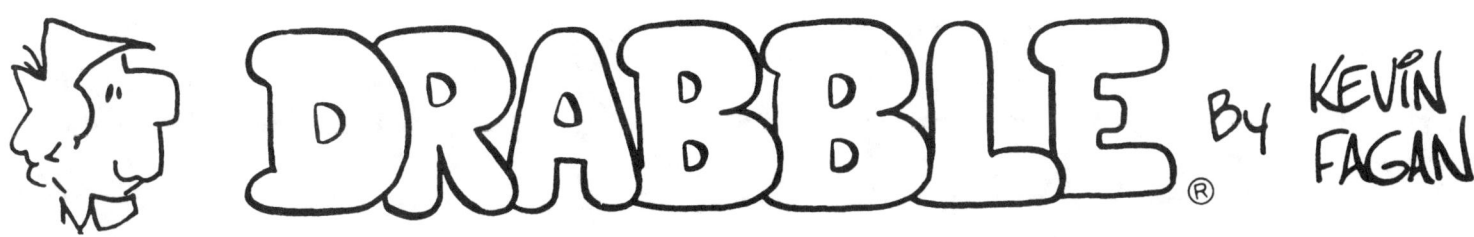

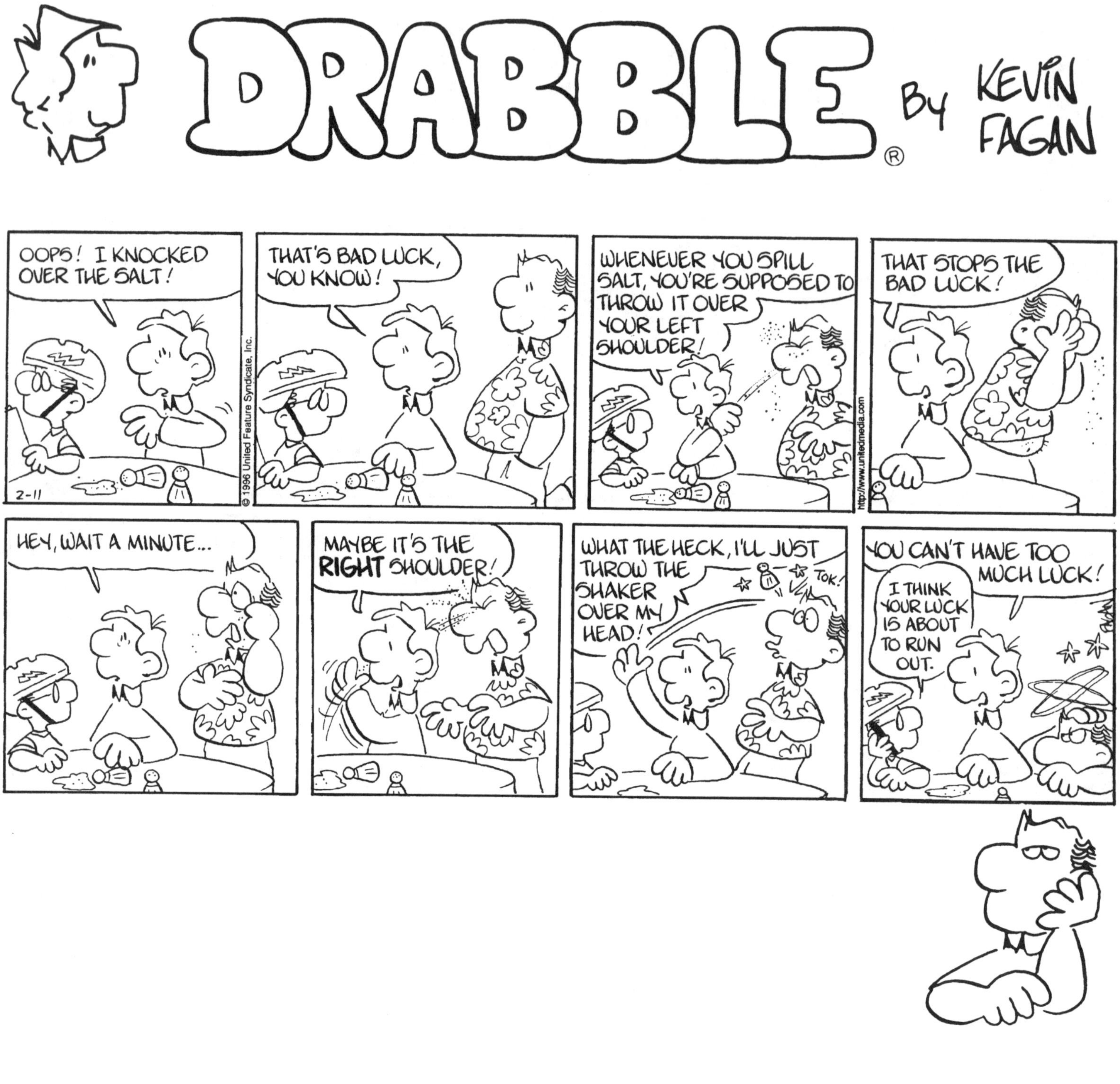
DRABBLE
BY KEVIN FAGAN
OOPS! I KNOCKED OVER THE SALT!
2-11
© 1996 United Feature Syndicate, Inc.
THAT'S BAD LUCK, YOU KNOW!
WHENEVER YOU SPILL SALT, YOU'RE SUPPOSED TO THROW IT OVER YOUR LEFT SHOULDER!
http://www.unitedmedia.com
THAT STOPS THE BAD LUCK!
HEY, WAIT A MINUTE...
MAYBE IT'S THE RIGHT SHOULDER!
WHAT THE HECK, I'LL JUST THROW THE SHAKER OVER MY HEAD!
TOK!
YOU CAN'T HAVE TOO MUCH LUCK!
I THINK YOUR LUCK IS ABOUT TO RUN OUT.

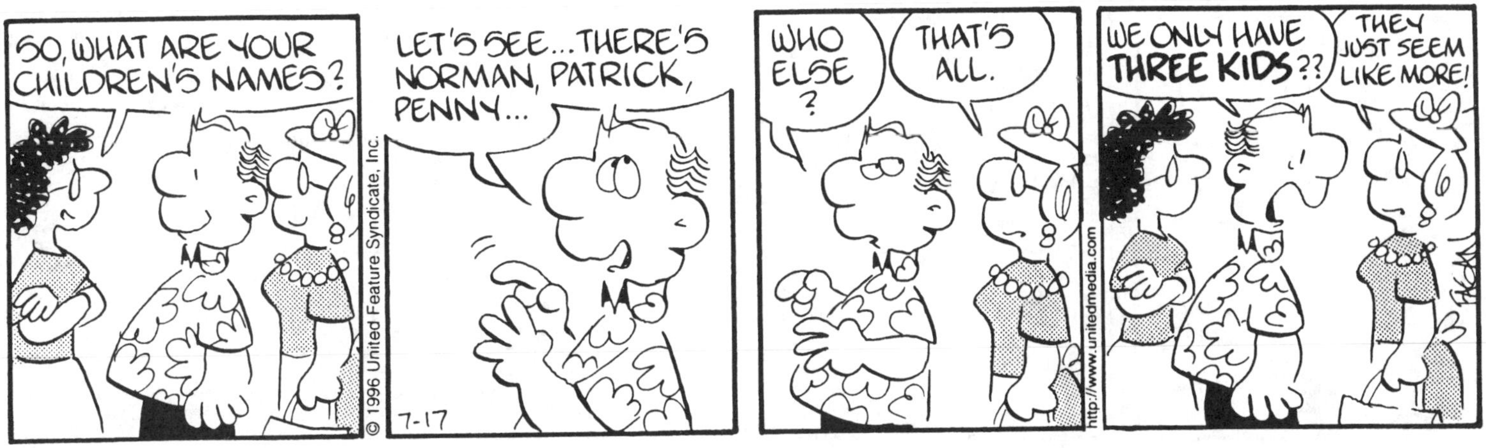
SO, WHAT ARE YOUR CHILDREN'S NAMES??
© 1996 United Feature Syndicate, Inc.
LET'S SEE...THERE'S NORMAN, PATRICK, PENNY...
7-17
WHO ELSE?
THAT'S ALL.
http://www.unitedmedia.com
WE ONLY HAVE THREE KIDS??
THEY JUST SEEM LIKE MORE!

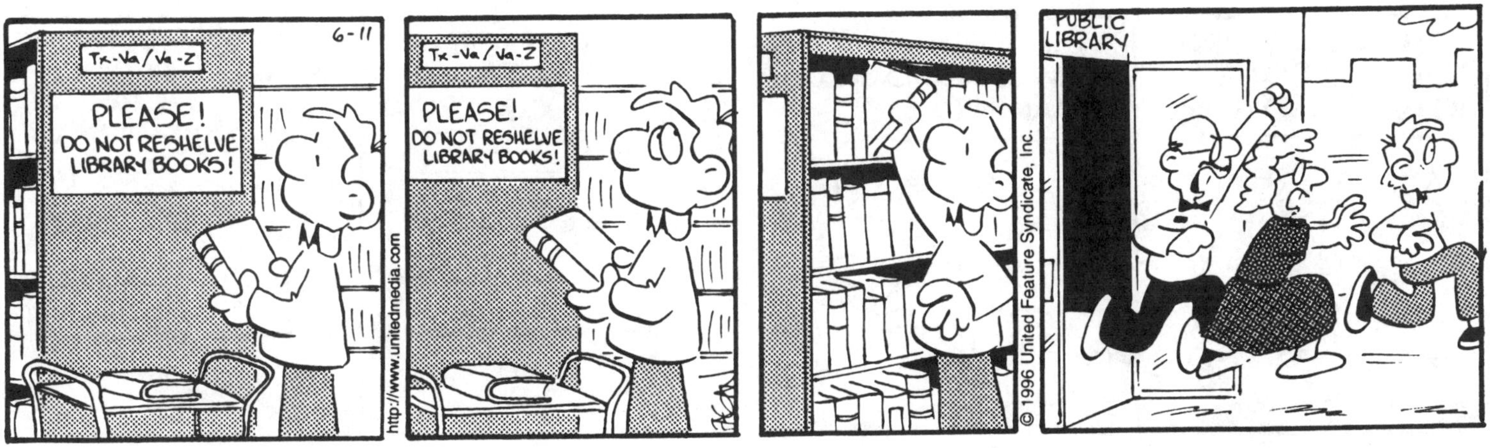
6-11
Tx-Va / Va-Z
PLEASE! DO NOT RESHELVE LIBRARY BOOKS!
http://www.unitedmedia.com
Tx-Va / Va-Z
PLEASE! DO NOT RESHELVE LIBRARY BOOKS!
© 1996 United Feature Syndicate, Inc.
PUBLIC LIBRARY

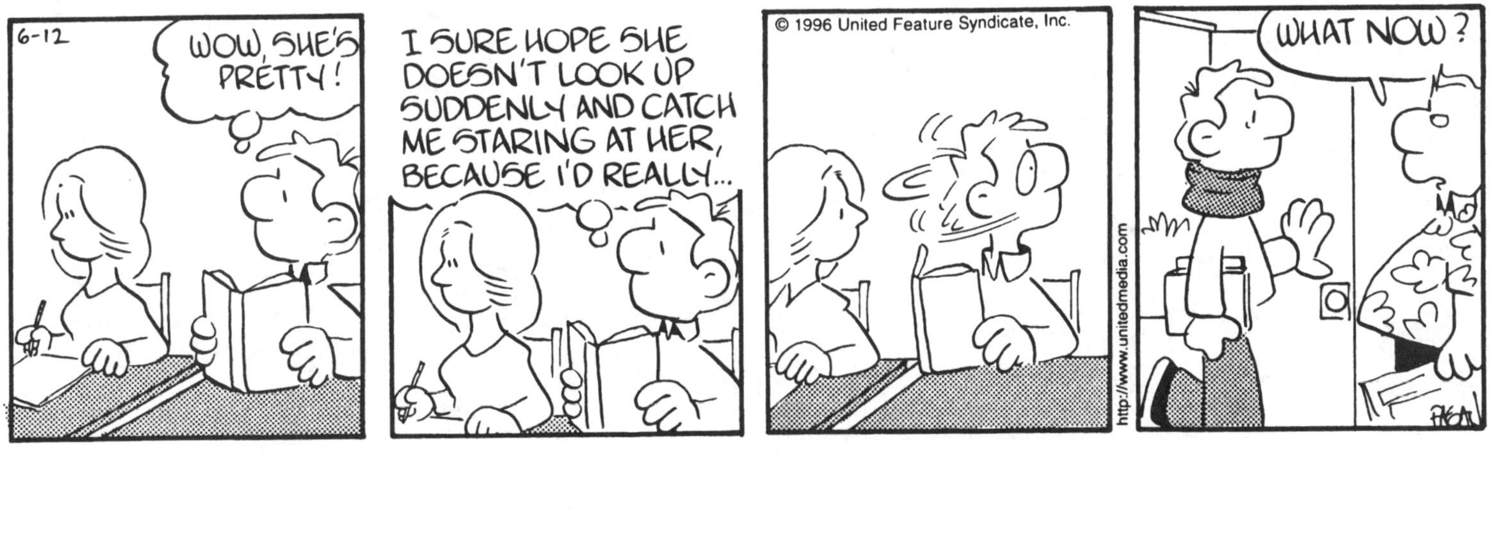
6-12
WOW, SHE'S PRETTY!
I SURE HOPE SHE DOESN'T LOOK UP SUDDENLY AND CATCH ME STARING AT HER, BECAUSE I'D REALLY...
© 1996 United Feature Syndicate, Inc.
http://www.unitedmedia.com
WHAT NOW?

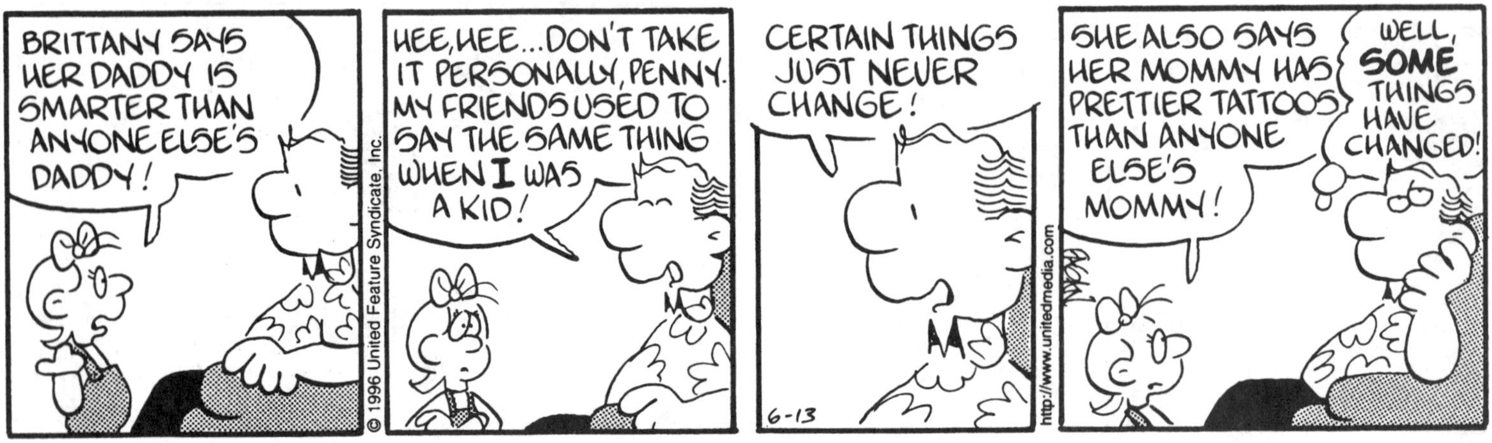
BRITTANY SAYS HER DADDY IS SMARTER THAN ANYONE ELSE'S DADDY!
© 1996 United Feature Syndicate, Inc.
HEE, HEE... DON'T TAKE IT PERSONALLY, PENNY. MY FRIENDS USED TO SAY THE SAME THING WHEN I WAS A KID!
CERTAIN THINGS JUST NEVER CHANGE!
6-13
http://www.unitedmedia.com
SHE ALSO SAYS HER MOMMY HAS PRETTIER TATTOOS THAN ANYONE ELSE'S MOMMY!
WELL, SOME THINGS HAVE CHANGED!

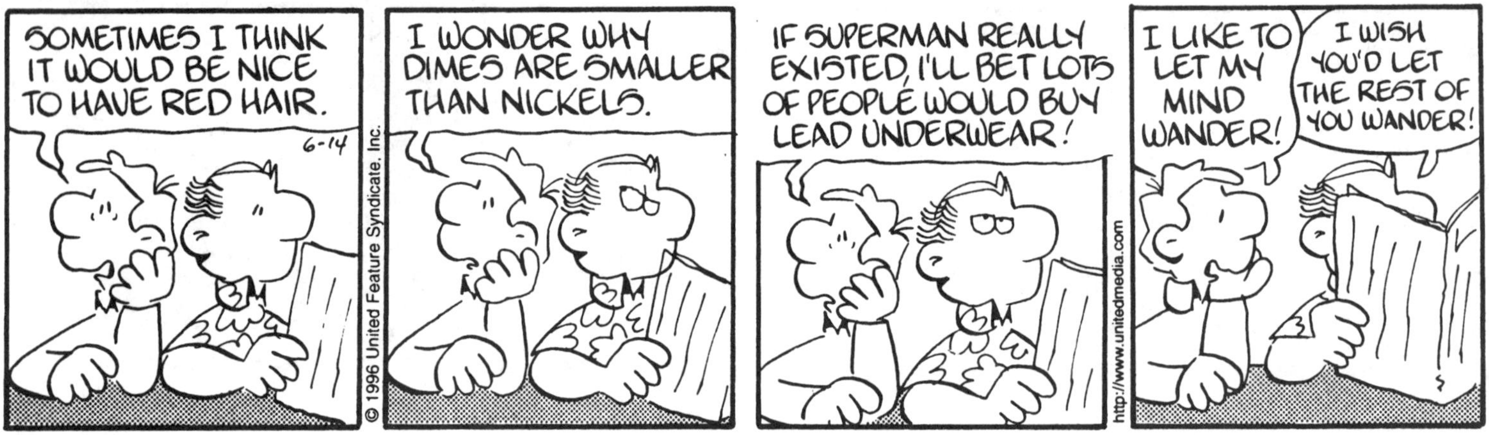
SOMETIMES I THINK IT WOULD BE NICE TO HAVE RED HAIR.
6-14
© 1996 United Feature Syndicate, Inc.
I WONDER WHY DIMES ARE SMALLER THAN NICKELS.
IF SUPERMAN REALLY EXISTED, I'LL BET LOTS OF PEOPLE WOULD BUY LEAD UNDERWEAR!
http://www.unitedmedia.com
I LIKE TO LET MY MIND WANDER!
I WISH YOU'D LET THE REST OF YOU WANDER!

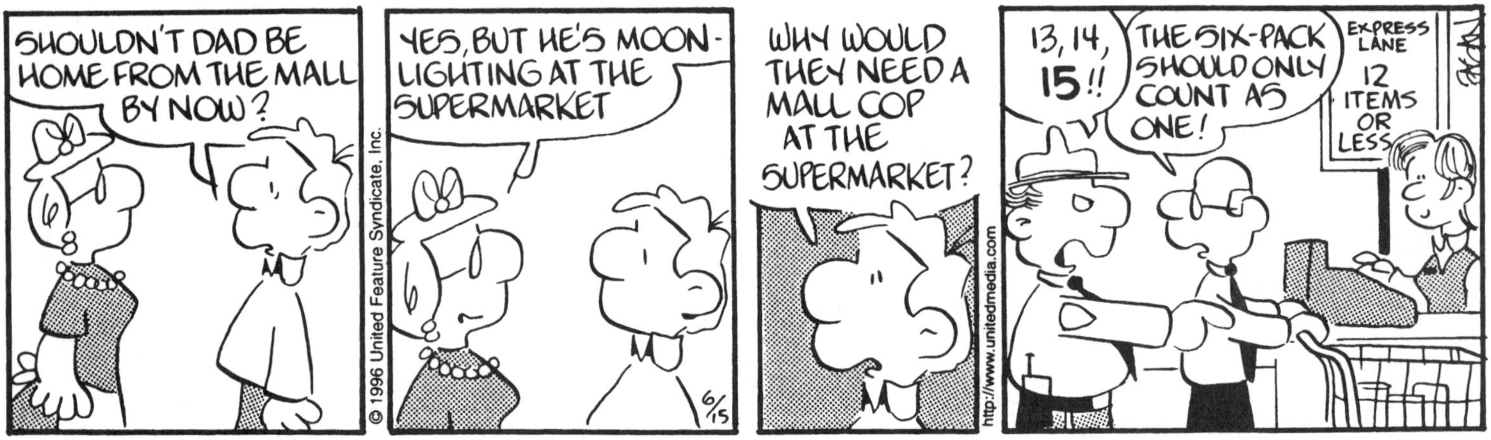
SHOULDN'T DAD BE HOME FROM THE MALL BY NOW?
© 1996 United Feature Syndicate, Inc.
YES, BUT HE'S MOONLIGHTING AT THE SUPERMARKET
6/15
WHY WOULD THEY NEED A MALL COP AT THE SUPERMARKET?
http://www.unitedmedia.com
13, 14, 15!!
THE SIX-PACK SHOULD ONLY COUNT AS ONE!
EXPRESS LANE
12 ITEMS OR LESS

DRABBLE®

By KEVIN FAGAN

3-3
DAD, THE OWNER OF THE DONUT SHOP IS HERE TO SEE YOU.
?
HI, ERNIE!
HELLO, MR. DRABBLE! I THOUGHT YOU MIGHT LIKE TO MEET MY FAMILY...
THIS IS MY WIFE, WILLAMINA!
HELLO
AND OUR DAUGHTER, DEBBIE. SHE'S GOING TO NEED BRACES, AS YOU CAN SEE!
http://www.unitedmedia.com
AND THESE ARE OUR TWINS. WE WON'T BE ABLE TO AFFORD PRE-SCHOOL MUCH LONGER, SO THEY'LL JUST HAVE TO...
ALL RIGHT! ALL RIGHT!! I'VE CHANGED MY MIND!!
I WILL NOT GO ON A DIET!!
BLESS YOU, MR. D!
DAD, THE GUY FROM THE YOGURT SHOP IS HERE!
© 1996 United Feature Syndicate, Inc.

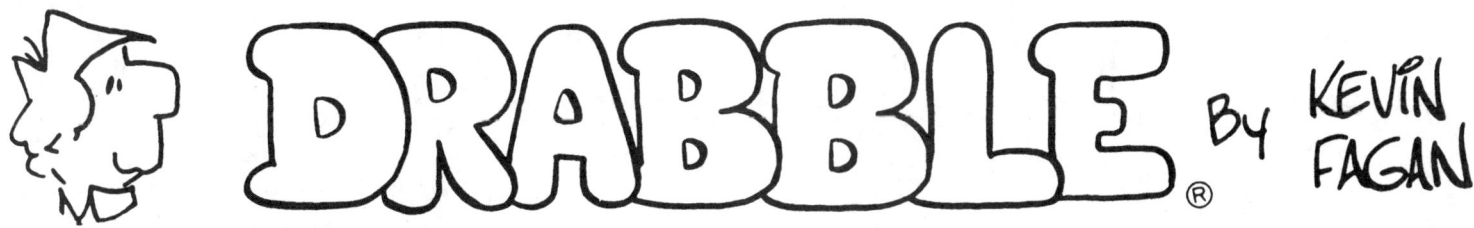

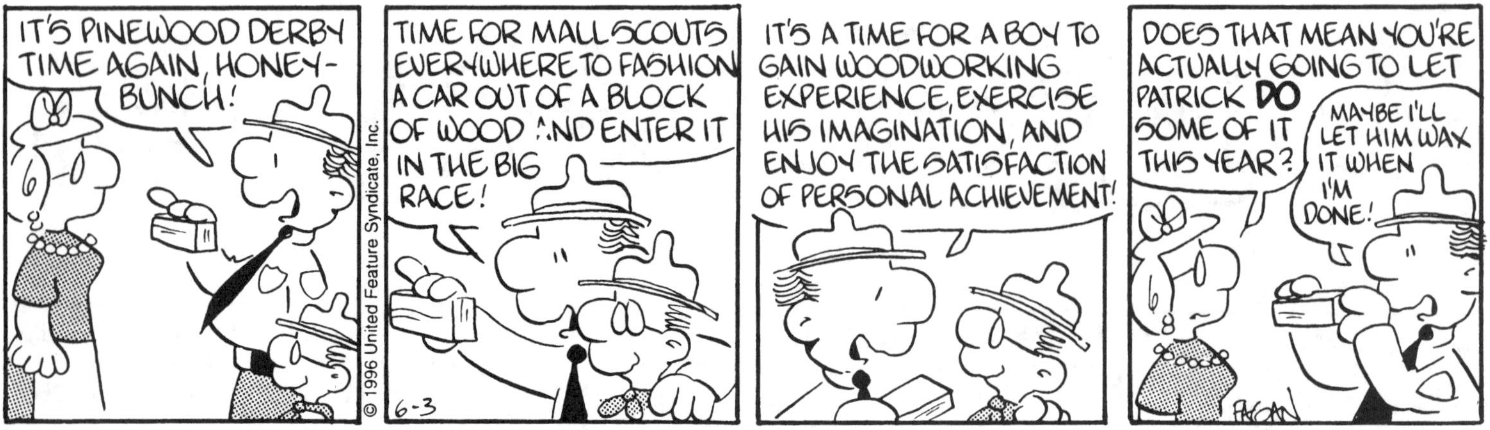
IT'S PINEWOOD DERBY TIME AGAIN, HONEY-BUNCH!
© 1996 United Feature Syndicate, Inc.
6-3
TIME FOR MALL SCOUTS EVERYWHERE TO FASHION A CAR OUT OF A BLOCK OF WOOD AND ENTER IT IN THE BIG RACE!
IT'S A TIME FOR A BOY TO GAIN WOODWORKING EXPERIENCE, EXERCISE HIS IMAGINATION, AND ENJOY THE SATISFACTION OF PERSONAL ACHIEVEMENT!
DOES THAT MEAN YOU'RE ACTUALLY GOING TO LET PATRICK DO SOME OF IT THIS YEAR?
MAYBE I'LL LET HIM WAX IT WHEN I'M DONE!
FAGAN

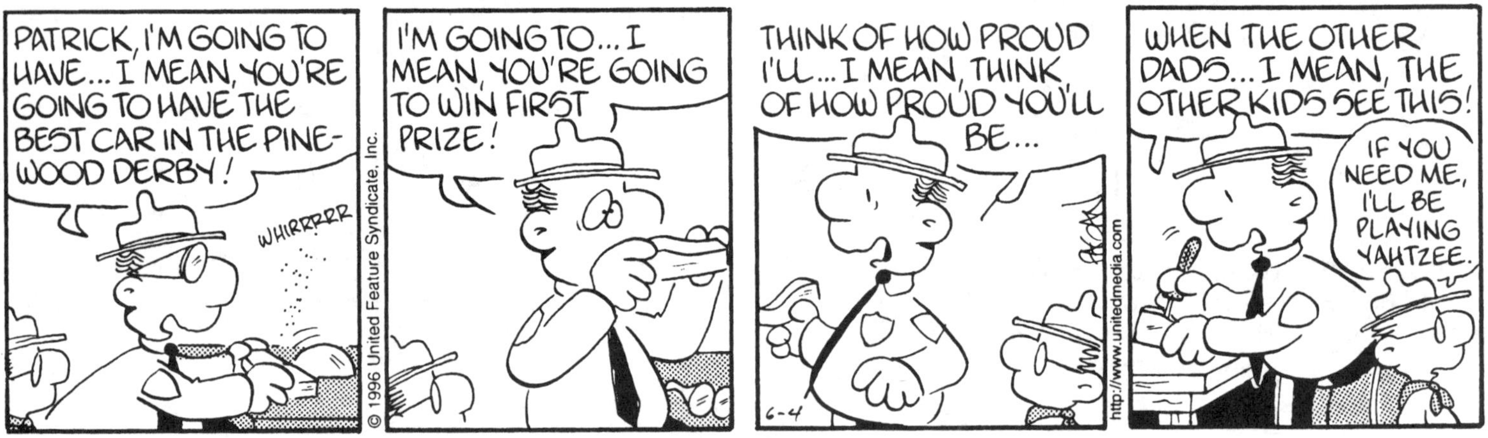
PATRICK, I'M GOING TO HAVE... I MEAN, YOU'RE GOING TO HAVE THE BEST CAR IN THE PINE-WOOD DERBY!
WHIRRRRR
© 1996 United Feature Syndicate, Inc.
I'M GOING TO... I MEAN, YOU'RE GOING TO WIN FIRST PRIZE!
THINK OF HOW PROUD I'LL... I MEAN, THINK OF HOW PROUD YOU'LL BE...
6-4
http://www.unitedmedia.com
WHEN THE OTHER DADS... I MEAN, THE OTHER KIDS SEE THIS!
IF YOU NEED ME, I'LL BE PLAYING YAHTZEE.

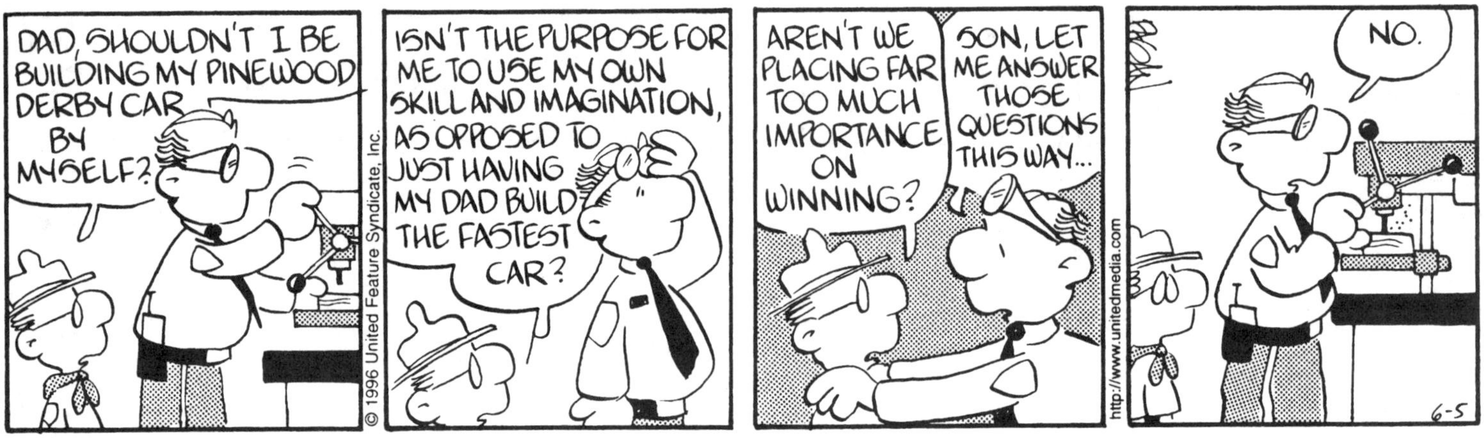
DAD, SHOULDN'T I BE BUILDING MY PINEWOOD DERBY CAR BY MYSELF?
© 1996 United Feature Syndicate, Inc.
ISN'T THE PURPOSE FOR ME TO USE MY OWN SKILL AND IMAGINATION, AS OPPOSED TO JUST HAVING MY DAD BUILD THE FASTEST CAR?
AREN'T WE PLACING FAR TOO MUCH IMPORTANCE ON WINNING?
SON, LET ME ANSWER THOSE QUESTIONS THIS WAY...
http://www.unitedmedia.com
NO.
6-5

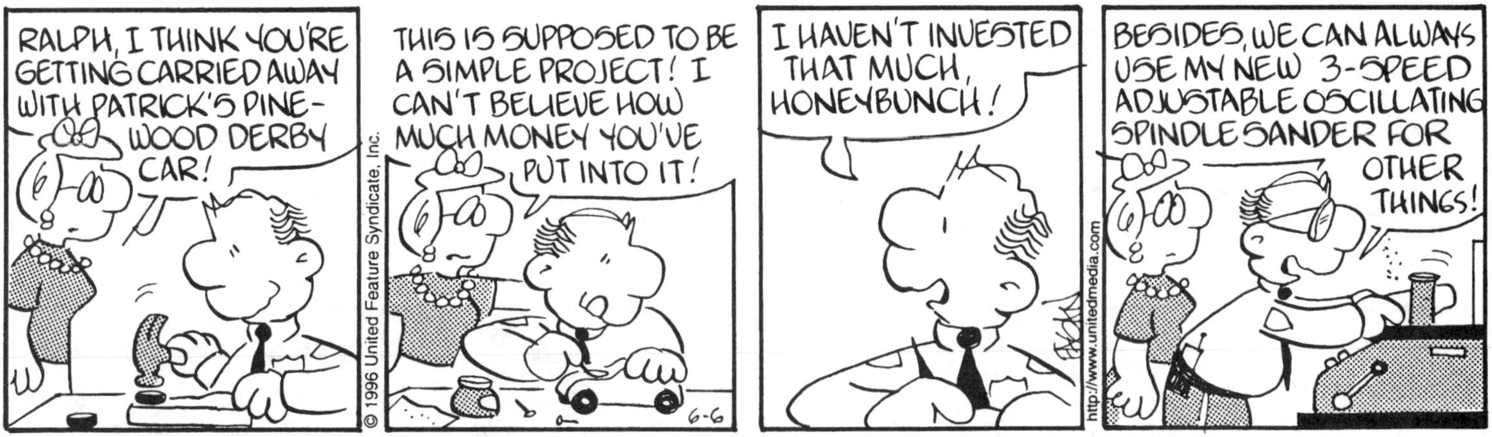
RALPH, I THINK YOU'RE GETTING CARRIED AWAY WITH PATRICK'S PINE-WOOD DERBY CAR!
THIS IS SUPPOSED TO BE A SIMPLE PROJECT! I CAN'T BELIEVE HOW MUCH MONEY YOU'VE PUT INTO IT!
© 1996 United Feature Syndicate, Inc.
6-6
I HAVEN'T INVESTED THAT MUCH, HONEYBUNCH!
http://www.unitedmedia.com
BESIDES, WE CAN ALWAYS USE MY NEW 3-SPEED ADJUSTABLE OSCILLATING SPINDLE SANDER FOR OTHER THINGS!

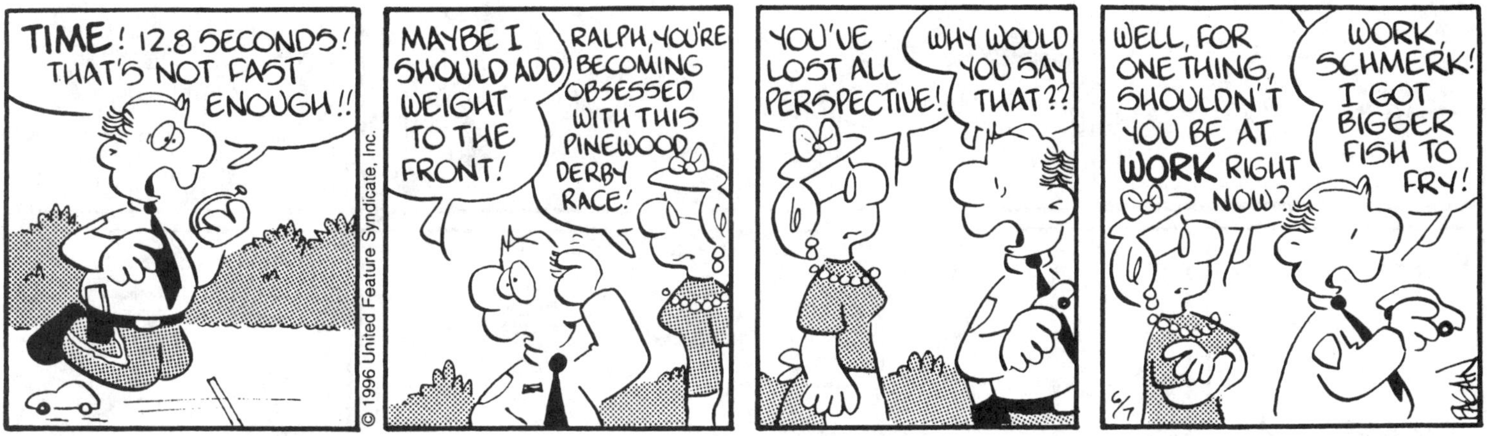
TIME! 12.8 SECONDS! THAT'S NOT FAST ENOUGH!!
© 1996 United Feature Syndicate, Inc.
MAYBE I SHOULD ADD WEIGHT TO THE FRONT!
RALPH, YOU'RE BECOMING OBSESSED WITH THIS PINEWOOD DERBY RACE!
YOU'VE LOST ALL PERSPECTIVE!
WHY WOULD YOU SAY THAT??
6/7
WELL, FOR ONE THING, SHOULDN'T YOU BE AT WORK RIGHT NOW?
WORK, SCHMERK! I GOT BIGGER FISH TO FRY!

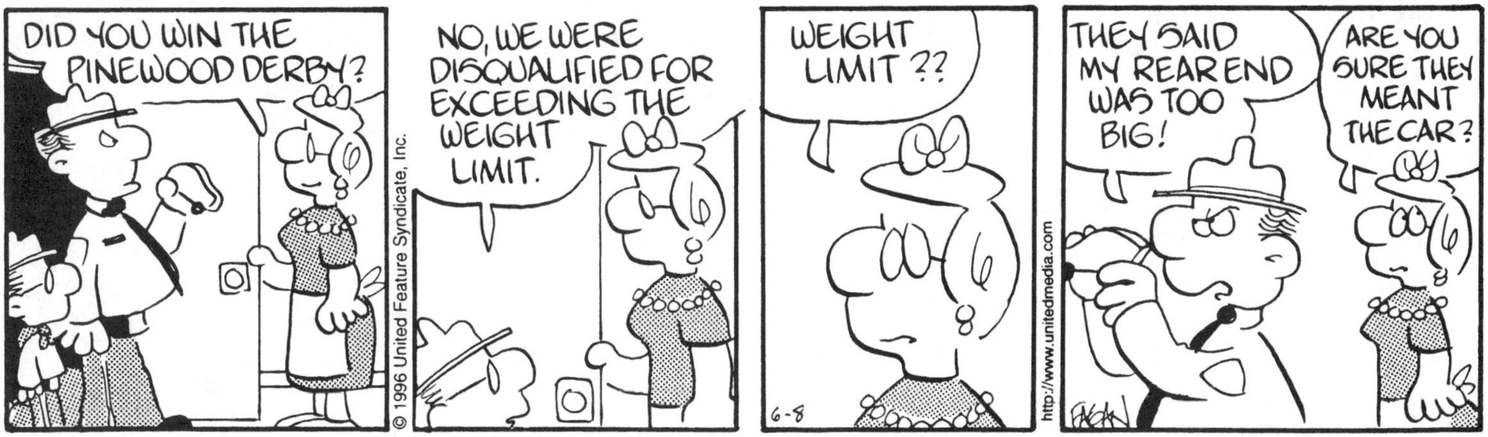
DID YOU WIN THE PINEWOOD DERBY?
NO, WE WERE DISQUALIFIED FOR EXCEEDING THE WEIGHT LIMIT.
© 1996 United Feature Syndicate, Inc.
WEIGHT LIMIT??
6-8
http://www.unitedmedia.com
THEY SAID MY REAR END WAS TOO BIG!
ARE YOU SURE THEY MEANT THE CAR?

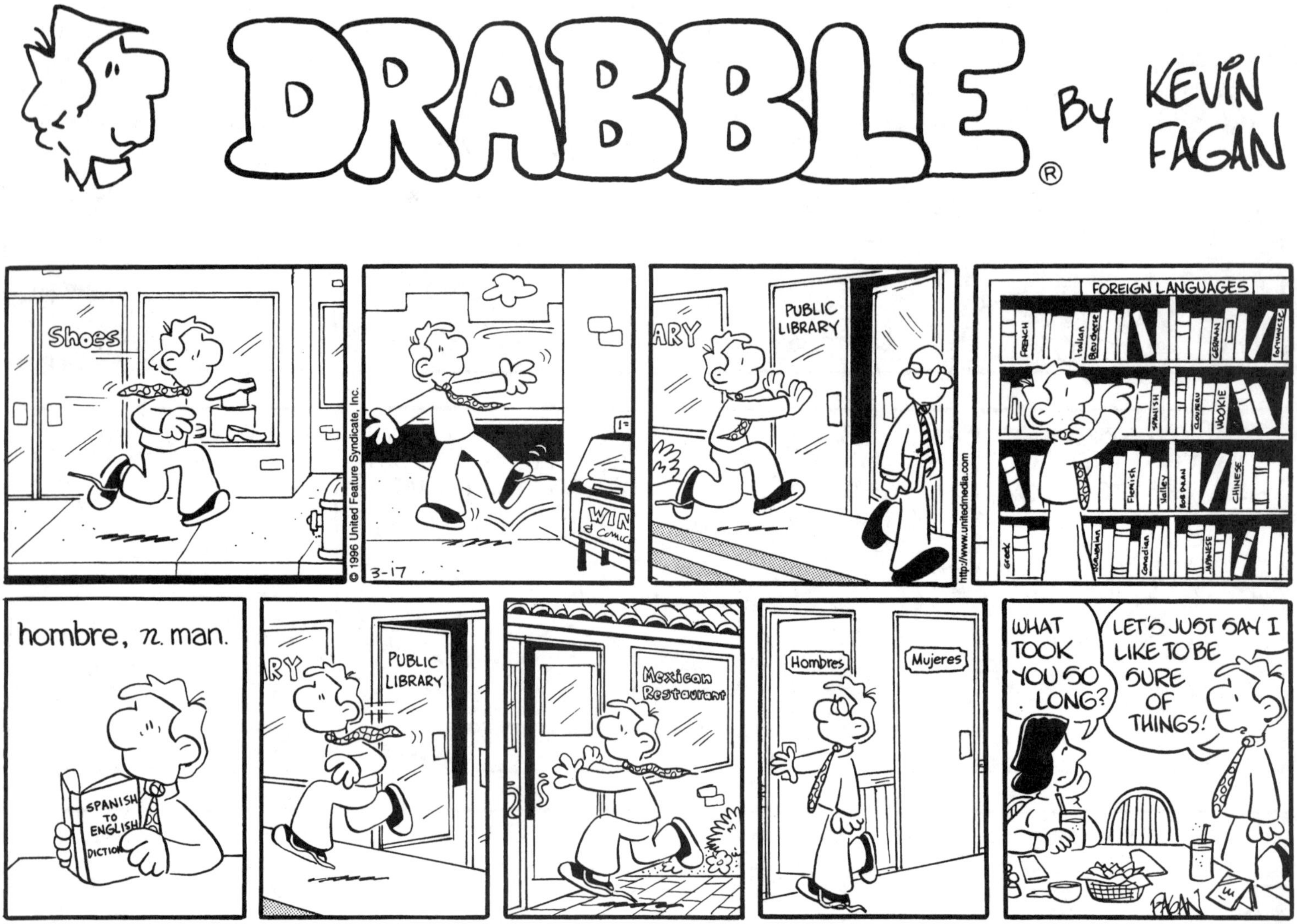
DRABBLE
By KEVIN FAGAN
Shoes
© 1996 United Feature Syndicate, Inc.
3-17
ARY
PUBLIC LIBRARY
http://www.unitedmedia.com
FOREIGN LANGUAGES
hombre, n. man.
SPANISH TO ENGLISH DICTION
ARY
PUBLIC LIBRARY
Mexican Restaurant
Hombres
Mujeres
WHAT TOOK YOU SO LONG?
LET'S JUST SAY I LIKE TO BE SURE OF THINGS!
FAGAN

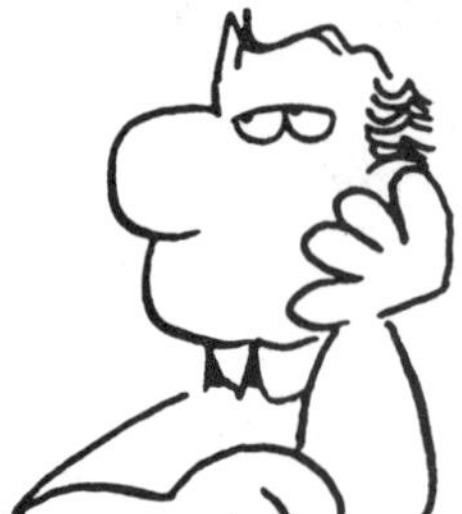

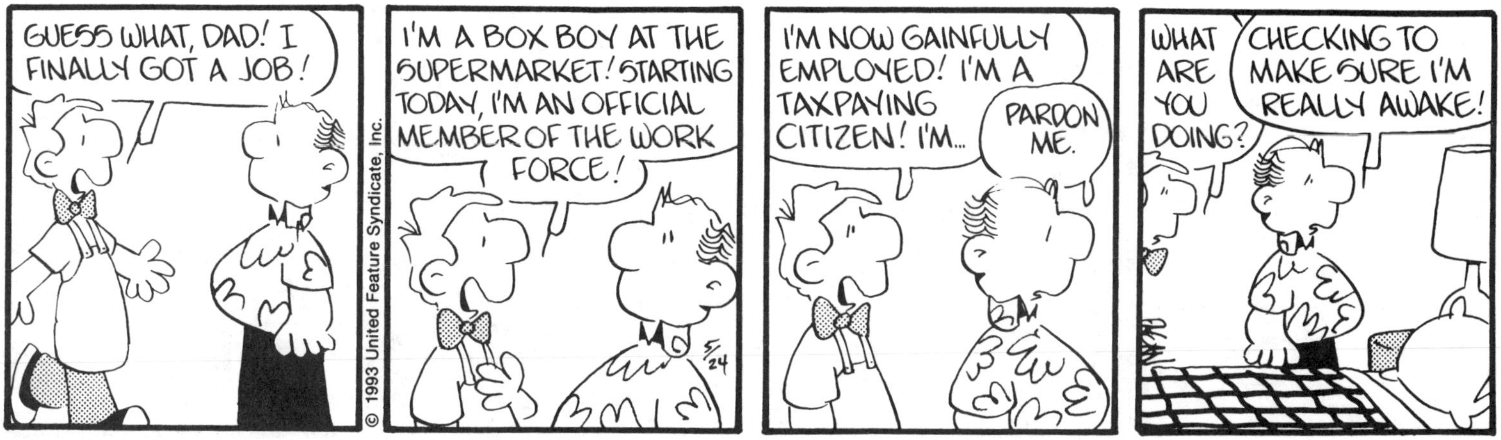
GUESS WHAT, DAD! I FINALLY GOT A JOB!
© 1993 United Feature Syndicate, Inc.
I'M A BOX BOY AT THE SUPERMARKET! STARTING TODAY, I'M AN OFFICIAL MEMBER OF THE WORK FORCE!
5/24
I'M NOW GAINFULLY EMPLOYED! I'M A TAXPAYING CITIZEN! I'M...
PARDON ME.
WHAT ARE YOU DOING?
CHECKING TO MAKE SURE I'M REALLY AWAKE!

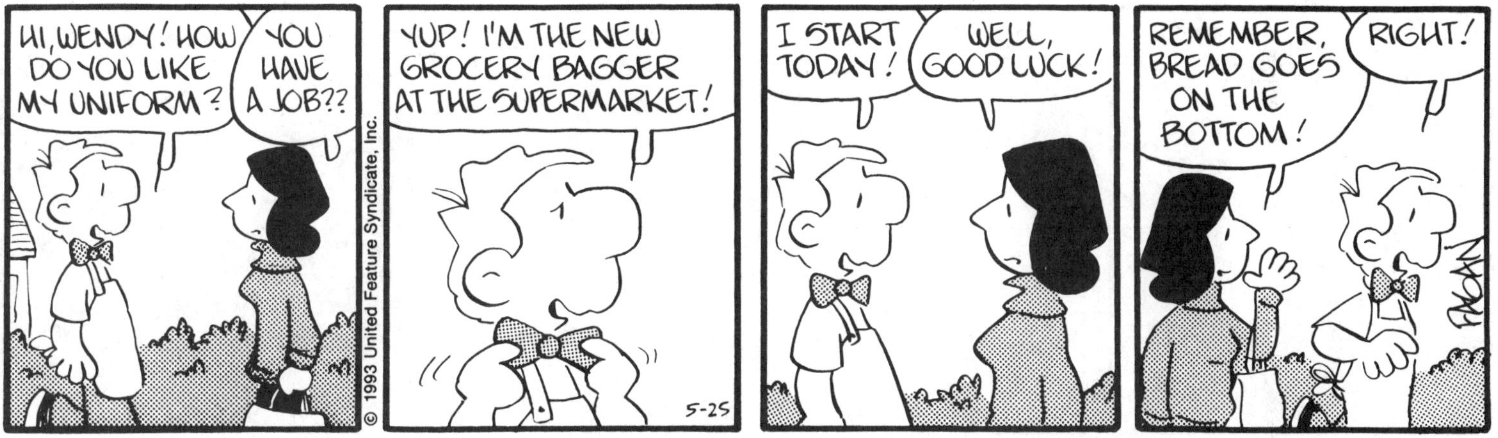
HI, WENDY! HOW DO YOU LIKE MY UNIFORM?
YOU HAVE A JOB??
© 1993 United Feature Syndicate, Inc.
YUP! I'M THE NEW GROCERY BAGGER AT THE SUPERMARKET!
5-25
I START TODAY!
WELL, GOOD LUCK!
REMEMBER, BREAD GOES ON THE BOTTOM!
RIGHT!

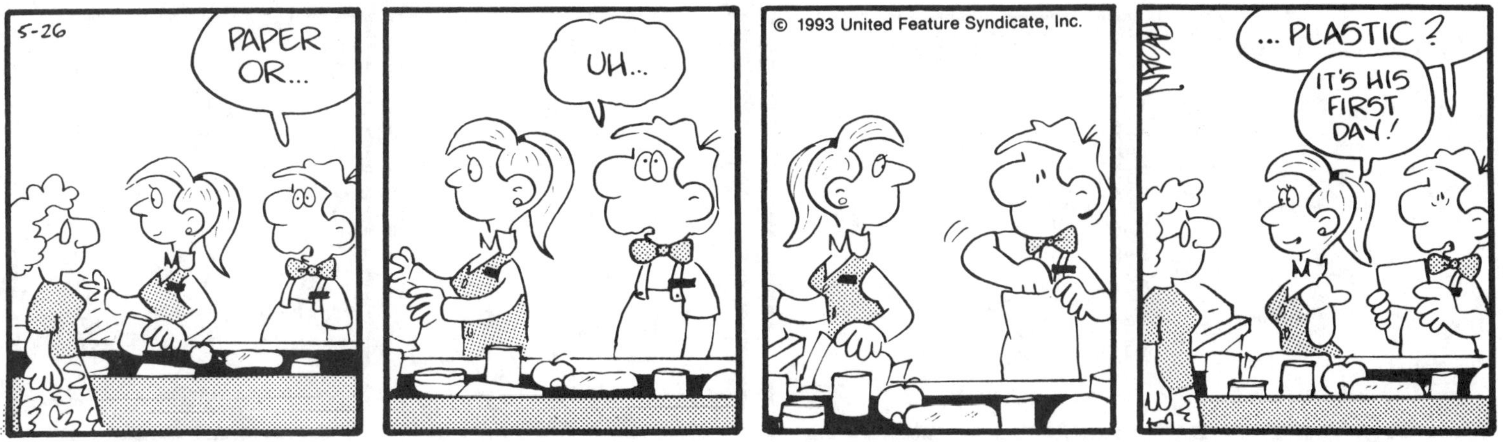
5-26
PAPER OR...
UH...
© 1993 United Feature Syndicate, Inc.
... PLASTIC?
IT'S HIS FIRST DAY!

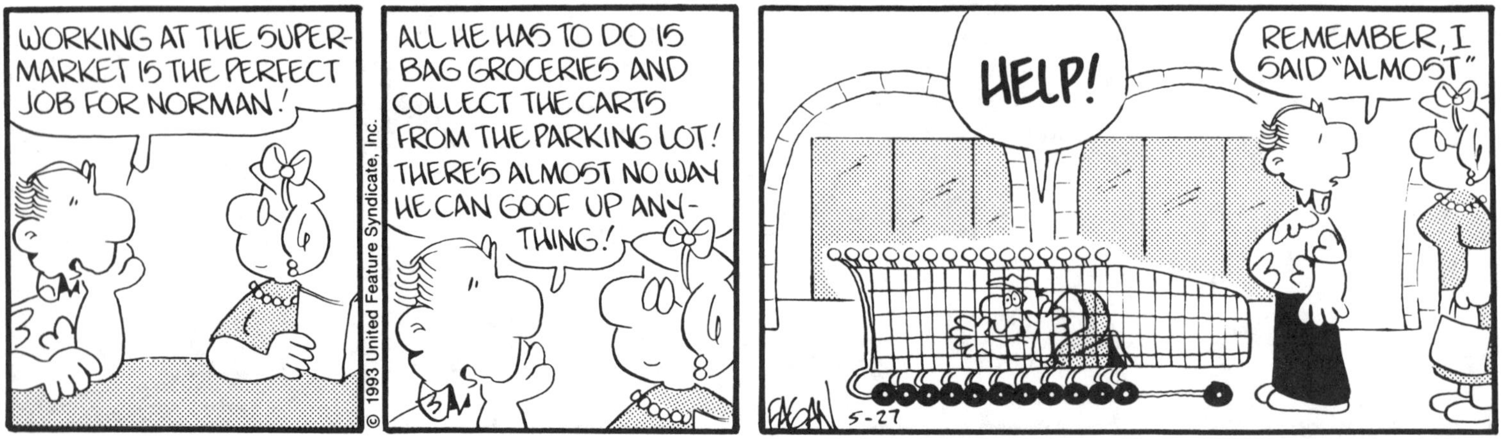
WORKING AT THE SUPERMARKET IS THE PERFECT JOB FOR NORMAN!
© 1993 United Feature Syndicate, Inc.
ALL HE HAS TO DO IS BAG GROCERIES AND COLLECT THE CARTS FROM THE PARKING LOT! THERE'S ALMOST NO WAY HE CAN GOOF UP ANYTHING!
HELP!
REMEMBER, I SAID "ALMOST"
5-27

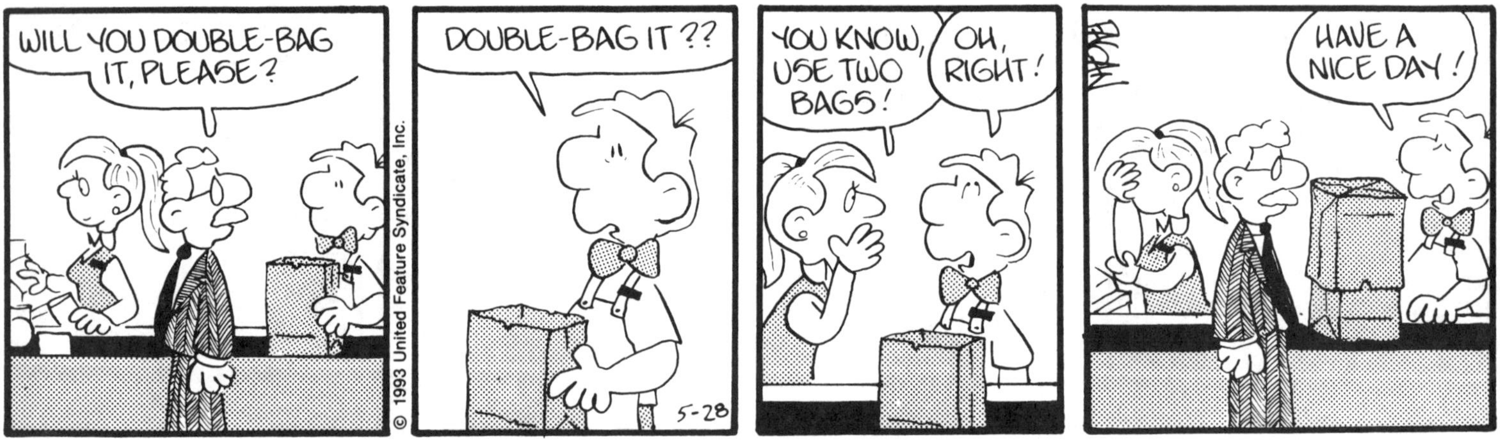
WILL YOU DOUBLE-BAG IT, PLEASE?
© 1993 United Feature Syndicate, Inc.
DOUBLE-BAG IT??
5-28
YOU KNOW, USE TWO BAGS!
OH, RIGHT!
HAVE A NICE DAY!

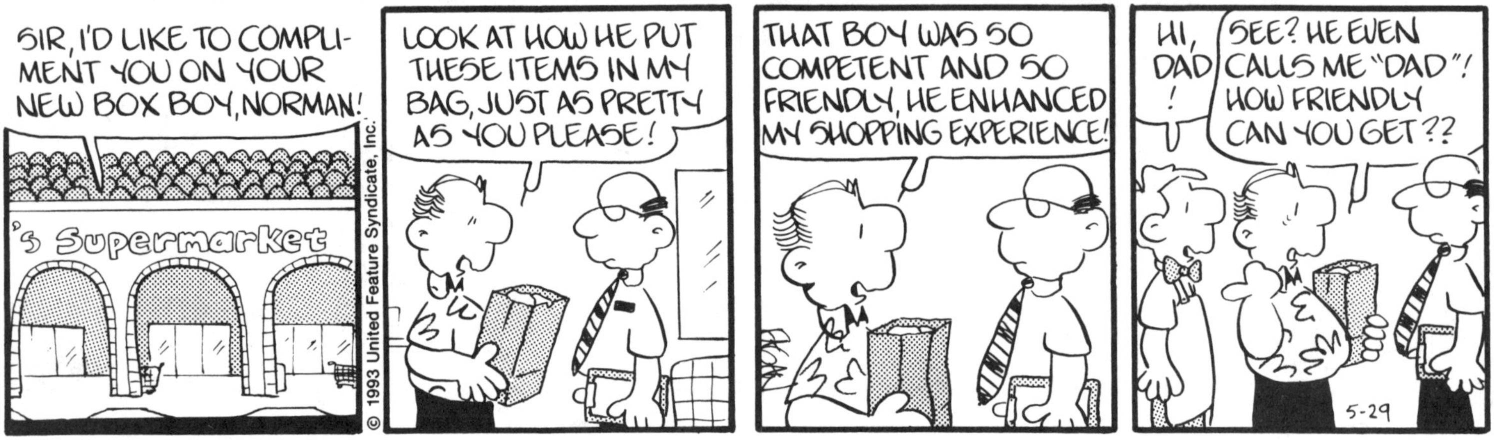
SIR, I'D LIKE TO COMPLIMENT YOU ON YOUR NEW BOX BOY, NORMAN!
'S Supermarket
© 1993 United Feature Syndicate, Inc.
LOOK AT HOW HE PUT THESE ITEMS IN MY BAG, JUST AS PRETTY AS YOU PLEASE!
THAT BOY WAS SO COMPETENT AND SO FRIENDLY, HE ENHANCED MY SHOPPING EXPERIENCE!
HI, DAD!
SEE? HE EVEN CALLS ME "DAD"! HOW FRIENDLY CAN YOU GET??
5-29

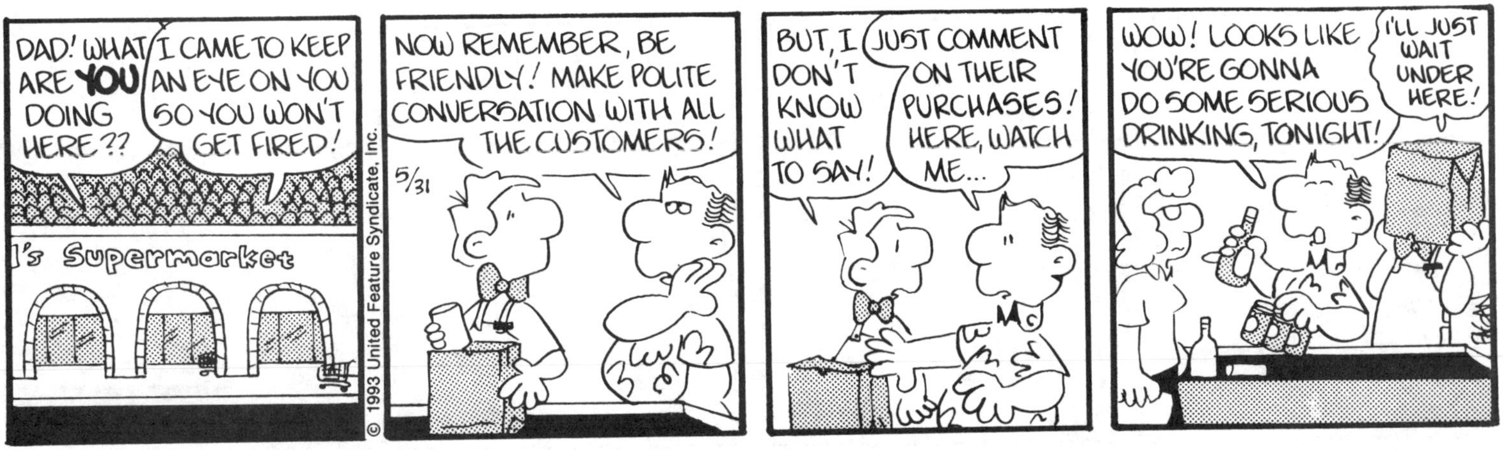
DAD! WHAT ARE YOU DOING HERE??
I CAME TO KEEP AN EYE ON YOU SO YOU WON'T GET FIRED!
'S Supermarket
© 1993 United Feature Syndicate, Inc.
5/31
NOW REMEMBER, BE FRIENDLY! MAKE POLITE CONVERSATION WITH ALL THE CUSTOMERS!
BUT, I DON'T KNOW WHAT TO SAY!
JUST COMMENT ON THEIR PURCHASES! HERE, WATCH ME...
WOW! LOOKS LIKE YOU'RE GONNA DO SOME SERIOUS DRINKING, TONIGHT!
I'LL JUST WAIT UNDER HERE!

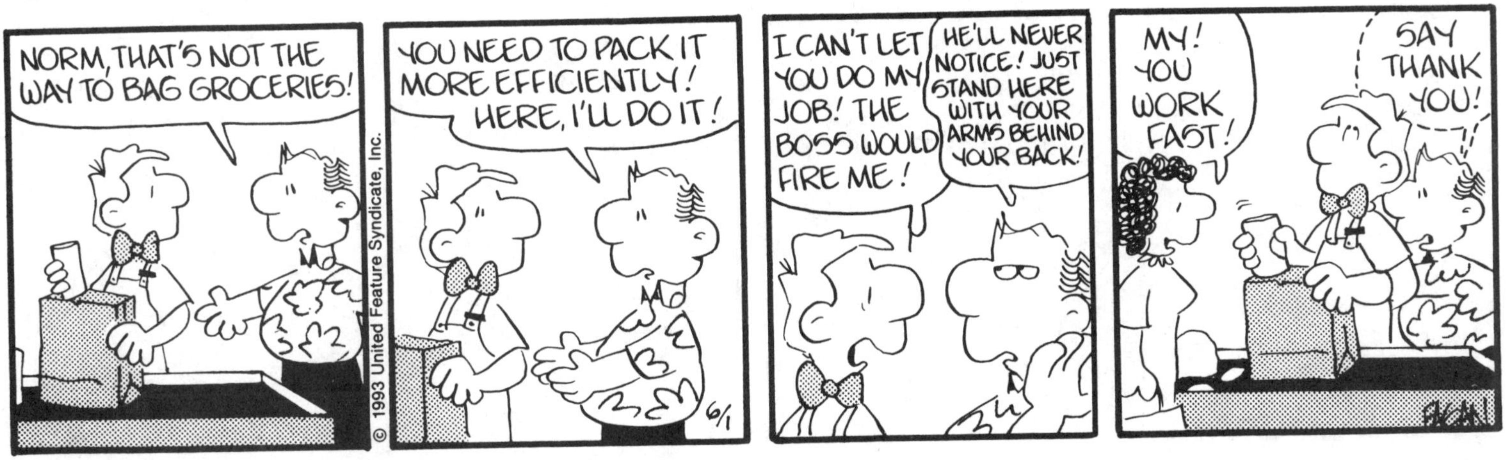
NORM, THAT'S NOT THE WAY TO BAG GROCERIES!
© 1993 United Feature Syndicate, Inc.
YOU NEED TO PACK IT MORE EFFICIENTLY! HERE, I'LL DO IT!
6/1
I CAN'T LET YOU DO MY JOB! THE BOSS WOULD FIRE ME!
HE'LL NEVER NOTICE! JUST STAND HERE WITH YOUR ARMS BEHIND YOUR BACK!
MY! YOU WORK FAST!
SAY THANK YOU!

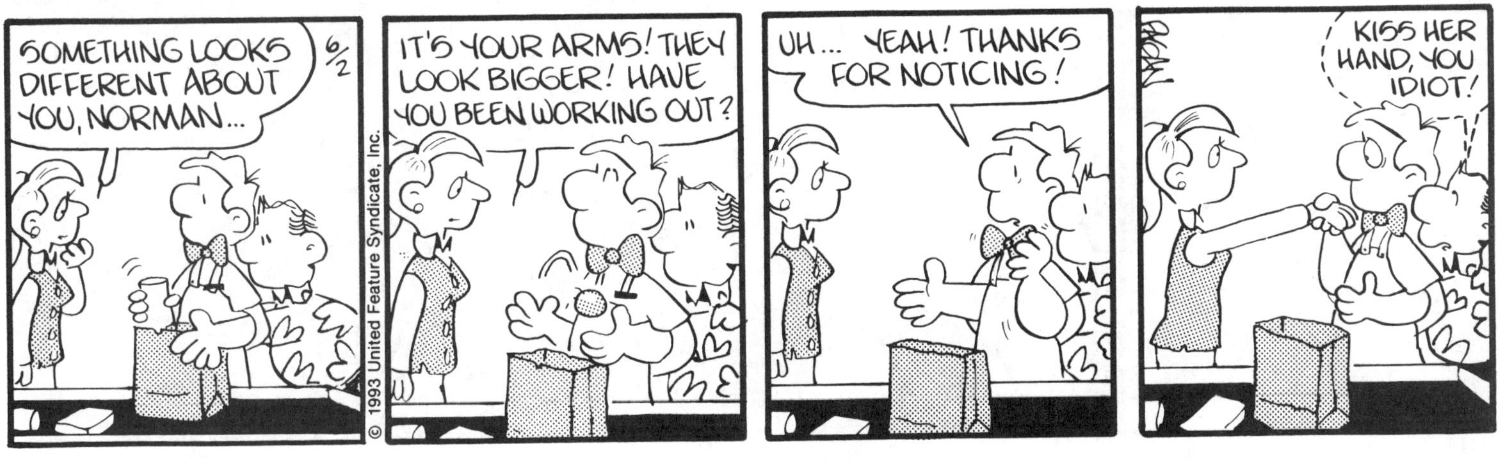
SOMETHING LOOKS DIFFERENT ABOUT YOU, NORMAN...
6/2
© 1993 United Feature Syndicate, Inc.
IT'S YOUR ARMS! THEY LOOK BIGGER! HAVE YOU BEEN WORKING OUT?
UH... YEAH! THANKS FOR NOTICING!
KISS HER HAND, YOU IDIOT!

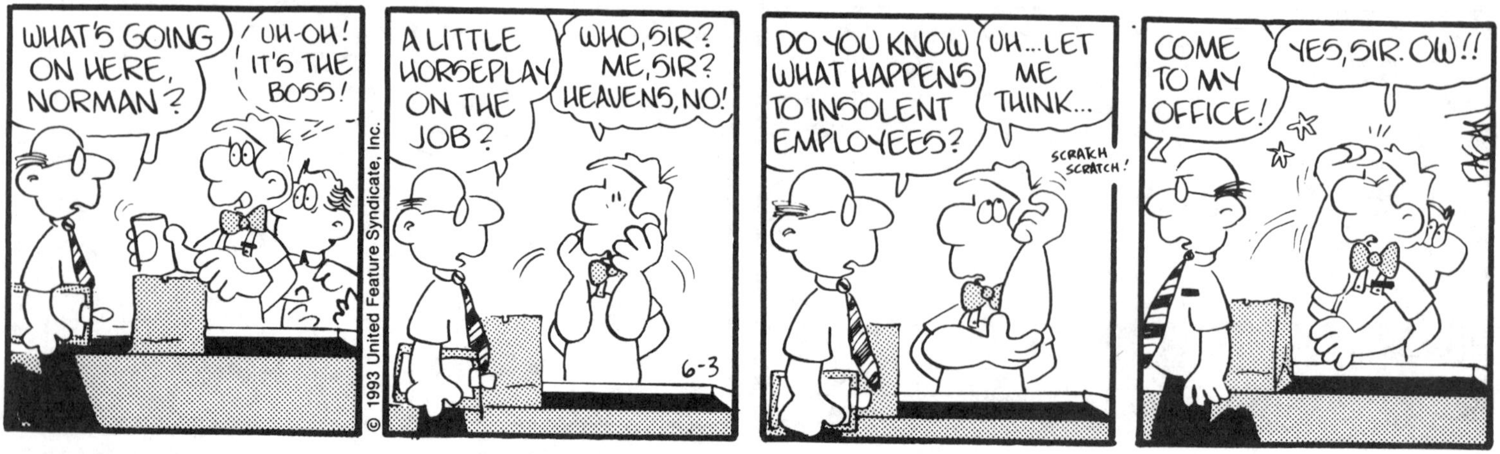
WHAT'S GOING ON HERE, NORMAN?
UH-OH! IT'S THE BOSS!
© 1993 United Feature Syndicate, Inc.
A LITTLE HORSEPLAY ON THE JOB?
WHO, SIR? ME, SIR? HEAVENS, NO!
6-3
DO YOU KNOW WHAT HAPPENS TO INSOLENT EMPLOYEES?
UH...LET ME THINK...
SCRATCH SCRATCH!
COME TO MY OFFICE!
YES, SIR. OW!!

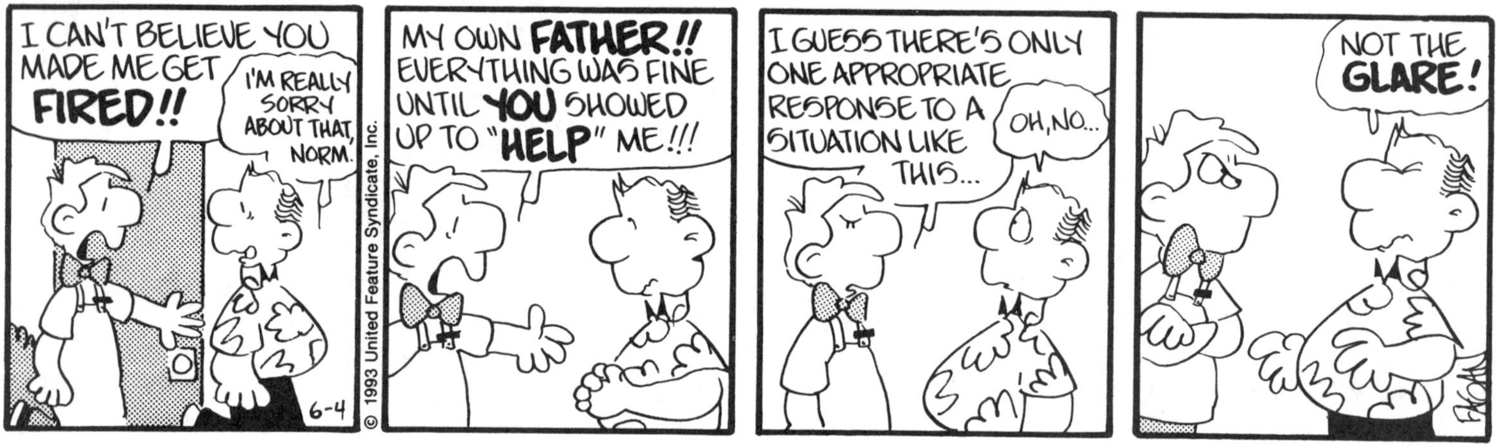
I CAN'T BELIEVE YOU MADE ME GET **FIRED**!!
I'M REALLY SORRY ABOUT THAT, NORM.
6-4
© 1993 United Feature Syndicate, Inc.
MY OWN **FATHER**!! EVERYTHING WAS FINE UNTIL **YOU** SHOWED UP TO "**HELP**" ME!!!
I GUESS THERE'S ONLY ONE APPROPRIATE RESPONSE TO A SITUATION LIKE THIS...
OH, NO...
NOT THE **GLARE**!

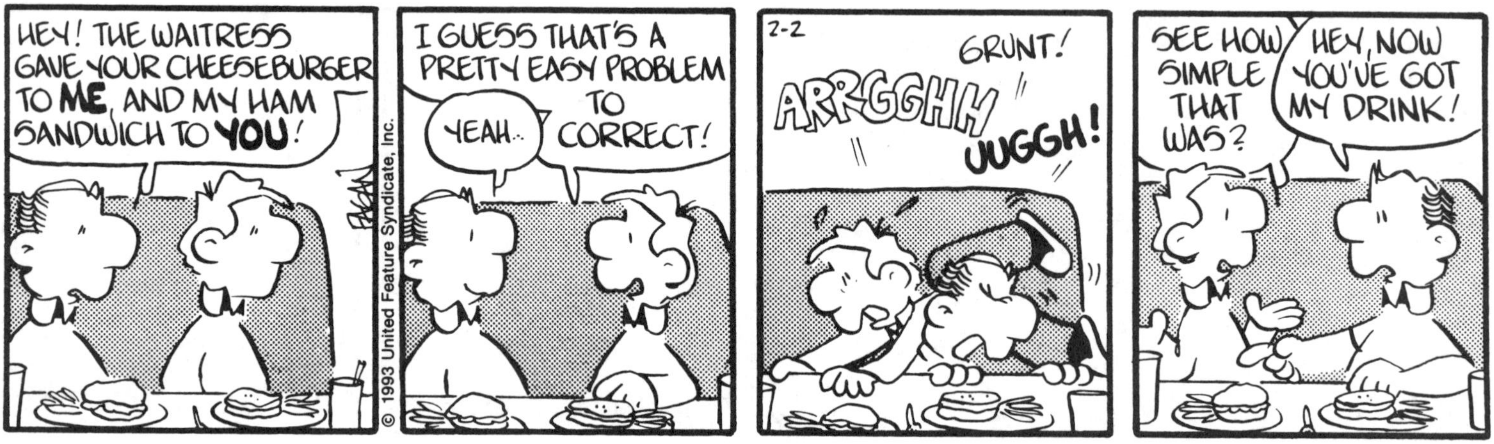
HEY! THE WAITRESS GAVE YOUR CHEESEBURGER TO **ME**, AND MY HAM SANDWICH TO **YOU**!
© 1993 United Feature Syndicate, Inc.
I GUESS THAT'S A PRETTY EASY PROBLEM TO CORRECT!
YEAH..
2-2
GRUNT!
ARRGGHH
UUGGH!
SEE HOW SIMPLE THAT WAS?
HEY, NOW YOU'VE GOT MY DRINK!

DRABBLE® By KEVIN FAGAN

Z
© 1996 United Feature Syndicate, Inc.
WHAM!
10-20
http://www.unitedmedia.com
RALPH DRABBLE, IF YOU EVER GO OUT WITH ANOTHER WOMAN AGAIN IN ONE OF MY DREAMS, YOU'LL LIVE TO REGRET IT!!
KEVINFAGAN@AOL.COM
HOW COME YOU'RE UP, DAD? DID YOU HAVE A BAD DREAM?
WORSE... I WAS IN ONE!

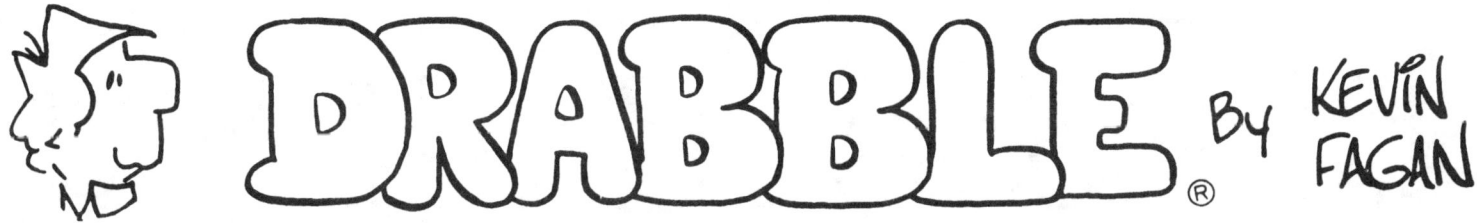

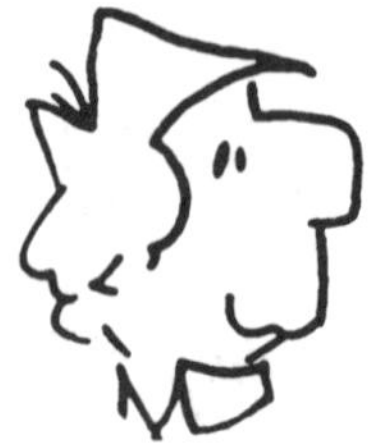

DRABBLE®

By KEVIN FAGAN

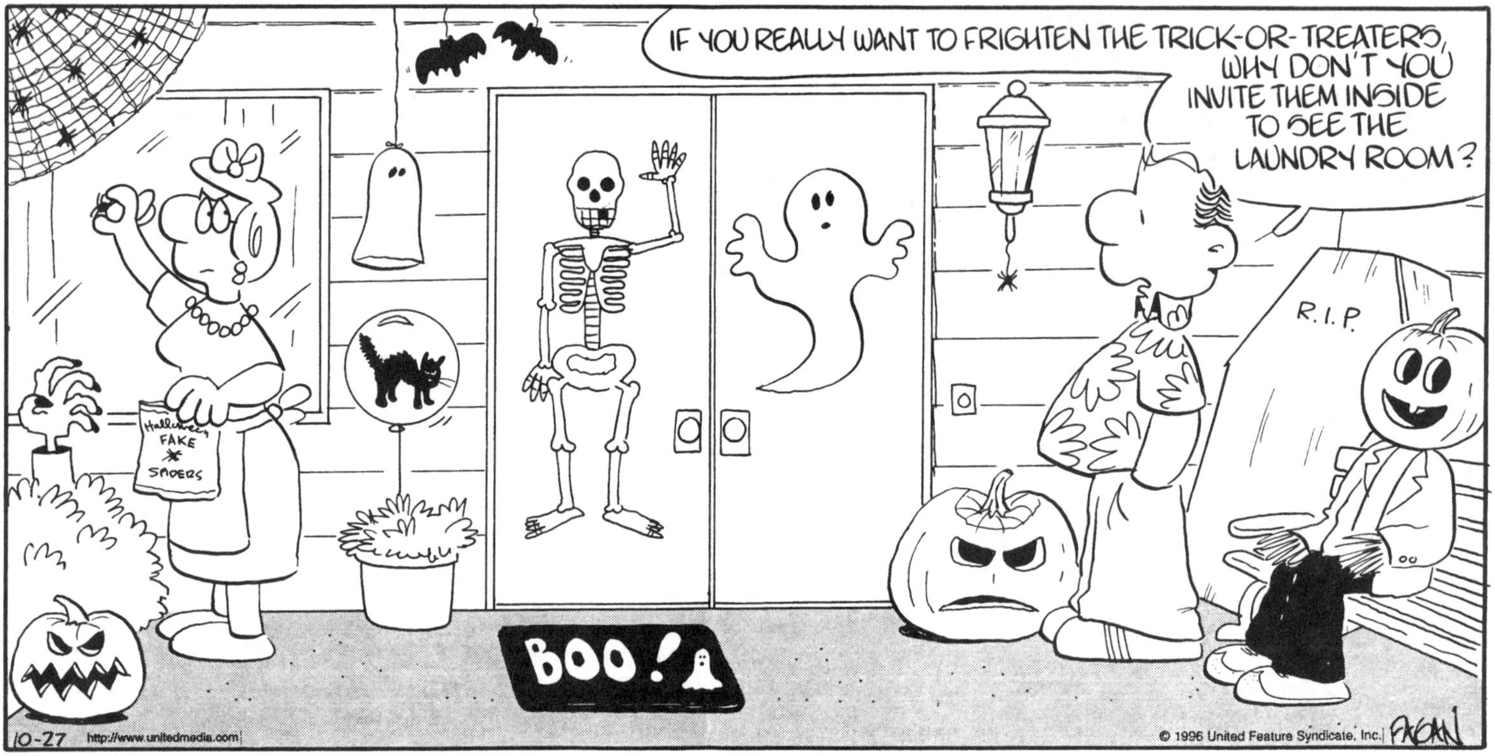

IF YOU REALLY WANT TO FRIGHTEN THE TRICK-OR-TREATERS, WHY DON'T YOU INVITE THEM INSIDE TO SEE THE LAUNDRY ROOM?
FAKE SPIDERS
BOO!
R.I.P.
10-27
http://www.unitedmedia.com
© 1996 United Feature Syndicate, Inc.
FAGAN

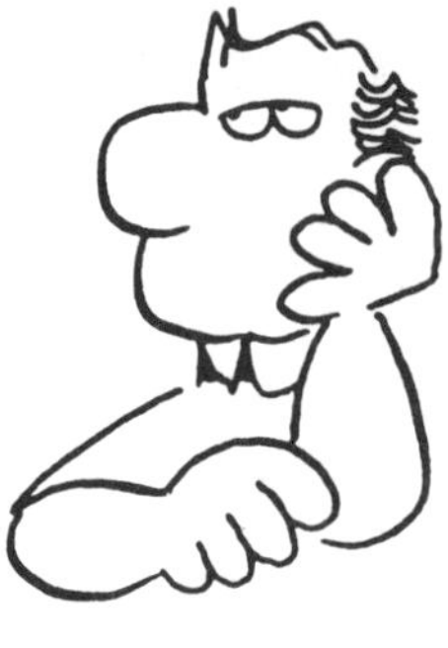

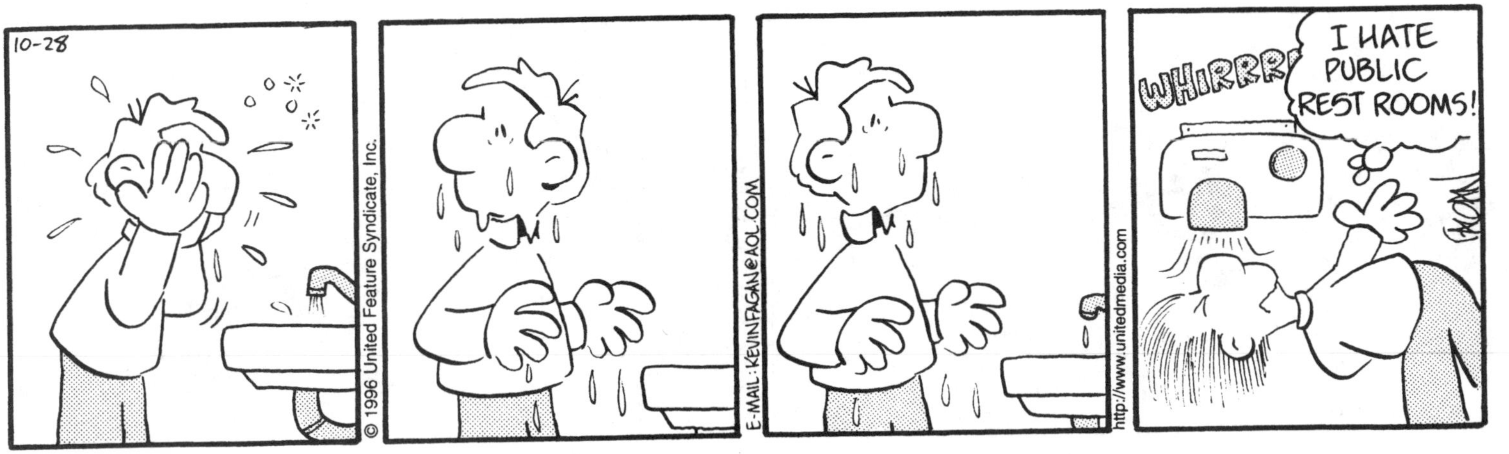
10-28
© 1996 United Feature Syndicate, Inc.
E-MAIL: KEVINFAGAN@AOL.COM
http://www.unitedmedia.com
WHIRRR
I HATE PUBLIC REST ROOMS!

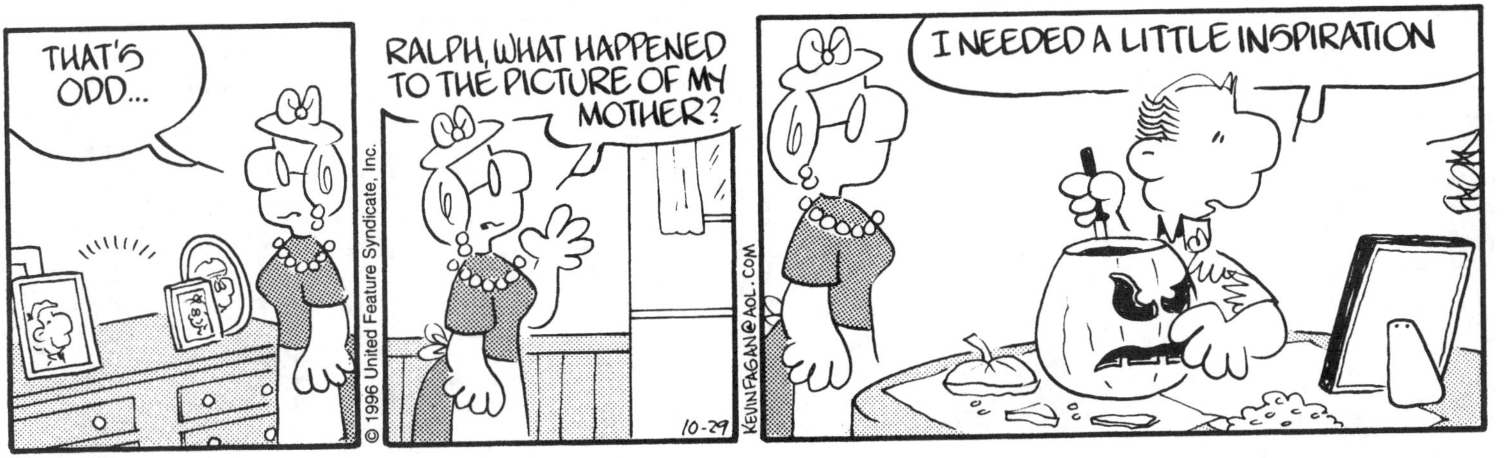
THAT'S ODD...
© 1996 United Feature Syndicate, Inc.
RALPH, WHAT HAPPENED TO THE PICTURE OF MY MOTHER?
10-29
KEVINFAGAN@AOL.COM
I NEEDED A LITTLE INSPIRATION

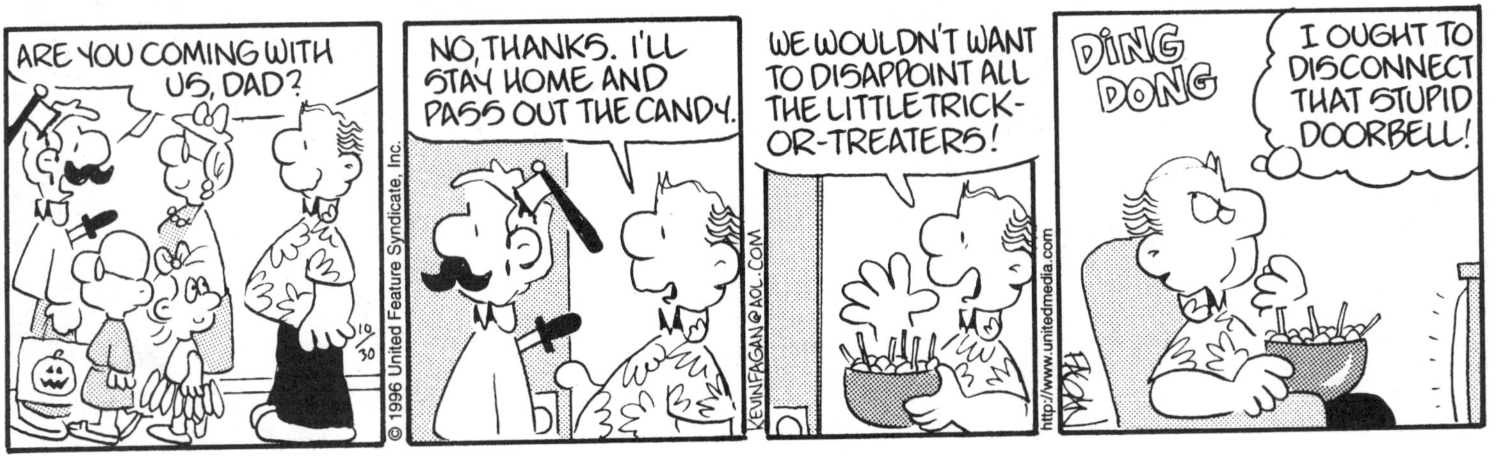
ARE YOU COMING WITH US, DAD?
10/30
© 1996 United Feature Syndicate, Inc.
NO, THANKS. I'LL STAY HOME AND PASS OUT THE CANDY.
KEVINFAGAN@AOL.COM
WE WOULDN'T WANT TO DISAPPOINT ALL THE LITTLE TRICK-OR-TREATERS!
http://www.unitedmedia.com
DING DONG
I OUGHT TO DISCONNECT THAT STUPID DOORBELL!

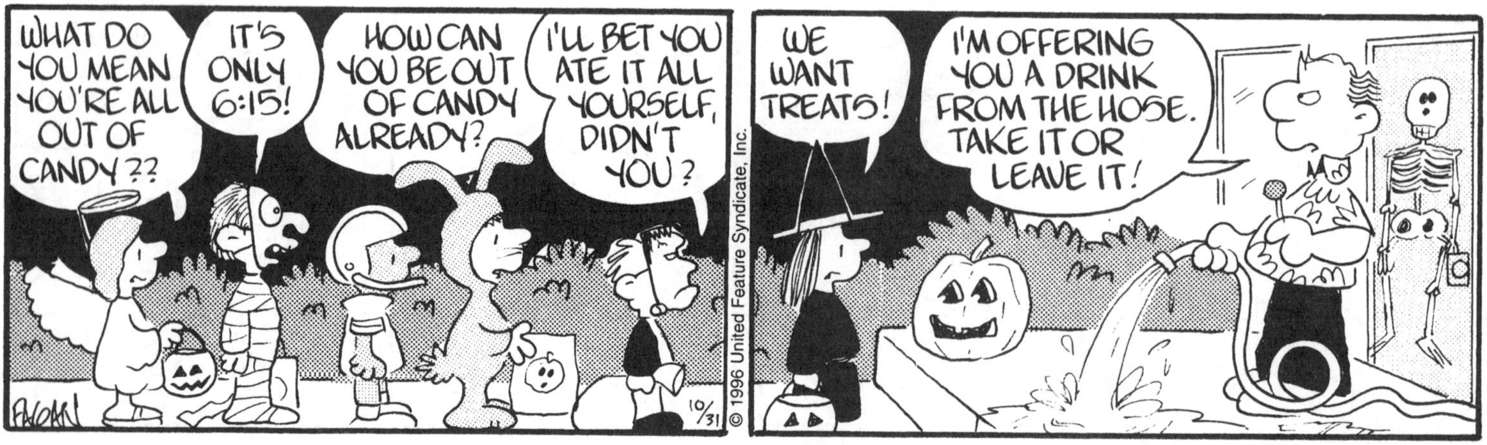
WHAT DO YOU MEAN YOU'RE ALL OUT OF CANDY??
IT'S ONLY 6:15!
HOW CAN YOU BE OUT OF CANDY ALREADY?
I'LL BET YOU ATE IT ALL YOURSELF, DIDN'T YOU?
FAGAN
10/31
© 1996 United Feature Syndicate, Inc.
WE WANT TREATS!
I'M OFFERING YOU A DRINK FROM THE HOSE. TAKE IT OR LEAVE IT!

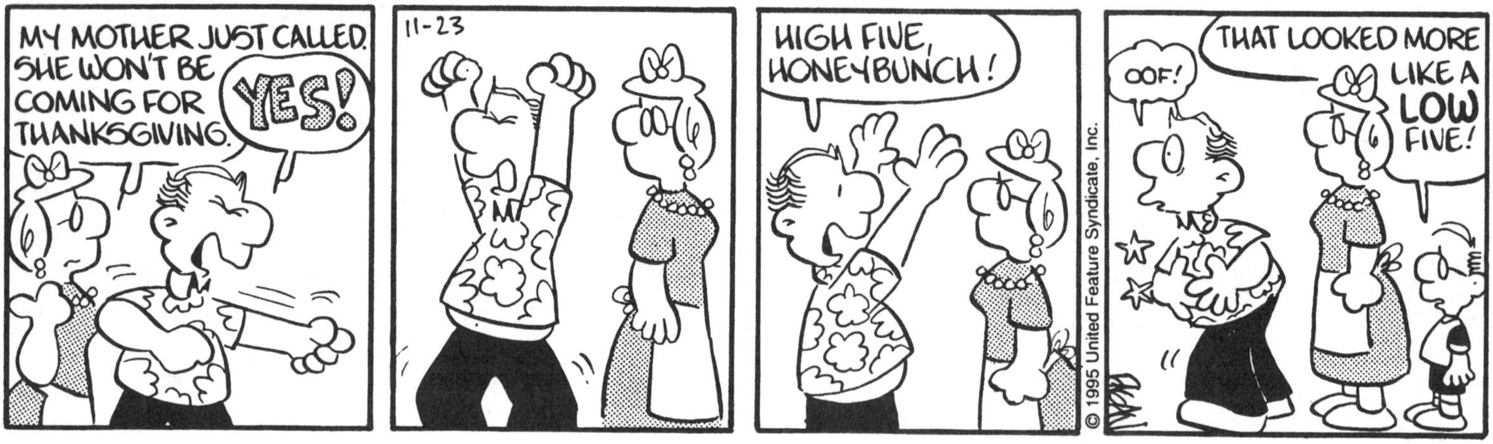
MY MOTHER JUST CALLED. SHE WON'T BE COMING FOR THANKSGIVING.
YES!
11-23
HIGH FIVE, HONEYBUNCH!
© 1995 United Feature Syndicate, Inc.
OOF!
THAT LOOKED MORE LIKE A LOW FIVE!

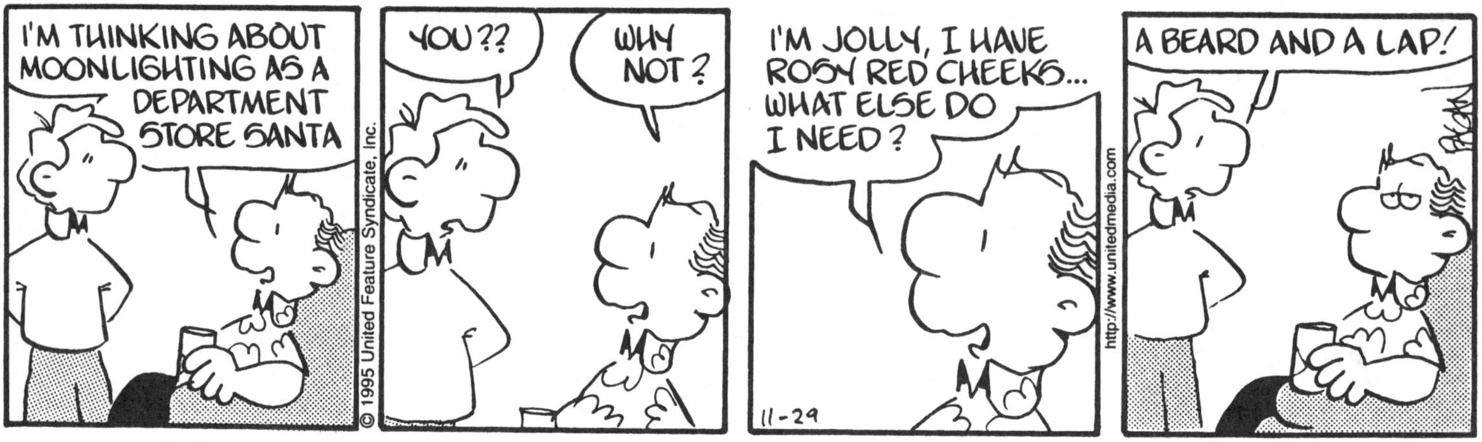
I'M THINKING ABOUT MOONLIGHTING AS A DEPARTMENT STORE SANTA
© 1995 United Feature Syndicate, Inc.
YOU??
WHY NOT?
I'M JOLLY, I HAVE ROSY RED CHEEKS... WHAT ELSE DO I NEED?
11-29
http://www.unitedmedia.com
A BEARD AND A LAP!
FAGAN

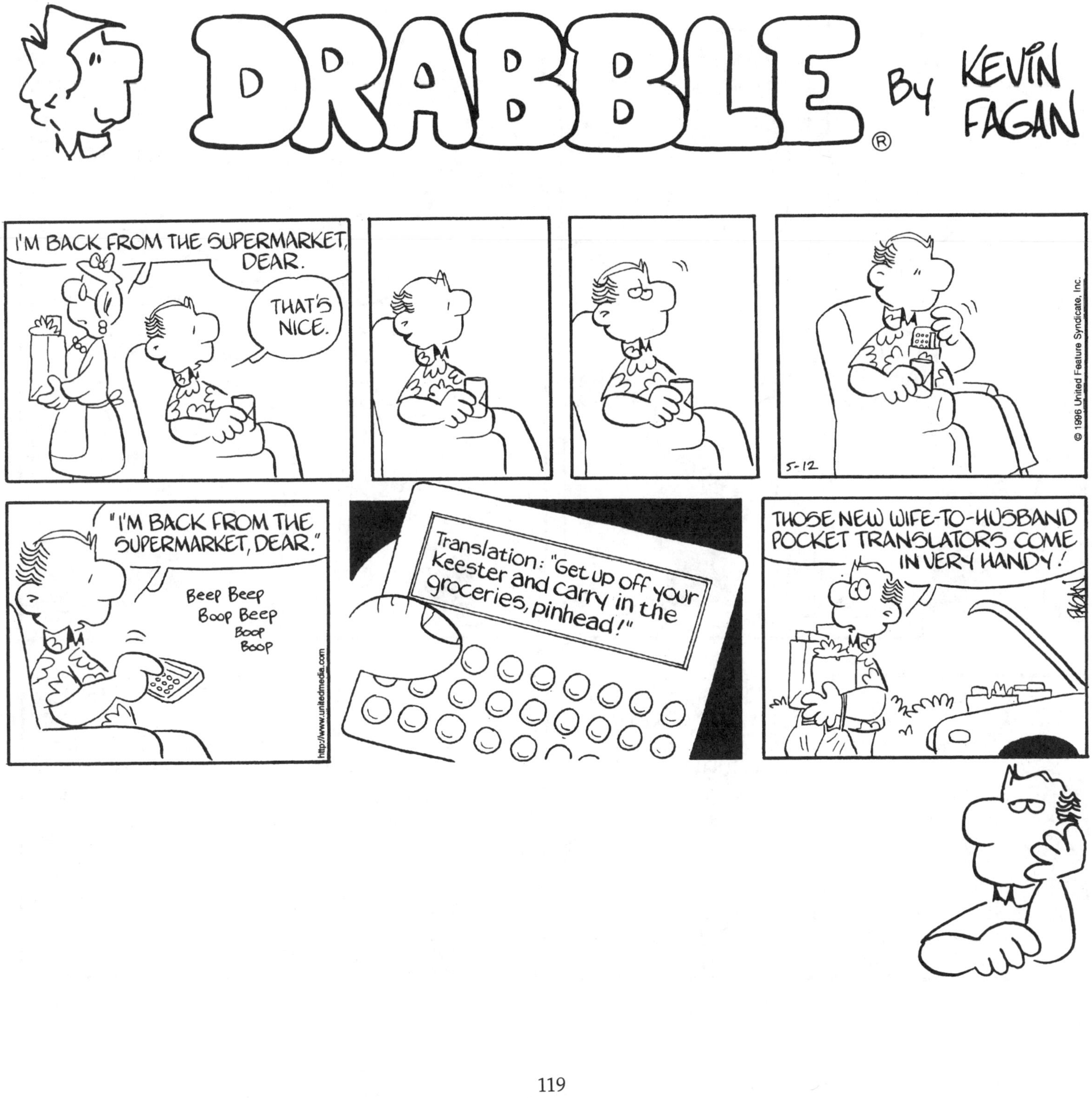
DRABBLE
By KEVIN FAGAN
I'M BACK FROM THE SUPERMARKET, DEAR.
THAT'S NICE.
5-12
© 1996 United Feature Syndicate, Inc.
"I'M BACK FROM THE SUPERMARKET, DEAR."
Beep Beep
Boop Beep
Boop
Boop
http://www.unitedmedia.com
Translation: "Get up off your Keester and carry in the groceries, pinhead!"
THOSE NEW WIFE-TO-HUSBAND POCKET TRANSLATORS COME IN VERY HANDY!

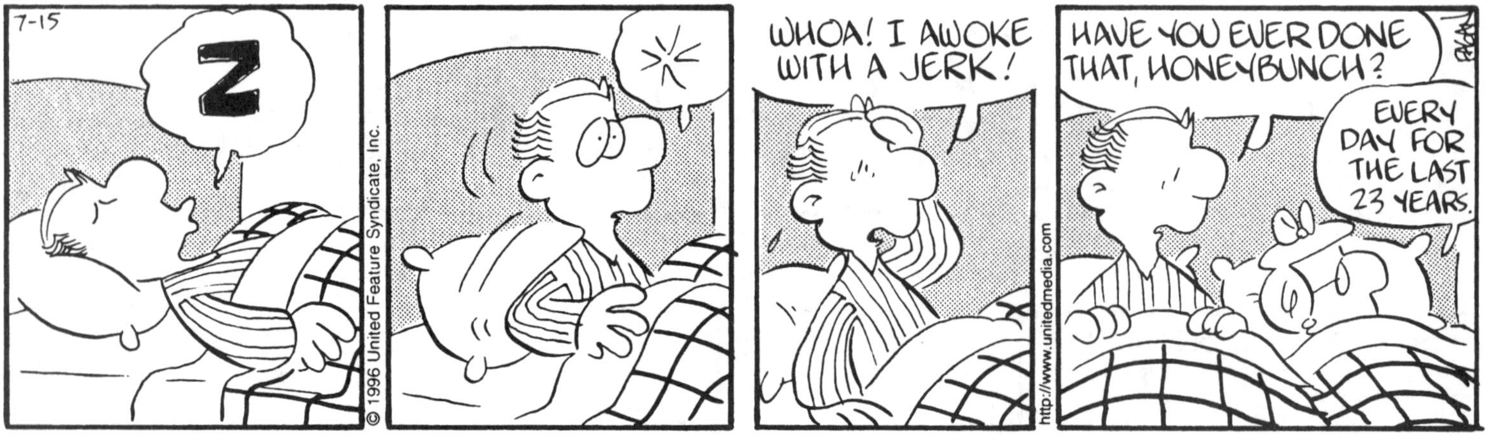
7-15
Z
WHOA! I AWOKE WITH A JERK!
HAVE YOU EVER DONE THAT, HONEYBUNCH?
EVERY DAY FOR THE LAST 23 YEARS.
© 1996 United Feature Syndicate, Inc.
http://www.unitedmedia.com

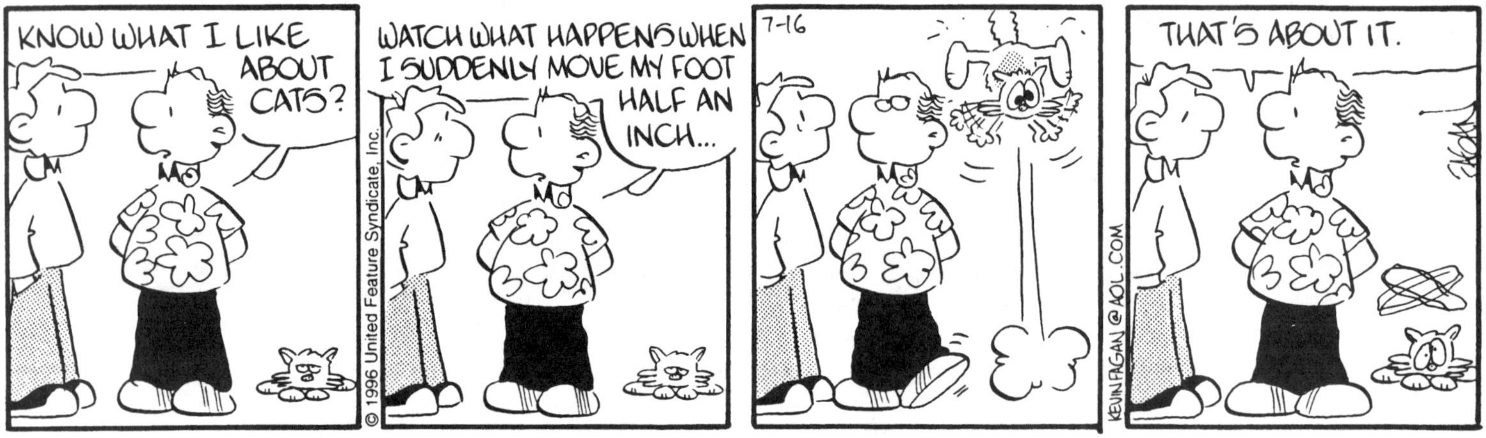
KNOW WHAT I LIKE ABOUT CATS?
WATCH WHAT HAPPENS WHEN I SUDDENLY MOVE MY FOOT HALF AN INCH...
7-16
THAT'S ABOUT IT.
© 1996 United Feature Syndicate, Inc.
KEVINFAGAN@AOL.COM

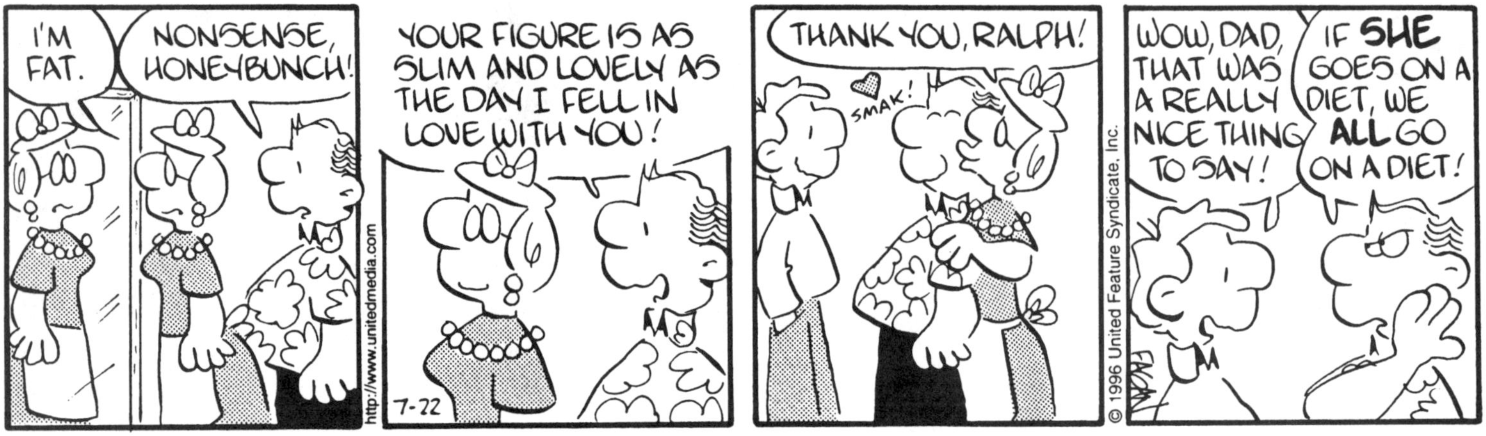
I'M FAT.
NONSENSE, HONEYBUNCH!
YOUR FIGURE IS AS SLIM AND LOVELY AS THE DAY I FELL IN LOVE WITH YOU!
7-22
THANK YOU, RALPH!
SMAK!
WOW, DAD, THAT WAS A REALLY NICE THING TO SAY!
IF **SHE** GOES ON A DIET, WE **ALL** GO ON A DIET!
http://www.unitedmedia.com
© 1996 United Feature Syndicate, Inc.

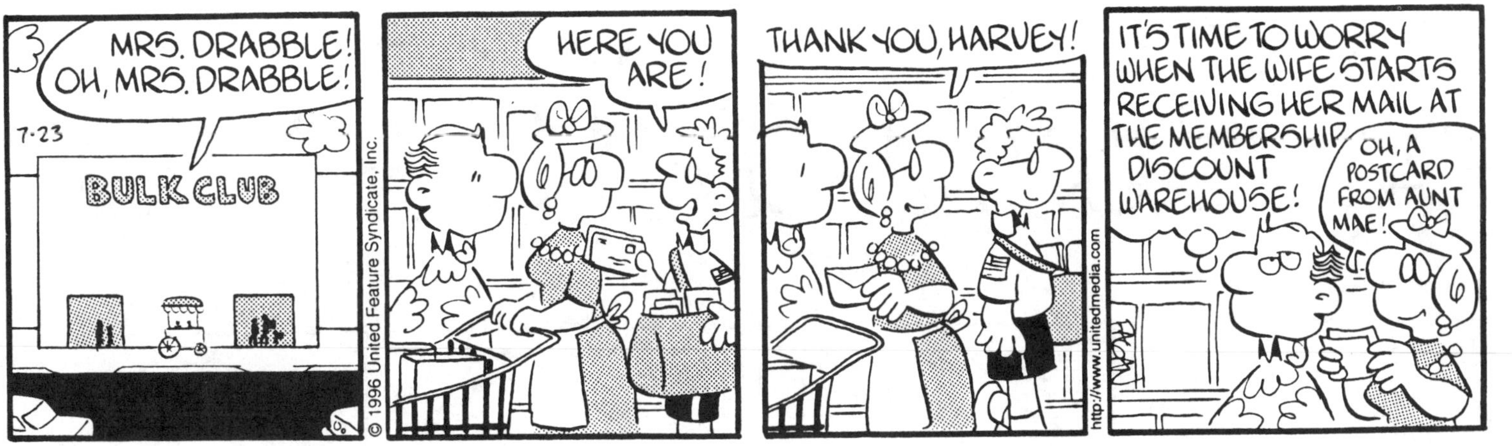

MRS. DRABBLE! OH, MRS. DRABBLE!
7-23
BULK CLUB
© 1996 United Feature Syndicate, Inc.
HERE YOU ARE!
THANK YOU, HARVEY!
http://www.unitedmedia.com
IT'S TIME TO WORRY WHEN THE WIFE STARTS RECEIVING HER MAIL AT THE MEMBERSHIP DISCOUNT WAREHOUSE!
OH, A POSTCARD FROM AUNT MAE!
FAGAN

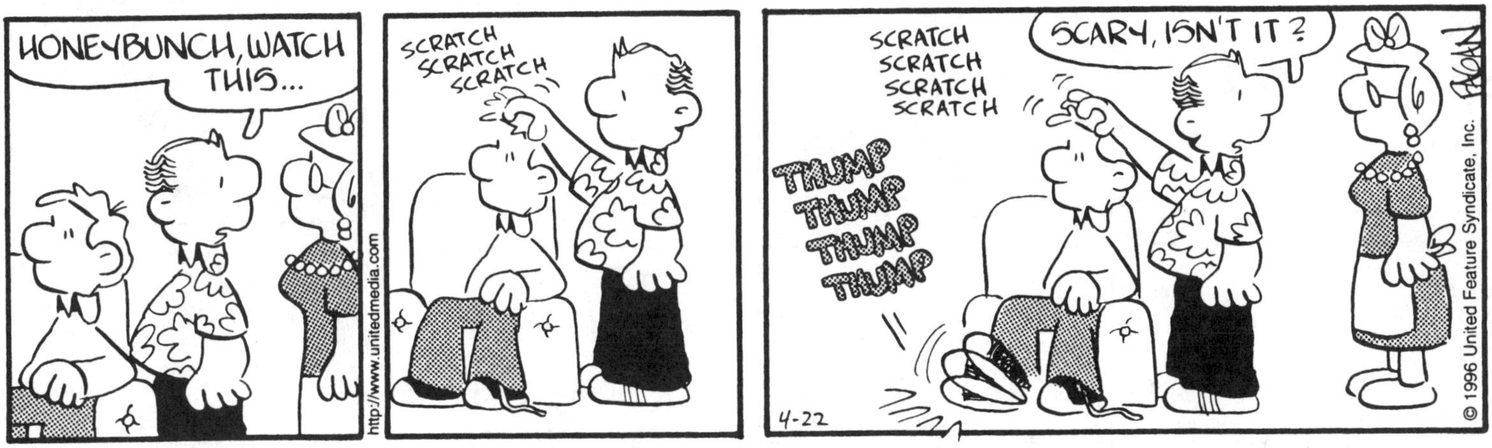

HONEYBUNCH, WATCH THIS...
http://www.unitedmedia.com
SCRATCH SCRATCH SCRATCH
SCRATCH SCRATCH SCRATCH SCRATCH
THUMP THUMP THUMP THUMP
SCARY, ISN'T IT?
4-22
FAGAN
© 1996 United Feature Syndicate, Inc.

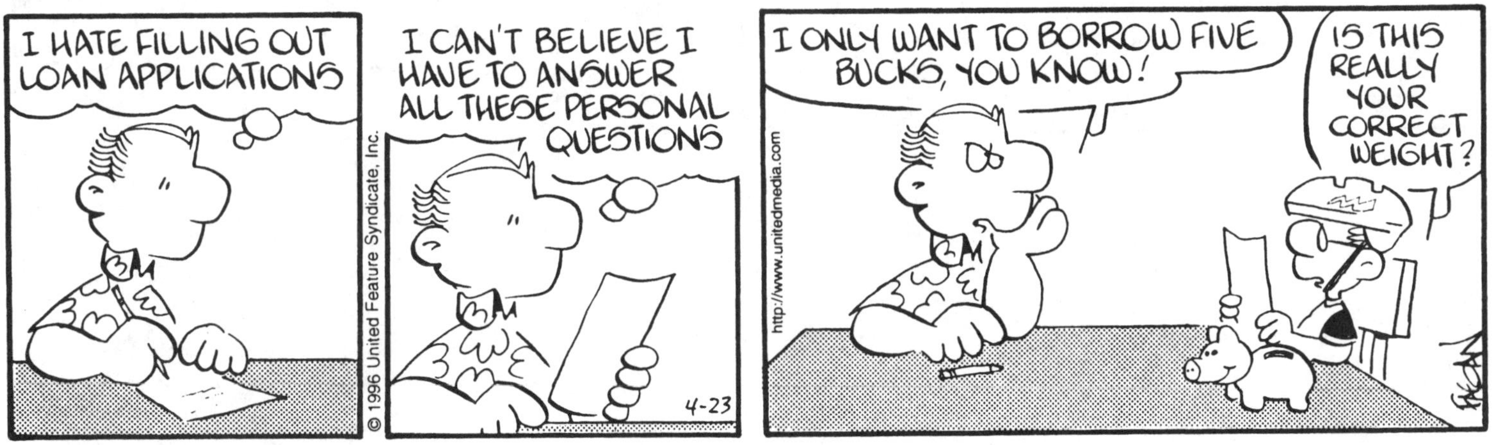

I HATE FILLING OUT LOAN APPLICATIONS
© 1996 United Feature Syndicate, Inc.
I CAN'T BELIEVE I HAVE TO ANSWER ALL THESE PERSONAL QUESTIONS
4-23
http://www.unitedmedia.com
I ONLY WANT TO BORROW FIVE BUCKS, YOU KNOW!
IS THIS REALLY YOUR CORRECT WEIGHT?
FAGAN

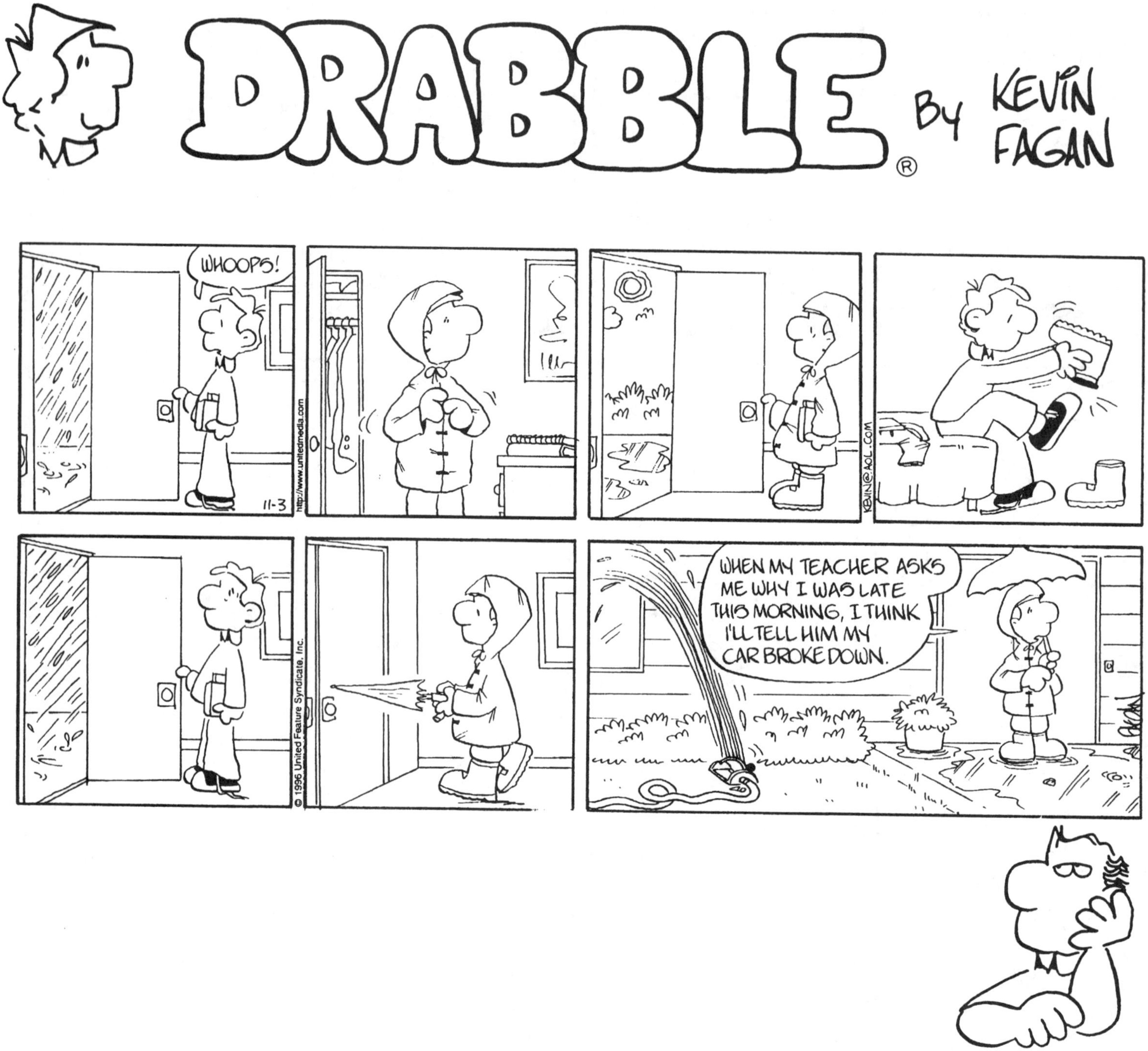
DRABBLE®
By KEVIN FAGAN
WHOOPS!
11-3
http://www.unitedmedia.com
KEVIN@AOL.COM
© 1996 United Feature Syndicate, Inc.
WHEN MY TEACHER ASKS ME WHY I WAS LATE THIS MORNING, I THINK I'LL TELL HIM MY CAR BROKE DOWN.

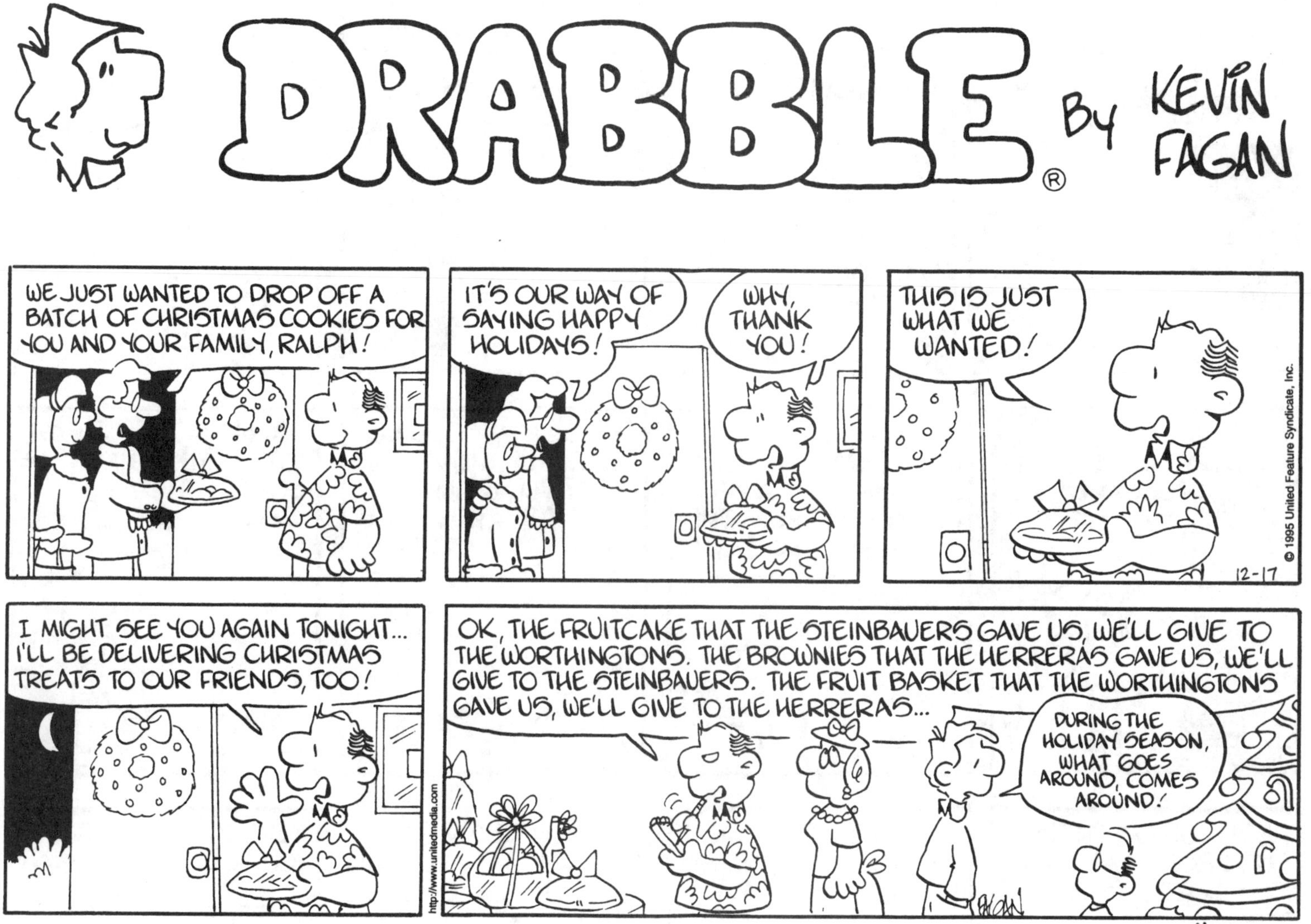
DRABBLE®
By KEVIN FAGAN
WE JUST WANTED TO DROP OFF A BATCH OF CHRISTMAS COOKIES FOR YOU AND YOUR FAMILY, RALPH!
IT'S OUR WAY OF SAYING HAPPY HOLIDAYS!
WHY, THANK YOU!
THIS IS JUST WHAT WE WANTED!
© 1995 United Feature Syndicate, Inc.
12-17
I MIGHT SEE YOU AGAIN TONIGHT... I'LL BE DELIVERING CHRISTMAS TREATS TO OUR FRIENDS, TOO!
http://www.unitedmedia.com
OK, THE FRUITCAKE THAT THE STEINBAUERS GAVE US, WE'LL GIVE TO THE WORTHINGTONS. THE BROWNIES THAT THE HERRERAS GAVE US, WE'LL GIVE TO THE STEINBAUERS. THE FRUIT BASKET THAT THE WORTHINGTONS GAVE US, WE'LL GIVE TO THE HERRERAS...
DURING THE HOLIDAY SEASON, WHAT GOES AROUND, COMES AROUND!
FAGAN

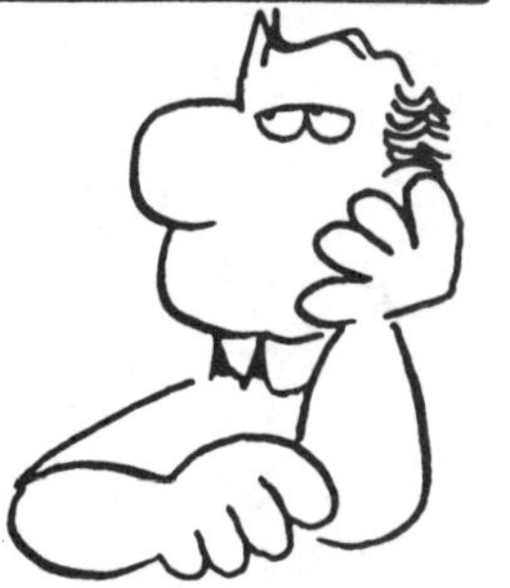

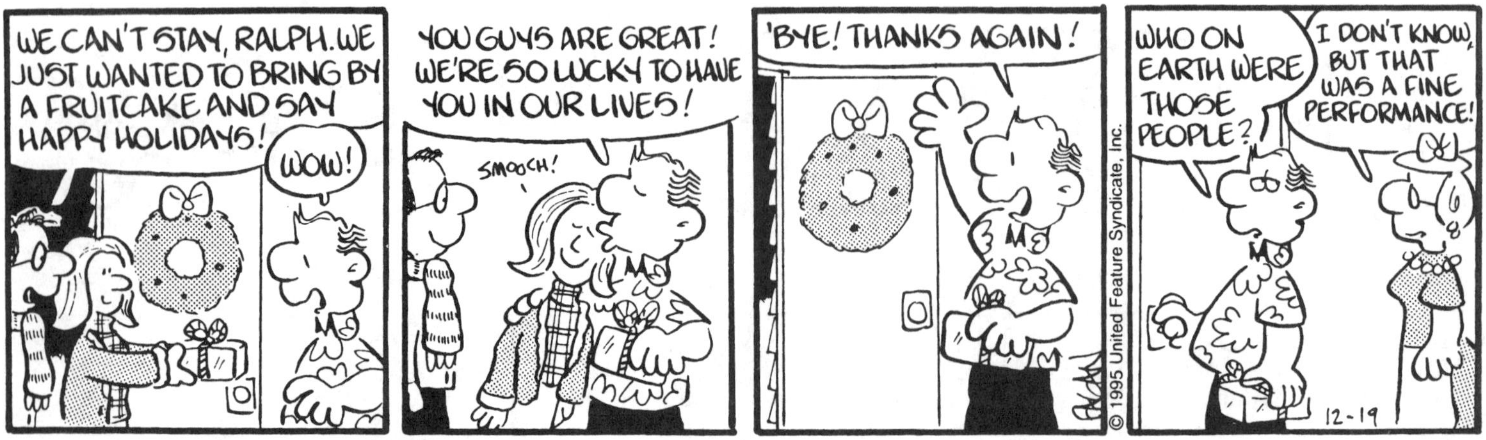
WE CAN'T STAY, RALPH. WE JUST WANTED TO BRING BY A FRUITCAKE AND SAY HAPPY HOLIDAYS!
WOW!
YOU GUYS ARE GREAT! WE'RE SO LUCKY TO HAVE YOU IN OUR LIVES!
SMOOCH!
'BYE! THANKS AGAIN!
© 1995 United Feature Syndicate, Inc.
WHO ON EARTH WERE THOSE PEOPLE?
I DON'T KNOW, BUT THAT WAS A FINE PERFORMANCE!
12-19

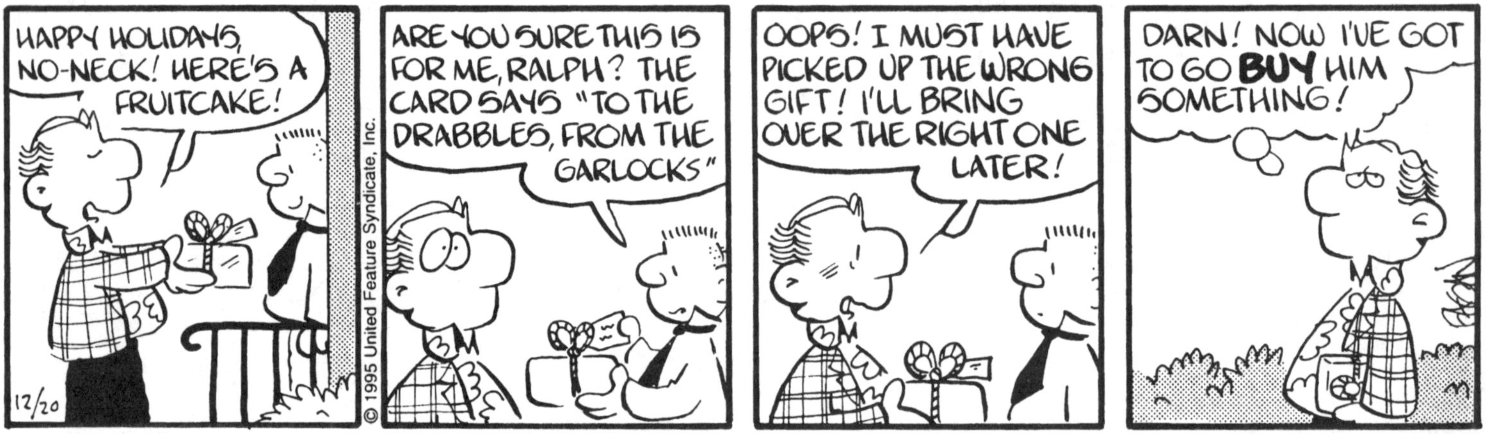
HAPPY HOLIDAYS, NO-NECK! HERE'S A FRUITCAKE!
12/20
© 1995 United Feature Syndicate, Inc.
ARE YOU SURE THIS IS FOR ME, RALPH? THE CARD SAYS "TO THE DRABBLES, FROM THE GARLOCKS"
OOPS! I MUST HAVE PICKED UP THE WRONG GIFT! I'LL BRING OVER THE RIGHT ONE LATER!
DARN! NOW I'VE GOT TO GO **BUY** HIM SOMETHING!

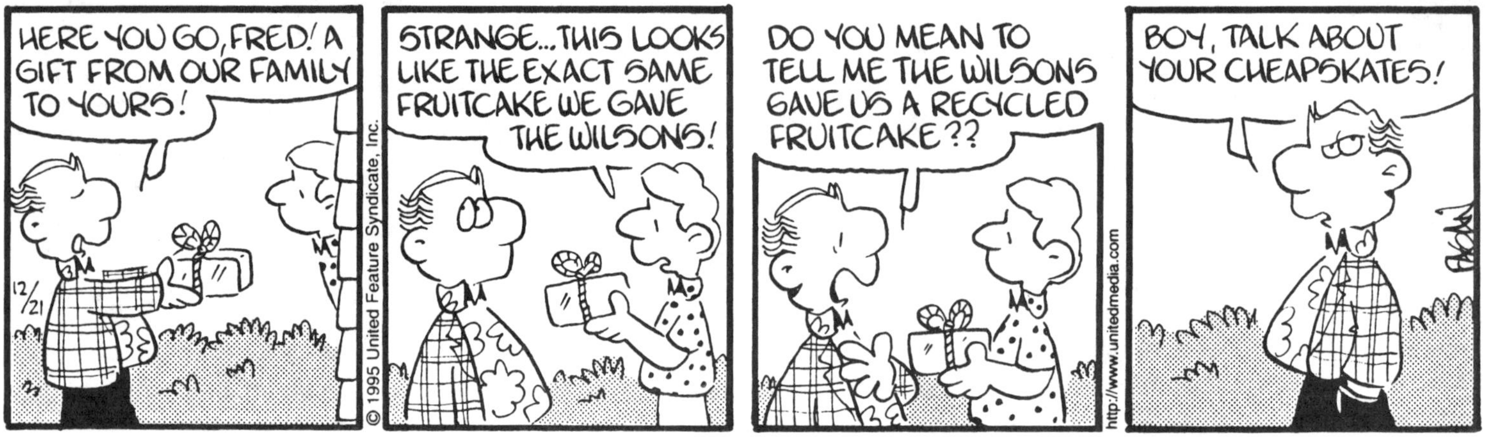
HERE YOU GO, FRED! A GIFT FROM OUR FAMILY TO YOURS!
12/21
© 1995 United Feature Syndicate, Inc.
STRANGE...THIS LOOKS LIKE THE EXACT SAME FRUITCAKE WE GAVE THE WILSONS!
DO YOU MEAN TO TELL ME THE WILSONS GAVE US A RECYCLED FRUITCAKE??
http://www.unitedmedia.com
BOY, TALK ABOUT YOUR CHEAPSKATES!

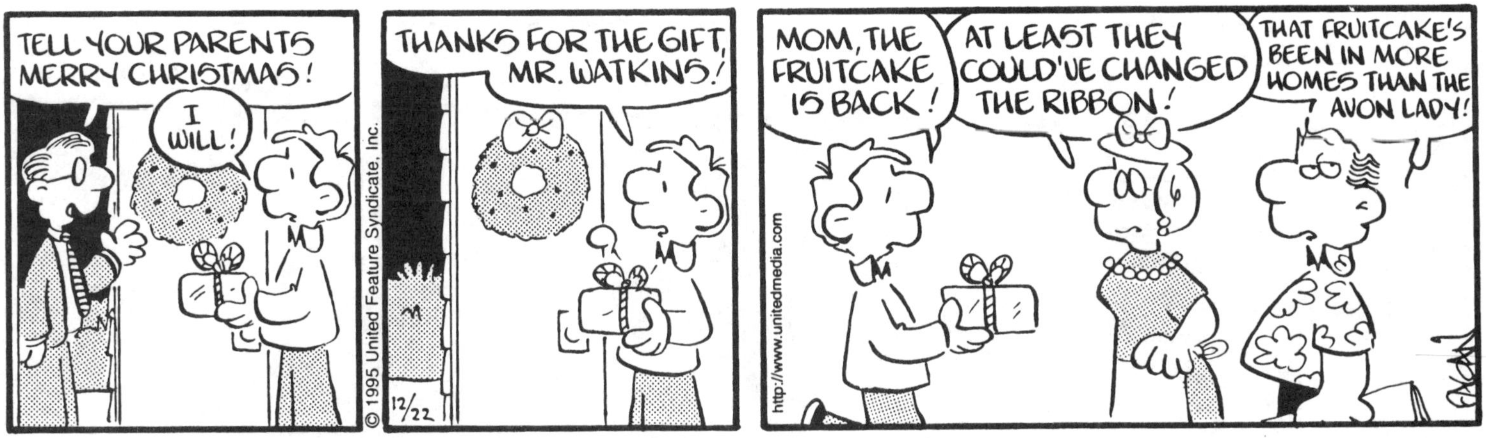
TELL YOUR PARENTS MERRY CHRISTMAS!
I WILL!
© 1995 United Feature Syndicate, Inc.
THANKS FOR THE GIFT, MR. WATKINS!
12/22
MOM, THE FRUITCAKE IS BACK!
AT LEAST THEY COULD'VE CHANGED THE RIBBON!
THAT FRUITCAKE'S BEEN IN MORE HOMES THAN THE AVON LADY!
http://www.unitedmedia.com

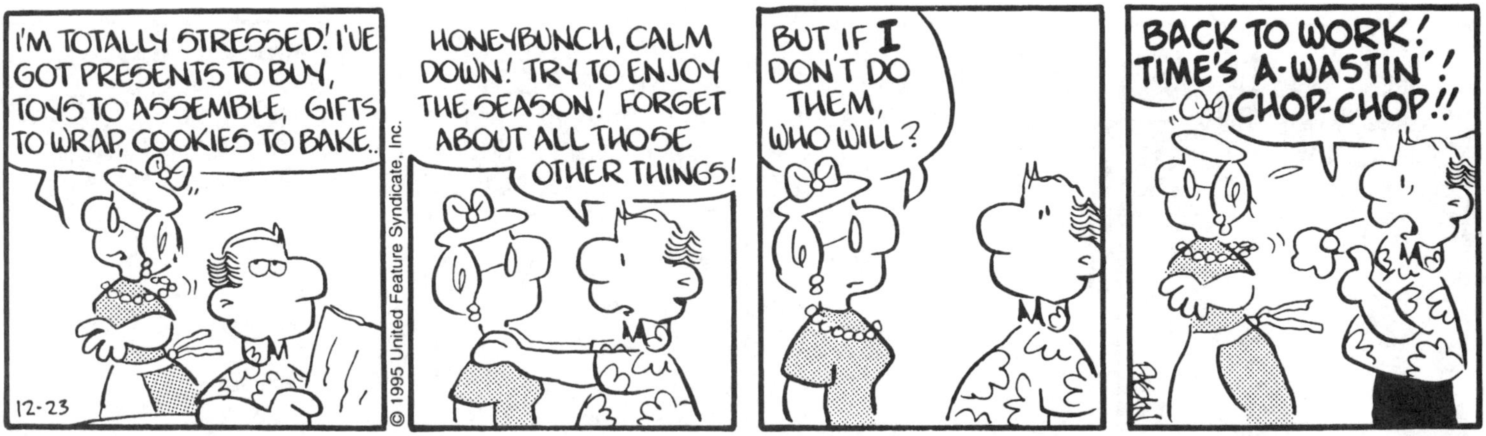
I'M TOTALLY STRESSED! I'VE GOT PRESENTS TO BUY, TOYS TO ASSEMBLE, GIFTS TO WRAP, COOKIES TO BAKE..
12-23
© 1995 United Feature Syndicate, Inc.
HONEYBUNCH, CALM DOWN! TRY TO ENJOY THE SEASON! FORGET ABOUT ALL THOSE OTHER THINGS!
BUT IF I DON'T DO THEM, WHO WILL?
BACK TO WORK! TIME'S A-WASTIN'! CHOP-CHOP!!

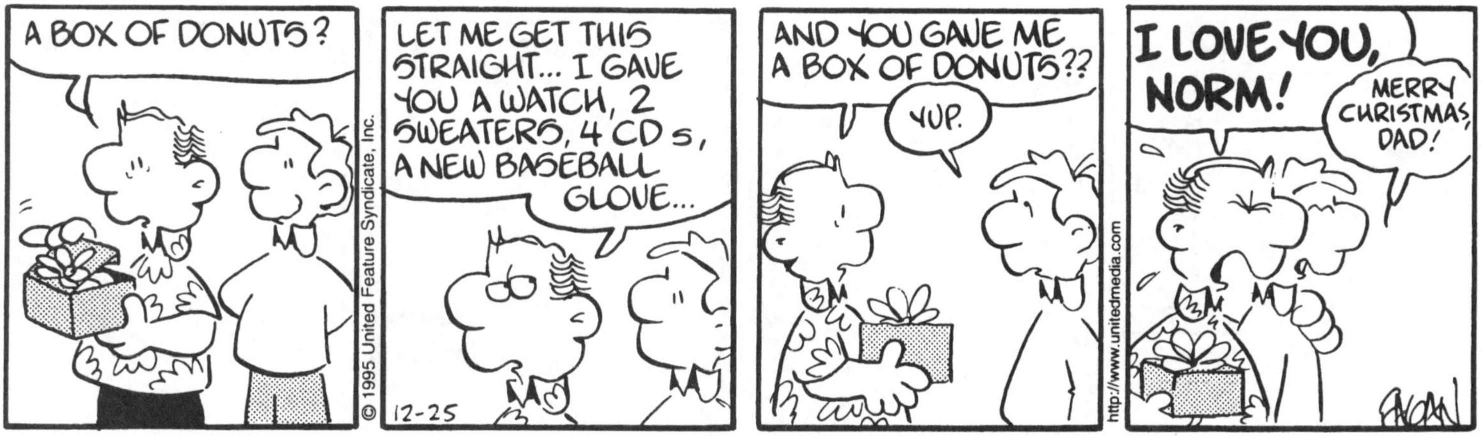
A BOX OF DONUTS?
© 1995 United Feature Syndicate, Inc.
LET ME GET THIS STRAIGHT... I GAVE YOU A WATCH, 2 SWEATERS, 4 CDs, A NEW BASEBALL GLOVE...
12-25
AND YOU GAVE ME A BOX OF DONUTS??
YUP.
http://www.unitedmedia.com
I LOVE YOU, NORM!
MERRY CHRISTMAS, DAD!

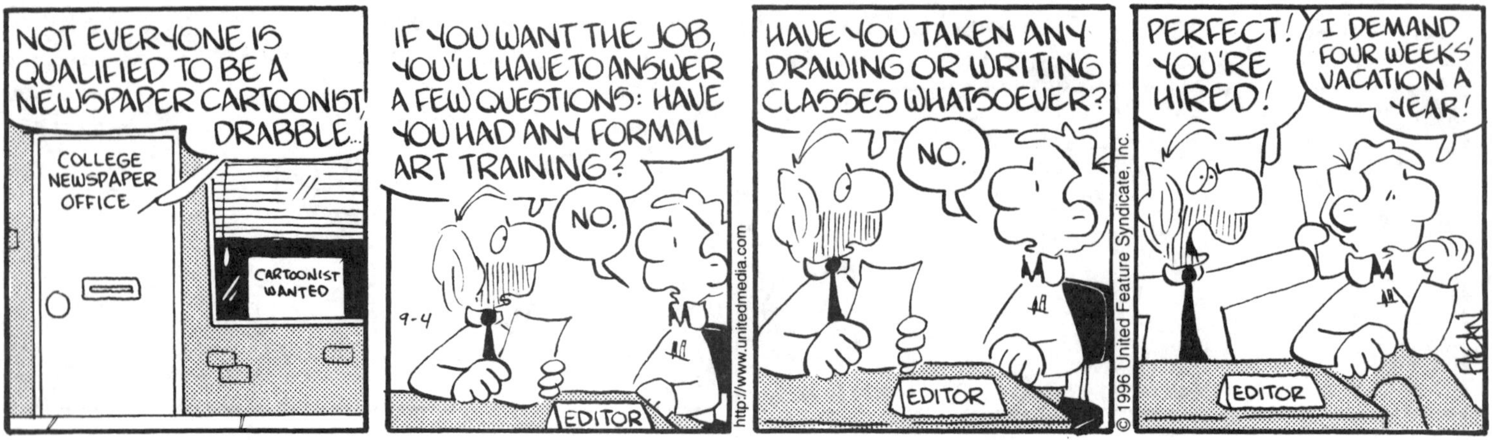

NOT EVERYONE IS QUALIFIED TO BE A NEWSPAPER CARTOONIST, DRABBLE...
COLLEGE NEWSPAPER OFFICE
CARTOONIST WANTED
9-4
IF YOU WANT THE JOB, YOU'LL HAVE TO ANSWER A FEW QUESTIONS: HAVE YOU HAD ANY FORMAL ART TRAINING?
NO.
EDITOR
http://www.unitedmedia.com
HAVE YOU TAKEN ANY DRAWING OR WRITING CLASSES WHATSOEVER?
NO.
EDITOR
© 1996 United Feature Syndicate, Inc.
PERFECT! YOU'RE HIRED!
I DEMAND FOUR WEEKS' VACATION A YEAR!
EDITOR

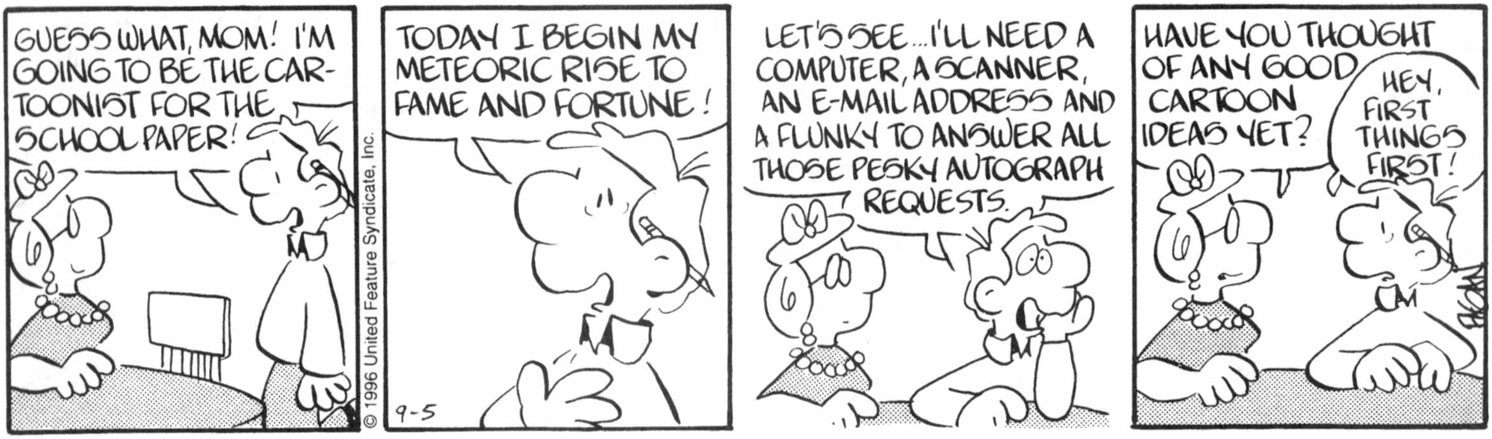

GUESS WHAT, MOM! I'M GOING TO BE THE CARTOONIST FOR THE SCHOOL PAPER!
© 1996 United Feature Syndicate, Inc.
9-5
TODAY I BEGIN MY METEORIC RISE TO FAME AND FORTUNE!
LET'S SEE...I'LL NEED A COMPUTER, A SCANNER, AN E-MAIL ADDRESS AND A FLUNKY TO ANSWER ALL THOSE PESKY AUTOGRAPH REQUESTS.
HAVE YOU THOUGHT OF ANY GOOD CARTOON IDEAS YET?
HEY, FIRST THINGS FIRST!

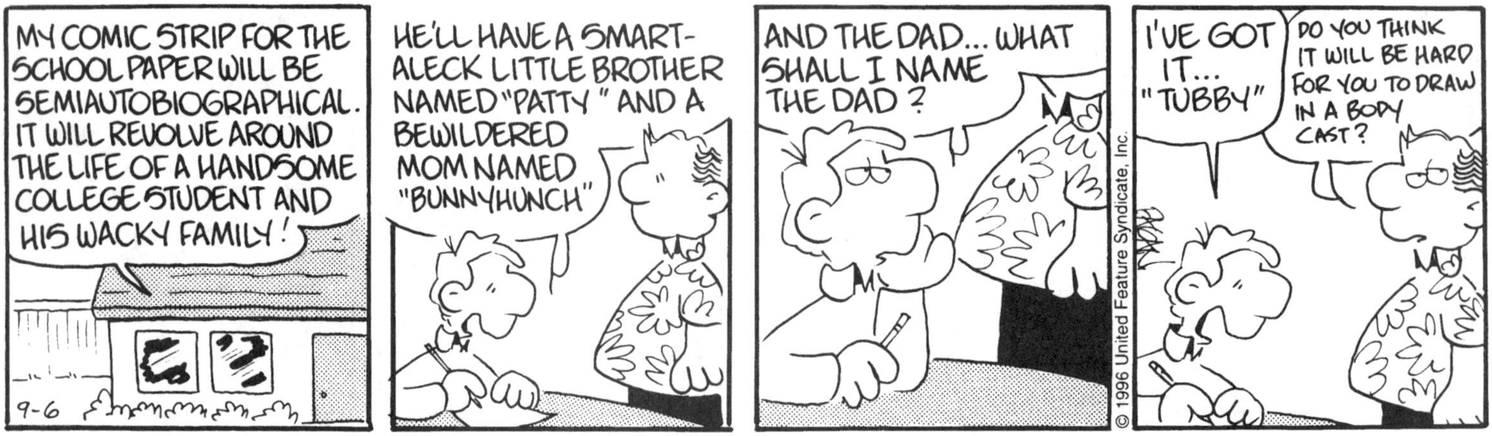

MY COMIC STRIP FOR THE SCHOOL PAPER WILL BE SEMIAUTOBIOGRAPHICAL. IT WILL REVOLVE AROUND THE LIFE OF A HANDSOME COLLEGE STUDENT AND HIS WACKY FAMILY!
9-6
HE'LL HAVE A SMART-ALECK LITTLE BROTHER NAMED "PATTY" AND A BEWILDERED MOM NAMED "BUNNYHUNCH"
AND THE DAD... WHAT SHALL I NAME THE DAD?
© 1996 United Feature Syndicate, Inc.
I'VE GOT IT... "TUBBY"
DO YOU THINK IT WILL BE HARD FOR YOU TO DRAW IN A BODY CAST?

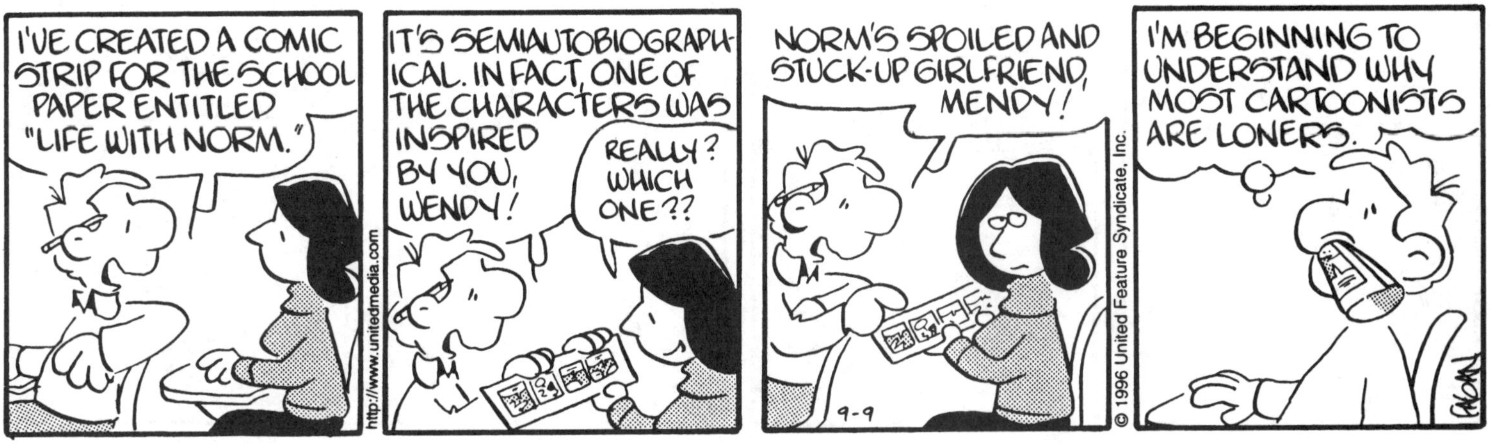
I'VE CREATED A COMIC STRIP FOR THE SCHOOL PAPER ENTITLED "LIFE WITH NORM."
http://www.unitedmedia.com
IT'S SEMIAUTOBIOGRAPHICAL. IN FACT, ONE OF THE CHARACTERS WAS INSPIRED BY YOU, WENDY!
REALLY? WHICH ONE??
NORM'S SPOILED AND STUCK-UP GIRLFRIEND, MENDY!
9-9
© 1996 United Feature Syndicate, Inc.
I'M BEGINNING TO UNDERSTAND WHY MOST CARTOONISTS ARE LONERS.

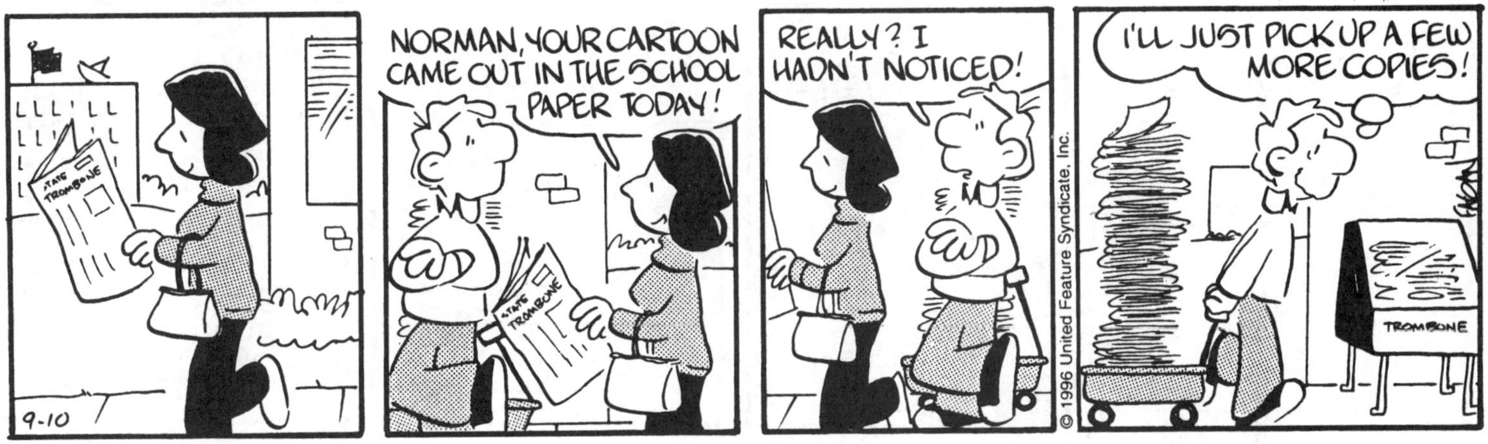
STATE TROMBONE
9-10
NORMAN, YOUR CARTOON CAME OUT IN THE SCHOOL PAPER TODAY!
STATE TROMBONE
REALLY? I HADN'T NOTICED!
© 1996 United Feature Syndicate, Inc.
I'LL JUST PICK UP A FEW MORE COPIES!
TROMBONE

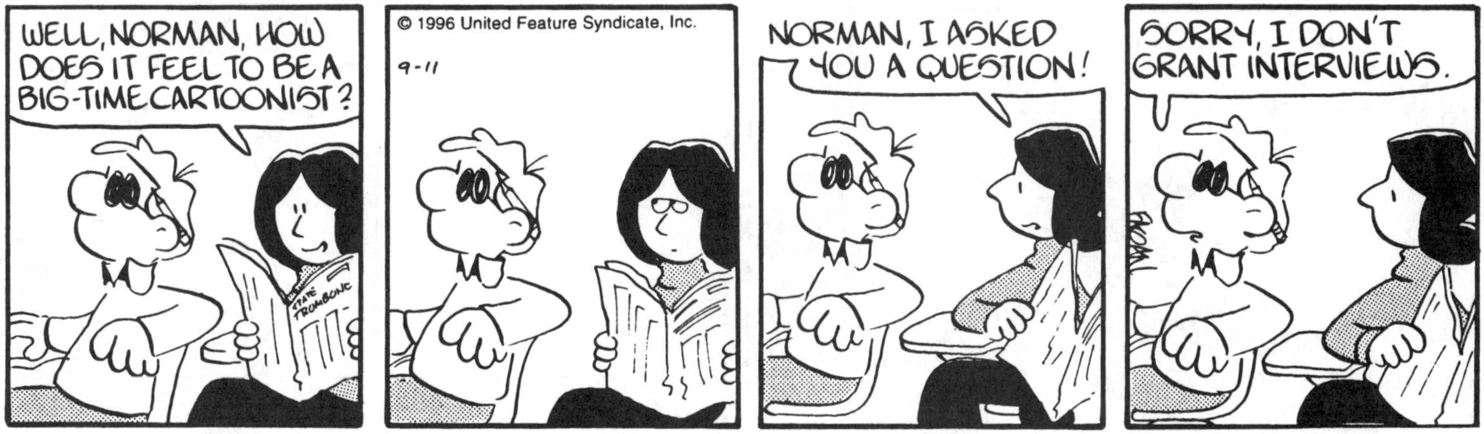
WELL, NORMAN, HOW DOES IT FEEL TO BE A BIG-TIME CARTOONIST?
STATE TROMBONE
© 1996 United Feature Syndicate, Inc.
9-11
NORMAN, I ASKED YOU A QUESTION!
SORRY, I DON'T GRANT INTERVIEWS.

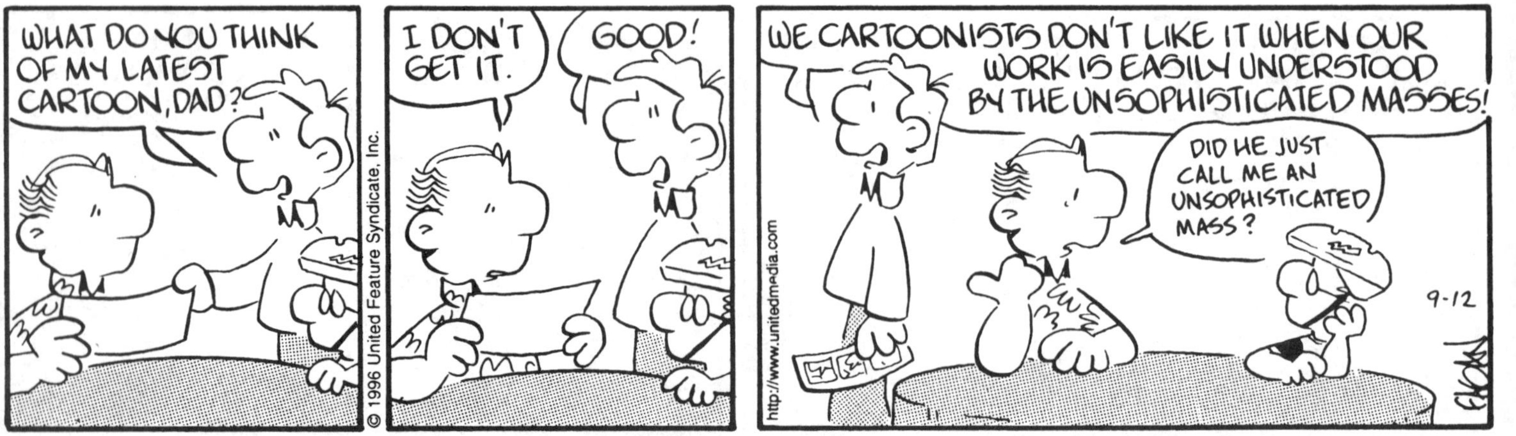
WHAT DO YOU THINK OF MY LATEST CARTOON, DAD?
I DON'T GET IT.
GOOD!
WE CARTOONISTS DON'T LIKE IT WHEN OUR WORK IS EASILY UNDERSTOOD BY THE UNSOPHISTICATED MASSES!
DID HE JUST CALL ME AN UNSOPHISTICATED MASS?
9-12
© 1996 United Feature Syndicate, Inc.
http://www.unitedmedia.com

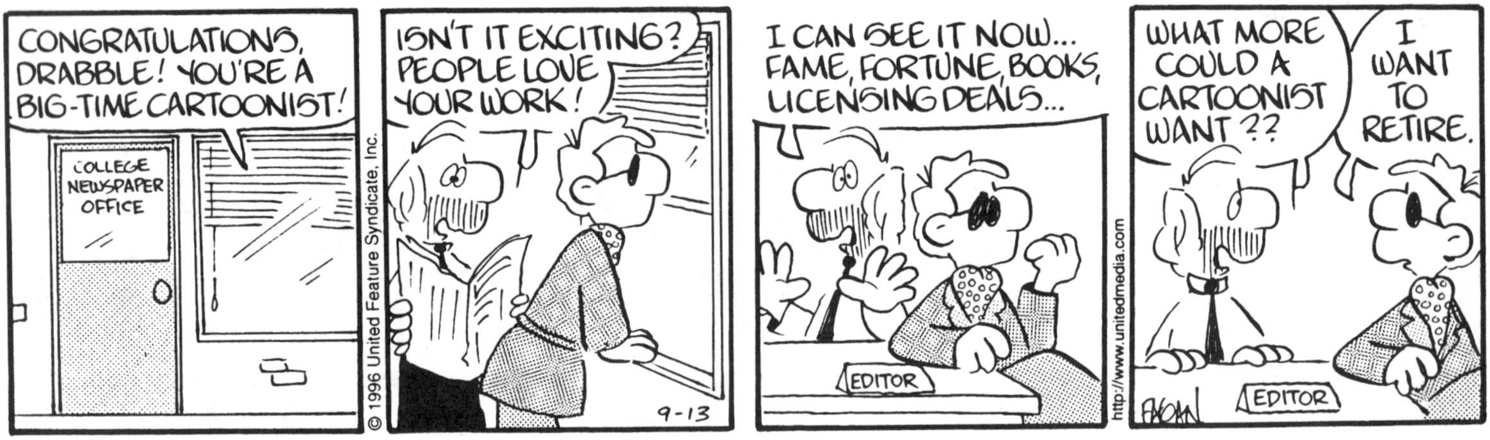
CONGRATULATIONS, DRABBLE! YOU'RE A BIG-TIME CARTOONIST!
COLLEGE NEWSPAPER OFFICE
ISN'T IT EXCITING? PEOPLE LOVE YOUR WORK!
9-13
I CAN SEE IT NOW... FAME, FORTUNE, BOOKS, LICENSING DEALS...
EDITOR
WHAT MORE COULD A CARTOONIST WANT??
I WANT TO RETIRE.
EDITOR
© 1996 United Feature Syndicate, Inc.
http://www.unitedmedia.com

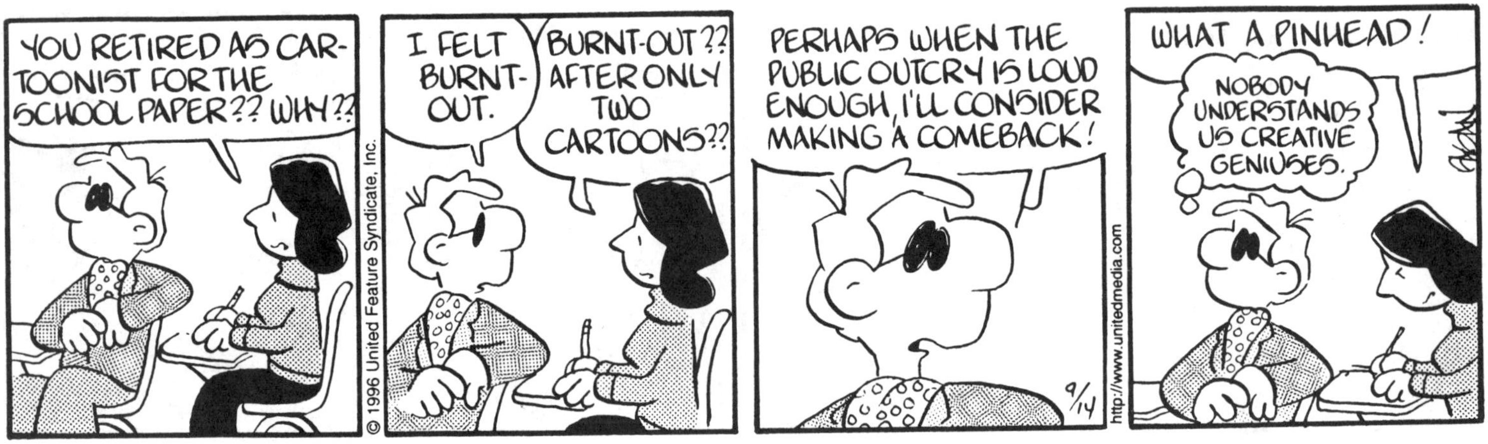
YOU RETIRED AS CARTOONIST FOR THE SCHOOL PAPER?? WHY??
I FELT BURNT-OUT.
BURNT-OUT?? AFTER ONLY TWO CARTOONS??
PERHAPS WHEN THE PUBLIC OUTCRY IS LOUD ENOUGH, I'LL CONSIDER MAKING A COMEBACK!
9/14
WHAT A PINHEAD!
NOBODY UNDERSTANDS US CREATIVE GENIUSES.
© 1996 United Feature Syndicate, Inc.
http://www.unitedmedia.com